WITHDRAWN

The Geometries
of Visual Space

The Geometries
of Visual Space

Mark Wagner
Wagner College

LAWRENCE ERLBAUM ASSOCIATES, PUBLISHERS
2006   Mahwah, New Jersey   London

Lawrence Erlbaum Associates, Inc., Publishers
10 Industrial Avenue
Mahwah, New Jersey 07430
www.erlbaum.com

Cover design by Kathryn Houghtaling Lacey

Library of Congress Cataloging-in-Publication Data

Wagner, Mark.
    The geometries of visual space / Mark Wagner.
        p. cm.

Includes bibliographical references and index.

ISBN 0-8058-5252-2(cloth : alk. paper)
ISBN 0-8058-5253-0 (pbk. : alk. paper)
1. Space perception. 2. Visual perception.   I. Title.
BF469.W35   2005
152.14'2—dc22   2005051008
                                                                                    CIP

Books published by Lawrence Erlbaum Associates are printed on acid-free paper, and their bindings are chosen for strength and durability.

Printed in the United States of America
10   9   8   7   6   5   4   3   2   1

This book is dedicated to John C. Baird

—mentor, collaborator, friend, and psychophysical wise man.

It is also dedicated to Susan Bernardo and Katie MacDonald,

for their love and support over the years.

Contents

Preface

When most people think of space, they think of physical space. *Physical space*, which is primarily the concern of physicists and geometers, is defined in reference to objective, physical measures such as rulers and protractors. As a perceptual psychologist, I am interested in another sort of space: Visual space. *Visual space* concerns space as we consciously experience it, and it is studied through subjective measures, such as asking people to use numbers to estimate perceived distances, areas, angles, or volumes.

Space perception is an important area to consider for a number of reasons. First, the study of space perception has a long pedigree. Many of the greatest philosophers and scientists in history including Descartes, Reid, Berkeley, Hume, and Kant have examined how well our perceptions of space match physical reality. The space perception problem has concerned some of the greatest minds in the history of psychology as well, including Helmholtz, Luneburg, Titchener, Wundt, James, and Gibson. Space, together with time, is the fundamental basis of all sensible experience. Understanding the nature of our spatial experience, then, addresses one of the most basic intellectual problems. Second, psychology began as the study of conscious experience. Behaviorism arose in the 1920s by asserting the proposition that it is impossible to say anything significant about conscious experience. Behaviorism is just part of a larger materialist philosophy that pervades modern science and medicine. I believe this materialist philosophy is over emphasized, and that consciousness is at least as fundamental and important as the physical world. This work on space perception is an attempt to show that one can develop a sophisticated and coherent understanding of conscious experience. Finally, there are potential practical applications of work on this topic. In the real world, predictable errors in spatial perception can have very real consequences, from landing planes badly to driving mistakes that can cost lives.

Numerous studies have found that physical space and visual space can be very different from each other. This past work has demonstrated that mismatches between physical and visual space are not isolated occurrences, but that large, systematic mismatches regularly occur under ordinary circumstances. This book reviews work that explores this mismatch between perception and physical reality. In addition, this book describes the many factors that influence our perception of space including the meaning we assign to geometric concepts like distance, the judgment method we use to report our experience, the presence or absence of cues to depth, the orientation of a stimulus with respect to our point of view, and many other factors.

Previous theorists have often tried to test whether visual space is best described by a small set of traditional geometries, such as the Euclidean geometry most of us studied in High School or the hyperbolic and spherical geometries introduced by 19th-century mathematicians. This "synthetic" approach to defining visual space relies on laying out a set of axioms characteristic of a geometry and testing the applicability of the axioms. This book describes this sort of research and demonstrates that the synthetic approach has largely failed because the empirical research commonly does not support the postulates or axioms these geometries assume.

I take a different approach based on what mathematicians call *metric functions*; that is, I attempt to specify the measurable properties of visual space, such as distances, angles, and areas, using functions that take into account the location of a stimulus in physical space and other psychological factors. The main theme of this book is that no single geometry describes visual space, but that the geometry of visual space depends on stimulus conditions and mental shifts in the subjective meaning of size and distance. Yet, despite this variation, our perceptions are predictable based on a set of relatively simple mathematical models.

Although this work is primarily intended for scholars in perception, mathematical psychology, and psychophysics, I have done my best to make this discussion accessible to a wider audience. For example, chapter 2 reviews the mathematical, philosophical, and psychophysical tools on which this book relies at what I believe is a very readable level. Because of this, I believe this book would also make for a good graduate-level textbook on space perception.

Plan of the book. The first two chapters contain philosophical, mathematical, and psychophysical background material. Visuals space is defined, and I explain why the problem is important to study. These chapters trace the history of philosophical work on space perception, which antedates psychology. They also explain how mathematicians approach geometry, describe some of the most important and widely known geometries, and discuss the psychophysical techniques used to explore visual space.

Chapter 3 looks at synthetic approaches to space perception including work on hyperbolic, spherical, and Euclidean geometries. I lay out the axioms for geometries of constant curvature and consider the extent to which these axioms are supported by empirical work. Chapter 4 proposes an alternative way to investigate the geometry of visual space, the analytic approach. Here, geometries are defined by using coordinate equations to express the metric properties of the space, such as distance, angle, area, and volume. I describe ways of assigning coordinates to visual space, talk about the origin of visual space —the egocenter, and talk about the general form of equations to describe metrics. Finally, I demonstrate that visual space violates the assumptions of one of the most general types of geometries, metric spaces.

The next three chapters review the three other major domains of psychophysical research on space perception. Chapter 5 presents a meta-analysis of studies that ask observers to directly estimate size, distance, area, angle, and volume. This meta-analysis examines how judgments of the measurable properties of visual space depend on contextual factors such as instructions, cue conditions, memory vs. direct judgment, the range of stimuli, judgment method, and so on. Chapter 6 looks at the size constancy literature in which observers are asked to adjust a comparison stimulus to match a variety of standards at different distances away. This chapter discusses the history of this literature and considers the effects of many variables on size constancy judgments such as instructions, cue conditions, age, and stimulus orientation. Chapter 7 discusses research that takes a multi-dimensional approach toward studying visual space. These studies look at how size and angle judgments change when stimuli are oriented horizontally, vertically, or in-depth. In all three chapters, mathematical models are presented that integrate data presented in the literature reviews.

Chapter 8 talks about how spatial experience is influenced by memory. In particular, I review factors that affect the development and structure of cognitive maps, including individual difference variables such as age, navigational experience, gender, and personality. In addition, it describes the types judgment errors that are unique to cognitive maps. Chapter 9 summarizes and synthesizes the data and theories discussed in the earlier chapters of the book. In addition, this chapter discusses spatial experience arising from modalities other than vision.

Acknowledgments. This book would not have been possible without the assistance of many people. First of all, I would like to thank my editors at Lawrence Erlbaum Associates, Bill Webber and Lori Stone, who helped guide me through the publication process in a gentle and professional way. In addition, I wish to thank Nadine Simms for her help with the production process. I'd also like to thank Jim Brace-Thompson of Sage Publications for the encouragement and help he provided shortly after I began writing this book.

I am also grateful to Elaina Shapiro, my undergraduate assistant, who helped me track down many hundreds of the articles that have gone into this work. She always approached this monumental task with good humor and enthusiasm. In addition, I would like to express my appreciation to Evan Feldman and Heather Kartzinel, whose research has contributed to this book.

I'd like to thank Stephen W. Link and several anonymous reviewers who gave me sage advice that helped improve the quality of the final product. Steve, in particular, gave me incredibly detailed feedback and much needed encouragement. Thanks, Steve!

I'd also like to acknowledge Susan Bernardo and Katie MacDonald for their love, tolerance, and support. Finally, I'd like to thank John C. Baird, my mentor, collaborator, and friend. This book would not have been possible without the vision and professionalism he displayed throughout our many collaborations.

—*Mark Wagner*

1

Introduction
Contrasting Visual, Experiential, and Physical Space

Time and space are the two pure forms of all sensible perception, and as such they make *a priori* synthetic propositions possible.
Immanuel Kant, *Critique of Pure Reason*

Contrasting Conceptions of Space

This book will investigate the properties of our visual perceptions of space. The concept of space has been an object of speculation and dispute throughout the history of philosophy and science. Great philosophers and scientists—Immanuel Kant, Thomas Reid, Henri Poincaré, Issac Newton, and Albert Einstein (to name a few)—have considered space (together with time) to be one of the cornerstones on which existence is based and from which philosophy and science arise.

At the outset, two terms need to be defined and distinguished: *physical space* and *visual space*. While it is tempting to distinguish between the two by saying that the latter reflects conscious experience and the former does not, I believe one must resist this temptation. Both concepts reflect aspects of our experience of the world. But the attitude we take toward that experience differs between physical and visual space. Perhaps, I risk offending some readers by reviving the shadows of Wundt and Titchener, but in perception at least, Titchener was accurate in observing:

All human knowledge is derived from human experience; there is no other source. But human experience, as we have seen may be considered from different points of view.... First, we will regard experience as altogether independent of any particular person; we will assume that it goes

1

on whether or not anyone is there to have it. Secondly, we will regard experience as altogether dependent on the particular person; we will assume that it goes on only when someone is there to share it. (Titchener, 1900/1909, p. 6)

However, conscious experience can be a rather slippery conceptual fish to grapple with. A scientist can only theorize based on solid data, and consciousness does not itself make marks on paper nor does it directly leave other physical traces that can be studied at leisure.

Harvey Carr once noted, "Consciousness is an abstraction that has no more independent existence than the grin of a Cheshire cat" (Carr, 1925). To open our experience to scientific investigation, we must rely on objectively observable behaviors and verbal reports that attempt to capture some aspect of experience, and we must resort to operational definitions of our concepts in order to render them concrete enough to use.

With this in mind, let me define my terms. By physical space I mean the space revealed to us by measuring devices such as rulers and protractors. Physical space is objectively defined; that is, the properties of physical space are largely observer independent. By visual space, I mean the space revealed by the psychophysical judgments of an observer. Visual space is not objectively defined; that is, the properties of visual space may depend critically on certain aspects of the observer, such as location in physical space, experimental conditions, and the mindset of the observer.

Defining visual space this way sidesteps the central issue: do the judgments people give accurately reflect their subjective experience of the world? Are the introspective reports that people generate a fair reflection of what is really witnessed internally? No doubt I would be wisest to simply drop the issue; however, I am too much of a philosopher to pass on without venturing an opinion.

Let me boldly state my own equivocal belief. While I believe that observers do attempt to base their judgments on their subjective experience of the world and I believe they really do try to be accurate, it is impossible to say how well they accomplish their goal. It is impossible to independently verify what is really in the subjective experience of an observer. The closest proxies we have are the judgments themselves.

Of course, if we did not believe that the numbers generated in psychophysical experiments reflected something of a person's internal experience, we would quickly lose interest in the subject. Why would one really care about mere number generating responses? A true behaviorist should find perception boring.

Geometry and space. A variety of geometries have been employed to describe physical space at different levels of scale. When the distances under consideration are large, Einstein (1922) pointed out that a hyperbolic geometry might best describe physical space. When the slightly less grandiose distances of the earth's surface are considered, a spherical (or elliptical) geometry makes sailing or flying around the world quicker and more efficient. Yet, if we confine ourselves to that range of distances which humans commonly experience; that is, if we confine ourselves to the ecological level of analysis mentioned by Gibson (1979); then any curvature in the earth's surface or in the fabric of space itself is small enough to be ignored. The world is Euclidean. When distances are measured by a ruler, the square of the hypotenuse of a right triangle is equal to the sum of the squares of the two legs to a high degree of approximation—just as Euclidean geometry would predict. When angles are measured by a protractor, the sum of the angles of any triangle is always very, very, very close to 180°—just as Euclidean geometry would predict.

The same definite conclusions cannot be made regarding visual space. People are capable of thinking about geometric concepts in different ways. By a simple mental shift, we can think of the distance from home to work as the crow flies, as the length of the path to get there, as the time it takes to drive, or as a segment of the "great circle" that intersects the two points. We can think of distance as the physicist sees it or take the artist's perspective and see distance as the amount of canvas lying between two objects in a painting. One time we can use category estimation to judge distance and try to keep differences between categories subjectively identical while another time we use magnitude estimation and try to reflect the ratio of the subjective sizes of targets; and emphasizing these different mathematical aspects of the situation leads to very different psychophysical functions. Which of the geometries of visual space that result from these different perspectives is correct? I believe it is best to simply admit that no single view is correct, but that they all are. All may be valid descriptions of our varying subjective experience.

In addition, our experience is influenced by the situation we find ourselves in. Trying to judge the distance to an on-coming car is more difficult at night than it is during the day. Things that are far away can seem different than when they are brought close to us, and the angle from which we regard an object can make a difference to our perceptions of it. The world can seem large in the mind of a child, but the adult who returns to the old neighborhood is struck by how small and underwhelming things seem.

As we will see later, many have attempted to specify *the* geometry of visual space, but in my view that enterprise is hopeless from the outset. There is no single geometry that describes visual space, but there are many. The geometries of visual space vary with experience, with mental set, with conditions, and with time.

The purpose of this book is to determine how the geometry of visual space changes along with conditions. In addition, as part of that, this book will look at the changing relationship that exists between physical space and our visual perceptions of it.

Memory and space. The foregoing hints that physical and visual spaces are not the only ones of interest to the psychologist. What of memorial space, space as we remember it based on a past viewing of an object or setting? Even if one believed that space as it is directly perceived is both accurate and Euclidean as a Gibsonian would suggest, a psychologist would have good reason to suppose that the process of memory would distort our judgments into a very non-Euclidean form. Memories are incomplete and reconstructed.

Cognitive maps are another step away from direct perception. Cognitive maps refer to our mental representations of the layout of our surrounding environment. Cognitive maps generally concern large-scale environments that are too big to ever be seen at one time (except perhaps from an airplane or a space ship); so, cognitive maps are constructed across time based on our unfolding experience. As we will see later, cognitive maps are riddled with holes (that represent unexperienced territories), distortions, discontinuities, and non-spatial associations. A complete characterization of cognitive space is not only non-Euclidean; it is probably non-Riemannian. In fact, there may be no simple mathematical system that could ever fully characterize the richly chaotic nature of our cognitive maps. Cognitive maps may consist of a patchwork of loosely connected parts.

From a psychological standpoint, memorial space and cognitive maps certainly deserve our attention, and this book will describe something of their nature. Once more, the family of geometries that describe human experiences expands. Who could think there might be only one?

Experiential space. Of course, one need not stop here. A more general conception than visual space is that of experiential space. By experiential space I refer to our experience of space of any kind. By its very nature, the term visual space excludes spatial perceptions based on the other senses. Yet, clearly we do perceive space in extra-visual ways. Not only does it make sense to speak of visual space, but one may also meaningfully speak of auditory space, haptic space, gustatory space, kinesthetic space, proprioceptive space, and olfactory space. This book will largely confine itself to vision because the vast majority of research studies on spatial perception concern visual stimuli, but I will have a few words to say about these other spaces in various places in this book.

Why Is This Problem Important?

A noble intellectual pedigree. The problem of space perception is one with a long and prestigious pedigree. According to Wade (1996), ancient Greek philosophers including Aristotle and Euclid recognized that spatial perception did not always correspond to physical measures and that variables such as binocularity, aerial perspective, and distance to the stimulus can alter size estimates. Roman era thinkers including Galen, Lucretius, and Ptolemy noted that variables like linear perspective and the orientation of a stimulus can lead to breakdowns in size constancy. The great 11th Century Islamic philosopher, Ibn al-Haytham, spoke of the effects of stereopsis and familiar size on spatial perception. Leonardo da Vinci reiterated the importance of binocularity and aerial perspective on size perception.

Philosophers throughout the modern era often wrote about spatial experience as part of their systems of philosophy. Wade (1996) mentions Francis Bacon's and René DesCartes's interest in the problems of space perception. As will be discussed at length in Chapter 2, Berkeley, Hume, Kant, Reid, Poincaré, and Husserl all held well-developed views on the geometric character of our spatial experience.

Interest in the problem of space perception also played an integral role in the development of psychology as a discipline. Helmholtz (1868/1921) extensively wrote about space perception and empirically investigated the problem as part of his assault on Kantian philosophy. Weber's studies of two-point limen in touch were largely motivated by his wish to understand how humans develop our sense of space. Other early founders of psychology, including Titchener and James, wrote extensive chapters (or even multiple chapters) on space perception in their foundational works on psychology. In fact, the longest single chapter in James's two-volume *The Principles of Psychology* is dedicated to the subject. Wundt, whom some consider the founder of psychology, was so dedicated to studying the nature of space perception that James said of him: "Wundt has all his life devoted himself to the elaboration of space theory" (James, 1890, p. 276). (By the way, I tend to agree with Link (1994, 2002) that Fechner is a better candidate for the role of psychology's founder than Wundt. While Wundt may have been better at self-promotion, psychology was alive and well before he ever came on the scene.)

Harvey Carr (1935), the great American Functionalist, wrote an entire book on space perception. In addition, when G. Stanley Hall was granted the first Ph.D. ever awarded in psychology in America, his dissertation was on (you guessed it) space perception (Boring, 1950).

In short, some of the greatest philosophers and psychologists in history focused considerable attention on the problems of space perception. The present book follows this rich tradition and reconceptualizes our spatial experience in the light of the massive body of empirical research performed in more recent years.

Space is foundational. These great minds devoted so much of their attention of spatial experience for a very good reason. Space is foundational. The universe itself may represent little more than the interplay of space, time, and energy. Modern physics seeks to explain gravity, black holes, and the expansion of the universe in terms of alterations in the fabric of space.

Psychologically, space is one of the fundamental building blocks of human experience. Without a conception of space, object perception and meaningful interaction with the world would be impossible. One literally could not live without some ability to sense the layout of the world. At times, one literally cannot live when this perception is in error at a critical time.

Kant (1781/1929) firmly believed that spatial experience served as the base out of which our phenomenal experience grows. In his words:

> Space is a necessary *a priori* representation, which underlies all outer intuitions. We can never represent to ourselves the absence of space, though we can quite well think it as empty of objects. It must therefore be regarded as the condition of the possibility of appearances, and not as a determination dependent on them. (Kant, 1781/1929, p. 24)

Like Kant, I feel that spatial experience represents something particularly fundamental that deserves detailed study. Unlike Kant, I believe that explicating the nature of visual space is an empirical, rather than a logical, *a priori* issue. This book describes the nature of visual space as revealed by the research literature.

A paradigm for measuring mind. Fechner (1860) and Wundt (1874/1904) attempted to apply mathematical tools and the scientific method to the study of consciousness, and for a while all of psychology focused on the study of conscious mind. But as time passed, psychology became ever less interested in consciousness and ever more interested in behavior. Why did this happen? Some believe early Structural Psychology died due to its methodological defects. Carr (1925), who did not wholly reject the introspective method of the Structuralists, pointed out the defects of introspection. He felt that introspection was too difficult to do to give much detailed information about consciousness, that introspective reports were not subject to independent verification, and that Structuralists tended to rely on trained observers whose observations were too easily influenced by their knowledge of the research hypotheses—what James (1890) referred to as the Psychologist's Fallacy.

A more fatal line of attack on introspection came from Watson (1914, 1919, 1924, 1925). Watson felt that it was impossible to make any real progress with a science based on introspection and that the whole enterprise could be dismissed as irrelevant. "The psychology begun by Wundt has thus failed to become a science and has still more deplorably failed in contributing anything of a scientifically usable kind to human nature" (Watson, 1919, p. 3).

While I realize that modern psychology has lost much of its behaviorist character, Watson's challenge is still one I take very seriously. Is it possible to take introspective reports and develop them into an organized, sophisticated, developing body of knowledge? If Watson is right, then it is not only difficult to study the mind, but mind becomes a mere wisp or vapor of no importance.

But, one can develop a sophisticated science based on introspective reports. And I believe no area of psychology is fitter to demonstrate this point than the spatial perception literature. Space perception can be seen as a paradigm of success in the study of mind. This book is an attempt to answer Watson's charge.

More recently, a second serious charge was leveled against the whole enterprise of psychophysics. Lockhead (1992) accused psychophysicists of generating a sterile discipline that consists of a series of unidimensional investigations that fail to adequately grapple with the effects of context on judgments. I see the present book as a lengthy refutation of Lockhead's charge. When taken together the spatial perception literature paints a rich, multidimensional picture that dynamically changes as a function of contextual variables.

Practical applications of visual space perception. James (1907/1964) felt that scientists could be divided into two groups based on their temperaments. The forgoing justifications might appeal to those with what James referred to as a "tender-minded make-up," but might not convince those with a more "tough-minded make-up." A final justification for the study of space perception might even satisfy readers of the hard-nosed persuasion. Space perception research can have many practical applications.

For example, Kong, Zhang, Ding, and Huikun (1995) found that accident-prone railroad drivers had poorer spatial perception skills, particularly those related to depth perception, than safe railroad drivers. Another group of Chinese researchers divided drivers into excellent, regular, relatively poor, and accident prone groups based on driving test scores and accident records and found that the worst drivers had significantly poorer visual depth perception (Zhang, Huang, Liu, & Hou, 1995). Hiro (1997) noted that the faster people drive, the more they underestimate the distance to the car ahead of them. Given that it takes more time to stop at faster speeds, this underestimation of distance could prove to be fatal.

Another skill that drivers need is the ability to read maps accurately. Gillan, Schmidt, and Hanowski (1999) found that contextual variables such as Müller-Lyer Illusion elements in the map can lead to map reading errors.

Pilots need to perceive accurately spatial layout in order to land their planes safely. Lapa and Lemeshchenko (1982) found that pilots who use an egocentric coordinate system have slower reaction times and make more errors in judging layout than those using a geocentric coordinate system. Of course, these pilot errors can cost lives.

Other pilot tasks involving spatial perception include searching for places or landing fields, flying in formation, aerial refueling, collision avoidance, weapons targeting, and low-level flight (Harker & Jones, 1980). Westra, Simon, Collyer, and Chambers (1982) found that landing on aircraft carriers depended more on a pilot's spatial abilities and training than on equipment factors. Unfortunately, distance judgments made from up in the air often lack many of the cues to depth usually found for terrestrial observers. Roscoe (1979) found that spatial perception was particularly difficult at dusk or in the dark, when flying over water, and when coming out of a bank of clouds. Roscoe (1982, 1985) also found that inaccuracies in spatial perception occur when pilots accommodate to their dark focus depth or on the cockpit window rather than on objects external to the cockpit.

If pilots have difficulty judging spatial layout because cues to depth are often absent, astronauts are likely to experience even more difficulty in determining the location of objects external to their capsule since many cues to depth are totally absent in space. Understanding spatial perception in outer space can be an important area of future research to assist the development of projects such as the International Space Station.

Space perception can also be critical for sports performance. For example, Issacs (1981) found that poor depth perception was an important variable in free-throw shooting in basketball. Similarly, McBeath, Shaffer, and Kaiser (1995) and Shaffer, Karauchunas, Eddy, and McBeath (2004) have shown how complicated the simple process of catching a baseball can be. In fact, Oudejans, Michaels, Bakker, and Dolne (1996) indicate that stationary observers are very poor at judging the catchableness of a baseball compared to moving observers. Obviously, this suggests that a running start may be an essential trick to being a good outfielder.

Another place where the ability to accurately perceive spatial layout is important is in surgery. Reinhardt and Anthony (1996) found the ability to engage in remote operation procedures involving internal cameras depended on the adequacy of depth and distance information. Conflicts between monocular and stereoscopic cues proved particularly problematic.

In another recent medical study, Turano and Schuchard (1991) found spatial perception deficits often result from macular and extramacular-peripheral visual field loss. (Although some subjects with quite extensive loss showed normal space perception.) What is more, these perceptual deficits occurred even outside of the damaged areas and when visual acuity is good.

Inaccuracy in distance estimates can also be an issue in some court cases. At least as far back as Moore (1907) legal scholars have been aware of a multitude of variables that negatively affect the reliability of witness testimony regarding spatial layout and the speed of movement. These variables include the amount of time witnesses observe a layout, the passage of time since the incident, the emotional state of the witness, motion in the object observed, darkness, and whether the incident is seen through water or air. At times witness estimates of layout can be critical information in courtroom testimony.

Because our ability to correctly perceive spatial layout is necessary for proper performance in so many areas, it is important to know which factors lead to spatial estimation errors so that we may engage in actions that may eliminate those errors. This book will examine many of these factors.

The Plan of the Book

All of the chapters of this book are directed at two central purposes: to describe our perceptions of visual space and to compare these perceptions to physical layout. The domain delimited by these objectives still covers a vast amount of material, because these two problems have many facets and can be approached from many different directions. The remainder of this chapter describes the various approaches this book takes toward addressing these central objectives. It lays out the basic plan of the book, briefly describing the contents of each of the chapters that follow.

Chapter 2. Like all issues in psychology, the questions discussed in this book arise within a larger historical context. As someone who has a deep interest in the history of psychology—I even co-edited a book on American Functionalism (Owens & Wagner, 1992)—I believe it is important to set up the discussion that follows by providing a bit of this historical background. Chapter 2 also describes some of the mathematical and psychophysical tools that may be used to characterize the geometries of visual space.

In particular, this chapter first discusses the ways mathematicians addressed geometry across history. Secondly, like the rest of psychology, the study of visual space grew out an attempt to apply scientific methods to a long-standing philosophical problem. This chapter speaks about early philosophical approaches to space perception. Finally, Chapter 2 discusses how the study of space perception fits into the wider domain of psychophysics, which provides the basic techniques necessary to paint a picture of visual space.

Chapter 3. Mathematicians define a space in two ways: synthetically and analytically. In the synthetic approach to geometry, the mathematician lays out a set of postulates that define a geometry and deduces theoretical statements that are the consequence of these statements. Chapter 3 describes the work of psychologists who applied this synthetic approach to visual space, particularly emphasizing Luneburg's hyperbolic model. Theoretical works proposing Euclidean and other more exotic geometries are also mentioned. Chapter 3 discusses the assumptions made by these theorists, the predictions made by each theory, and the degree to which empirical research supports these synthetic models.

Chapter 4. My approach to describing visual space is analytic. In an analytic geometry, a set of coordinates is assigned to a space and equations are used to describe the measurable properties of the space like distance, angles, and area. This chapter discusses the advantages of the analytic approach. It describes methods for assigning coordinates to visual space, the location of the origin of visual space, and general formulas for distance, area, and volume judgments. The chapter also talks about how visual space sometimes fails to satisfy the axioms of a metric space, one of the most general forms of an analytic geometry, and describes some dramatic consequences of this failure.

Chapter 5. An expansive literature shows that judgments of the measurable properties of visual space depend on contextual factors such as instructions, cue conditions, memory vs. direct judgment, the range of stimuli, judgment method, etc. Chapter 5 performs a meta-analysis of the effects of these factors on the parameters of psychophysical functions and on the goodness of fit of these psychophysical functions. This meta-analysis is based on over seven times as many studies and experimental conditions than any previously published meta-analysis on space perception. Multiple regression analyses of this data produce a set of general psychophysical equations for distance, area, and volume judgments as a function of contextual conditions. Angle judgments are also briefly examined.

Chapter 6. A second spatial perception literature concerns the perception of size constancy. In this literature, a near comparison is adjusted to match the size of standard stimuli at varying distances from the observer, at varying orientations, and under varying cue conditions. This chapter discusses the history of this literature and considers the effects of many variables on size constancy judgments. It also develops a theory to explain the results that is a generalization of the classic Size-Distance-Invariance Hypothesis. The virtue of the present theory is that it allows one to unify the size constancy literature and the psychophysical literature addressed in the previous chapter. Finally, the chapter briefly talks about the link between size-constancy and the moon illusion.

Chapter 7. The vast majority of the psychophysical literature is based on unidimensional judgments, where depth and egocentric distance are looked at independently from frontal size perception. Chapter 7 talks about a few exceptions to this unidimensional rule that look at spatial judgments as a function of two or even three dimensions simultaneously. I describe two of my own studies of this type and present several models to describe this data. Here, at last, we create models that fully specify the geometry of visual space under a given set of conditions. The rest of the chapter discusses other work of this type. These studies look at changes in visual space as a function of distance from the observer, elevation of gaze, and the presence of context-defining objects. The chapter also mentions evidence for the presence of multiple visual systems, one that guides motion and the other that produces visual experience.

Chapter 8. Memory adds yet another layer of complexity to the analysis of spatial experience. This chapter contrasts the data and theoretical approaches produced by the direct perception and memory literatures, particularly focusing on the cognitive mapping literature. It describes the structural elements of cognitive maps and how cognitive maps are acquired across time. I look at the affect of individual difference factors on cognitive maps such as age, navigational experience, gender, and personality. I also look at the nature of the errors that cognitive maps contain. After this, Chapter 8 compares the psychophysical judgments of size and distance that observers give under direct perception, memory, and cognitive mapping conditions. The chapter also develops a theoretical framework for understanding these data. Finally, I list a few objections to the cognitive-science paradigm that pervades much of this literature and mention an alternative way to think about memory.

Chapter 9. The final chapter summarizes and synthesizes the data and theories discussed in the earlier chapters of the book. In addition, Chapter 9 will touch on spatial experience arising from modalities other than vision. Finally, the chapter discusses the ecological, philosophical, and practical implications of the spatial perception literature.

The End of the Beginning

In summary, a wealth of data that are discussed in the following chapters indicates that visual space is different from physical space. In fact, the geometry that best describes visual space changes as a function of experimental conditions, stimulus layout, observer attitude, and the passage of time.

In addition, the problem of human spatial perception is one of great antiquity, long-standing philosophical import, and considerable practical significance. The spatial perception literature is well enough developed to convincingly show that a sophisticated science can be based on the introspective reports of observers.

2

Traditional Views of Geometry and Vision

Like most psychological problems, the problem of space perception exists within a context larger than itself. This chapter provides a bit of this context. In particular, this chapter examines the historical background of the problem and looks at the empirical and analytical tools available to describe visual space.

The first leg of this contextual tour looks at the approaches mathematicians use to define the geometry of a space. Following this, we discuss the works of early philosophers whose views about visual space naturally led to more recent psychological developments. Finally, this chapter briefly discusses the psychophysical methods that are employed to empirically measure visual space perception.

Geometry as the Mathematician Sees It

Because the problem of visual space perception is explicitly geometric in nature, a logical place to begin searching for tools to work on the problem is with geometry. How do mathematicians define a space? According to Kline (1972), there are two general approaches to geometry. One is synthetic, and the other is analytic.

Synthetic approaches. Ancient Babylonia and Egypt possessed forms of geometry; however, these geometries were concrete, primitive, and lacked unifying principles. This early work focused on solving practical problems associated with flood control, building, and trade. They relied on approximation rather than exact numbers. For example, π was thought to be three. While these ancient mathematicians anticipated many important elements of geometry (such as the Pythagorean Theorem), their works were empirically derived. They lacked the modern concept of proof, and the various mathematical findings were not integrated into a coherent structure.

The first real sophistication in mathematics began with the classical Greeks, who created many geometry theorems. The earliest proof is generally attributed to Thales about 600 BC. Over the next few centuries, the Pythagoreans and others added many new geometrical proofs. Euclid theorems organized these theorems into a coherent structure in his book *Elements*.

In this book, Euclid laid out proofs for 465 geometrical propositions. Euclid's method, however, was of far greater importance than this impressive number of proofs. Euclid began his development by making a list of definitions and postulates. His ten postulates consisted of global, rather than algebraic, assumptions. The most famous example is the Parallel Postulate that states "Through a point P not on a line L, one and only one parallel to L can be drawn." Euclid (and others subsequently) then deduced his many theorems based on these definitions and postulates. Such a geometry, consisting of global definitions, postulates, and theorems, is called a synthetic geometry.

For over a millennium, mathematicians believed that Euclid's geometry was the only one possible. Asking what geometry best describes visual space would have made no sense to them. Visual space could only be Euclidean.

The self-evident certainty of Euclidean geometry crumbled in the early 19th century as a result of mathematical investigations of the Parallel Postulate. Euclid's Parallel Postulate had always been unsatisfactory to mathematicians. In 1733, the Jesuit mathematician Saccheri vainly attempted to prove the Parallel Postulate based on the other nine postulates. While other mathematicians largely rejected the "proof" he generated, his work induced others to take an interest in the problem.

Finally, in 1829, Lobatchevsky demonstrated not only that the Parallel Postulate could not be proved but that a perfectly consistent geometry could be constructed from the assumption that more than one parallel exists to a line through a point not on the line. A few years later Bolyai (1833) published his work demonstrating the same point. (Gauss's notes indicated that he had developed similar proofs earlier than Lobatchevsky and Bolyai, but he never published the work).

The geometry defined by this new form of parallel postulate is called a hyperbolic geometry. A hyperbolic geometry has many properties that are different from those in Euclidean geometry. In a hyperbolic geometry, the sum of the angles of a triangle is less than 180°. The "straight" lines of the space are shaped like hyperbolas. No infinity exists in the hyperbolic space; that is, the space is bounded.

In 1854, Riemann invented a third type of synthetic geometry that arises from another variant of the Parallel Postulate. In this case, Riemann assumed that no parallels to a line could be drawn through a point not on the line. Such a geometry is called a spherical geometry. A simple example of a spherical geometry is the surface of the earth. Here, "straight lines" are circles whose centers are coincident with the center of the earth. All lines (known as Great Circles) defined this way must intersect at two points.

A spherical geometry has a number of other interesting characteristics. First of all, all lines have a finite length. Because pairs of lines intersect at two points, spherical geometry violates Euclid's postulate that two straight lines cannot enclose a space. The sum of the angles of a triangle is always greater than 180° (but less than 540°). The perimeter and area of all figures cannot exceed a maximum size.

Analytic approaches. Geometry was almost exclusively synthetic in nature until the 17th century. In 1637, René Descartes introduced analytic geometry. He established what we now call the Cartesian coordinate system (although he only defined the first or positive quadrant). He demonstrated that many hitherto unsolved geometric problems were solvable by means of analytic geometry. Three key ideas separate analytic from synthetic geometry. First, numbers are associated with the locations or coordinates of points. Second, equations are associated with curves. Third, coordinate equations are used to define distance and other metric properties.

Descartes's ideas proved to be extremely important. Algebra and geometry merged into one discipline. As geometry could now be quantitative, mathematicians put more effort into the study of algebra. The calculus became possible. In short, mathematics became far more flexible and powerful. This analytic approach to mathematics and geometry made many of the profound discoveries of Newtonian physics possible.

The analytic approach can be used to describe all of the synthetic geometries we just mentioned. For a time after Lobatchevsky, synthetic and analytic geometry contested for supremacy. In the end, analytic geometry won the battle. In 1854, Riemann introduced an extremely general form of geometry. The synthetic Euclidean, hyperbolic, and spherical geometries were simply special cases of this more general analytic geometry. Where synthetic geometry had only introduced a handful of possible geometries, Riemannian geometry allowed for a potentially infinite variety. In addition, analytic geometries can make use of powerful tools such as algebra and calculus. Since Riemann's time, synthetic geometry gradually faded from the mathematical world. In fact, one of the few places where it still finds adherents is in psychology (as we will see later).

In Riemann's terms, Euclidean, hyperbolic, and spherical geometries are referred to as geometries of constant curvature. A Euclidean geometry is considered flat and has a curvature of zero. A spherical geometry has a constant positive curvature, and a hyperbolic geometry has a constant negative curvature.

Metric spaces. A Riemannian geometry has two essential characteristics (Eisenhart, 1925): First, the space must be a manifold. That is, there must be some way to assign coordinates to the points in the space, and functions assigning these coordinates must be smooth. (There should be no discontinuities between the coordinates of points lying close to each other.) Second, the nature of the space is critically related to the distance function that is defined on the space. Different distance functions are indicative of different spaces. In fact, in 1871

Klein showed that Euclidean, hyperbolic, and spherical geometries essentially only differ in their respective distance functions.

Riemann's ideas are stated in their most general form in modern topology and real analysis. One of the most general types of distance-defined spaces is called a *metric space*. A metric space consists of two parts. First, there must be a non-empty set of points (X). Second, there is a function (d) defined on the set which assigns a distance to any pair of points (x,y). Such a distance function, called a metric, must satisfy four conditions:

Let x, y, and z be elements of set X, then d(x,y) is a metric on X if

(1) Distance is always non-negative. That is,

$$d(x,y) \geq 0. \tag{2.1}$$

(2) Non-identical points have a positive distance. That is,

$$d(x,y) = 0 \text{ if and only if } x = y. \tag{2.2}$$

(3) Distance is symmetric. That is,

$$d(x,y) = d(y,x). \tag{2.3}$$

(4) Distance is the shortest path between points. In other words, a path between two points which is traced through a third point can never be shorter than the distance between the two points. (There are no short cuts.) This property is often called the triangle inequality. That is,

$$d(x,y) \leq d(x,z) + d(z,y). \tag{2.4}$$

These metric axioms express much of what is essential to our every day concept of distance.

The metric axioms are also quite general. An infinite variety of possible metric spaces exist. Three of the most well known metrics are the Euclidean, city block, and Minkowski metrics. Let's look at these three metrics as examples of metric functions.

In a two dimensional Cartesian coordinate system, the Euclidean distance between two points P_1 and P_2 located at the coordinates (x_1,y_1) and (x_2,y_2) respectively is

$$d(P_1,P_2) = \sqrt{(x_1-x_2)^2+(y_1-y_2)^2}. \tag{2.5}$$

This is the typical "straight line" distance between two points. The metric space defined in this way has all the properties of a Euclidean space.

Distance need not be defined in a Euclidean manner. Other metrics may be more natural under various circumstances. For instance, imagine that you are in New York City at 96th street and 1st Avenue, and you want to walk to a diner at 90th street and 3rd Avenue. Unless you can walk through buildings, the distance you would need to walk would not be the Euclidean, as-the-crow-flies distance. In this case a more realistic conception of distance is that your destination is six blocks downtown and two blocks cross-town. In other words, the diner is eight blocks away. The metric we have just described is appropriately called the city block metric. It is expressed mathematically as

$$d(P_1,P_2) = |x_1\text{-}x_2| + |y_1\text{-}y_2|. \tag{2.6}$$

A final example shows how general and powerful metrics can be. A third type of metric is the Minkowski metric, defined as

$$d(P_1,P_2) = [|x_1\text{-}x_2|^R + |y_1\text{-}y_2|^R]^{1/R}. \tag{2.7}$$

Here, R may take on any positive value greater than or equal to one. If R=1, the city block metric results and we have Equation 2.6. If R=2, the Euclidean metric results and we have Equation 2.5. Clearly, R can take on an infinite number of values resulting in a infinite number of potential metric spaces. Metrics also exist for hyperbolic and spherical geometries.

People are capable of looking at distance, of creating metrics, in more than one way, and stimulus conditions can also influence the metric used. As a simple example, most city dwellers tend to think of the distance between places in terms of a driving time metric. Because different roads travel at different speeds at different times of the day, this driving time metric would be quite complicated and very non-Euclidean.

A second more whimsical metric should be familiar to anyone who lives in a cold climate. I might call it the pain metric. People are often willing to walk a bit out of their way as long as they can stay out of the cold. The pain metric, then, would be the path that produces the minimum amount of pain from the cold.

An interesting account of metrics and their applications can be found in Shreider (1974). In terms of the psychology literature reported later in this book, we will see that the metric of visual space under laboratory conditions varies depending on which instructions are given to the subject and stimulus conditions. One of the primary themes of this book is that there is no single metric that describes visual space.

Metrics are sometimes stated in a differential form. Here we assume that if the metric function is true on a large scale it is also true on an infinitesimal scale. In terms of differentials, we would express the Euclidean metric (Equation 2.5) as

$$ds^2 = dx^2 + dy^2 . \tag{2.8}$$

Here, dx indicates a very small change in the x-dimension, dy indicates a very small change in the y-dimension, and ds indicates the change in distance. This form of the distance equation makes it possible to use differential equations and tensors when working with geometrical problems. You will notice throughout this book that I will tend to prefer algebraic expressions most of the time, because I believe that clarity demands using the simplest form of an equation possible.

Banach spaces and other more esoteric variations. Another way to employ spatial coordinates is to think of them as representing vectors. The length of vectors is expressed in terms of norms. In a normed-linear space, the norm is a function that assigns a number $\|x\|$ to each vector such that:

(1) The norm is always non-negative and only zero if the vector has no length. That is,

$$\|x\| \geq 0, \text{ and } \|x\| = 0 \text{ if and only if x is the zero vector.} \tag{2.9}$$

(2) The triangle inequality holds

$$\|x+y\| \leq \|x\| + \|y\|. \tag{2.10}$$

(3) Multiplying the coordinates by a scalar increases the norm by that scalar

$$\|ax\| = |a| \, \|x\|. \tag{2.11}$$

A normed-linear space that is also a complete metric space is called a Banach space. Thus, a Banach space is a metric space that assumes that distances have a ratio property in addition to the other assumptions. The distance between two points in a Banach space is simply $\|x-y\|$.

Even more general spaces exist such as Hausdroff spaces, Normal spaces, T1 spaces, and topological spaces. For the most part, these spaces are of lesser importance to the present enterprise because the concepts of size and distance are not as central in these spaces. The most general form of geometric space is a topological space. Topology looks at the properties of a space that remain invariant under continuous transformations. A continuous transformation is one in which two points that are close to each other to begin with will still be close to each other after the transformation, i.e., a bend or a stretch, but not a break or a tear. We will examine some of the topological properties of visual space later.

Quasimetrics. Angles and areas are also types of measures on a space. Many of their properties may be described by metric-like axioms. Angles may be defined on three points x, y, and z (where y is the vertex) by the function $A(x,y,z)$ where $0° \leq A \leq 180°$. The area of a triangle defined by three points x, y, and z may be expressed by the function $T(x,y,z)$. Thinking in terms of a Euclidean space as an example, both of these functions should have the property of being non-negative. Angles are symmetric in that

$$A(x,y,z) = A(z,y,x). \qquad (2.12)$$

Areas are entirely symmetric in that all six possible orders for x, y, and z produce the same area. A form of the triangle inequality also holds. That is, including a fourth point t,

$$A(x,y,z) \leq A(x,y,t) + A(t,y,z). \qquad (2.13)$$

$$\text{And } T(x,y,z) \leq T(x,y,t) + T(x,t,z) + T(t,y,z). \qquad (2.14)$$

I will call measures that satisfy metric-like axioms *quasimetrics*. The quasimetrics and metrics of a space taken together will be referred to as the metric properties of the space. Geometry is largely the study of distances, angles and areas and there interrelationships. By defining the metric properties of a space, we can set down a reasonably complete description of the geometry of that space.

I will also use the term quasimetric in another sense. Distance functions may satisfy some, but not all of axioms of a metric space. That is, we will find that peoples' judgments of size and distance do not always satisfy all of the axioms of a metric space, but still express peoples' perceptions of these quantities. I will also call distance functions that don't quite satisfy metric assumptions, but still reflect our mental conceptions of distance, quasimetrics. Failures to meet the metric axioms will make us question how well visual space fits together into a coherent structure.

Geometry as transformation. Because the same objects exist in both physical and visual spaces, points that exist in one space should also exist in the other. Once approach to understanding visual space then is to ask how points in physical space are transformed or mapped onto visual space. In 1872, Felix Klein, a German mathematician, proposed that different geometries can be defined by the transformations they permit and the properties that remain invariant in an object's structure after these transformations. (See Tittle, Todd, Perotti, and Norman (1995) for a excellent review of Klein's concepts and an empirical investigation of how they apply to visual space.) For example, Euclidean geometry allows an infinite variety of translations and rotations of coordinates which still preserve the distance between any two points in a space.

One of the simplest possible transformations between visual space and physical space would be a *similarity transformation*. Here, visual space would simply be a larger or smaller version of physical space, while the basic structure of physical space would be preserved in all other ways. After a similarity transformation, observers would report the absolute sizes of objects in visual space to be larger or smaller than the corresponding size in physical space, but they would be able to accurately report on ratios of distances, angles should be accurately perceived, and factors such as orientation and position in space should have no affect on judgments.

Another transformation that could be involved in transforming physical space to visual space would be a *conformal transformation*. The geometries of constant curvature mentioned earlier are of this type. While these geometries allow a considerable degree of distortion to exist between the two spaces on the macro level, they assume that both spaces are locally Euclidean. That is distance and angle relations in sufficiently small, local regions of the space are essentially Euclidean. On the macro level, however, straight lines in physical space may appear curved in visual space.

Another sort of transformation that proves to be very relevant in describing visual space is an *affine transformation* (c.f., Tittle, Todd, Perotti, & Norman, 1995; Todd & Bressan, 1990; Todd & Norman, 1991; Wagner, 1985; Wagner & Feldman, 1989). An affine transformation would allow space to be stretched in one direction compared to physical space. After such a transformation, the curvature constants of the space would remain the same and parallel lines would still look parallel. The geodesic, or the shortest path between two points, would remain the same. Observers would be able to correctly judge distance ratios for stimuli with the same orientation; however, the judged size of an object would systematically change along with changes in stimulus orientation.

A final transformation allowed in a Klein geometry is a *topological transformation*. A topological transformation would allow very complicated distortions to exist in visual space relative to visual space subject to the constraint that points adjacent to each other in physical space must still be adjacent to each other in the transformed space. Visual space is almost certainly of this type; however, the same cannot be said for memorial space or cognitive maps. Cognitive maps have many gaps and discontinuities that make them difficult to describe in geometric terms.

Philosophical Approaches to Visual Space Perception

The concept of visual space has a long history that antedates psychology as a discipline. Physical space, experiential space, and mathematical space occupied the attention of many great philosophers. In a recent article reviewing the history of a broad range of perceptual phenomena, Wade (1996) repeatedly demonstrates that pre-20th century philosophers and scientists often anticipated the observations of their modern counterparts. Experiential geometry is no exception to this rule.

According to Kline (1972), the ancient Greeks recognized a difference between the mathematical space described by their geometry and experiential space. Many subsequent philosophers lost this subtle distinction.

Newton pointed out that all mathematicians up to his time were convinced that Euclidean geometry correctly represented the properties of physical (and experiential) space. Isaac Barrow listed eight reasons for the absolute truth of Euclidean geometry. Hobbes, Locke, and Leibniz believed that Euclidean geometry is inherent in the design of the universe.

Bishop Berkeley (1709/1910) rediscovered the distinction between physical space, mathematical space, and visual space. Berkeley believed that nothing exists outside of conscious experience. Berkeley went on, however, to distinguish between the space defined by touch ("tangible extension") and the space defined by vision ("visible extension"). The tangible space was thought to be primary and is equivalent to the space revealed by measuring devices (what I call *physical space*). Visible space, on the other hand, was thought to be derived through associations between vision and touch. However, Berkeley clearly declared that tangible space, visible space, and the abstract space of mathematicians need not be the same.

Having made this bold statement, Berkeley then retreated into showing why the two types of space are equivalent. Berkeley believed that the eye itself is incapable of depth perception because objects at different distances can fall on the same point of the retina. Visual sensations of distance were said to arise because "when we look at a near object with both eyes, according as it approaches or recedes from us, we alter the disposition of the eyes, by lessening or widening the interval between the *pupils*. This disposition or turn of the eyes is attended with a sensation ... " from which perceptions of distance arise. These perceptions of distance are not direct, however, but rather arise from the repeated association of tangible experience with visible experience. Thus, Bishop Berkeley concluded that visual space ends up being identical to physical or tangible space. That is, visual space is Euclidean.

On the other hand, Berkeley argued that visual space is not continuous. He believed there exists a *minima visibilia* or a minimum size visible that we can perceive. Visual experience is composed of these small, but finitely-sized components. This viewpoint would imply that visual space does not satisfy one of the axioms of a Riemannian geometry of which Euclidean space is a subset. As Berkeley lived before Riemann's time, he did not see this implication. Once again, Berkeley believed visual space is Euclidean and is equivalent to tangible space.

Berkeley's idea that touch is the basis of all spatial knowledge and that *minima visibilia* exist would later influence psychology through the work of Weber. Weber's creation of the just noticeable difference (JND) concept came from his studies of touch and how touch is the basis for our concept of space. Weber later influenced Fechner, and Fechner influenced Helmholtz.

The first major philosopher to deviate from Berkeley's position was David Hume in his *Treatise of Human Nature* (1739/1896). Hume did not deny the existence of a world outside of human experience. He did feel, however, that no one could justify such a belief. Thus, all statements made by philosophers and scientists concerning space must be in regard to experiential space. Hume also felt that there were no self-evident truths or universal laws. As such, Euclidean geometry could not be thought of as a certain truth. Like any other question, the validity of Euclidean geometry is subject to empirical investigation. Even if scientific investigation proved to support the Euclidean position, there is no guarantee that the universe will always be Euclidean or is Euclidean everywhere.

Immanuel Kant reacted violently to Hume's nihilism. In his *Critique of Pure Reason* (1781/1929) Kant asserted that the Euclidean nature of space is a synthetic *a priori* truth. In other words, it is a truth which goes beyond logic *per se* but which nevertheless is certain. This certainty does not arise from knowledge of a pre-experiential world. Instead, space is a fundamental element of human experience; it is a necessary precondition for a person to experience anything at all.

In Kant's words:

Space is not an empirical concept which has been derived from outer experiences. For in order that certain sensations be referred to something outside me (that is, to something in another region of space from that in which I find myself), and similarly in order that I may be able to represent them as outside and alongside one another, and accordingly as not only different but as in different places, the representation of space must be presupposed. The representation of space cannot, therefore, be empirically obtained from the relations of outer appearance. On the contrary, this outer experience is itself possible only through that representation. (Kant, 1781/1929, p. 23)

Kant made no distinction between space as the individual experiences it and as the physical scientist experiences it. Both represent phenomenal experience as opposed to the "noumenal world" that lies beyond experience. The geometry of the noumenal world is unknown. The Euclidean geometry reflected in our experience and in our physical science is a function of the organizing power of the human mind. The visual world has three dimensions not because this is the true nature of the universe but because our mind gives it to us in this form.

Helmholtz (1869/1921) was drawn to the study of geometry and experience by his opposition to Kantian nativism. While he did agree with Kant that some sort of basic concept or intuition of space must exist before we can perceive the world spatially at all, Helmholtz believed that determining the specific geometries that best describe visual experience and the physical universe were empirical problems to be settled by observation rather than philosophical analysis. Because more than one consistent geometry can be imagined, Euclidean spatial axioms can not be considered necessary for us to conceive of space. A general spatial sense can be transcendentally given without the axioms that govern it being so. The axioms that are expressed in spatial experience can be empirically investigated.

Helmholtz (1868/1921) believed that he could establish three axioms which described visual and physical space. In particular, he believed the following three characteristics describe our spatial experience: 1) Space is a three dimensional manifold. That is space can be coordinatized, and motion produces a continuous change in the coordinates. 2) Rigid objects display the property of free mobility such that moving from one part of space to another does not change the structure of the object. 3) Space is *monodromic*. A complete rotation of an object around any axis will produce a figure that is congruent to the original figure. Helmholtz believed that these three axioms taken together imply that experiential space is a geometry of constant curvature. That is, experiential space must be either Euclidean, spherical, or hyperbolic.

Helmholtz (1868/1921) felt that one could show empirically that physical space is Euclidean, at least within the limits of measurement possible for terrestrial measures. Experiential space, on the other hand, could be consistent with any of the geometries of constant curvature. Helmholtz went on to describe how the world would be experienced if our perceptions were spherical or hyperbolic. Which of these geometries best describe visual space is an open empirical question.

Meanwhile, back on the British Isles, Thomas Reid, a Scottish philosopher, published a book entitled *Inquiry into the Human Mind* (1764/1813). With this book, the study of visual space *per se* began.

Thomas Reid was interested in "what the eye alone can see" without regard to deeper processing due to cognition, experience, or motion. Indeed, Reid rejected the representational view of mind altogether (Ben-Zeev, 1989,1990). With this view of perception in mind, Reid developed a geometry for this visible space which was synthetic in nature. As summarized by Daniels (1974), Reid's geometry was presented in four steps: (1) He used standard notions of points, lines, angles, etc.; (2) he applied these notions to what an idealized eye would see; (3) he claimed that the eye itself is incapable of depth perception for much the same reason as Berkeley; as such, he stated that his "visible" space can be represented by a sphere of arbitrary radius encompassing the space; (4) he deduced some central theorems of the geometry. (For example, no parallel lines exist is the space. The sum of the angles of a triangle is greater than 180°. A straight line in visual space will cut the space in two and come around to meet itself if followed through its whole circuit.) Mathematically, these assumptions are consistent with a spherical geometry (technically called a doubly elliptic Riemannian geometry).

Reid conducted a thought experiment with a hypothetical race called the Idomenians who could see, but not touch the world. He believed that such creatures would possess no conception of depth. Like Berkeley, Reid believed that depth perception arises from our sense of touch.

Thomas Reid's theory is significant for several reasons. First, his statement of a non-Euclidean geometry antedates Lobatchevsky's mathematically rigorous work. Second, Reid's geometry is explicitly applied to a visual space as opposed to physical space (which Reid also believed existed) and as opposed to a purely mathematical space. Third, Reid was also interested in how observers were capable of depth perception. He may be the first to submit that frontal and in-depth perceptions of extent might come from different sources. If frontal and in-depth perceptions of extent might come from different sources, we might conjecture that it is possible that the two spatial dimensions could be perceived differently.

Henri Poincaré, one of the greatest mathematical philosophers of the 20th century, wrote extensively about the nature of space. Poincaré concluded that there is no "true" geometry. Many geometries may be applied to experience. Some geometries are simpler and more convenient than others, however.

Poincaré spoke explicitly about visual space in one section of his *Science and Hypothesis* (1905). In several respects, Poincaré's views were similar to Reid's. The eye itself only receives a two dimensional view of the world. This visual space is clearest at the center of the field of vision. More importantly, Poincaré reiterated that perception of depth arises from "sensations quite different from the visual sensations which have given us the concept of the first two dimensions. The third dimension will therefore not appear to us as playing the same role as the two others. What may be called complete visual space is not therefore an isotropic space" (p. 53). Once again, the untested possibility exists that frontal and in-depth perception of space may be quite different.

The viewpoint that visual space is represented by a spherical geometry is common among more modern philosophers who have been influenced by Husserl's (1910) phenomenological approach. Husserl felt that during most of their lives people assume a natural attitude in which the focus of our awareness is turned outward toward the world and we experience it without examining our thoughts. In contrast, the phenomenological attitude of Husserl involves turning ones mind inward and attempting to "bracket out" all presuppositions arising from our knowledge of and theories about the outer world.

In terms of space perception, Husserl believed that our experience of space is layered (Scheerer, 1985). His first layer is the visual field. The *visual field* is similar to an artist's canvas on which sensations are spread out left and right, and up and down, but the visual field lacks depth. Objects only present one face to the observer. In other words, we see what Idhe (1986) referred to as the manifest profile of an object. His second layer involves eye movement. In this *occulomotor field*, visual and kinesthetic experiences are integrated to produce a wider area of clear visual experience. The third layer involves head movement; this *kephalomotor field* exposes us to a hemisphere of visual experience. Up to this point, Husserl's analysis produces an experience similar to being inside a sphere of arbitrary size. The third dimension of depth is only added to our experience through motion. In this *locomotor field*, the horizon of my experience shifts with the movements of my body and the properties of three-dimensional space begin to emerge. Locomotion within the field produces an experience of expansion of approaching objects and contraction of receding objects. This expansion and contraction of objects is correlated with our perception of distance and depth. In other words, we experience visual flow patterns similar to those Gibson (1950) describes.

This description of the world reminds me of Helmholtz (1868/1921) who described the experiences of a person living in a hyperbolic space (which he termed a "pseudospherical" space) in a similar fashion to this analysis. According to Helmholtz, if the experiences of a person were hyperbolic they would "give him the same impression as if he were at the center of Beltrami's spherical image. He would believe he could see all round himself the most distant objects of this space at a finite distance, let us for example assume a distance of 100 feet. But if he approached these distant objects they would expand in front of him, and indeed more in depth than in area, while behind them they would contract" (p. 21).

More recently, Daniels (1974) and Angell (1974) have proposed that visual space is phenomenologically best represented by a spherical geometry, just as Reid (1764/1813) suggested. Along similar lines, French (1987) published an excellent philosophical treatise on space perception that also takes a phenomenological point of view. French contrasts his conception of "visual space" with a naive realist view of space. To French, visual or phenomenal space is defined by an attitude shift from the outward-oriented view of a physical scientist to an inward-oriented view of the world which examines the experience of space that is phenomenally immediately present.

French believes that phenomenological space is continuous and bounded within a region of about 170° horizontally and 120° vertically. Phenomenal space is two-dimensional because it does not possess thickness. In fact, to French, phenomenal space is like seeing a projection onto part of a sphere where the viewer is located at the center of the sphere. Depth perception is a distinctly different topic and may be thought of as a separate dimension, separately determined. On the other hand, depth does influence our perception. French believes that objects at different distances are projected onto spheres of varying curvature and that this curvature is a function of distance from the observer.

In my opinion, the various philosophers who argue that visual space is spherical are not wrong, but they are incomplete. Under monocular conditions where binocular depth cues are unavailable (and head and body movement are not allowed) and when the observer is asked to assume a phenomenal attitude in which cognitive cues to depth are ignored, the spherical model probably does describe our perceptions of visual space. Although these conditions seem rather narrowly drawn, humans are capable of assuming such an attitude under such conditions and therefore the spherical models deserves a legitimate place among the geometries of visual space. However, the phenomenological attitude is not the only attitude that may be included sensibly within the definition of visual space. Our ordinary understanding of space as we manipulate it to achieve our ends is certainly a very different experience of space than the phenomenological view, but it is none-the-less an experience of space. In fact, it is the more common and useful experience of space. Neither of these sorts of spatial experience need correspond to space as physical measures reveal it to us. A complete understanding of visual space then, must take into account the varying attitudes that people are able to assume when thinking about space. We will speak more of this matter when we discuss the effects of instructions on spatial judgments in Chapters 5 and 6.

Opening the Psychophysical Toolbox to Build a Window into Visual Space

Physical space can be measured using a variety of physical instruments such as rulers and protractors. The results of these measures are objective in that more than one observer can simultaneously examine the results of the measurement and different observers should come up with precisely the same results through repeated measurement. Unfortunately, experiential space (and visual space in particular) is subjective by its very nature. It is impossible to open up a person's conscious experience to allow multiple observers to make observations. The only route available to investigate visual space is to allow people to report on their own experiences using the tools of psychophysics.

The purpose of the last section of this chapter is to briefly introduce the tools available for examining visual space perception and to say a few words about their weaknesses and the meaning that can be assigned to the results they produce. Subsequent chapters will contain a more complete discussion of the issues and techniques raised here, but saying a few words now will make it easier to develop those other points later.

Psychophysical tools and their limitations. Psychophysical methods are of three basic types: numeric estimation, magnitude production, and sensitivity measures. Numeric estimation techniques require an observer to assign a number to a perceived intensity or extent. Two commonly employed numeric estimation methods are magnitude estimation and category estimation. In magnitude estimation observers attempt to preserve ratios, that is, if one stimulus seems twice as large another, the observer is asked to assign a number that is twice as big. In category estimation, observers are asked to assign each stimulus to a limited number of perceptually equal categories. In space perception, numeric estimation techniques have been used to estimate perceived areas, volumes, angles, and other metric characteristics of a space, but they have been employed primarily for estimating size and distance.

Magnitude production techniques require an observer to match perceptions. In a perceptual matching task, the observer may be asked to adjust the intensity or extent of a stimulus under standard conditions until it is perceived to be equivalent to a fixed stimulus under varying conditions or they may be asked to pick which of a series of standard stimuli best matches their perception of a comparison stimulus. Alternatively, the observer might be asked to draw or physically produce their impressions of a stimulus arrangement. For example, the observer might be asked to draw a map of the perceived layout of a set of stimuli. This mapping technique is most commonly employed in cognitive mapping studies that involve large-scale environment whose spatial layout is learned across time. It is seldom used for the perception of smaller-scale stimuli that are physically present and simultaneously observable at the time of the testing (although there are exceptions).

Sensitivity measures ascertain the smallest physical difference between stimuli that observers can discriminate. The most common sensitivity measurement techniques are the method of constant stimuli, the method of limits, and the method of adjustment. These techniques are typically directed at small-scale stimuli such as the perception of line length and seldom employed to measure perceptions of large-scale environments. In general, sensitivity measures give two sorts of information (Ono, Wagner, & Ono, 1995; Wagner, Ono, & Ono, 1995). First, one can determine the accuracy of a perception; that is, how much a perception deviates from some objective value. This is particularly useful in quantifying spatial illusions. Second, one can determine the precision of perceptual processing; that is, how little must a stimulus change before the observer notices a difference. These just noticeable differences may be thought of as measures of perceptual sensitivity where sensitivity is highest when the just noticeable difference is small.

All of these psychophysical methods have been applied extensively to the spatial domain. From a geometric point of view, this extensive body of literature suffers from several weaknesses. First of all, psychophysical work has been concerned almost exclusively with unidimensional stimuli (Lockhead, 1992), although there are exceptions to this rule (Wagner, 1992). Distance perception, for instance, has been extensively investigated. Many studies explore perception of distance in-depth (stretching away from the observer). Other studies explore distance perception in the frontal plane. Yet, few studies systematically explore depth and frontal perception simultaneously. The infinite number of possible orientations for distances in between frontal and in-depth orientations is virtually an untapped void. We will mention a few studies that apply psychophysical methods to multidimensional stimuli in Chapter 7, but these studies are rare. Second, the psychophysical literature on space perception is largely disorganized. Providing a multidimensional geometric model for visual space may allow us to fit unrelated studies into a more coherent framework. This is the goal of Chapters 5, 6, and 7. Third, it is rare for any researcher to report results from more than one method in the same paper. This makes it impossible to know whether the psychophysical functions found in any given study are due to perception itself or due to response processes inherent in the method. A few studies will be mentioned later that do apply several alternative techniques at once. Commonalties resulting from these converging measures are more likely to represent aspects of visual space that are independent of the methods employed. Yet, few studies bother to take this step.

Fechner, Stevens, and the power function. When people are asked to report on their spatial perceptions using numeric estimation methods, the relationship between judged (J) and actual (D) distance is most often described by a power function (Baird, Wagner, & Noma, 1982; Cadwallader, 1979):

$$J = \lambda D^{\alpha} \tag{2.15}$$

where α is an exponent and λ is usually thought of as a scaling constant (although it has other possible meanings such as indicating the existence of an illusion as we will see later). In psychophysics, this equation is sometimes known as Steven's Law and it is commonly thought to describe the relationship between magnitude estimates and almost any unidimensional stimulus continua (Stevens, 1957, 1975). Theoretically, category estimates are said to follow a logarithmic function (Galanter, 1962), but a many researchers (Krueger, 1989; Wagner, 1982, 1989) feel that Equation 2.15 also describes these judgments and is the more useful and meaningful formulation.

If our perceptions perfectly matched reality, we would expect that the exponent for the power function should be exactly 1.0. Yet, past research has shown that there is no single exponent that holds under all conditions (Wiest & Bell, 1985). In fact, there are times when the exponent is considerably higher than 1.0, and conditions under which it is considerably lower than 1.0. The exponent in perceptual studies depends on instructions, the richness of depth information, and stimulus orientation (Baird, 1970). Similarly, when people are asked to judge distance from memory, as in cognitive mapping studies, exponents are typically less than one and often range widely depending on factors such as the familiarity of the environment, the presence of barriers, and the informational density of the environment (Wagner, 1998; Wiest & Bell, 1985). In summary, the exponent is not a constant, nor is it generally equal to 1.0 in either the direct perception or recall of spatial information.

What does the exponent to the power function mean? Wagner (1998) purposed that the exponent for the power function is related to the concept of uncertainty reduction. Uncertainty about spatial layout in turn should influence judgment precision. Conditions that make our knowledge of stimuli less precise should in theory lead to a decline in the exponent.

Baird and Noma (1978) and Teghtsoonian (1971) believe the exponent reflects the relative sensitivity of the subject to the response and stimulus dimensions. Teghtsoonian (1971) also believed that the exponent is directly related to the stimulus range. When a broad range of stimuli are presented the exponent should decline compared to presenting a narrow range of stimuli.

Warren (1958, 1969, 1981) proposed a Psychophysical Correlate Theory. He believed that subjects do not always directly estimate the stimulus dimension that the experimenter intends them to, but rather base their judgments on some other aspect of the stimulus. For example, instead of actually judging area, estimates may actually reflect the size of a single dimension of the stimulus. Variations in exponents result when the experimenter attempts to compare the subject's estimates to the wrong stimulus dimension.

Steven's (1970, 1971) felt variations in the exponent result from the varying degrees of transformation that occur in the process of transducing stimulus energy into neural firing and in the process of carrying that information up to and through the brain. Similarly, Baird's Complementrity Theory (1996) posits that the exponent arises from the competition of two processes, a sensory process that depends on the activation of neural populations by stimuli and a second cognitive process that reflects the subject's uncertainty when giving a response on a given trial.

Whatever the true meaning of the exponent, we may think of the process of arriving at a psychophysical judgment as having two stages. First, the perceptual process produces a sensation that we experience, and then a judgment process operates on this sensation to produce a number that represents our judgment. So the exponent of the power function really has two parts and Equation 2.15 can be rewritten as in the following equation:

$$J = \lambda \, (D^s)^r \tag{2.16}$$

Where s indicates that some portion of the exponent is determined by sensory factors, and r indicates that some portion of the exponent is determined by response factors. (For some even this may be too strong a formulation. Perhaps such a reader will accept that the exponent is some function of sensory and response factors.)

The Holy Grail for a psychophysicist interested in space perception would be to determine the equation that truly reflects a person's experience of world as a function of physical layout. Unfortunately, if Equation 2.16 or something like it is correct, this Holy Grail will be forever out of reach. We will never know the degree to which the judgments observers produce reflect their conscious experience as opposed to judgment factors related to number usage or production errors.

However, because this issue cannot be resolved, the theorist is forced to take the data as it is and define visual space in terms of the data. The geometry of visual space is really the geometry of the judgments subjects produce.

There is one final issue I would like to discuss concerning psychophysical functions. Generally, the parameters of Equation 2.15 are thought of as being constants. Lockhead (1992) criticized psychophysical work for not sufficiently taking into account context when generating psychophysical equations, and I have agreed with him that it is important to take such things into account (Wagner, 1992). In truth the parameters of Equation 2.15 should be thought of as being functions of these contextual conditions, not constants. Perhaps Equation 2.14 is better rewritten as

$$J = \lambda(\beta, \gamma, \delta, \ldots) \, D^{\alpha(\beta, \gamma, \delta, \ldots)} \qquad (2.17)$$

where β, γ, and δ represent varying experimental conditions. Here, the "scaling constant" and the exponent are no longer thought of as constants, but as functions of judgment conditions such as instructions, cue conditions, etc. This final equation reflects the essential spirit of this book. There is no single geometry for visual space perception, but the geometry of the space is a function of conditions.

3

Synthetic Approaches to Visual Space Perception

As is often the case with problems in perception, psychology took over where philosophy left off. The Kantian (1781/1923) notion that only one geometry for phenomenal space was possible, because this way of seeing the world is one of the organizing structures of the mind without which perception is impossible, gave way to Helmholtz's (1869/1921) view. According to Helmholtz, because more than one geometry may be consistently apprehended by the mind, the nature of space as it is experienced is an empirical question best left to scientific investigation.

Visual Space as a Hyperbolic Geometry

The empirical investigation of visual space also began with Helmholtz (1867, 1896/1925). (Although a good case could be made for Götz Martius's (1889) work on size constancy which we will discuss in Chapter 6.) Helmholtz found that when an observer is asked to arrange three luminous points in the horizontal plane in a straight line, the resulting arrangement is not always physically straight. The configuration can be physically concave toward the observer for near points, physically straight at a small range of intermediate distances, or convex relative to the observer for physically distant triplets.

In another classic experiment, Hillebrand (1902) asked observers in a darkened room to arrange pairs of luminous points stationed at various distances from the observer to form an alley with walls equidistant from each other. The resulting arrangement was not physically straight, but both walls of the alley curved outward with increasing distance from the observer.

Blumenfeld (1913) replicated Hillebrand's work and extended it in important ways. Like Hillebrand, Blumenfeld asked observers to arrange two rows of luminous points to form an alley whose walls were equidistant. The most distant pair of points was fixed. The resulting "distance alley" arrangement was neither physically straight nor were the walls parallel in a Euclidean sense. As before, the physical distance between pairs of points gradually increased with increasing distance of the pair from the observer. Blumenfeld also asked the observers to arrange the points to form straight lines parallel to each other. The resulting "parallel alley" arrangement is similar to that obtained for the "distance alleys." The distance between pairs of points gradually increases as the pairs lie farther from the observer. The parallel alleys were consistently different from the dis-

30

tance alleys in one respect, however. The parallel alleys were always located inside the distance alleys; that is, the distance between pairs of points is always smaller for parallel alleys than it is for distance alleys. Blumenfeld's experiments have been replicated many times by other observers (Hardy, Rand, & Ritter, 1951; Hardy, Rand, Rittler, Blank, & Boeder, 1953; Higashiyama, Ishikawa, & Tanaka, 1990; Indow, Inoue, & Matsushima, 1962b, 1963; Indow & Watanabe, 1984a). However, attempts to extend this work to the fronto-parallel plane have generally found distance and parallel alleys to coincide and not display significant curvature (Indow, 1988; Indow & Watanabe, 1984b, 1988).

Luneburg's theory of binocular space perception. Luneburg (1947, 1948, 1950) used Helmholtz and Blumenfeld's demonstrations as evidence that visual space is hyperbolic. Luneburg's approach was synthetic in nature. He began by listing a series of axioms about visual space similar to those Helmholtz proposed (which we discussed in the previous chapter). Based on these axioms, Luneburg concluded that visual space is a hyperbolic geometry.

After Luneburg's death in 1949, a number of talented mathematical psychologists have kept Luneburg's work alive by proposing modified versions of the theory. Blank (1953, 1957, 1958, 1959) refined Luneburg's theory somewhat along the same synthetic path. Blank more explicitly laid out the axioms and hypotheses on which the theory was based and accounted for the experimental evidence that existed at the time. Following Blank, Indow (1967, 1974, 1979, 1990, 1995) became the primary proponent of the theory, producing a series of mathematically sophisticated papers and empirical tests of the theory. More recently, Aczél, Boros, Heller, & Ng (1999) and Heller (1997a, 1997b) have written clear papers that present additional refinements of the theory.

Luneburg's theory was based on a fairly sizeable set of axioms. First, Luneburg assumed that visual space is a metric space as defined in the last chapter. Second, the theory assumes that visual space is convex. This axiom says that for any two points $(P_1$ and $P_3)$ on a line a third point (P_2) exists on the line between them such that

$$D(P_1,P_2) + D(P_2, P_3) = D(P_1,P_3) \qquad (3.1)$$

where D is the metric for the space.

Third, the theory assumes that visual space is compact. This means that for any point P_1 and any number ε, there exists another point P_2 such that

$$0 < D(P_1,P_2) < \varepsilon \qquad (3.2)$$

This axiom allows one to assume that the metric is continuous and well-behaved. It also allows one to express the metric in a differential form, because the distance function is defined at the smallest levels.

Fourth, the theory assumes that visual space is locally Euclidean. This means that, within a sufficiently small neighborhood, metric relationships between points are essentially Euclidean, even though the space as a whole may not be.

For example, the surface of the earth may best be described by a spherical geometry, but within any local region we get along rather well using Euclidean concepts of measurement to perform our daily tasks.

Fifthly, the theory assumes that visual space is Desarguesian. This says that for any two points on a visual plane, the geodesic (or shortest path between the points) does not depart from the plane.

Finally, Luneburg assumed visual space has the property of free mobility. That is a rigid structure moved through visual space should retain its distance and angular relationships. In other words, visual space is homogenous, and one can construct visually congruent configurations at any location and orientation.

Taken together, these axioms imply that visual space is a Riemannian geometry of constant curvature. Riemannian geometries of constant curvature are of three types: Euclidean, elliptical (spherical), and hyperbolic. Blumenfeld's demonstration that more than one set of "parallels" could be produced by different instructions led Luneburg to conclude that visual space is non-Euclidean. The fact that the "parallel alleys" tend to be inside the "distance alleys" allowed Luneburg to conclude that visual space is hyperbolic.

Knowing the visual space is a Riemannian geometry of constant curvature also defines the metric function that allows us to specify the distance between points in space. Using differential form, the length of a line element ds is

$$ds^2 = \frac{dx^2 + dy^2 + dz^2}{[1 + \frac{K}{4}(X^2+Y^2+Z^2)]} \tag{3.3}$$

where dx, dy, and dz represent small changes in the x, y, and z dimensions of a point located at coordinates X, Y, and Z. Here, K is the curvature of the space. If K is positive, the space is spherical. If K is zero, the space is Euclidean. In Luneburg's theory, K takes on the negative value of a hyperbolic space.

In this hyperbolic space, points lying along the same Vieth-Müller circle are perceived as being equidistant from the observer. Here, Vieth-Müller circles are circles that contain the center of each eye as part of their circumference. (See Figure 3.1.) Under idealized assumptions about the structure of the eye, the Vieth-Müller circle consists of stimulus locations that are projected on corresponding places on the two retinas when the observer fixates on one point of the circle (Howard & Rogers, 1995). The lines in the hyperbolic space consist of Hillebrand hyperbolae. These lines should be perceived to have a constant visual direction. If the observer fixates on a point along an Hillebrand hyperbola, other points along the hyperbola are projected on retinal points that deviate the same extent from the fovea in both eyes but in opposite directions.

Luneberg's theory makes several testable predictions outside of those already mentioned. First of all, the sum of the angles of any triangle should always be less than 180°. Second, Luneburg established a correspondence between physical space and visual space. This correspondence yields a metric formula (in terms of physical coordinates) that relates physical space to distance in visual space. This formula could be tested empirically. Third, the mapping from physical space to visual space is conformal. That is, an angle in physical space is mapped onto an equal angle in visual space. (The validity of each of these predictions will be discussed in detail in Chapter 7.) In addition, Luneburg's formulation requires visual space to be bounded. The most distant objects in physical space should seem to lie at a finite distance from the observer.

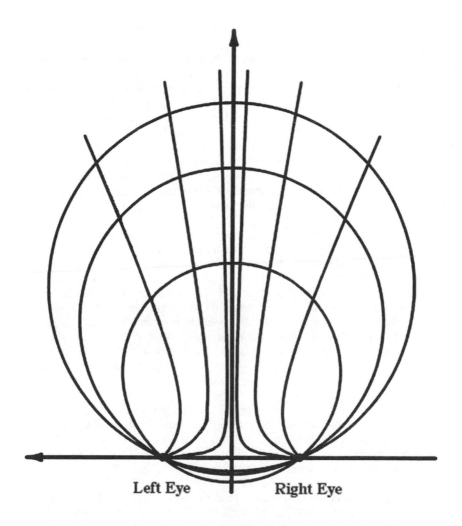

Figure 3.1. Vieth-Müller circles and hyperbolae of Hillebrand. Points lying along Vieth-Müller circles are theoretically perceived as being equidistant from the observer, while points on Hillebrand hyperbolae are theoretically perceived as having the same visual direction.

A beautiful theory, but does it work? Anyone who has worked with Luneburg's theory is impressed by its brilliance, precision, and scope. The theory stands as one of the most sophisticated and beautiful contributions ever made to psychology. (Interestingly, Luneburg was actually a physicist rather than a psychologist.) This very elegance may account for the fact that the theory has survived over 50 years. As Blank (1959) said "There is something more to be said for an apt mathematical model. So elegant was Luneburg's theoretical development that it was not abandoned despite the initial failure of experimental results to conform to theory" (p. 398). Despite the brilliance of Luneburg's theory, empirical results have not always supported it.

Of course, the weakest point of any well-developed axiomatic system is in the axioms themselves. Luneburg's theory is no exception. Luneburg's first axiom is that visual space is a metric space. A number of researchers have disputed this claim. For example, Cadwallader (1979), Codol (1985), and Burroughs and Sadalla (1979) report that distance judgments are not always symmetrical; that is, the distance from point A to point B is not always the same as the distance from point B to point A. Baird, Wagner, and Noma (1982) demonstrated that distance judgments often violate the triangle inequality. Baird et al. also show that another of Luneburg's assumptions, that visual space is convex, routinely fails to describe distance judgments. We'll speak more about the logic and evidence behind these statements and the consequences of their violations in the next chapter of this book.

Convexity and metricity are not the only axioms of Luneburg's system that may be open to doubt. For example, is visual space really compact? This axiom requires that for any detectable distance percept, yet finer discriminations must be possible. In other words, there should be no limit to our ability to discriminate stimuli. However, all psychophysical dimensions have a threshold for detection and a finite just noticeable difference for distinguishing between stimuli. Similarly, there is a minimum size to allow detection of an object, and there is a minimum difference between sizes that is distinguishable. For example, the Weber fraction for line lengths is about .04 (Baird & Noma, 1978). While this is very good, it is not good enough to satisfy the compactness axiom. Bertrand Russell (1971) expressed this conclusion eloquently

> We must do one of two things: either declare that the world of one man's sense-data is not continuous, or else refuse to admit that there is any lower limit to the duration and extension of a single sense-datum. The later hypothesis seems untenable, so that we are apparently forced to conclude that the space of sense-data is not continuous... (p. 107)

The compactness axiom is necessary to allow the expression of distance metrics in differential form. Luce and Edwards (1958) argue that existence of finite sized just noticeable differences makes the use of differential form illegitimate. If taken seriously, this objection is general enough to lead us to reject more than Luneburg's hyperbolic model; without the compactness axiom, we also need to conclude that visual space is not even Riemannian.

Similarly, the rejection of the compactness axiom casts into doubt Luneburg's axiom that visual space is locally Euclidean. The local Euclidean property states that metric relations are Euclidean in a sufficiently small neighborhood. Yet, if one can't speak of differential sized regions, one also can't speak of the metric relations within such a region. Under such circumstances, it is hard to assign any meaning to the locally Euclidean axiom.

Another critical axiom is that visual space is Desarguesian. According to this axiom, the visual geodesic (the shortest distance) connecting any two points in a perceptual plane should not depart anywhere from that plane. Foley has tested this property. Foley's early work (1964a, 1964b) supported the Desarguesian property, while his later work (1972) denies it.

Foley's (1972) work also casts into doubt the free mobility axiom. Foley asked observers to construct two separate triangles that seemed identical to the observer in different positions in space. Having constructed the triangles, observers make judgments about the corresponding portions of the triangle. The judgments of corresponding sides were not congruent, showing that what seemed to be the same configuration as a whole was not the same in terms of its parts.

Similarly, according to this axiom, it should be possible to move figures through visual space without distortion. Moving an object through space should preserve distances and angles. Angles in particular should be conformal; an angle in physical space should correspond to the same angle in visual space. Wagner (1985) showed that distance and angle judgments for physically similar objects changed dramatically depending on the location and orientation of the object in space. In particular, objects oriented frontally with respect to the observer were seen as much larger than those oriented in depth, and angles facing toward or away from an observer where seen as much larger than those seen to the side. Thus, it would seem that the location and orientation of an object in space will influence our perceptions of it, and the free mobility axiom does not hold.

Based on Foley (1972) and Wagner (1985), Suppes (1995) concluded that describing visual space would require radically different assumptions than those of Luneburg. Suppes believed that visual space was unlikely to be any of the geometries of constant curvature. Instead, Suppes believed that visual space is not unitary, but that different geometries may be required to describe different experimental results.

Cuijpers, Kappers, and Koenderink (2001) also challenged the free-mobility axiom using a different method. The authors presented reference targets at various orientations and locations relative to the observer. Observers were asked to rotate a comparison target until it appeared parallel to the reference target. Contrary to the Luneberg's predictions (or that of any geometry of constant curvature), the comparison's orientation systematically deviated from the reference orientation and that the degree of deviation varied as a function of relative location of the stimuli in space. They also found that the degree of deviation was influenced by how the stimuli were oriented compared to the walls of the room in which the experiment was conducted. Thus, the angular judgments not only varied with position in space, but also were influenced by the presence of reference stimuli. Cuijpers et al. hold out the possibility that free mobility might hold in an environment free of reference stimuli, such as a completely darkened room (conditions similar to the parallel alley experiments that Luneberg's proponents have used to support the Hyperbolic model), but the authors feel that geometries of constant curvature can not account for their data when reference information is present. Because most ordinary perception takes place under information rich conditions with many reference stimuli present, Cuijpers et al's data rules out the applicability of Luneberg's theory under most ordinary conditions.

Taken together Luneberg's axioms imply that visual space is a Riemannian geometry of constant curvature. What is more, Luneburg used the alley experiments to conclude that this curvature was negative. Is visual space a geometry of constant negative curvature? Some evidence indicates that this may not be the case. Based on alley experiments, Hardy, Rand, and Rittler (1951) and Ishii (1972) found that for about half of their observers, the curvature was negative and for the remainder it was positive. Higashiyama, Ishikawa, and Tanaka (1990) found that the parallel and distance alleys did not differ under a variety of conditions, indicating a curvature of zero. On the other hand, Indow, Inoue, and Matsuchima (1962a, 1962b, 1963), Hagino and Yoshika (1976), Higashiyama (1976), and Zajaczkowska (1956a, 1956b), have found negative curvature for the great majority of their observers. If one steps away from alley experiments, however, the picture changes. Higashiyama (1981, 1984) asked observers to move a light until it generated either a right triangle or an equilateral triangle relative to a second point and the observer's location. Based on this experiment, he concluded that the curvature of visual space is variable, depending on how far points range from the median plane and how far they are away. Koenderink, van Doorn, and Lappin (2000, 2003) also used triangle adjustment to determine that the curvature of visual space was positive for near stimuli and negative for distant stimuli. The curvature ranged from very negative to very positive. Similarly, Ivry and Cohen (1987) determined that the curvature varied from positive to negative for different stimulus configurations. Therefore, it would seem that visual space does not consistently display negative curvature. In fact, the curvature may not be constant at all, just as French (1987) proposed.

On the other hand, Cuijpers, Kappers, and Koenderink (2003) derived metric functions for visual and haptic space using a parallelity task. Their model found that a model assuming zero curvature fit data related to fronto-parallel horopters, parallel alleys, and distance judgments (based on data from Gilinsky (1951) and Wagner (1985)). A zero curvature would signal a Euclidean space rather than a hyperbolic one.

Luneberg's theory predicts that the sum of the angles of a triangle should be less than 180°. Moar and Bower (1983) had subjects estimate the direction from a location to two other locations, and calculated the angle between these direction estimates. They then asked the subjects to make similar judgment from each of the other two locations. The sum of the derived angles tended to be consistently greater than 180°, a result that is inconsistent with both the Euclidean and hyperbolic geometry formulations, and more consistent with a spherical geometry model. Of course, the direction estimates were based on memory; so, it is possible that they do not apply to direct perception. Lucas (1969) made a similar observation from a phenomenological standpoint. Based on careful introspection he observed that the sum of the angles of a quadrilateral appear to sum to more than 360°, once again consistent with a spherical geometry and not a hyperbolic one.

Luneburg's theory asserts that visual space is bounded; that is, the most distant objects should seem to lie at a finite distance from the observer. While no definite conclusions can be reached about the boundedness of visual space, a few studies bear on this issue somewhat. Plug (1989) investigated the measurement systems of ancient astronomers. He concluded that the Babylonians, Arabs, Greek, and Chinese believed the stars to lay no more than 10 to 40 meters away from the observer. Similarly, Rock and Kaufmann (1962) attempted to explain the moon illusion through a similar conception that the night sky is perceived as being a finite length away. In the case, of Rock and Kaufmann, the sky was thought to have the shape of an upside-down soup bowl. Baird and Wagner (1982) refuted this claim. They had subjects use magnitude estimation to have observers judge the distance to the night sky at various elevations. They found that some observers saw the zenith sky as being closer than the horizon just as Rock and Kaufmann predicted. On the other hand, slightly more observers saw it the other way around, the zenith was seen as being farther away than the horizon. Other subjects were in the middle, with the horizon and zenith being perceived as equally far away. What is more, the judgments of distance to the horizon sky were highly correlated with the physical distances to objects located along the horizon. Baird and Wagner concluded that the night sky is not perceived as a surface located at a specific distance away from the observer. As the article summarized "To the query 'How high is the sky?' we suggest the retort, 'What a meaningless question?'" (p. 303).

If the distance to celestial objects is indeterminate except in terms of our perceptions of distance along the ground, the next question that needs to be asked is whether our perceptions of distance along the ground are bounded. The exponent for egocentric distance judgments is typically greater than one (Wiest & Bell, 1985). This would indicate that the distance to physically far away stimuli is actually overestimated, and this over-estimation increases with increasing distance from the observer. Thus, not only do distance judgments not approach a limit, but the precise opposite appears to obtain. In addition, while there are circumstances where judgments of egocentric distance from the observer do show a tendency for judgments to distant objects to be compressed relative to what we would expect based on the judgments made toward nearer objects (because the exponent for the power function relating perceived distance to physical distance is often less than one), even these judgments do not approach a limit.

I might offer one observation that I have made introspectively that shows there to be no obvious limit to our ability to perceive that one object along the ground is farther away than another object. Anyone who has ever climbed a mountain knows that as one ascends the distance one can see continues to expand. From the top of the mountain, one can see that one hill is farther away than another even though the hills are many miles away. If visual space is bounded, the boundary must lie further away than one can see along the surface of the earth.

Another aspect of the theory can also be questioned. According to the theory, points along the Vieth-Müller circles should be perceived as being an equal distance from the observer. Yet, Hardy et al. (1953), Foley (1966), and Higashi-yama (1984) have shown that distance judgment deviate systematically from this prediction. In particular, perceived equidistance lies between the Vieth-Müller circle and physical equidistance, where this deviation from prediction is greatest for stimuli close at hand. A number of theorists have attempted to modify Lu-neburg's theory (Aczél et al., 1999; Blank, 1978; Heller, 1997) or proposed their own theories (Foley, 1980) to account for these deviations. None of these at-tempts have been completely satisfactory (Higashiyama, 1984).

Battro, di Piero Netto, and Rozenstraten (1976) found highly variable fronto-parallels under full-cue conditions that varied as a function of distance from the observer and varied between observers considerably. These results also challenge Luneburg's conceptualization.

Koenderink, van Doorn, Kappers, and Lappin (2002) present an even greater challenge to the traditional view of the Vieth-Müller circles. They asked observ-ers to adjust a central point until it appeared to form a straight line with two flanking points along the fronto-parallel plane. The adjustments observers made were slightly concave toward the observer, but the curvature was very small. (The radius of curvature was 21 m for stimuli 2 m from the observer and 178 m for stimuli 10 m from the observer.) A second pointing task actually found fronto-parallel planes that were concave toward the observer, a result directly the opposite of the traditional form of Vieth-Müller circles.

Finally, I'd like to add a theoretical objection on top of the empirical discon-firmation just mentioned. Our perceptions of visual space are the result of a long process that begins in the retina, follows along ganglion cells, and continues into the visual cortex. At no stage do we expect the end product of perception to be identical to the physical instantiation of the information. We do not perceive the world as being upside-down like the image of light on the retina. We do not perceive the world as being larger in the middle of the field of vision than in the periphery even though the visual cortex devotes more space to the middle of the visual field. Why would we expect equal perceived distance from the observer to fall along the Vieth-Müller circle or for parallel lines in the space to follow Hillebrand hyperbolea just because such circles and lines fall along corresponding points on the retina. Visual space is a unified whole, not the image on the ret-ina. Similarly, French (1987) feels that visual space must be spherical because stimulation falls on a circular retina, and geometrically this can't be projected onto a flat surface without adding distortion. Because no distortion is evident, French feels this is evidence for a spherical geometry for visual space. To both Luneburg and French I have the same basic objection: visual space is the end product of a process which includes a great deal of cognitive embellishment and which is designed to give the person access to the most veridical picture of the world possible. We should not expect it to coincide with the physical structures of the eyes or the brain. They are means to an end, but not an end in themselves.

Alternative accounts for the alley experiments. Although many objections can be raised to Luneburg's theory, it does have the virtue of accounting for the data from the often-repeated alley experiments. Numerous experimenters (Hardy, Rand, & Ritter, 1951; Hardy, Rand, Rittler, Blank, & Boeder, 1953; Indow,

Inoue, & Matsushima, 1962b, 1963) have found that when subjects are asked to adjust lights to form alleys in the dark, there is a strong tendency for points nearest to the observer to be set closer together than those fartherest away, and for "parallel" alleys to fall inside "distance" alleys. How can one account for this data outside of Luneburg's formulation?

A number of researchers (Baird, 1970; Battro, Reggini, & Karts, 1978; French, 1987; Wagner, 1982) have posited that the alley experiments are special cases of the more general phenomena of size constancy, which we will discuss in greater detail in Chapter 6. In the typical size constancy experiment, a near comparison stimulus is adjusted until it is perceptually equal to a standard stimulus placed at various distances from the observer. When such adjustments take place under reduced-cue conditions (such as a darkened room with most cues to distance eliminated), observers tend to perceive standard stimuli (as reflected by their adjustments of the comparison stimulus) as being progressively smaller as distance away from the observer increases—a phenomena known as underconstancy. Conversely, if observers were asked to adjust stimuli to be perceptually equal in length to a standard at one distance, they would be expected to adjust the length of more distant stimuli to be larger than they would for stimuli closer to the observer. This is exactly what is found in the alley experiments.

How can one explain the fact that the parallel alleys are often, but not always (Hardy, Rand, & Rittler, 1951; Higashiyama, Ishikawa, & Tanaka, 1990; Ishii, 1972) inside of the distance alleys? One possibility is that the data result from instruction effects. Underconstancy is least for objective instructions in which observers are asked make their adjustments reflect physical reality. Underconstancy is greater for apparent instructions in which observers are asked to make adjustments reflect their perceptions or how things "look." Underconstancy is greatest under projective instructions in which the observer is asked to take an artist's eye view of distance and have their adjustments reflect the amount of the visual field taken up by a stimulus. Projective instructions imply the observer should ignore depth cues. In terms of the alley experiments, this would mean that the alleys should be straightest (and on the outside) with objective instructions and most curved (and on the inside) for projective instructions.

In fact, Battro, Reggini, and Karts (1978) were able to precisely predict the shape of parallel alleys by assuming that judgments reflect a constant Thouless ratio (which will be defined and discussed in Chapter 6). Later experimental work confirmed that Thouless ratios were indeed constant for all distances when subject performed the alley task. According to their model, alleys should be straightest with Thouless ratios close to 1 (which generally occurs with objective instructions under full-cue conditions) and most curved and located inside with Thouless ratios close to 0 (which generally occurs with apparent or projective instructions under reduced cue conditions). Battro et al. found their size-constancy based model better fit the parallel alley data than Luneburg's hyperbolic model.

A careful look at the instructions used to generate distance and parallel alleys shows they may not be exactly of the same type. For example, Indow and Watanabe (1984a) gave the clearest description of their instructions in their methods section of any study I've found. Here is what they told subjects:

Please keep in your mind the following points.

(1) In the case of the parallel series, you are not requested to place two series to be physically parallel like railway tracks. Perceptually they appear
to converge at a certain distance because they are physically parallel. The
series you construct have to be perceptually parallel. You need not care
about what are physical positions of light points. Rely solely on your
perceptual impression...

(2) In the case of equi-distance series, you have to equate lateral distances
you perceive between two lights on the left and on the right. Farther pairs
may look inside of nearer pairs though all pairs look equally separated,
i.e., being spanned by the same invisible string if the string is moved
back and forth between pairs appearing at different distances from you.
(pp. 149, 151)

It would seem from the above description that great emphasis is placed on
judgments not reflecting physical reality in the parallel alley instructions. They
seem to fall somewhere between apparent and projective instructions. The distance alley instructions put much less emphasis on judgments not reflecting
reality. In fact, the reference to the invisible string is similar to asking subjects
to make their judgments according to a ruler. These instructions appear to fall
closer to the objective type. Baird (1970) and French (1987) find that this difference in instructions is common for alley experiments. If true, this would account
for parallel alleys being inside distance alleys as explained before.

Higashiyama, Ishikawa, and Tanaka (1990) directly tested the effects of instruction type on alley settings. They found that objective instructions consistently lead to straighter alleys that lie on the outside of alleys generated from
apparent instructions. If the same type of instructions were used, parallel and
distance alleys did not differ from each other under most conditions. Objective
alleys were outside of apparent alleys, but parallel alleys did not differ from distance alleys.

Indeed, the classic Blumenfeld alley experiment has probably been misinter-
preted. The defining feature of a hyperbolic geometry is the restatement of the
Parallel Postulate in the form: through a point P not on a line L, there is more
than one parallel to L. The Blumenfeld alleys might support the hyperbolic
model if more than one parallel existed *using the same instructions*. As a matter
of fact, only one parallel is produced for each instruction set. The reason different
parallels exist across different instructions is that *observers are performing different tasks*. As evidence for this, I cite a phenomenon mentioned by Luneburg
(1948) himself. Observers report that "parallel alleys" do indeed seem parallel;
however, "distance alleys" do not seem parallel. In fact, distance alleys do not
even appear to be composed of straight lines.

With this in mind a second alternative explanation of the alley results can be
offered that does not rely on objective vs. apparent instruction effects: The distance alley and parallel alley data may result from very separate mechanisms.
Let's consider how each data set might arise in turn.

(1) *Distance alleys*: Distance alley instructions ask to observer to maintain a constant distance between pairs of luminous points. According to Holway and Boring (1941) frontal judgments under reduced-cue settings (such as being in the dark) tend to be nearly proportional to the visual angle of the stimulus. (Presumably this is because the visual angle is the only information that the observer has to determine size.) If observers are asked to adjust stimuli to be the same perceived size, then actual size must systematically increase with increasing distance in order to maintain the same visual angle. The function that describes the relationship between visual angle and distance from the observer will be discussed in Chapter 6. For now it is enough to say that this function is exponential like (it looks a bit like an exponential equation, but is not) and would produce a curved alley just as in the Blumenfeld experiment.

(2) *Parallel alleys*: Wagner (1982, 1985) and Wagner and Feldman (1990) have shown that angle perception is powerfully influenced by the orientation of an angle with respect to the observer. Angles facing either directly toward the observer or directly away from the observer are perceptually expanded while those viewed from the side are perceptually compressed. That is, when an angle is seen on its side, a line from the observer can cut through both legs of the angle. For an angle seen facing directly toward or away from the observer, the opposite would be true. A line from the observe could only cut through one leg of the angle.

As shown in Figure 3.2a, asking observers to make parallel alleys is equivalent to asking them to make the angle defined by a given pair of points and one more distant one equal to 90°, a right angle. This angle is seen on its side. As such it should be seen as perceptually contracted. In order to achieve an angle that is perceptually equal to 90°, the physical angle must be expanded slightly. If this expansion is applied to each pair of points (successively working inward) a curve like that seen in the parallel alleys will result. Because this curve arises from a separate mechanism than the distance alley, we would not necessarily expect the two curves generated to coincide.

By the way, this logic can generate an interesting prediction that (to my knowledge) no one has ever tested before. Let us say that instead of asking observers to make two straight lines, they are asked to create two outward bending arcs as seen in figure 3.2b (perhaps by showing the curve to the subjects on a card presented frontally near the observer). This time the angle ($\emptyset_1$) will be seen frontally. This angle should seem perceptually expanded compared to physical reality. To adjust, the observer will need to set the points so that they curve less physically than the curve they were asked to produce. This is precisely the opposite of what occurred with the parallel alleys, and different from what a hyperbolic geometry would predict. (Note that the second curve is not really necessary.)

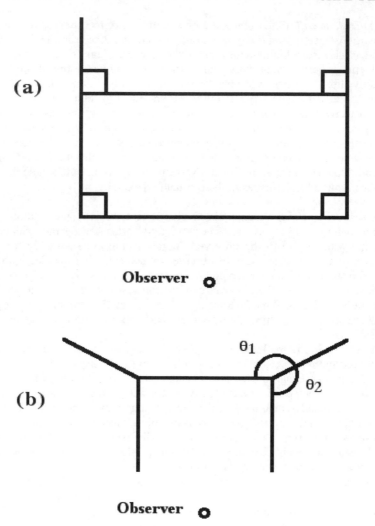

Figure 3.2. (a) The visual display observers are trying to produce in the parallel alley experiment. (b) The visual display observers are trying to produce in the experiment proposed in the text. (Observers are trying to produce two bending arcs.)

If we just look at the right hand curve in Figure 3.2b, we see that $\varnothing_2$ is seen on its side. As such, it should seem perceptually contracted. To compensate, the observer will need to expand this angle in order to generate the curve they were asked to produce.

Although this prediction has not been tested empirically, I have confirmed it to my own satisfaction introspectively. When driving along the interstate, I often notice that moderately sharp curves seem sharper at a distance than when I am on the curve and thus seeing it in a more frontal orientation.

A few final comments on Luneburg's theory. You might be surprised, given the foregoing analysis, to hear me express my admiration for Luneburg's theory. His theory is eloquent and sophisticated. It represents a paradigm for model building. Given the right conditions, his theory may also represent a reasonable description of visual space. Yet, like the spherical model of Reid (1764/1813), Angell (1974), Daniels (1974), and French (1987), Luneburg's model probably only works well under a fairly narrow set of conditions.

The Luneburg theory applies to stimuli that lie on the horizontal plane that passes through the eyes. Indow and Watanabe (1984a, 1988) show that the curvature of the fronto-parallel plane does not differ significantly from the Euclidean value of zero. It is only when stimuli are arrayed in depth that the hyperbolic model applies. Secondly, most of this work is done in the dark with luminous points under controlled conditions that eliminate all other cues to depth outside of binocular disparity and vergence. Such cues are limited in scope—primarily useful within two meters from the observer (Baird, 1970). As such, the most dramatic departures from what we might expect compared to a Euclidean model are for stimuli that are close at hand. Indow (1974) and Indow, Inoue, and Matsushima (1963) found that certain predictions of the hyperbolic model were somewhat "disappointing" when applied to a large-scale spacious field. In addition, the curvature of visual space seems to be attenuated under full-cue conditions, like a well lit field with plenty of monocular cues to depth (Battro et al., 1976; Hardy, Rand, & Rittler, 1951; Koenderink et al., 2002). While other experimenters sometimes find a general tendency toward negative curvature even under these conditions (Indow & Watanabe, 1984; Higashiyama, Ishikawa, & Tanaka, 1990), even these later researchers did not find negative curvature with all of their subjects under illuminated conditions, arguing for at least some attenuation in the effect.

In summary, within its restricted domain, Luneburg's theory holds a place as one of the geometries of visual space. However, I do not believe that it is the only geometry that applies. As with the spherical model of the phenomenologists, the geometry of visual space varies with observer attitude and stimulus conditions.

Visual Space as a Euclidean Geometry

Why list Euclidean geometry second? You may wonder at why I chose to start this chapter on synthetic approaches to visual space by discussing the hyperbolic model instead of beginning with the traditional Euclidean approach. The reason for this organizational tack is that relatively few perception researchers have explicitly supported the Euclidean model for visual space. Compared to the hyperbolic model that has attracted some of the top minds in mathematical psychology, the Euclidean model seems to be something of a unwanted step child; perhaps, because there is little excitement attached to proposing the traditional view.

Having said this, Euclidean geometry is not without its supporters. Fry (1950) constructed a synthetic model that describes visual space as Euclidean. Like Luneburg, Fry proposed a set of axioms that he thought were self-evident facts. For example, Fry asserts that physically straight lines are seen as straight, physically right angles are seen as right angles; physically parallel lines are seen as parallel. Such observations, if true, would indicate that visual space is more or less equivalent to physical space and this would support a Euclidean model (if one assumes that physical space is Euclidean). His primary empirical evidence to back up the claim that visual space is Euclidean is based on his observation that subjects (with fixation held constant) can reliably arrange eight points to form a square that has straight lines, right angle corners, and sides of equal length. The constructed object was said to not only be physically square, but it looked physically square to the observer. If true, this observation would be strong evidence for the Euclidean character of visual space. Unfortunately, Fry did not give any details for this experiment, and to my knowledge, no one has replicated his findings. Fry dismissed Blumenfeld and Helmholtz's work as being artifacts of allowing free eye movement and the distortions that occur in visual perception due to asymmetrical convergence angles in the two eyes. Fry (1952) argued that some of the theoretical and empirical work on size constancy designed to support Luneburg's theory (i.e., Gilinsky, 1951) actually are better explained via a Euclidean geometry.

A model for visual space that assumes constant fixation and symmetrical convergence angles would seem to be even more restrictive than the assumptions of Luneburg's model which does allow free eye movement (but no monocular cues to depth). In addition, Fry's model needs more empirical support.

More fundamentally, proponents of a Euclidean model for visual space face many of the same objections as discussed for the hyperbolic model. The Euclidean model also assumes that visual space is a metric space in which distance perceptions should display symmetry (the distance from point A to point B is the same as the distance from B to A) and the triangle inequality should hold. The Euclidean model also assumes that visual space is convex, compact, and Desarguesian. The Euclidean model requires free mobility to hold. All of these assumptions are necessary for visual space to be a Riemannian geometry of constant curvature of which Euclidean geometry is a special case. All of the empirical work that attacks these assumptions not only casts into doubt Luneburg's hyperbolic model, but the Euclidean model of visual space as well.

Higashiyama (1981, 1984) and Ivry and Cohen's (1987) determination that the curvature of visual space is not constant, but ranges between negative and positive values, is no more consistent with an Euclidean model than it is with a hyperbolic model because both require a constant curvature. Nor is the Euclidean model consistent with Moar and Bower (1983) who found that subjects tended to perceive the angles of a triangular structure to be greater than 180°.

Modern Euclidean philosophers. A number of modern philosophers take a tack similar to Kant (1781/1923) to arrive at the conclusion that visual space is

Euclidean. For example, Ewing (1974) and Strawson (1976) believe that although we are able to conceive of non-Euclidean geometries in the abstract, the Euclidean conception of space is perceptually necessary in order to experience the world at all. Unlike the empirically derived observations we make about our world which often have exceptions, the structure of our phenomenal world is universal. For example, we cannot experience the world, except in terms of three dimensions, try as we might.

Ewing and Strawson do not distinguish between the physical space and visual space because both are aspects of phenomenal space. To them, the observations of physics are as much a part of this phenomenal space as our everyday experiences as individuals. All of these observations, of the scientist and of the average individual, reflect a coherent conception of space, not a randomly selected set of propositions that vary across time and space. The evidence from physical science is that visual space is Euclidean, at least at the terrestrial level. Where can this coherence arise from if it is not built into the universe or imposed as an organizing structure of the human mind?

One can make the same reply to these modern philosophers that Helmholtz (1869/1921) made to Kant. While it is certainly possible that Euclidean conceptions are built into our perceptual apparatus as part of the act of experiencing the world, this model can be subjected to empirical test. The axioms and metric relations found in perception can be tested through the judgments people make. It is also possible to empirically compare the judgments people make based on their perceptions to the measurement made by physical scientists to determine if indeed the phenomenal world is a coherent whole in which our perceptions match reality. The conception that our perceptions of space are universal can also be tested; in other words, we can determine if our perceptions of the world change under varying conditions and shifts in mental attitude. In truth, the data is in and few of these propositions hold. As we will see in subsequent chapters, visual space is clearly different from physical space and its nature depends on conditions. However logical the argument in favor of the necessity of Euclidean space, if the data contradict it, the theory of Euclidean necessity must be rejected.

J. J. Gibson's model. Gibson (1950, 1959, 1966) also argues that visual space is Euclidean, although he comes to this conclusion from a very different direction. Gibson begins his development by attacking conventional views of space and vision. Gibson believes that visual space is neither an abstract structure as in mathematics nor a structure created by the human mind to organize experience as in Kant. To Gibson, the traditional viewpoint implies that the perception of space is totally divorced from the real world. Gibson feels that these abstract structures are empty vessels that evaporate into nothingness unless stimulation is presented to the observer. Rather than objects fitting into an abstract space, spatial perception arises from our perception of surfaces whose structure already exists in the real world and whose layout is specified by invariant patterns in stimulation (Cutting, 1993; Gibson, 1979; Turvey & Carello, 1986). The invariant patterns that specify the location of objects include occlusion, texture gradients, flow gradients, and motion parallax.

Furthermore, Gibson is a Naive Realist (Henle, 1974; Gibson, 1959, 1979). That is, he believes that the perceptual systems of people and animals have evolved to allow us to perceive the world veridically. In other words, our perceptions closely match physical reality under ordinary circumstances. If our perception of the world did not match reality, then we would be locking ourselves into a world of subjectivity. We would be making the error of "concluding that we can know nothing but our perceptions.... Once having made this argument, a theorist is trapped in a circle of subjectivism and is diverted into futile speculations about private worlds" (Gibson, 1959, pp. 462-463). In addition, if our perceptions did not match reality, then we would constantly be making perceptual errors that would handicap us in the struggle for survival.

Thus, Gibson submits that humans are capable of almost perfect perceptual constancy; that is, humans perceive the metric attributes of the world correctly under virtually all ordinary circumstances. Because an almost perfect relationship exists between physical space and visual space, and because physical space is Euclidean, visual space must also be Euclidean.

Ironically, Gibson's assumption of perceptual constancy allies him with Luneburg, in that Luneburg's free mobility axiom was motivated by this assumption of constancy. Gibson (1959) referred to his own early empirical work to bolster his claim of perfect constancy. Gibson (1933, 1947, 1950) had subjects estimate the size of objects at various distances from the subject under information rich natural conditions and in a cluttered office space, and he found that judgments matched physical reality to a high degree.

Of course, the problem here is that other researchers do not find perfect constancy. As summarized in Baird (1970), frontally oriented objects tend to exhibit overconstancy under full-cue conditions like Gibson employed; that is, distant objects tend to be seen as larger than near objects of the same physical size. Wagner, Kartzinel, and Baird (1988) found that objects lying on the ground oriented in-depth tend to exhibit strong underconstancy; that is, distant objects tend to be seen as smaller than near objects. Many other studies have also found a lack of perceptual constancy under a variety of conditions. Outside of constancy studies, illusions also represent occasions when constancy breaks down.

Gibson was aware that such contrary data existed. Yet, he swept this data aside as irrelevant. Gibson (1979) referred to data collected under controlled conditions as "aperture vision" or "bite-board vision" as opposed to the natural vision relevant to human and animal adaptation to the world in which he was interested. Gibson (1977) felt that perceptual error only arises under two conditions: when the perceptual system breaks down such as with eye injury or when the information necessary for accurate perception is denied to the perceiver. Thus, Gibson was convinced that laboratory studies controlled the phenomena of interest out of existence because they failed to provide the information necessary for veridical perception. In particular, Gibson stressed the importance of exploration and motion to provide the information necessary for veridical perception.

Following Gibson's death, ecological psychologists have followed up on his theory along a number of different lines. Some, like Feldman (1985) and Turvey and Carello (1986), have attempted to quantify the invariant patterns in stimulation that specify location and guide motion. Others have shown the importance of motion to perceiving perceptual constancy (Clocksin, 1980; Johansson, 1986; Johansson, von Hofsten, & Jansson, 1980). Others still have emphasized that perception is most accurate in information rich environments that provide plenty of redundant cues to depth (Bruno & Cutting, 1988). For example, Runeson (1988) explained how the environment normally provides enough redundant information to specify spatial layout even under static viewing conditions, and the distorted perceptions reported for the Ames' Room are generated by eliminating much of this information.

Other researchers have presented evidence opposing the ecological viewpoint. Gehringer and Engel (1986) found that much of the Ames' room illusion remained even after observers were allowed unrestricted head movement and binocular viewing, indicating that rich information conditions do not always produce perceptual constancy. Domini and Braunstein (1998) found that three-dimensional layout produced by motion does not yeild perceptions with a Euclidean structure. Similarly, Loomis and Beall (1998) found that optic flow does not fully explain control of locomotion, and that other more cognitive information is necessary to guide action.

While I greatly admire the Gibsonian perspective (as any of my students would quickly attest to), I feel that it has three essential weaknesses in the present context. First, the assumption of perfect perceptual constancy, which lies at the heart of Gibson's doctrine of Naive Realism, should not be taken on faith. This assumption can and has been tested empirically. Even under the most information rich conditions, perceptions do not always match physical reality as we will see in subsequent chapters. Second, cognitive factors such as the meaning the observer attaches to the concepts of size and distance will influence our judgments. Gibson too quickly derides the importance of such factors when he argues that perception is direct. Third, Handel (1988) points out that although perception can be thought of as exploration, we are often not explicitly interested in layout; so, we don't always move around to explore the environment. Even under these static conditions, we still have an impression of the layout of a scene. Thus, static viewing is really no less natural than dynamic viewing. Static viewing conditions are a part of our ordinary life experience. Similarly, I would add that we experience information poor viewing conditions every day when the lights go out at night. We should not so narrowly define what is natural enough to be studied. The most complete understanding of visual space arises from looking at how the geometry of the space changes with conditions. Gibson's desire to limit the domain of perceptual research would leave us with an incomplete understanding at best.

Crypto-Euclidean spaces. Although few theorists go out of their way to positively assert that visual space is Euclidean, the Euclidean perspective may still be the dominant perspective in space perception. This oxymoronic statement is possible because the Euclidean position pervades much of the theoretical work in perception without the assumption ever being acknowledged. For example, the trigonometry underlying the Size-Distance Invariance Hypothesis is Euclidean trigonometry. Many of the classic explanations for the moon illusion including the flattened-dome theory assume a Euclidean space in the process of their development. Much of the logic behind the classical explanations for why cues to depth work have an Euclidean assumption at their root.

To give one example, Gogel has often used a head motion measure for perceived distance (Gogel, 1990, 1993, 1998; Gogel, Loomis, & Sharkey, 1985; Gogel & Tietz, 1973, 1980). This measure is based on the fact that the height of a triangle (perceived distance) can be calculated by knowing the length of the base of a triangle (the degree of head movement) and the angles that form the triangle (directions to fixated object) based on trigonometry. However, using this trigonometry presupposes that the space is Euclidean.

There is nothing wrong with assuming that visual space is Euclidean as part of the process of model building. This assumption should be made explicit however. In many cases, Euclidean mathematics is taken for granted without being acknowledged. In other words, Euclidean assumptions slip into the model building process, to give us a sort of crypto-Euclidean space.

Other Geometries Applied to Visual Space

Other geometries have been proposed to describe visual space. In most cases, these models are variations on the hyperbolic or Euclidean models. For example, Hoffman (1966) suggested that visual space displays the properties of a Lie transformation group. Hoffman uses his theory to explain size and shape constancy, motion perception, and rotational perception. Hoffman and Dodwell (1985) extend this theory to account for some of the Gestalt properties of visual perception. In the case of static perception, Hoffman's model reduces to something similar to Luneburg's theory of perception. I am not familiar with any independent empirical work that followed up on this theory to test its assumptions and predictions.

Drösler (1979, 1988, 1995) generalizes Luneburg's theory. Drösler (1979) described visual space as a Cayley-Klein geometry. His more recent work attempts to tie space perception to more fundamental psychophysical invariance relations. Drösler (1988) assumes that the free mobility axiom holds, while Drösler (1995) attempts to tie space and color perception into a generalized version of Weber's Law. In all cases, the metric of visual space is thought to be a variation on Luneburg's model.

Yamazaki (1987) revisited the data used to support Luneburg's theory. Yamazaki explained this data without assuming that visual space is Riemannian by thinking of visual space as being composed of a set of connected affine spaces. In this space, curvature need not be constant because visual space may be stretched slightly in one direction in a given location and stretched in a different direction in another location in the space. One consequence of this structure is that a line element that travels a complete circuit through these connected spaces need not end up in the same perceived location. Yamazaki applied this model to explain Blumenfeld's visual alley data.

Dzhafarov and Colonius (1999) generalize the Fechnerian integration (that we will talk about in Chapter 5) to describe space perception. According to this approach, stimuli are associated with psychometric functions that determine the probability that they will be discriminated from other stimuli. This function is assumed to vary smoothly from one stimulus to adjacent stimuli and to be defined on an infitesimal level. The metric is determined by integrating along a path between two stimuli and using the minimum distance to define the metric. Of course, the assumptions of compactness and the ability to express JND's as differentials are open to question, but the approach does integrate information from different psychophysical domains.

One may also doubt about whether Dzhafarov and Colonius's approach really is a legitimate generalization of Fechner's work. Dzhafarov and Colonius use a concept of similarity that Fechner avoided. See Link (1994) for a discussion of Fechner's original approach.

Final Comments on the Synthetic Approach

Thus, a virtual plethora of geometries have been proposed for visual space. Given the appropriate axioms, each approach is internally consistent and undeniable. Unfortunately, the various proposed geometries are not mutually compatible. Visual space cannot be doubly elliptical, hyperbolic, Euclidean, a Lie group, and a non-Riemannian affinely connected space all at the same time. Perhaps one geometry may hold under one set of conditions and another may hold under another set of conditions, and we must accept that there is no single geometry that works under all conditions.

Yet, the difficulties for the synthetic approach run deeper than this. The various critical studies, such as the Blumenfeld alleys, that are meant to help us choose between models can be reinterpreted to support other geometrical formulations (c.f., Fry, 1952, Hoffman, 1966). It is not clear that a critical test exists that can differentiate between the models.

In addition, the validity of each synthetic model rests on the veracity of the axioms on which the theory is based. There are a host of studies reported earlier in this chapter that call into question the most fundamental of these axioms. It is not clear that any synthetic geometry except perhaps the most global topological systems (which would be able to make only the vaguest of predictions) can pass this rigorous test. In many ways, the synthetic approach to visual perception has failed.

I believe that an alternative approach is possible. Rather than indirectly attempt to specify the geometry of visual space through postulates and critical experiments, it may be possible to take a more direct approach. Rather than attempt to define the geometry of visual space synthetically, one can take an analytic approach. In this approach, observers are asked to judge the metric properties of visual space directly using the methods of psychophysics. In turn, these judgments can serve as the basis for deriving functions that relate the observer's judgments to physical coordinates as a function of experimental conditions. These functions can be used to directly specify the metric of visual space, and the geometry of the space can be defined in terms of this metric. The next chapter will begin to develop this alternative.

4

An Analytic Approach to Space and Vision

In mathematics, there are two ways to approach the geometry of a space: synthetic geometry and analytic geometry. The previous chapter considered attempts to define visual space synthetically; that is, by listing a set of postulates meant to describe visual space and determining what geometry best fits the proposed postulates. While the synthetic approach has successfully accounted for a small set of classic experiments, none of the models presented can account for the effects of stimulus conditions and observer attitudes that are found in the literature. In addition, research does not appear to support the foundational axioms of the synthetic models.

I would like to propose a more direct way to define visual space by using the tools of analytic geometry. To apply this approach to visual space one must first assign coordinates to locations in visual space. Secondly, one must seek out equations based on these coordinates that describe our perceptions of distance and other metric properties such as angles, areas, volumes, etc.

Advantages of the Analytic Approach

Using an analytic approach has a number of advantages. First of all, the analytic approach is more general. While the synthetic approach has largely focused on the three geometries of constant curvature (hyperbolic, Euclidean, and spherical geometry), the analytic approach is under no similar restraint. An infinite variety of coordinate equations are potentially available to describe metric relationships. As an example of this flexibility, consider the Minkowski metric that we discussed in Chapter 2. According to this equation, distance between points is defined as

$$d(P_1, P_2) = [|x_1 - x_2|^R + |y_1 - y_2|^R]^{1/R} \tag{4.1}$$

where the distance between points P_1 and P_2, $d(P_1, P_2)$, is a function of the coordinates of the two points, (x_1, y_1) and (x_2, y_2), and the Minkowski parameter R. This single equation expresses an infinite number of geometries. If R is equal to 2, this metric equation specifies a Euclidean space. If R is equal to 1, the equation specifies a city-block space. Yet, these are only two of an infinite number of values that the Minkowski parameter can assume.

As flexible as the Minkowski metric is, it is only one of an infinite number of possible metric equations that can be defined on a set of coordinates. Clearly, the analytic approach to defining a space is both general and powerful.

Second, the analytic approach is more direct than the synthetic approach and is more applicable to modeling the psychophysical literature as a whole. The synthetic approach relies on a small number of critical experiments that attempt to test the axioms of the synthetic models in order to specify the geometry of visual space. The vast majority of studies on space perception, however, are not directed at testing these axioms, but instead ask observers to judge various metric properties (particularly size and distance) as a function of conditions and instructions. From a synthetic viewpoint, these studies are essentially irrelevant.

The analytic approach, however, easily incorporates this corpus of the space perception literature. Indeed, according to the analytic approach, the judgments that observers give for size and distance directly *define* visual space. The theorist's goal is to find coordinate equations that predict the judgments that observers generate. Thus, instead of being irrelevant, psychophysical studies of space perception provide the basic data that specify the geometry of visual space.

Third, the synthetic approach cannot easily incorporate the effects of stimulus conditions, stimulus layout, judgment methods, and instructions. As such, synthetic theorists tend to carefully limit the domain to which their theories apply. Luneburg (1947) and the other advocates for the hyperbolic model, for instance, make it clear that the theory applies only to binocular space perception in the dark with luminous points of light for stimuli and a stationary head position. Although it usually not explicitly stated, the modeling is also limited to data collected through various methods of adjustment, and numeric estimation methods are excluded. Similarly, Foley (1980) explicitly limits himself to binocular viewing conditions under which no other cues for depth are allowed except eye position and binocular disparity. He also rules out the use of verbal reports. This tendency to limit the domain to which a theory applies and to exclude large bodies of data seems to universally describe synthetic models for space perception. In fact, most of these models explicitly exclude from consideration the natural viewing conditions typically found in every day life.

The analytic approach does not need to be so exclusive. In fact, variations in method and conditions can be incorporated into the metric equations that define visual space. When quantifiable, these conditions can be included as parameters in the coordinate equations that predict the size and distance judgments people generate. Some conditions are not directly quantifiable, such as using different sorts of judgment methods or varying judgment instructions. In this case, one could develop separate metric equations for each condition to specify how the geometry of visual space changes from one condition to another or use "dummy coding" to incorporate the affects of these qualitative dimensions within a single equation. In short, the analytic approach need not exclude data, but can incorporate changes in stimulus conditions and experimental methods into the definition of the geometry of visual space.

Indeed, one should not be too quick to exclude data generated from any source. In general, most psychologists would feel more confidence in any conclusion if converging measures for the same concept yield similar results. Certainly, this also applies to space perception. When only a single method is applied, it is impossible to know whether the resulting function is due to perception or due to response processes inherent in the method. Both numeric estimation and adjustment methods are influenced by various response factors (Ono, Wagner, & Ono, 1995; Wagner, 1989; Wagner, Ono, & Ono, 1995). If several alternative psychophysical techniques are used to probe an observer's perceptions, then commonalties resulting from these converging measures should represent aspects of visual space that are largely independent of the methods employed. Using a large number of methods also allows for a comparison of the methods themselves. In the analytic approach, judgment method can be thought of as another parameter to take into account when modeling spatial judgments.

Finally, before moving on, I must admit that the distinction I have drawn between the synthetic and analytic approaches to space perception is not as cut and dry as I may have made it seem. Most synthetic theorists do attempt to derive metric functions to describe distance perception. Similarly, the analytic approach has synthetic axioms buried implicitly within it. For example, the geometries of constant curvature can be approached analytically because their metric functions are well known. In fact, one can think of these synthetic geometries as simply being special cases of the more general analytic approach. The difference between the synthetic and analytic approaches really lies in a difference in emphasis. The synthetic approach to visual perception starts by listing the axioms of a limited set of synthetic geometries and attempts to validate those axioms and chose between the geometries considered. Metric functions are derived as an after thought. The analytic approach begins with metric judgments and attempts to model them directly, spending little thought on whether fundamental axioms hold.

Analytic Geometry and Visual Space

To implement the analytic approach to space perception, two questions must be answered. (1) How will the locations of stimulus points be specified? That is, what coordinates are most appropriate for visual space? (2) What function relates these coordinates to the judgments observers give for the metric properties of visual space? Let us deal with each of these questions in turn.

The coordinates of visual space. How should the locations of stimulus points be specified? In general, the location of a point in a plane may be specified by two coordinates, and the location of a point in three dimensions may be specified by three coordinates. Similarly, the locations of two points involve four coordinates in a plane and six coordinates in three dimensions. The exact nature of these coordinates is somewhat arbitrary. Points could be located by sets of Cartesian coordinates, (x_1, y_1), (x_2, y_2), etc. They could be located by sets of polar coordinates, (R_1, θ_1), (R_2, θ_2), etc. They could also be located in many other ways.

I believe the way one specifies point locations should ultimately depend on four criteria: (1) The method must locate points using a disjoint set of coordinates. That is, the coordinate system must completely specify point locations while at the same time not *over specify* the points by including the same information more than once. (2) The method must be reasonably simple. The coordinate dimensions must be easy to understand and interpret. (3) Because one cannot directly examine conscious experience to determine coordinates, the only way to assign coordinates is by basing them on the physical position of stimuli. Some might object to this, because the goal is to describe visual space, not physical space, and it would seem more appropriate to assign coordinates to visual space directly. Unfortunately, one could never be certain that the set of coordinates assigned based on one person's introspection are equivalent to the set derived from another's. To operationalize our variables in a way that allows for scientific investigation requires us to tie the observer's judgments to something concrete, such as physical position. In truth, little is lost here because the assignment of coordinates is somewhat arbitrary, and the differences between physical layout and experienced layout will find their expression in the metric functions that we derive from the observer's judgments. (4) The method should be ecologically valid. That is, the method should naturally relate the person making the judgment to the points being judged. In so doing, an attempt should be made to specify point locations in a manner that a person might normally use to specify them. A coordinate system designed with this ecological criterion in mind is likely to be both easy to interpret and sensitive to systematic trends which might exist.

The classic Cartesian coordinate system certainly passes the first three of these tests, but I feel that it fails the fourth criterion. For example, if a person was facing north and looking at a point one meter away to the northeast, it is unlikely that the observer would conceptualize the point as being located $\sqrt{2}/2$ to the right and $\sqrt{2}/2$ forward. The polar coordinate system is a more natural way to locate a single point because people do think in terms of how far away something is and how much something deviates from straight ahead.

Another coordinate system that has been used extensively by Luneburg and others (Aczél et al., 1999; Blank, 1953, 1958, 1959; Foley, 1980, 1985; Heller, 1997a, 1997b; Indow, 1974, 1979, 1982, 1990; Luneburg, 1947, 1948) is bipolar coordinates. As shown in Figure 4.1, if the two eyes are fixated on a point in space, the bipolar coordinates (α, β) are determined by the angular deviation from straight ahead from the center of the two eyes.

This coordinate system makes if easy to work with the Vieth-Müller circles which in the idealized case represent those stimuli which fall on corresponding points of the two retina when one point on the circle is fixated; that is, the two eyes would need to change direction by the same amount to fixate on another point of the circle. To Luneburg, points lying along the same Vieth-Müller circle are perceived as being equidistant from the observer. Similarly, this coordinate system makes it easy to describe the hyperbolae of Hillebrand that form the

parallel lines in Luneburg's hyperbolic space. If the observer fixates on a point
along an Hillebrand hyperbola, other points along the hyperbola are projected
onto retinal points that deviate the same angular extent from the fovea in both
eyes but in opposite directions.

To Luneburg, the points along a Hyperbola of Hillebrand are perceived to lie
in the same visual direction from the observer. Because both the Vieth-Müller
circle and the hyperbola of Hillebrand can be described most simply in such angular terms, the bipolar coordinate system is probably the simplest and most
elegant way to express them.

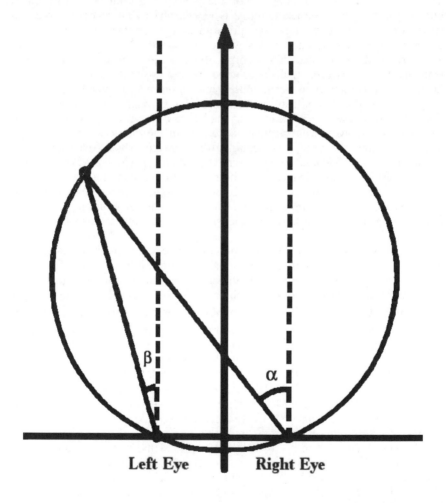

Figure 4.1. Bipolar coordinates for a point in space in terms of angular deviation
from straight ahead for the right eye (α) and the left eye (β).

Unfortunately, when one leaves the world of Vieth-Müller circles and hyperbolae of Hillebrand and one attempts instead to model the size and distance judgments found in the bulk of the space perception literature, the bipolar coordinate system is awkward to use at best. Using the bipolar coordinate system also implies a number of implicit assumptions about the nature of space perception that I find questionable. First of all, most of the theorists who use this coordinate system act as though the only cues to depth that matter are binocular ones like disparity and convergence angle. In truth, there are a host of monocular cues to depth perception that also influence spatial perception (such as texture gradients, linear perspective, motion parallax, etc.), which have no place in a bipolar system. In addition, under most circumstances, our perception of space is a unitary phenomenon. We seem to be looking on the world from one place, one origin, not from two places at once. The origin of visual space is not in the eyes, but it is the mind, and it is located at a singular egocenter. Thus, in terms of the criterion mentioned earlier, bipolar coordinates pass the tests of being disjoint and defined physically, but fail the tests of simplicity and naturalness.

Implicit natural coordinates. A fourth coordinate system implicitly underlies the bulk of the space perception literature. In truth, most space perception studies don't bother with specifying a coordinate system at all, but define stimuli in terms of egocentric and exocentric distance, stimulus orientation, and eccentricity (deviation from straight ahead of the observer). The following is an attempt to explicitly layout the coordinate system implicitly employed by the majority of space perception research. This "Natural Coordinate System" is not as simple as the previous systems, but it corresponds more closely to our ordinary, common-language conceptions of space.

For the location of a single point, as in egocentric distance estimation tasks, the "natural" way to assign coordinates is with a polar coordinate system. Here the two coordinates are R and θ. To make this definition more concrete, let us define the radius (R) as the straight-line Euclidean distance from the observer to the point, and the polar angle (θ) as the counter-clockwise angle measured between an arbitrarily defined axis and the direction to the point. In my formulation, the arbitrarily defined axis extends from the observer directly to his or her right. Thus, a point directly to the observer's right is at 0°, a point located directly in front of the observer is at 90°, and a point directly to the observer's left is at 180°. I use this convention to avoid needing to talk about negative angles or constantly having to specify on which side of the observer each stimulus lies, although I recognize that it might be even more natural to think of straight ahead as being 0°, and other angles could be thought of as being so many degrees to the right and so many to the left. While most experiments present stimuli along a plane defined by the ground or a table, one could extend this coordinate system by including a third coordinate that specifies the elevation of the stimulus. This coordinate would also be expressed as a polar angle relative to some arbitrarily defined axis.

For size and exocentric-distance estimation, four Natural Coordinates are needed to capture the location of the two points that define the object being judged. Figure 4.2 displays these coordinates. Here, the four coordinates are: the distance from the observer to the nearest point (R), the polar angle or the direction the nearest point lays relative to an arbitrarily defined axis to the observer's right (θ), the orientation of the points with respect to the observer's frontal plane (φ), and the Euclidean distance between the two points (D). This coordinate system for distance judgments can be easily extended to three-dimensional space by including polar and orientation coordinates that express elevation.

The coordinate system thus defined is disjoint. The location of the near point is defined by R and θ; while φ and D define the location of the far point (with respect to the near one). The inclusion of D as one of the coordinates is particularly noteworthy. In this way, inter-point distance is factored out of the other coordinate dimensions. When determining judged distance as a function of actual distance and other factors about the location of the stimulus (as well as other non-spatial factors), factoring out distance prevents recursive effects of including

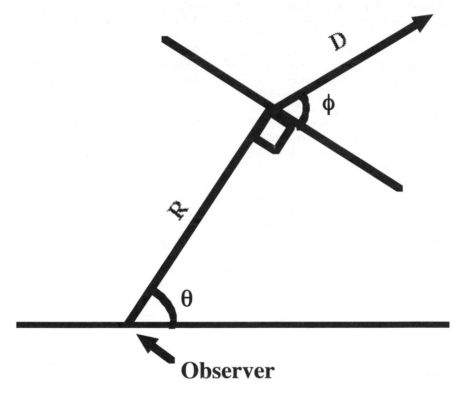

Figure 4.2. Natural coordinate system used to specify object locations for distance estimation. The four coordinates are: the distance from the observer to the nearest point (R), the polar angle or the direction the nearest point lays relative to an arbitrarily defined axis to the observer's right (θ), the orientation of the points with respect to the observer's frontal plane (φ), and the Euclidean distance between the two points (D).

distance twice in the formula, once as the distance itself and once hidden in the coordinates. It also allows one to directly address the effects of stimulus orientation, which turns out to be a critical factor in size judgments. Typically, stimuli are either presented frontally or in-depth relative to the observer (although seldom both at once). The natural coordinate system allows this experimental factor to be directly represented in a model.

This coordinate system is also easy to interpret, and it is defined in terms of the objectively observable physical layout of the stimuli. In addition, the coordinate system is relatively ecologically valid. The coordinate dimensions are defined with respect to the observer much as a naive observer might describe them. That is, an object could be described as far away (or near), to the right (or left), see straight on (or in-depth), and is so long. (At least, the specification is more ecologically valid than the obvious alternatives.)

On the other hand, Natural Coordinates fail the test of simplicity. Instead of each point being defined by two equivalent coordinates as in other systems, the four coordinates describe different aspects of the stimulus constellation as a whole. Despite this complexity, this coordinate system more directly relates to the size and distance estimation literature than other systems. Egocentric distance judgments involve estimating R; exocentric distance judgments (or size judgments) involve estimating D; and ϕ corresponds to variations in stimulus orientation found in different experiments.

One may also use a similar Natural Coordinate System to describe angle judgments. The smallest number of points that may define an angle is three. One point specifies the vertex, while two other points lay along the two legs. Because three points are involved a total of six coordinates will be needed to completely specify the position of the points. As seen in Figure 4.3, the six coordinates that define an angle are: the distance from the observer to the vertex of the angle (R), the polar angle between the vertex and an arbitrarily defined axis (θ), the orientation of the angle relative to the observers frontal plane (ϕ) where orientation is defined by the vector that bisects the angle, the physical size of the angle (A), and (to be complete) the length of the two legs of the angle (D1 and D2). Like the Natural Coordinate System for distance judgment, this one has the advantages of being disjoint, physically defined, and ecologically valid. It is also defined in terms of important experimental variables in a fashion that will make modeling easier. In this book, I will tend to prefer Cartesian coordinates when modeling metric functions for visual space as a whole, but Natural Coordinates will be used when reviewing the direct estimation and size constancy literature because this corresponds to the variables researchers typically emphasize.

The origin for visual space. Idhe (1986) points out that spatial localization is reciprocal. Looking out at the world, we are able to localize the position of objects relative to our own position and see each object from a certain point of view. This same information, however, also can serve to localize the point from which the observation occurs. Our point of view, the exact direction from which we look on an object, points back toward the direction that the observer him/herself lies. By a process of triangulation, the position of the self can be unambiguously identified, if the visual direction to more than one object is known. This location from which observation occurs is known as the egocenter, and I believe that it is the logical origin of any coordinate system for visual space.

Where does the egocenter lie? One simple hypothesis might be that we see the world from the point of view of our dominant eye, and thus the origin of visual space lies there. This does not seem to be the case. Barbeito (1981), Ono (1979), and Ono and Barbieto (1982) have shown that our perception of visual direction does not originate in either eye, but from a point in between that they refer to as the cyclopean eye after Homer's mythological Cyclopes.

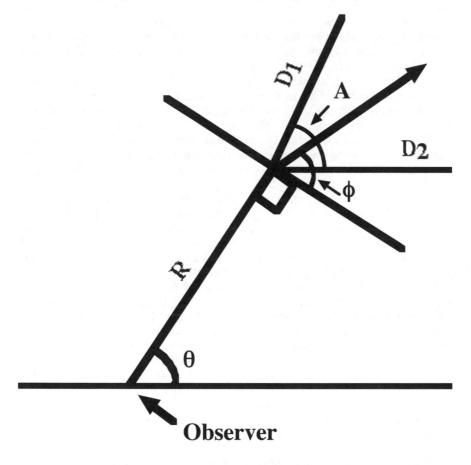

Figure 4.3. Natural coordinate system used to specify object locations for angle estimation. The four coordinates are: the distance from the observer to the nearest point (R), the polar angle or the direction the nearest point lays relative to an arbitrarily defined axis to the observer's right (θ), the orientation of the bisector of the angle with respect to the observer's frontal plane (ϕ), the length of the two legs (D_1 and D_2), and the physical size of the angle (A).

If the egocenter is not coincident with either of the eyes, then where does it lie? Four methods have been proposed for locating the egocenter. Funaishi (1926) had subjects fixate a point straight ahead of them and equidistant between the two eyes (the median plane) and judge the direction to non-fixated targets in the same depth plane as the fixation point by pointing toward each target with their hands (which are out of sight). Judgments are made at two different fixation distances with stimuli placed at the same visual directions from the subject in each depth plane. Lines are drawn through corresponding judgments from the two depths and projected back toward the observer. The point of intersection for more than one of these lines is said to define the egocenter. One can criticize this method, because the experimenter has made a determination of what the visual direction is physically and not allowed subjects to make their own determination. In addition, pointing may be a very poor measure because the arm is in a different place than the egocenter and the mechanics of the arm might conceivably influence directional estimates.

Fry (1950) tried a more indirect method. He had subjects fixate the more distant of two stimuli along the median plane (straight ahead from the middle of the observers head). Subjects were asked to point at the locations of the two diplopic images produced by the non-fixated stimulus by pointing with their hands (which were out of sight). He derived the location of the egocenter from this information based on Hering's (1879/1942) principles of visual direction. Once again, pointing may be a poor estimate of visual direction.

Roelofs (1959) had subjects look with one eye through a tube that is physically pointing toward the fovea of the eye, while the other eye is occluded. Subjects do not see the tube as pointing at the eye, but as pointing at their face in between the two eyes. Subjects indicate the point on the face where the tube appears to point, and a line is defined from the front of the tube through the point on the face. The point where the lines defined by each eye intersect is the egocenter.

Howard and Templeton (1966) developed the most direct method for measuring the egocenter, and one that does not require pointing. Subjects rotate a rod presented at eye level until it appears to be pointing directly at the self. That is, the front and back ends of the rods appear to lie in along the same visual direction. The rod is moved to different locations and the rod is once again rotated until it appears to point at the observer. The place where lines traced along the axis of the rod intersect is the egocenter.

Not only is this later method the most direct (and to me the most intuitively appealing), it also appears to work the best. While Mitson, Ono, and Barbeito (1976) found that all methods where highly reliable, producing consistent egocenter locations both within experimental sessions and between different experimental sessions, Barbeito and Ono (1979) found that the Howard and Templeton method had the highest levels of internal consistency and test-retest reliability. In addition, the Howard and Templeton method had the highest predictive validity for three experimental tasks involving locating the subjective median plane, judging the relative direction of three points, and an accommodative convergence task. The Howard and Templeton method also produced less variable estimates of egocenter location.

So, where is the egocenter located? According to Barbeito and Ono (1979), Funaishi's (1926) method places the egocenter .28 cm to the right of the median plane and 2.69 cm behind the plane defined by the cornea of the eyes. Fry's (1950) method places it .28 cm to the right of the median plane and 15.07 cm behind the corneal plane. Roelof's (1959) method places it .29 cm to the left of the median plane and .99 cm in front of the corneal plane, a seemingly unlikely result. Finally, the Howard and Templeton (1966) method places it .28 cm to the right of the median plane and 1.16 cm behind the corneal plane. Given the greater reliability, predictive validity, and intuitive superiority of the Howard and Templeton method, I believe the later figure represents our best estimate for the location of the egocenter. Most recent research is consistent with the idea that the egocenter is located halfway between the two eyes and slightly behind the corneal plane (Mapp & Ono, 1999; Nakamizo, Shimono, Kondo, & Ono, 1994; Ono & Mapp, 1995; Shimono, Ono, Saida, & Mapp, 1998).

Blumenfeld (1936) believed that the egocenter might not be located at one fixed place, but it might shift location depending on attentional factors and the sense modality employed. A number of research studies appear to support Blumenfeld's conclusion.

In an unpublished undergraduate project (Krynen & Wagner, 1983), we once attempted to replicate Howard and Templeton's work and extend it to auditory space. In the auditory condition, two tiny speakers located at two different distances from the subject would alternately make a beeping sound. Subjects were asked to align the nearer of the two speakers so that the two appeared to lie in the same direct from the subject. In the visual condition, the subject aligned the speakers visually. The average location for the egocenter in the visual condition was .76 cm to the right of the median plane and 1.32 cm behind the corneal plane. For audition, the average location for the ego center was .71 cm to the right of the median plane and 10.11 cm behind the corneal plane. Thus, the auditory egocenter would appear to lie more or less between the two ears. The localization of the auditory egocenter was quite variable however. The standard deviation for both of the two coordinates was almost four times greater in the auditory condition than it was in the visual condition.

Shimono, Higashiyama, and Tam (2001) attempted to locate the egocenter for kinesthetic space in four experiments. Overall, they found that the kinesthetic egocenter is located in the middle of the body, on the surface of the skin or just below it. Thus, the location of the egocenter appears to change across sense modalities, although the location of the egocenter appears to be relatively fixed within a given sense modality.

The metrics of visual space. Although much will be said about metric functions that describe visual space, something should be said about the general form of these functions in terms of the coordinate systems I have just introduced.

Stevens (1975) demonstrated that judgments of unidimensional stimuli almost universally fit a power function. For distance estimation, Baird (1970) showed that the power function describes estimates of stimulus size both in the frontal plane and in depth. Thus, if we examine judged distance as a function of actual distance for points in a given location and orientation in space, we would expect to obtain a power function of the form

$$J = \lambda D^\gamma \tag{4.2}$$

where λ and γ are constants for that particular location and orientation and J and D are judged and actual distances, respectively. Stevens (1975) argues that all unidimensional estimates of the magnitude of stimuli (prothetic continuum) are best fit by a power function irrespective of the method employed (whether magnitude estimation, category estimation, etc.). Different methods, however, will give rise to different power function exponents. Following Stevens's example, I will often use a power function to describe the metrics of visual space. In this way, cross-method consistency is gained and distortions in judgments due to the response method can be accounted for by alterations in the exponent.

The parameters λ and γ need not be the same for stimuli at all positions in space. More specifically, the values of these parameters may vary as a function of the Natural Coordinate dimensions developed in this chapter such that

$$J = \lambda(R,\theta,\phi) \, D^{\gamma(R,\theta,\phi)} \tag{4.3}$$

where R, θ, and ϕ are the coordinates mentioned above.

As mentioned in Chapter 2, these functions need not depend on the coordinate dimensions alone, but may also vary with stimulus conditions and instructions. Hence, a more complete form for this general metric function could be

$$J = \lambda(R,\theta,\phi,\alpha,\beta,\delta, \ldots) \, D^{\gamma(R,\theta,\phi,\alpha,\beta,\delta, \ldots)} \tag{4.4}$$

where α, β, and δ represent varying experimental conditions.

While the idea that exponents might be functions of stimulus conditions is not entirely new (Stevens & Hall, 1966; Stevens & Rubin, 1970; Teghtsoonian & Teghtsoonian, 1978; Wagner, 1982, 1985, 1992), it is rarely done in practice. In fact, Lockhead (1992) criticized psychophysical work for not sufficiently taking into account context when generating psychophysical equations. Treating λ as a function of conditions is rare indeed.

Does the power function always work? While this formulation of the power function is very general, even this formula may not describe all metric judgments that observers give. The human mind is capable of conceptualizing distance in many ways. Different judgments are given in response to objective, apparent, and projective instructions that respectively ask people to objectively report distance, to say what things look like, or to take on a artist's eye view and report how much of the visual field a stimulus takes up.

Yet, these common instructions only scratch the surface of the variation possible in the human conception of distance. People are able to view distance in terms of the shortest route between two places. In fact, peoples' conception of the "shortest" route between two places deviates greatly from their as-the-crow-flies estimates and the nature of these judgments can be quite complex. Bailenson, Shum, & Uttal (1998) found that people tend to engage in "route climbing." That is, they tend to begin their trip by selecting the longest and straightest route segment available heading in the direction of their goal even when another overall shorter path is available that is slightly less direct to begin with. This heuristic can lead to asymmetric path selection because the longest and straightest route segment heading out of point A in the direction of point B may place the subject on a different overall path than the longest and straightest route segment heading out of point B in the direction of point A.

Raghubir and Krishna (1996) found that paths with many sharp turns and switchbacks tend to be perceived as shorter than paths of the same length that move generally in the same direction along their whole route. Here, perceived path length may be biased toward the as-the-crow-flies distance traversed (without being identical to it).

Metric functions can also be influenced by cognitive factors and categorization effects. Howard and Kerst (1981) found that people tend to alter their distance judgments between locations on a rectangular map in a way that causes the map to "square up;" in other words, the left-right dimensions of the judged space are made to seem roughly equal to the up-down dimension even though this is physically untrue. In addition, near by objects tend to be perceived as being clustered together more tightly than they actually are, particularly in memory conditions.

In summary, although a power function appears to describe many distance judgments, people are mentally flexible enough to conceive of distance in very complex ways—particularly, when judgments are based on memory. One must be prepared to abandon the power function under these circumstances.

A Cautionary Note: Is Visual Space Metric?

It is tempting to think of the effects of instructions and the judgments of route length as being exceptions. According to this view, we know what we normally mean by perceived size and distance, and these other sorts of judgments are not what we mean by those words. Perhaps, if one eliminated these pesky exceptions, then a unitary view of visual space would be possible. Perhaps, if one eliminated the exceptions, the geometry of visual space would be singular.

I believe this viewpoint implicitly pervades much of the space perception literature. According to this standard view, people perceive the world in a single, internally consistent fashion, which they (more or less) accurately report on with the various judgment methods. Because all of the judgment methods are getting at the same underlying perceptual object, each of these methods should produce results that are largely consistent with each other. That is, they do not change the basic structure of visual space, but accurately reflect it.

What do I mean by our perceptions of visual space being internally consistent? In an internally consistent space, the judgments people give for each of the parts of visual space should fit together again to produce a coherent whole. If an object is broken into two parts, the sum of the perceived sizes of the parts should equal the perceived size of the whole. At the very least, visual space should be internally consistent enough to qualify as a metric space.

Is the standard view right? Is there a single visual space? Do the various judgment methods produce results that are consistent with each other? Is visual space internally consistent? Is it even a metric space?

Baird, Wagner, and Noma (1982) explored these questions and concluded that visual space, as reflected by the judgments that observers give, appears to fail each of these criteria. This paper is not very well known among psychologists because it was published in a geography journal. I will lay out the basic argument here.

Does visual space satisfy the metric axioms? To be considered a metric space, the distance function on that space must satisfy the four axioms mentioned in Chapter 2 (Equations 2.1 to 2.4). Let us examine whether or not these axioms hold for visual space.

Let x, y, and z be elements of set X, then $d(x,y)$ is a metric on X if

(1) Distance is always non-negative. That is,

$$d(x,y) \geq 0 \tag{4.5}$$

(2) Non-identical points have a positive distance. That is,

$$d(x,y) = 0 \text{ if and only if } x = y \tag{4.6}$$

(3) Distance is symmetric. That is,

$$d(x,y) = d(y,x) \tag{4.7}$$

(4) The triangle inequality holds. In other words, a path between two points which is traced through a third point can never be shorter than the distance between the two points. That is,

$$d(x,y) \leq d(x,z) + d(z,y) \tag{4.8}$$

No one quarrels with the first of these axioms, but one can dispute the other three. For example, all psychophysical modalities have a smallest stimulus that can be detected, an absolute threshold. This is also true of distance perception; non-identical points may seem to be in the same place if the distance between them is very small.

Similarly, there is evidence that distance perception is not always symmetric. This violation of symmetry is most often found in memory or cognitive mapping conditions (Burroughs & Sadalla, 1979; Cadwallader, 1979; Codol, 1985).

While neither of these violations of the metric axioms seems particularly serious, we will see that violations of the triangle inequality are common and that they have far reaching consequences for the internal structure of visual space.

The primary reason for the failure to satisfy the triangle inequality is that the power function exponent (seen in Equation 4.2) relating judged distance to perceived distance is almost never equal to precisely one. Wiest and Bell (1985) report that an average exponent for the direct perception of distance using magnitude estimation is 1.1 with wide variation around this number. In some cases, the exponent is much greater than one. On the other hand, the exponent is typically significantly less than one when other methods are used such as category estimation and mapping (Baird, Merrill, & Tannenbaum, 1979; Sherman, Croxton, & Giovanatto, 1979; Stevens, 1975; Wagner, 1985), under memory conditions (Weist & Bell, 1985), or under reduced-cue conditions (Baird, 1970). Chapter 5 will explore variations in the exponent as a function of stimulus conditions, instructions, and method in great detail.

Yet, we will see that the problems relating to the triangle inequality are even deeper than the power function, and apply to any concave or convex transformation of physical distance into perceived distance.

Concave and convex functions. A positive function, f, is said to be concave (downward) if it satisfies the following inequality

$$f(a) + f(b) > f(a+b) \qquad (4.9)$$

and is said to be convex (downward) if it satisfies the inequality

$$f(a) + f(b) < f(a+b) \qquad (4.10)$$

The power function is either a concave or convex transformation unless the exponent is precisely equal to 1.0. In fact, it is easy to show that the following theorem holds (For the proof, see Baird, Wagner, & Noma, 1982.):

$$a^\gamma + b^\gamma > (a+b)^\gamma \text{ if } a,b > 0, \alpha < 1 \qquad (4.11)$$
$$a^\gamma + b^\gamma < (a+b)^\gamma \text{ if } a,b > 0, \alpha > 1 \qquad (4.12)$$

Thus, the power function is concave when the exponent is less than one and convex if the exponent is greater than one. To see why this is problematic, consider three points that lie along a line in physical space. Let us say the distance from the first point to the second is a, and the distance from the second point to the third is b, and the distance from the first to the third is $a+b$. Now let us say that the perceived distances (a', b', (a+b)') between the points is a power function of the physical distance; that is, the judged distances are

$$a' = a^\gamma \qquad (4.13)$$
$$b' = b^\gamma$$
$$(a+b)' = (a+b)^\gamma$$

Equations 4.11 and 4.12 imply that the straight line is only preserved as a unified whole when the exponent is equal to one. When the exponent is greater than one, the triangle inequality (Equation 4.8) does not hold because the total distance from the first point to the last $(a+b)^\gamma$ is greater than the sum of its parts. Because the exponent for size and distance judgments is often greater than one, this implies that the triangle inequality is violated on a regular basis.

Even if the exponent is less than one, the perceived line can no longer be straight because the perceived distance between the first and last points is less than the sum of the two parts. In fact, this is a best case scenario, because any other path from the first point to the third that passes through a second point will produce parts whose perceived lengths will sum to an even larger number. The parts can never fit together to make the whole. In fact, contrary to the old Gestalt saying, the whole is always less than the sum of it parts. (Of course, one can make the parts fit together by moving into a higher dimension. The line segments could be plotted on a plane, although the line would not be straight. Conceptually, one might be able to keep a perception of straightness by moving this construction of pieces into an even higher dimension. Because visual space is three dimensional, the parts could fit together by moving to four dimensions, with the projection into three dimensions seeming straight. It's not clear how to interpret the outcome of this operation that would be in the spirit of the classic book *Flatland* (Abbott, 1884).)

What is more, one can't escape these difficulties by turning to one of the non-Euclidean geometries discussed in the previous chapter. Luneburg laid out the axioms that visual space must satisfy to be a geometry of constant curvature. As I said in the last chapter (Equation 3.1), one of these axioms (which Luneburg referred to as convexity — using the term in a different way than I am here) requires that for any two points (P_1 and P_3) on a line a third point (P_2) must exist on the line between them such that

$$D(P_1, P_2) + D(P_2, P_3) = D(P_1, P_3) \tag{4.14}$$

where D is the metric for the space. Equations 4.11 and 4.12 flatly contradict this axiom and thus rule out any of the geometries of constant curvature.

By the way, Equations 4.11 and 4.12 can be extended to subtraction as well through a few simple substitutions to yield the following equations:

$$a^\gamma - b^\gamma < (a-b)^\gamma \text{ if } a > b > 0, \gamma < 1 \tag{4.15}$$
$$a^\gamma - b^\gamma > (a-b)^\gamma \text{ if } a > b > 0, \gamma > 1 \tag{4.16}$$

(A result which I have used to explain several spatial illusions such as the Müller-Lyer Illusion, the Delbouef Illusion, and the moon illusion — although I have never published the theory.)

Spatial distortions implied by the power function. None of the forgoing has assumed that visual space had any particular geometry. Yet, to give you a idea of the sorts of distortions in visual space implied by the power law, let's see what would happen if we suppose that visual space were Euclidean. Let us say that we had three points on a plane in a triangular arrangement whose inter-point distances were a, b, and c as seen in Figure 4.4a.

Here, ϕ is the angle opposite side c. If perceived distance is related to physical distance by a power function, then

$$a' = a^\gamma \qquad\qquad\qquad (4.17)$$
$$b' = b^\gamma$$
$$c' = c^\gamma$$

If we try to map these perceived distances back onto a Euclidean plane, the resulting triangle is seen in Figure 4.4b. Let us see how θ, the perceived angle opposite c', changes as a function of the exponent.

By the Law of Cosines, c in Figure 4.4a can be reexpressed as

$$c^2 = a^2 + b^2 - 2ab \cos\phi \qquad\qquad\qquad (4.18)$$

Thus, c' in Equation 4.17 may be rewritten as

$$c' = (a^2 + b^2 - 2ab \cos\phi)^{\gamma/2} \qquad\qquad\qquad (4.19)$$

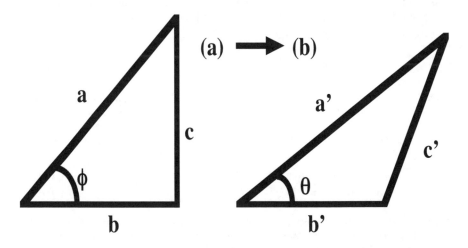

Figure 4.4. Transformation of triangle 4.4a into triangle 4.4b after a power function is applied to distances between vertices. (Based on a figure from Baird, Wagner, and Noma, 1982. Copyright 1982 by the Ohio State University Press. Reprinted by permission.)

In perceived space, the Law of Cosines gives us

$$\cos\theta = \frac{a'^2 + b'^2 - c'^2}{2a'b'} \tag{4.20}$$

Substituting for a', b', and c' and solving for θ yields

$$\theta = \text{Arccos}\left[\frac{a^{2\gamma} + b^{2\gamma} - (a^2 + b^2 - 2ab\cos\phi)^\gamma}{2a^\gamma b^\gamma}\right] \tag{4.21}$$

Figure 4.5 shows the relationship between the original physical angle, φ, and the new angle in visual space, θ, based on Equation 4.21 for two different triangles: one where side *a* is equal in length to side *b*, and one where side *a* is ten times longer than *b*. Each curve displays this relationship based on a single exponent. Notice that the original angle equals the new angle only when the exponent is equal to one. The more the exponent deviates from one, the more the new angle is distorted from the original. The distortion is particularly extreme when *a* and *b* are very unequal in length.

The figure also shows that when the exponent is less than one, certain angles do not exist in the transformed space. For example, there are no straight lines through three points in the perceptual space because 180° angles are not represented in the space. If the exponent is greater than one, many larger physical angles cannot even be represented in the perceptual space.

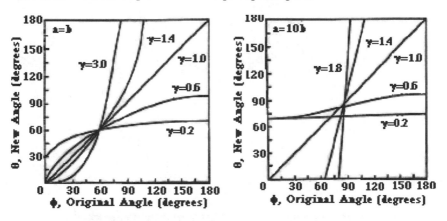

Figure 4.5. Relationship between the Angle in a Triangle (φ, Figure 4.4a) and the Angle (θ, Figure 4.4b) after a power transformation of distances between vertices. Data are based on an evaluation of Equation 4.21 for the exponents (γ) listed on the graph (left, enclosing sides of are equal, a = b; right, a = 10b). From Baird, Wagner, and Noma, 1982. Copyright 1982 by the Ohio State University Press. Reprinted by permission.

Not only do these findings cast doubt on the viability of geometries of constant curvature to describe visual space, but they may be generalized in yet another way. They also apply to any n-dimensional Minkowski space (as defined by Equation 2.7). More formally, if R^n is a complete n-dimensional Minkowski space (every n-tuple of real numbers is defined on the space), S^m is a complete m-dimensional Minkowski space, and there is a concave or convex mapping of distances between R^n and S^m, then it can be shown that one or the other of these spaces can no longer be complete if the mapping generally holds. For example, if the mapping is concave, then straight lines will not exist in S^m. If the mapping is convex, then a straight line in R^n cannot be mapped into S^m (Baird, Wagner, & Noma, 1982).

Examples of impossible figures. While it is possible to systematically explore how power function transformations distort the distance and angular relationships between three points, when the layout of four or more points is examined, distance and angular relations can break down altogether. Let's look at two examples of this that were presented in Baird, Wagner, and Noma (1982).

In Figure 4.6, two line segments intersect at right angles ($\phi = 90°$) to form a cross where the end points of the cross (A, B, C, and D) are all the same distance (a) from the center point (O).

To find the angle in the perceptual space, we can substitute $a = b$ and $\phi = 90°$ into Equation 4.21 to yield

$$\theta = \text{Arccos}\left[\frac{a^{2\gamma} + a^{2\gamma} - (a^2+a^2)^\gamma}{2(aa)^\gamma}\right]$$

or

$$\theta = \text{Arccos}\left[\frac{2a^{2\gamma} - (2a^2)^\gamma}{2(a)^{2\gamma}}\right]$$

$$\theta = \text{Arccos}\left[\frac{2a^{2\gamma} - 2^\gamma a^{2\gamma}}{2(a)^{2\gamma}}\right]$$

$$\theta = \text{Arccos}\left[\frac{2 - 2^\gamma}{2}\right]$$

$$\theta = \text{Arccos}\left[1 - 2^{\gamma-1}\right] \tag{4.22}$$

Here, θ is only equal to 90° when $\gamma = 1$. Otherwise, the four angles that make up a complete circuit do not sum to 360°, which would contradict the predictions of a Euclidean geometry. If the exponent is less than one (but still positive),

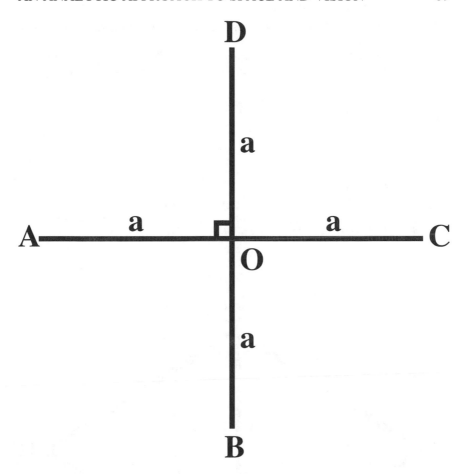

Figure 4.6. Diagram representing four points (A, B, C, and D) equidistant from a common origin (O). Based on a figure from Baird, Wagner, and Noma, 1982. Copyright 1982 by the Ohio State University Press. Reprinted by permission.

then the sum of the angles is less than 360°. This result would be similar to the predictions of a hyperbolic geometry. If the exponent is slightly larger than one, then the sum of the four angles would be greater than 360°. These results remind us of the predictions of a spherical geometry, although in both cases, we still have the problem we discussed earlier with Luneburg's "convexity" axiom.

A second example. As a second example of the difficulties that arise from power function transformations, consider Figure 4.7. In this figure, four points (A, B, C, and D) define two equilateral triangles. All five line segments that make up this figure have the same length (a). Each of the angles in the triangle

(ϕ), are equal to 60°. Putting two of these angles together to make up ϕ' should span a total of 120°.

Now, let's look at how each of these angles is affected by a power function transformation. Substituting $\phi = 60°$ and a = b into Equation 4.21 yields

$$\theta = \text{Arccos}\left[\frac{a^{2\gamma} + a^{2\gamma} - (a^2 + a^2 - 2a^2(.5))^\gamma}{2a^{2\gamma}}\right]$$

or

$$\theta = \text{Arccos}\left[\frac{2a^{2\gamma} - a^{2\gamma}}{2a^{2\gamma}}\right]$$

$$\theta = \text{Arccos}\left[\frac{1}{2}\right] = 60°$$

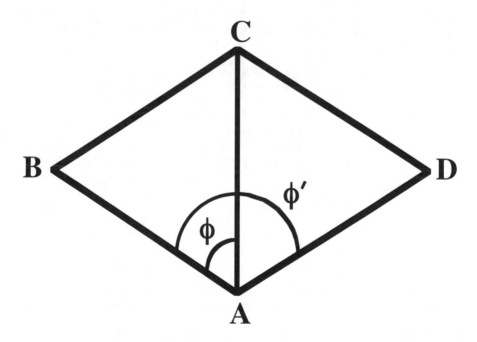

Figure 4.7. Diagram to represent four points (A, B, C, and D), where the lengths of line segments AB, BC, CD, and AD are all equal and = 60°, = 120°. Based on a figure from Baird, Wagner, and Noma, 1982. Copyright 1982 by the Ohio State University Press. Reprinted by permission.

Thus, the 60° angles that make up the two equilateral triangles remain the same after the power function transformation. The angle to the right of ϕ, $\angle CAD$, will also transform to 60°. The sum of these two angles should give us ϕ'. Now, let's see what happens to the combined angle, ϕ', when the formulas are applied to it directly. Substituting $\phi' = 120°$ and $a = b$ into Equation 4.21 yields

$$\theta = \text{Arccos}\left[\frac{a^{2\gamma} + a^{2\gamma} - (a^2 + a^2 - 2a^2(-.5))^\gamma}{2a^{2\gamma}}\right]$$

or

$$\theta = \text{Arccos}\left[\frac{2a^{2\gamma} - (3a^2)^\gamma}{2a^{2\gamma}}\right]$$

$$\theta = \text{Arccos}\left[\frac{2a^{2\gamma} - 3^\gamma a^{2\gamma}}{2a^{2\gamma}}\right]$$

$$\theta = \text{Arccos}\left[\frac{2 - 3^\gamma}{2}\right] \tag{4.23}$$

The transformed angle found in Equation 4.23 is only equal to 120° when $\gamma = 1$. Thus, unless the exponent is one, the larger angle is no longer the sum of its two parts.

Why visual space is not a Banach space. In Chapter 2, we mention another space that is important in mathematics, the Banach space. In a Banach space, spatial coordinates are thought of as vectors whose lengths are called norms ($\|x\|$). In terms of space perception, these norms may be thought of as the perceived distance from the self, or the origin of visual space, to objects. The above analysis indicates that visual space also fails to live up to the axioms of a Banach space.

First, a Banach space assumes that the norm is always non-negative and only zero if the vector has no length. Once again, the existence of thresholds for the detection of distance makes this unlikely. Second, a Banach space assumes that the triangle inequality holds, and we have seen that this is often untrue for egocentric distance judgments. Finally, a Banach space assumes that multiplying the coordinates by a scalar should increase the norm in a like manner. That is,

$$\|cx\| = |c| \, \|x\| \tag{4.24}$$

A power function transformation of physical distance into perceptual distance does not satisfy this final axiom either because if $D' = c\,D$ in physical space and judgments are transformed by the equation

$$J = \lambda\, D^{\gamma}$$

then substituting the value for D' into the equation yields

$$J' = \lambda\, (c\, D)^{\gamma} = c^{\gamma}\, \lambda\, D^{\gamma} \neq c\, J \qquad \text{if } \gamma \neq 1 \tag{4.25}$$

A Few Final Comments

A few general conclusions can be drawn from the preceding analysis. First of all, one may wonder if space perception data gathered using different methods are consistent with each other. If magnitude estimation gives rise to exponents greater than one, category estimation gives rise to exponents less than one, and mapping techniques force subjects judgments to fit onto a plane, it would seem that the methods are giving very incompatible results. Statements about the geometry of visual space may be conditioned on the method employed. One may need to derive different, incompatible models for visual space for data generated by each method.

This conclusion that the methods for exploring visual space lead to mutually inconsistent results led MacLeod and Willen (1995) to conclude that no unitary visual space exists. They used experiments involving sinusoidal stimuli and the classic Zollner and Müller-Lyer illusions to show that judgments of orientation and location do not always agree.

Second, if numeric estimation judgments are used as the basis for defining visual space, then we know quite a bit about what visual space can not be. It is not really a geometry of constant curvature because the judgments observers give are described by a power function which does not in general satisfy Luneburg's "convexity" axiom. Visual space is not satisfactorily described by any Minkowski metric (including the Euclidean metric) because the power function transformation would imply that either visual space or physical space is not complete. Under many circumstances, visual space is does not even satisfy the axioms of a metric space. At least three of the axioms are open to question, and whenever the exponent is greater than one, the triangle inequality is flatly violated. Visual space also does not satisfy the axioms of a Banach space.

This is one of the reasons for introducing the concept of a quasimetric in Chapter 2. Although visual space may not in general be a metric space, people do make metric-like judgments. That is, while an observer's judgments of size and distance may not always satisfy all of the axioms of a metric space, they may still reflect the observer's perceptions of these quantities.

One might wish that the data generated by subjects would fit a predetermined model more closely than it does. Yet, I believe that one should not reject data just because it does not fit our preconceptions. Data must be primary, and theory must follow to describe it. I feel that the only way to approach the problem of space perception is to rely on the judgment's generated by subjects, even though those judgments may lead one to conclude that visual space has a distorted structure.

The analytic approach is better able to handle this difficult data rather than the synthetic approach. The same logic that leads us to question the metric nature of visual space also leads us to question the synthetic models proposed by others. If visual space is not convex (in Luneburg's terms), then neither is it hyperbolic, spherical, or Euclidean.

On this sobering note, it is now time to examine the data in more detail. Subsequent chapters will look at the size and distance judgments subjects make under a variety of conditions. In particular, the next chapter will look at unidimensional judgments; that is, size and distance judgments when stimuli are all presented in a single orientation (e.g.., frontally or in-depth). Later chapters will look at the more complicated case of multidimensional stimuli.

5

Effects of Context on Judgments of Distance, Area, Volume, and Angle

In Chapter 4, I argued that judgments of the metric properties of space (distance, area, volume, etc.) can be related to their corresponding physical dimensions using a power function of the form

$$J = \lambda \, S^{\gamma} \tag{5.1}$$

where J represents the subject's judgments of distance, area, or volume, λ is a scaling constant, S is the physical distance, area, or volume and γ is an exponent. In addition, I argued that the parameters of this equation, λ and γ, are not constants, but rather vary as a function of stimulus location and experimental conditions.

This chapter presents the results of a meta-analysis on the space perception literature. Conditions that significantly influence spatial judgments and the degree to which they alter the parameters of the power function are examined. I also look at how well the power function fits spatial data and under which circumstances the fits are particularly good or particularly poor.

Previous Reviews

Prior to Stevens (1957) and Stevens and Galanter (1957) researchers seldom reported power function parameters. However, after Stevens convinced the majority of the psychophysical community that the power function was the best description of judgments for a wide variety of perceptual modalities, particularly for judgments arising from magnitude estimation techniques, researchers began to regularly report the power function parameters for experiments involving spatial judgments.

Eventually, researchers generated enough data that meta-analytic summaries began to appear. Perhaps the first review of the spatial literature may be attributed to Baird (1970). Baird reported 69 exponents from 14 studies on judgments of length, area, and volume. Baird found that exponents for length are largest when the standard is in the middle of the range. He also discussed the effects of average stimulus size, stimulus range, and instructions, but believed that these

74

variables had little influence of length judgments. For area, Baird indicated that objective instructions typically produced higher exponents than apparent instructions, but other contextual variables had little effect. In addition, he suggested that fits to the power function were poor for area judgments of complex shapes. Overall, Baird believed the average exponents for length, area, and volume averaged about 1.0, .8, and .6, respectively.

Two meta-analytic reviews of distance perception appeared in 1985. DaSilva (1985) reported 76 exponents from 32 studies on egocentric distance estimation, where egocentric distance refers to the distance from the observer to an object. DaSilva excluded exocentric distance judgments, which refers to the length or distance between two endpoints that are both located away from the observer. DaSilva indicated that a number of variables might potentially influence exponents including judgment method, whether the data is collected indoors or outdoors, instructions, size of the standard, size of the number assigned to the standard, range of stimuli, and stimulus cue conditions, although he did not produce any statistics from the 32 studies to examine these claims. Based on a number of his own experiments, DaSilva concluded that the typical exponent for egocentric distance estimation was about .90. He also found that magnitude estimation produces lower exponents that ratio estimation or fractionation, that increasing stimulus range produces lower exponents, and that the exponents for individual subjects are quite variable but less than 1.0 about 78% of the time.

Wiest and Bell (1985) analyzed 70 exponents taken from 25 studies on distance estimation. Their main finding concerned performance across perceptual, memory, and inference conditions. To Wiest and Bell, judgments are perceptual when the judged stimuli are available to the subject throughout the judgment process; memory judgments occur when stimuli are presented perceptually to the subject at one time but judgments are made at a later time when the stimuli are no longer available, and inference judgments occur when knowledge about stimulus layout is acquired across time such as in cognitive mapping. Wiest and Bell found that the average exponents were 1.08, .91, and .7 for the perceptual, memory, and inference conditions respectively. They also found that larger stimulus ranges are associated with smaller exponents and that judgments collected outdoors tend to produce smaller exponents than those collected indoors.

A great deal of spatial perception research has been reported in the decades following these prior reviews. The present review updates and greatly expands on them, because it is based on over seven times as much information as the most extensive previous work.

The Scaling Constant

A complete description of spatial judgments should include a discussion of variations in the scaling constant, λ, as a function of stimulus conditions. In truth, most all of the foregoing analysis will focus on the exponent and measures of goodness of fit, because the scaling constant is typically only meaningful within a single procedural context due to variations in the numerical scale used for judgments in different experiments.

In fact, Borg and Marks (1983) mention 12 factors that can influence the scaling constant. These factors include the units of measurement for the physical stimulus, the units of measurement for the psychological scale, the psychophysical method, sensory and processing variations across conditions, and individual differences. In addition, if the exponent is determined in the usual fashion by fitting a straight line through a log-log plot of the data and subjects accurately judge the size of the standard, then the scaling constant (which is the y-intercept) will vary along with the slope of the line and therefore along with changes in the exponent. Only when the exponent and experimental conditions are relatively constant will variations in the scaling constant be meaningful.

Given these conditions, however, variations in the scaling constant can be quite important because they indicate an across the board tendency for judgments under one set of conditions to be greater than under another. In fact, a number of experiments have uncovered interesting variations in the scaling constant.

Teghtsoonian (1980) had children of various ages engage in cross modality matching of length and loudness. She found that the scaling constant increased significantly with increasing age although the exponent did not differ significantly.

Butler (1983a) had subjects estimate the lengths of horizontal and vertical lines and found that the scaling constant for a vertical standard was about 12% greater than for a horizontal standard while exponents did not differ significantly across conditions. Butler thought of this variation in the scaling constant as a direct measure of the magnitude of the horizontal-vertical illusion. Butler (1983b) also found that the scaling constants associated with judgments of line length were significantly influenced by whether the line appeared in the context of the edges of a box or by itself. The scaling constant was significantly larger for lines viewed in the box context. Butler interpreted this difference as being an alternate measure of the constant error that is traditionally measured with discrimination techniques such as the method of constant stimuli.

Wagner (1985) and Wagner and Feldman (1989) had subjects estimate distances at various orientations with respect to the observer using four psychophysical methods. Wagner found that the scaling constant for stimuli oriented in-depth with respect to the observer tended to be about half as large as for stimuli oriented frontally, while exponents did not differ across conditions. Wagner felt this variation indicated a general tendency for in-depth stimuli to be seen as smaller than frontally oriented stimuli of the same physical length. In other words, Wagner viewed variations in the scaling constant to be indicative of the presence of a perceptual illusion.

Methodology

The remainder of this chapter will focus on variables that influence the exponent and the coefficient of determination (R^2) of the power function. This work is meta-analytic in that it statistically combines data gleaned from many sources to estimate the overall effects of different contextual variables on the exponent. However, I see the basic purpose of this investigation as being primarily descriptive; the amount of data collected and the number of variables involved are so large that the main points could easily be lost in a sea of convoluted statistical analysis. I aim to keep things as simple as possible.

The initial list of works to include in the analysis came from a computer search for articles on length, distance, size, area, volume, and space perception that included mention of power functions or exponents. I then eliminated non-English articles. This eliminated eight articles mentioned in the initial computer search. The list was then supplemented by adding references from the previous meta-analytic reviews (Baird, 1970; DaSilva, 1985; Wiest & Bell, 1985) and other articles.

In the end, the analysis includes 104 space perception articles and a total of 530 power function exponents. The later number is greater than the former because most articles reported exponents for multiple experimental conditions. In a few cases, the experimenters broke down the data into so many conditions that very few subjects participated in a given combination. In these cases, I would average exponents across variables that were not at issue in the present study. (Otherwise, some studies would carry more weight in the final analysis simply by virtue of multiple exponents being reported in the same study with no other useful information being added to the analysis.)[1]

For each study, 22 variables were recorded (when available). The effects of 13 of these variables on the power function exponent and coefficient of determination are listed in Table 5.1 and will be discussed in this chapter. The other 9 variables are not reported either because they are redundant re-expressions of reported variables or because they lacked sufficient variation to make analysis valid.

The results for distance, area, volume, and angle judgments will be reported separately, starting with distance estimates. For size and distance judgments, I will discuss the effects of each variable four ways. First, an analysis of the entire data set will be discussed. Second, the analysis will be repeated for perceptual data alone, excluding inference and memory conditions. Third, the analysis will be refined even further to focus on perceptual data collected using magnitude estimation or ratio estimation. (Two methods which Wiest and Bell (1985) and others argue are equivalent.) Finally, I will discuss the results of articles that specifically examine a given variable (if such articles exist).

The data are presented in a variety of formats in recognition of the dangers involved in meta-analytic research. Data collected under memory and inference conditions may not be equivalent to perceptual data. Similarly, certain judgment methods such as mapping, fractionation, or triangulation place physical constraints on the judgment process that may render them non-equivalent to numeric techniques like magnitude and ratio estimation.

---

[1]A complete copy of the Excel database which was used in the following analyses can be obtained from the author by sending a diskette (being sure to indicate if your computer is IBM compatible or Macintosh) to the following address: Mark Wagner, Psychology Department, Wagner College, 1 Campus Road, Staten Island, NY 10301.

Table 5.1

Mean Exponent and Coefficient of Determination (R^2) as a Function of Recorded Variables for Judgments of Distance Calculated from All Data, Perception Data, and Magnitude or Ratio Estimation Perception Data

Variable	Value of Variable	Exponent			Coefficient of Determination		
		All	Per.	Mag. Est.	All	Per.	Mag.Est.
Overall		0.96	1.02	1.04	0.91	0.95	0.96
Age	Pre Under.	0.93	0.92	1.05	0.97	0.97	0.99
	Undergrad.	0.95	1.02	1.02	0.91	0.97	0.96
	Post Under.	1.04	1.04	1.05	0.91	0.91	0.95
Cue Conditions	Full	1.00	1.02	1.04	0.92	0.94	0.95
	Reduced	0.99	0.99	1.01	0.98	0.98	0.99
Ego vs. Exocentric	Egocentric	0.99	1.01	1.06	0.96	0.98	0.99
	Exocentric	0.95	1.03	1.01	0.88	0.91	0.92
Immeadiacy	Perception	1.02		1.04	0.96		0.96
	Memory	0.87		0.90	0.87		0.85
	Inference	0.77		0.76	0.82		0.81
Inside or Outside	Inside	1.02	1.05	1.04	0.91	0.96	0.95
	Outside	0.89	0.97	1.03	0.91	0.95	0.97
Instructions	Objective	0.94	1.03	1.08	0.90	0.97	0.96
	Neutral	0.93	1.00	1.03	0.90	0.94	0.92
	Apparent	1.02	1.03	1.04	0.96	0.95	0.97
	Road Path	0.70			0.82		
Method	Fractionation	0.89	0.90		0.97	0.97	
	Ratio Est.	0.82	1.02	1.02			
	Mag. Est.	0.98	1.04	1.04	0.91	0.96	0.96
	Mapping	0.76	0.96		0.88		
	Production	1.02	1.06		0.92	0.99	
	Triangulation	0.96	0.96				
Number of Subjects	≤ 15	1.00	1.03	1.03	0.92	0.94	0.95
	> 15	0.90	1.01	1.04	0.91	0.97	0.97
Standard Used	No	0.96	1.03	1.05	0.93	0.98	0.98
	Yes	0.96	1.00	1.00	0.88	0.92	0.93
Standard Size	Small	0.94	1.02	1.02	0.84	0.82	0.86
	Midrange	0.96	0.94	0.96	0.93	0.92	0.93
	Large	1.04	1.03	1.03	0.98	0.98	0.98
Stimulus Orientation	Horizontal	1.02	1.01	1.02	0.95	0.93	0.86
	Vertical	1.04	1.04	1.04	0.91	0.91	0.91
	In-depth	1.01	1.04	1.09	0.95	0.98	0.98
Log Stimulus Range	< 1	1.06	1.06	1.10	0.97	0.97	0.96
	1 ≤ x ≤ 1.5	1.06	1.06	1.08	0.94	0.94	0.96
	> 1.5	0.86	0.89	0.91	0.98	0.97	0.98
Stimulus Size	< 1 m	1.04	1.04	1.02	0.95	0.95	0.94
	1m ≤ x ≤ 10m	1.10	1.09	1.11	0.99	0.99	0.99
	> 10m	0.88	0.93	0.99	0.90	0.94	0.96

More researchers focus on perception and most of those use magnitude estimation techniques, and so the more refined analyses reported here will conform to this emphasis. In addition, because conditions are not randomly assigned to researchers and some combinations of conditions may occur more frequently than others, it is possible for variables to be correlated with one another. Thus, the apparent influence of one variable on the exponent might really be due to it being correlated with another recorded variable. Examining studies that explicitly look at the effects of a given variable within a single experimental context can serve as a check to confirm or disconfirm meta-analytic conclusions.

Size and Distance Estimates

There were a total of 362 exponents for distance estimates that entered into the analysis. The perceptual data set had 257 exponents, while the magnitude/ratio estimation data set had 182 exponents. Table 5.1 summarizes the effects of different contextual variables on judgments of size and distance. I will discuss the effects of each variable in turn.

Overall. In general, exponents for distance estimation are very close to 1.0. For both perceptual data sets, it appears that the average exponent is slightly larger greater than 1.0, and the data are well-fit by a power function with coefficients of determination averaging about .95. The total data set shows a lower average exponent and a lower coefficient of determination due to the influence of memory and inference conditions.

Age. Only a small number of studies reported the average age of the subjects involved. Typically, studies either reported an age range or described the population from which subjects were drawn—such as undergraduates. I used this information to estimate the average age of the subjects. In truth, there was little variation in age because 84% of all studies were based on undergraduate students.

Based on the total data set, exponents appeared to significantly increase with age, $r = .15$, $p < .05$, but this trend is not significant for the other two data sets. Coefficients of determination appear to decline with age for the total data set, $r = -.19$, $p < .05$, and for perceptual judgments, $r = -.28$, $p < .05$.

Cue conditions. Some studies limit perceptual exploration and/or cues to distance more than others. Full-cue conditions allow relatively complete layout information, while reduced-cue conditions limit perceptual information in some way. In the present analysis, most studies (81.2%) were classified as full cue.

Exponents were significantly greater under full-cue conditions for all data combined and for perceptual magnitude estimates. In truth, the effects of cue conditions may be greater than the summary data would make it seem because 60.4% of the studies classified as "reduced-cue" only limited information by fixing head position with a bite bar. This attempt at increased experimental control may also explain why the coefficient of determination was significantly greater under reduced conditions.

One study that looked at cue conditions (Hagen & Teghtsoonian, 1981) found higher exponents for egocentric distance estimates under binocular conditions than monocular ones. Similarly, Kunnapas (1968) found a low exponent (.82) for monocular conditions, an intermediate exponent (.93) for binocular conditions with a fixed head position, and a high exponent (.97) for full cue conditions. Also consistent with this general tendency, Wagner and Feldman (1989) found much lower exponents for distance judgments collected under dark conditions (.70) than under full lighting (.99). Predebon (1992), however, found few consistent effects of head position or binocularity.

Egocentric vs. exocentric. There were no significant differences in the exponent between egocentric and exocentric distance judgments. Coefficients of determination, however, were significantly higher for egocentric judgments for all three data sets.

Immediacy. For want of a better word, immediacy here refers to the effects of perceptual, memory, and inference conditions as defined by Wiest and Bell (1985). The stimulus is most immediately available in perceptual conditions and never directly available under inference conditions.

The exponent is highest for perceptual conditions and lowest in the inference condition. In addition, coefficients of determination were highest for perceptual conditions and lowest for inference conditions. These differences in exponents and coefficients of determination between all three conditions are statistically significant at the .001 level according to Duncan follow up tests.

Wiest & Bell (1985) restricted their analysis to magnitude and ratio estimates. To make the present analysis equivalent, Table 5.1 also reports mean exponents for perceptual, memory, and inference conditions based exclusively on magnitude and ratio estimates. (This is the only time the third column of the table includes memory and inference conditions.) The exponents reported here are similar to those reported by Wiest and Bell; however, they deviate a bit less from 1.0 than in their report. Once again, coefficients of determination are highest for perceptual conditions and lowest for inference conditions.

The present results are also consistent with many individual articles examining the effects of memory on psychophysical judgment. Bradley and Vido (1984), Kerst, Howard, and Gugerty (1987), Moyer et al. (1978), Radvansky and Carlson-Radvansky (1995) all found higher exponents in perceptual than in memory conditions. DaSilva, Ruiz, and Marques (1987) found high exponents for perception, generally lower exponents for memory, and generally lowest exponents for inference conditions. However, there are two exceptions to this general rule. DaSilva and Fukusima (1986) and Kerst and Howard (1978) found perceptual exponents to be slightly greater than one and memory exponents to be even greater. One might be tempted to assume that memory exponents will be less than perceptual exponents if the perceptual exponent is less than one, and greater than perceptual exponents when the perceptual exponent is greater than one consistent with Kerst and Howard's reperception hypothesis, but three of the studies who found perceptual exponents to be greater than memory ones also had mean perceptual exponents greater than one.

For memory conditions, the amount of time that passed between stimulus presentation and the judgment process was recorded. One might expect than exponents would decline with increasing retention intervals, but the data did not support this. There was no consistent pattern in the size of exponents as a function of judgment interval and the correlation between retention interval and the exponent was not significant. Past studies that specifically looked at this variable are inconsistent regarding the effects of retention interval on the exponent (DaSilva & Fukusima, 1986; DaSilva, Ruiz, & Marques, 1987; Kerst, Howard, & Gugerty, 1987).

For inference conditions, Foley and Cohen (1984a, 1984b) and Wagner and Feldman (1990) found a tendency for the exponent to increase (and approach 1.0) the longer subjects reside in a location, but there was not enough data to test this hypothesis in the current meta-analysis.

Inside vs. outside. Experiments conducted indoors produce significantly higher exponents than those conducted outside for the two larger data sets. However, this difference is not significant for perceptual data collected using only magnitude/ratio estimation. Coefficients of determination do not differ significantly between inside and outside studies.

Teghtsoonian and Teghtsoonian (1970a) were the first to find higher exponents for distance judgments collected indoors. More recently, one condition of Higashiyama and Shimono (1994) directly tested this effect and found results consistent with the Teghtsoonians and those reported here.

Instructions. Studies differ in the way they describe the judgment task to subjects. In the present analysis, instructions were classified into four types. Apparent size instructions were the most commonly employed (39.2% of studies). These instructions ask subjects to judged how the distance "looks", "appears", or "seems to be" subjectively. Objective instructions, which explicitly emphasize physical accuracy, are less commonly employed (24.3% of studies). A third categorization used here was a neutral category, that neither emphasized physical accuracy nor how things appear subjectively, but rather simply asked subjects to judge the distance between two points. This categorization describes 34.3% of the studies. Finally, a relatively small number of studies (2.2%) asked subjects to judge the distance from one place to another, not as the crow flies, but according to the length of the route one would need to take to drive from one place to another.

Instructions appeared to have inconsistent effects on the exponent. For the complete data set, apparent instructions produced significantly higher exponents than objective or neutral instructions. For perceptual magnitude/ratio estimates, objective instructions tended to result in higher exponents than either apparent or neutral instructions although this trend is not significant. Road-path length produced consistently and significantly lower exponents and coefficients of determination than other instruction types.

The studies that directly looked at this issue generally either found little difference in exponents due to instructions or found objective instructions resulted in slightly higher exponents. Two experiments by DaSilva and DosSantos

(1984) found objective instructions produced slightly higher exponents (.88) than apparent instructions (.86). Similarly, Gogel and DaSilva (1987) found very slightly higher exponents with objective instructions (1.02) than apparent instructions (1.00). Teghtsoonian (1965) also found slightly higher exponents for objective instructions (1.00) than apparent instructions (.98). None of these differences were statistically significant, and they also do not seem to be "significant" in the common English meaning of that word.

Method of judgment. Analysis of variance indicates that the exponent differs significantly as a function of method used to collect judgments for the total data set at the .001 level. Duncan follow up tests indicate that mapping, complete ratio estimation, and fractionation exponents are significantly smaller than exponents based on magnitude estimation and production. Exponents also differ significantly (at the .001 level) as a function of method for the perceptual data set. Here, Duncan follow up tests reveal that the exponents for magnitude estimation, complete ratio estimation, and production are all significantly greater than those produced by fractionation. The magnitude/ratio estimation data set found no significant difference between magnitude and ratio estimation. There was too little data collected employing category estimation or absolute judgment to make meaningful statistical statements, but such as there is indicates that category estimation exponents seem to be low (.90) while absolute judgment exponents seem to be very high (2.44). Coefficients of determination did not differ significantly as a function of method.

Many studies have explicitly looked at how method influences exponents. Often, these studies have produced contradictory results. Baird, Merrill, and Tannenbaum (1979) and Bradley and Vido (1984) both found magnitude estimation produced higher exponents than mapping when testing knowledge of the spatial layout of a familiar environment. Wagner (1985) found that magnitude estimation exponents were higher than mapping exponents (and category estimates were the lowest) in a perceptual task. However, Kerst, Howard, and Grugerty (1987) found magnitude estimation produced lower exponents than mapping in a memory task. Baird, Romer, and Stein (1970) found that magnitude estimation led to much lower exponents than absolute judgment. Bratfisch and Lundberg noted that magnitude estimation exponents tended to be slightly larger than those associated with complete ratio estimation. In MacMillan et al. (1974) and Mershon et al. (1977), magnitude estimation exponents tended to be slightly higher than magnitude production exponents under similar conditions; however, Masin (1980) and Teghtsoonian and Teghtsoonian (1978) showed no consistent difference between magnitude estimation and magnitude production exponents and Pitz (1965) actually found higher exponents with magnitude production.

Number of subjects. The number of subjects in the experiment proved to be significantly negatively correlated with the size of the exponent for the total data set, r = -.30, p < .001. The most probable explanation of this relationship is that memory studies typically had many more subjects than perceptual ones. Because memory exponents are much lower than perceptual exponents, this would explain why exponents went down with the number of subjects under memory conditions. When memory is factored out as in the two perceptual data sets, the correlation between the number of subjects and the exponent disappears.

Standard. Although no difference is found with the total data set, studies using a standard had significantly lower exponents and coefficients of determination than studies that used no standard for perceptual data collected using magnitude or ratio estimation. Using a standard gave rise to more accurate judgments with the exponent averaging precisely 1.0. It would appear that putting the standard in the middle of the stimulus range gives rise to lower perceptual exponents than placing it at either extreme, but this trend is not significant.

Past research is equivocal. DaSilva and DaSilva (1983) and Kowal (1993) found the presence of a standard had little consistent influence on the exponent. On the other hand, Pitz (1965) found consistently lower exponents when the standard was present.

Stimulus orientation. The orientation of the stimulus did not significantly influence the exponent for any of the data sets. However, for both of the perceptual data sets, orientation significant influenced the coefficient of determination. In both data sets, Duncan follow up tests show that in-depth oriented stimuli gave rise to significantly higher R^2 values than frontally presented stimuli in a vertical orientation. For the magnitude/ratio estimates, in-depth stimuli were also associated with higher R^2 values than frontally presented stimuli oriented horizontally.

Butler (1983b), Hartley (1977), and Künnapas (1958) all found little difference in exponents between vertical and horizontal frontal stimuli. Baird and Biersdorf (1967) found higher exponents for frontally oriented stimuli than for those oriented in-depth. Unlike the analysis reported above, Teghtsoonian (1973) conducted four studies and also found a marked tendency toward higher exponents for frontally oriented stimuli than those oriented in-depth.

As mentioned before, even though exponents may not differ much due to stimulus orientation, orientation may still have profound effects on perception of distance. Butler (1983b) found the scaling constant differed significantly between horizontal and vertical stimuli. Similarly, Wagner (1985) and Wagner and Feldman (1989) found very different scaling constants between in-depth and frontally oriented stimuli. These studies indicate a general tendency for frontally oriented stimuli to seem larger than those oriented in-depth.

Stimulus range. Teghtsoonian (1971, 1973) proposed that the exponent was closely related to the range of stimuli presented to the subject. Large stimulus ranges should theoretically produce consistently smaller exponents. In the present study, the stimulus range was determined dividing the maximum stimulus presented to the subject by the smallest. To be consistent with Teghtsoonian's work, I then took the logarithm of this ratio.

Stimulus range proved to be one of the most powerful predictors of the exponent. The exponent was negatively correlated with log stimulus range at the .001 level for all three data sets (r = -.45 for all data, r = -.38 for perception data, r = -.44 for perceptual magnitude estimation data). The coefficient of determination was not significantly correlated with stimulus range for any of the data sets.

Past research is largely, but not entirely, consistent with Teghtsoonian's theory as well. Da Silva (1983b), DaSilva and DaSilva (1983), Gibson and Bergman (1954), Künnapas (1958), and Markley (1971) all found lower exponents for larger stimulus ranges than for smaller ones. A few other studies found no consistent effect of stimulus range (Galanter & Galanter, 1973; Kowal, 1993; Teghtsoonian & Teghtsoonian, 1970, 1978).

Stimulus size. For the total data set, stimulus size—defined as the midpoint of the stimuli presented to the subject—was significantly negatively correlated with the size of the exponent, r = -.16, p < .01. Once again, this correlation probably arises because inference conditions, which are associated with lower exponents, often use large-scale environments to test cognitive mapping knowledge. When memory and inference conditions are factored out, as in the two perceptual data sets, the correlation between stimulus size and the exponent is no longer significant.

Multivariate analyses. Of course, there are certain statistical dangers associated with conducting a large series of univariate significance tests. First of all, the more tests one conducts, the higher the likelihood that some of the significant findings arise by chance (Type I error). Secondly, it is possible that real trends in the data may be produced (or obscured) by the effects of secondary factors that are accidentally associated with the variable due to the non-random nature of the data collection process. Because some combinations of conditions may occur more frequently than others, it is possible for variables to be correlated with one another. Thus, the apparent influence (or lack of influence) of one variable on the exponent might really be due to it being correlated with another recorded variable.

To overcome these deficiencies, I performed a series of linear multivariate regression analyses. The exponent was the outcome variable and all variables that displayed any significant univariate associations with the exponent served as predictor variables. These predictor variables included age, cue conditions, immediacy, inside vs. outside location, instructions, method, number of subjects, standard presence, and log stimulus range. Mean stimulus size was not included as a predictor because its association with the exponent was non-linear. Variables with no significant univariate association with the exponent were excluded to limit the multivariate model to a reasonable size.

Categorical variables were recoded as dummy variables where "1" represented the presence of a factor and "0" represented the absence of a factor. If more than two levels existed for a categorical factor, a series of dummy variables were used to represent the information. For example, instructions were broken down into two variables, one for the presence of objective instructions and one for the presence of apparent instructions.

For the total data set, four factors proved to be significantly associated with the exponent in the multivariate analysis: inference conditions (t = 3.70, p < .001), the presence of a standard (t = 2.64, p < .01), judgment method (t = 2.84, p < .005), and log stimulus range (t = 9.54, p < .0001). Once the significant variables were determined, a second regression analysis was performed employing only these four significant variables to determine the best fitting equation to predict the exponent. This equation accounted for 42.03% of the variance in the exponent.

The results of the second regression equation can be substituted into equation 5.1 to yield the following general equation to predict distance judgments:

$$J = \lambda D^{[.083(\text{mag}) - .058(\text{stan}) - .210(\text{inf}) - .167(\log(\text{max/min})) + 1.172]} \quad (5.2)$$

where J is the subject's judgment for distance, λ is a scaling constant, D is the physical distance, "mag" is code "1" if the method is magnitude or ratio estimation and "0" otherwise, "stan" is coded "1" if a standard is used and "0" otherwise, "inf" is code "1" for inference stimuli and "0" for memory and perceptual stimuli, and log(max/min) refers to the base 10 logarithm of the ratio of the largest stimulus used in the experiment to the smallest.

Because there was a linear dependency between the way magnitude/ratio judgments and the various production methods were coded (by knowing that the method was not any of the production methods automatically implied that the method was magnitude or ratio estimation), a second equation could be generated based on the various production methods (fractionation, triangulation, mapping, and magnitude production) where magnitude estimation was coded as "0." Only one of these methods significantly predicted the exponent, fractionation. The linear regression including the influence of fractionation accounted for 47.76% of the variance in the exponent. When this regression equation was substituted into the power function it yields the following general equation to predict distance judgments:

$$J = \lambda D^{[-.264(\text{frac}) - .067(\text{stan}) - .249(\text{inf}) - .143(\log(\text{max/min})) + 1.232]} \quad (5.3)$$

where "frac" is coded "1" when the fractionation method was employed and "0" otherwise.

For the perceptual data set, three (of the eight remaining) variables proved to be significantly related to the exponent in the multivariate regression analysis. Consistent with the total data set, the three variables that were significantly related to the exponent were method (t = 2.75, p < .01), presence of a standard (t = 2.40, p < .05), log stimulus ratio (t = 8.17, p < .0001). (Of course, the inference condition could not be an element in the perceptual equation because inference data was factored out of this data set.) When a regression equation was generated based on these three factors it accounted for 29.46% of the data. Substituting this linear equation into the power function yields the following general equation to predict perceptual distance judgments:

$$J = \lambda D^{[.084(\text{mag}) - .055(\text{stan}) - .160(\log(\text{max/min})) + 1.161]} \quad (5.4)$$

Once again, if production methods are focused on, fractionation was the only method significantly associated with the exponent. The regression equation including fractionation accounts for 36.87% of the variance. The power function based on this regression equation is:

$$J = \lambda D^{[-.268(\text{frac}) - .065(\text{stan}) - .134(\log(\max/\min)) + 1.219]} \quad (5.5)$$

Finally, for the perceptual data set focusing on magnitude and ratio judgments, only two factors were significantly related to the exponent in the multiple regression equation, presence of a standard ($t = 3.02$, $p < .01$) and log stimulus ratio ($t = 6.25$, $p < .0001$). (Method is no longer a factor because it has been factored out of the data set.) This regression equation accounted for 23.48 % of the variance in the exponent. Substituting this equation into the power function yields the following equation to predict distance judgments:

$$J = \lambda D^{[- .071(\text{stan}) - .136(\log(\max/\min)) + 1.223]} \quad (5.6)$$

Area Estimates

A similar meta-analysis was performed for the effects of contextual variables on judgments of area. In this case, only two data sets were examined; one based on all area judgments and another solely based on perceptual judgments that excluded memory and inference conditions. There was no point to separately analyze perceptual judgments using magnitude or ratio estimation alone because almost all (95%) area judgments employed either magnitude or ratio estimation. There were 117 exponents in the total data set, and 91 exponents in the perceptual data set. Table 5.2 shows a summary of the effects of various contextual variables on area estimation exponents and power function coefficients of determination (R^2). The following looks at each of these variables in more detail:

Overall. In general, area exponents are smaller than those reported for distance judgments and are in line with Baird's (1970) estimate of .8. For perceptual judgments, area exponents averaged .84, and these judgments followed a power function quite well as indicated by the high average coefficient of determination of .95. The total data set showed somewhat lower exponents and coefficients of determination due to the influence of memory and inference conditions.

Age. There was a small, but significant, positive correlation between the age of subjects and the size of the exponent for the total data set ($r = .21$, $p < .05$). A similar correlation between age and the exponent is seen in the perceptual data set, but it is not significant ($r = .21$, $p > .05$). The coefficient of determination declines sharply with age for the perceptual data set ($r = -.58$, $p < .001$), but this trend is not significant for the total data set ($r = -.13$, $p >. 05$). These data are somewhat consistent with Borg and Borg (1990) who generally found higher area estimation exponents with older, more educated subject populations.

Table 5.2

Mean Exponent and Coefficient of Determination (R^2) as a Function of Recorded Variables for Judgments of Area Calculated from All Data and Perception Data

Variable	Value of Variable	Exponent All Data	Perception	Coefficient of Determination All Data	Perception
Overall		0.78 (.20)	0.84 (.18)	0.90 (.16)	0.95 (.11)
Age	Pre Under.	0.81 (.06)	0.81 (.06)	0.99 (.01)	0.99 (.01)
	Undergrad.	0.76 (.23)	0.83 (.21)	0.89 (.23)	0.97 (.03)
	Post Under.	0.80 (.18)	0.87 (.16)	0.87 (.18)	0.76 (.25)
Cue Conditions	Full	0.75 (.14)	0.80 (.11)	0.89 (.17)	0.94 (.13)
	Reduced	0.97 (.36)	0.97 (.36)	0.95 (.03)	0.95 (.03)
Immeadiacy	Perception	0.84 (.18)		0.95 (.11)	
	Memory	0.67 (.10)		0.81 (.15)	
	Inference	0.50 (.12)		0.81 (.24)	
Inside or Outside	Inside	0.79 (.20)	0.85 (.18)	0.92 (.14)	0.97 (.03)
	Outside	0.63 (.16)	0.63 (.16)	0.54 (.10)	0.54 (.10)
Instructions	Objective	0.96 (.47)	1.01 (.49)	0.99 (.01)	0.99 (.01)
	Neutral	0.79 (.18)	0.87 (.13)	0.90 (.16)	0.97 (.03)
	Apparent	0.75 (.13)	0.78 (.11)	0.90 (.16)	0.94 (.13)
Method	Ratio Est.	0.97 (.13)	0.97 (.14)		
	Mag. Est.	0.76 (.15)	0.82 (.11)	0.91 (.15)	0.96 (.07)
Number of Subjects	≤ 15	0.83 (.23)	0.86 (.23)	0.93 (.13)	0.92 (.14)
	> 15	0.72 (.14)	0.79 (.06)	0.87 (.18)	0.98 (.03)
Standard Used	No	0.77 (.16)	0.80 (.14)	0.97 (.01)	0.99 (.02)
	Yes	0.77 (.16)	0.83 (.12)	0.86 (.18)	0.92 (.14)
Standard Size	Small	0.82 (.21)	0.82 (.21)		
	Midrange	0.81 (.12)	0.81 (.12)		
	Large	0.64 (.13)	0.76 (.08)		
Stimulus Orientation	Frontal	0.80 (.19)	0.84 (.18)	0.93 (.13)	0.97 (.03)
	Flat	0.63 (.16)	0.63 (.16)	0.54 (.09)	0.54 (.09)
Log Stimulus Range	≤ 1.5	0.98 (.14)	0.98 (.14)	0.98	0.98
	1.5 ≤ x ≤ 2.0	0.84 (.25)	0.84 (.25)	0.99 (.01)	0.99 (.01)
	> 2.0	0.73 (.10)	0.73 (.10)	0.88 (.19)	0.88 (.19)
Stimulus Size	< 100 cm^2	0.87 (.14)	0.87 (.14)	0.98 (.01)	0.98 (.01)
	in between	0.85 (.37)	0.85 (.37)	0.98 (.00)	0.98 (.00)
	> 1000cm^2	0.75 (.11)	0.74 (.11)	0.89 (.21)	0.89 (.21)

Cue conditions. There appears to be a tendency for the exponent to be larger under reduced cue conditions than it is under full cue conditions, although this result is not statistically significant for either data set. The total data set shows a significantly higher coefficient of determination for reduced cue conditions, perhaps due to the greater experimental control often employed in reduced settings. In truth, there are too few experiments that have employed reduced cue settings to allow for any firm conclusions. Given only 12 reduced cue data points, one particularly large exponent (2.08) found using absolute judgment (which produced the largest exponents for distance judgments as well) may be responsible for the differences seen here (Baird, Romer, & Stein, 1970).

Predebon (1992) had subjects judge areas looking through an aperture both with binocular vision and free head movement and with monocular vision with head position fixed. Exponents for the binocular condition were identical to those in the monocular condition (.8) when no familiar size cues were present. Exponents were slightly lower in the binocular condition (.82) than in the monocular condition (.87) when familiar size cues were present.

Immediacy. Exponents varied significantly as a function of memory condition, $F(2,114) = 24.46$, $p < .001$. Duncan follow-up tests show that all three conditions differ significantly from each other. The highest exponents arose from perceptual conditions (.84), followed by memory conditions (.67), and inference conditions led to the smallest exponents (.50). Coefficients of determination were also highest in the perceptual condition while the two memory conditions did not differ significantly from each other.

Of course, this pattern is similar to what was found with distance judgments, and individual research studies also show the same tendencies. Algom, Wolf, and Berman (1985) found larger exponents for area judgments for perceptual conditions than in either memory or inference conditions. Similarly, other researchers have found higher exponents for perceptual conditions than in memory conditions (Chew & Richardson, 1986; Kerst & Howard, 1978; Moyer, Bradley, Sorensen, Whiting, & Mansfield, 1978). DaSilva, Marques, and Ruiz (1987) and Kemp (1988) found the largest exponents for perceptual conditions, followed by memory conditions, and trailed by inference conditions. In contrast, Björkman, Lundberg, and Tärnblom (1960) presented the lone study to find higher exponents for remembered area than perceived area in an experiment that employed complete ratio estimation.

Inside vs. outside. Exponents for judgments collected indoors were significantly larger than those gathered outdoors for the perceptual data set. Indoor conditions also produced much higher coefficients of determination. While these results are significant and consistent with what was found with distance estimation, they must be viewed with caution because the outdoor average is only based on 4 exponents. In addition, I found no individual studies that examined the effects of this variable in my literature search.

Instructions. Both data sets showed significantly higher exponents when objective instructions are used than when either neutral or apparent instructions are employed. For the perceptual data set, neutral instructions displayed higher exponents than apparent instructions. Gärling and Dalkvist (1977) also found higher exponents for objective instructions than apparent instructions when subjects judged the area rectangles, but found no difference when judging the area of ellipses. Teghtsoonian (1965) found objective instructions produced much higher exponents than apparent instructions when judging the area of circles, but found little difference between the two instructions when estimating the area of complex polygons. Thus it would appear that objective instructions boost exponents for simple figures, but not for more complex ones.

Method. Most of the area estimation studies either employed magnitude estimation or complete ratio estimation. For both data sets, complete ratio estimation yielded significantly higher exponents than magnitude estimation. While other judgment methods were seldom used (only one or two exponents based on each method), a preliminary list of exponents based on each method for the perceptual data is as follows: absolute judgment (2.08), complete ratio estimation (.97), mapping (.85), magnitude estimation (.82), magnitude production (.69), and category estimation (.46).

Four studies specifically looked at the effects of various methods on the exponent. Contrary to the meta-analytic conclusion presented above, Ekman and Junge (1961) found higher exponents with magnitude estimation than with complete ratio estimation. Employing other methods, Baird, Romer, and Stein (1970) displayed much higher area estimation exponents using absolute judgment (2.08) than magnitude estimation (.63). MacMillan, Moschetto, Bialostozky, and Engel (1974) showed higher exponents for magnitude estimation than for magnitude production both when a standard was present and when one was not. Wagner (1985) found the highest area estimation exponent using mapping (.85), the second highest exponent using magnitude estimation (.6), and the smallest exponent using category estimation (.46).

Number of subjects. The number of subjects employed in the experiment did not significantly influence either the exponent or the coefficient of determination.

Standard. Contrary to what one might imagine, the presence of a standard actually led to significantly lower coefficients of determination for both data sets; however, the exponent did not differ significantly as a function of the presence of a standard. In one individual study that looked specifically at the effects of the presence of a standard, MacMillan, Moschetto, Bialostozky, and Engel (1974) displayed higher exponents when a standard was present than when it was not under four different sets of conditions.

Having the standard at the high end of the stimulus range was associated with significantly lower exponents for the total data set, but not for the perceptual data set. Consistent with this, Mashhour and Hosman (1968) found smaller exponents when the standard was placed at the top of the stimulus range than when it was place in the bottom or the middle of the range.

Stimulus orientation. For the perceptual data set, exponents were significantly higher for frontally presented areas than for areas lying flat on a horizontal surface, and coefficients of determination were significantly larger for frontally presented stimuli for both data sets. No individual research studies specifically looked at the effects of stimulus orientation on area judgments.

Stimulus range. Once again, Teghtsoonian's (1971, 1973) prediction that wide stimulus ranges are associated with smaller exponents is dramatically confirmed. The log stimulus range (log(Maximum Stimulus/Minimum Stimulus)) was significantly negatively correlated with the exponent for both data sets (for the total data set r = -.42, p < .001, and for the perceptual data set r = -.42, p < .001). However, neither of the two individual research studies I found that systematically varied stimulus range for area judgments found a consistent pattern in the exponents as a function of stimulus range (Björkman & Strangert, 1960; Ekman & Junge, 1961).

Stimulus size. Stimulus size (defined as the midpoint of the stimulus range) was significantly negatively correlated with the coefficient of determination for both data sets, but stimulus size was not significantly correlated with the exponent (although it was close at p = .053). In particular, it appears that very large stimuli are associated with lower coefficients of determination than small- and mid-sized stimuli.

Multivariate analyses. Once again, I performed a series of linear multivariate regression analyses on the area judgment data. The exponent was the outcome variable and all variables that displayed any significant univariate associations with the exponent served as predictor variables. These predictor variables included age, immediacy, inside vs. outside location, instructions, method, standard size, stimulus orientation, and log stimulus range. Variables with no significant univariate association with the exponent were excluded to limit the multivariate model to a reasonable size.

For the total data set, two multiple regression analyses were performed. The reason why this was necessary was because all of the experiments involving memory and inference conditions did not specify their stimulus range; therefore, it was not possible to calculate the log stimulus range for any memory or inference studies. Because the log stimulus range only existed for perceptual data, no correlation is possible between the log stimulus range and immediacy conditions, and without this correlation, multiple regression cannot be performed. For this reason, I did two separate multiple regression analyses, one involving all significant factors but the log stimulus ratio and another involving all significant factors but immediacy. In both cases, once the significant variables were determined, a second regression analysis was performed employing only these significant variables to determine the best fitting equation to predict the exponent. When the log stimulus ratio was involved in the equation, two factors proved to be significantly related to the exponent: the log stimulus ratio and the use of objective instructions. This equation accounted for 30.37% of the variance in the exponent.

The results of the second regression equation can be substituted into equation 5.1 to yield the following general equation to predict area judgments:

$$J = \lambda A^{[.302(obj) - .103 \log(max/min) + 1.015]} \qquad (5.7)$$

where "A" is the physical area of a target and "obj" is coded "1" when objective instructions were employed and "0" otherwise.

When memory and inference variables were used for the regression instead of the log stimulus ratio, four variables proved to be significantly related to the exponent: use of inference conditions, use of memory conditions, age of subject, and use of objective instructions. This equation accounted for 39.41% of the variance. The power function based on this regression equation is:

$$J = \lambda A^{[.157(\text{obj}) - .320(\text{inf}) - .148(\text{mem}) + .006(\text{age}) + .689\,]} \qquad (5.8)$$

where "obj" is coded "1" when objective instructions were used and "0" otherwise, "inf" is coded "1" under inference conditions and "0" otherwise, "mem" is coded "1" under memory conditions and "0" otherwise, and "age" refers to the estimated average age of subjects in years.

For the perceptual data set, only one regression equation is necessary because memory and inference conditions are not included in this data set. Only two variables were significantly related to the exponent: use of objective instructions and the log stimulus ratio. (Two other variables were very close to significant, whether judgment took place indoors or outdoors— $p = .064$ —and stimulus orientation— $p = .072$.) The power function based on the two significant variables was:

$$J = \lambda A^{[.302(\text{obj}) - .103 \log(\text{max/min}) + 1.015\,]} \qquad (5.9)$$

Note that equation 5.9 is identical to equation 5.7 because all of the data entering into equation 5.7 were perceptual in nature.

Volume Estimates

While distance and area estimation are well explored, much less research has been conducted on volume estimation. My literature search only uncovered 44 volume exponents. About half of the exponents came from estimates based on actual volumes, while the other half were based on drawings or photographs of three-dimensional stimuli. All but one of the exponents involved perceptual conditions, and all of the exponents derived from either ratio or magnitude estimation.

Somewhat more troubling is the fact that more than half (24) of the exponents derive from a single source (Frayman & Dawson, 1981) who had subjects estimate the volumes of seven different shapes and three different presentation conditions. In another experiment, they had subjects judge the volumes of thin, normal, and fat cylinders. (Indeed, their experiment would have accounted for 45 exponents if I had not averaged the results of their within-subjects and between-subjects experiments.) Because so many of the exponents derive from this single source, I separately analyzed the data by summarizing Frayman & Dawson's data with a single exponent as a check on the excessive influence of this single source.

Certain variables that were looked at for distance and area estimation could not be analyzed due to insufficient data or lack of variation in the variable of interest. For example, all judgments involved full-cue conditions, and all judgments took place indoors. In addition, few studies reported coefficients of determination; so, it was not possible to meaningfully look at the effects of contextual variables on R^2 for volume estimation. The average value for R^2 base on the three coefficients of determination I found was .94, which is similar to the values found under perceptual conditions for distance and area estimation.

Table 5.3 summarizes the effects of various contextual variables on volume estimation exponents. The following looks at each of these variables in more detail:

Overall. Volume exponents are smaller on the average (.64) than exponents based on distance or area estimation, they are only somewhat larger than Baird's (1970) estimate of .6. Factoring out Frayman and Dawson, yielded a higher overall exponent of .72.

Age. As with both distance and area estimation, there was a significant positive correlation between age and exponent size, $r = .54$, $p < .001$ (without Frayman and Dawson, $r = .45$, $p < .05$). While this consistency is interesting, one should note that the only study that actually varied age across conditions (Teghtsoonian, 1965) found little difference between the exponents of graduate students and those of older professionals. Of course, it is possible that whatever influence age, experience, or training has on estimates has already fully taken effect by the time one is a graduate student.

Immediacy. All but one of the exponents derived from perceptual conditions; so, no statistically significant conclusions can be drawn. However, consistent with expectations, the single inference exponent was lower than the average for perceptual exponents. Moyer et al. (1978), the source for this inference exponent, compared volume estimation under perceptual and inference conditions. Their study also found the perceptual exponent (.73) to be greater than the inference exponent (.53).

Instructions. None of the experiments used objective instructions. However, there was a highly significant difference between the exponents for neutral and apparent instructions. Neutral instructions gave rise to significantly higher exponents than apparent instructions. However, no individual studies focused on this specific variable.

Method. While only three exponents were based on complete ratio estimation rather than magnitude estimation, the ratio estimation exponents still proved to be statistically greater on the average.

Table 5.3
Number of Exponents, Mean and Standard Deviation of Exponents as a Function of Recorded Variables for Judgments of Volume. Values excluding Frayman and Dawson are in parentheses.

Variable	Value of Variable	Number	Mean	Standard Dev.
Overall		44 (22)	.64 (.72)	.11 (.10)
Age	Undergraduate	36 (12)	.62 (.68)	.10 (.10)
	Post Undergrad.	8 (8)	.76 (.76)	.11 (.11)
Immeadiacy	Perception	43 (21)	.64 (.73)	.11 (.10)
	Inference	1 (1)	.53 (.53)	— —
Instructions	Neutral	9 (9)	.80 (.80)	.09 (.09)
	Apparent	35 (13)	.60 (.66)	.07 (.06)
Method	Ratio Estimation	3 (3)	.85 (.85)	.14 (.14)
	Magnitude Est.	41 (19)	.63 (.70)	.10 (.08)
Number of Subjects	< 40 (<12)	20 (10)	.73 (.77)	.10 (.10)
	≥ 40 (≥12)	24 (10)	.57 (.68)	.06 (.08)
Shape	Cube	14	.72	.13
	Sphere	9	.64	.10
	Octahedron	5	.60	.09
	Cylinder	6	.62	.07
	Other	9	.56	.04
Standard Used	No	4 (4)	.76 (.76)	.20 (.20)
	Yes	40 (16)	.63 (.70)	.09 (.08)
Standard Size	Small	2 (2)	.75 (.75)	.01 (.01)
	Midrange	28 (6)	.59 (.66)	.07 (.06)
Log Stimulus Range	≤ 2.0 (≤ 2.0)	8 (8)	.81 (.81)	.09 (.09)
	2.0 < x < 3.0	25	.57	.06
	≥ 3.0 (> 2.0)	7 (9)	.67 (.66)	.07 (.05)
Stimulus Size	< 1000 cm^3	12 (12)	.76 (.76)	.11 (.11)
	> 1000cm^3	29 (5)	.59 (.67)	.07 (.06)
Stimulus Type	Actual Volume	21 (11)	.68 (.70)	.11 (.13)
	Drawing	23	.60 (.73)	.10 (.08)

Number of subjects. There was a significant negative correlation between the number of subjects and the exponent, $r = -.39$, $p < .01$. However, this tendency although generally present is no longer significant if Frayman and Dawson's data are factored out. However, the only study to vary the number of subjects across conditions (Ekman, Lindman, & William-Olsson, 1961) found the opposite trend, small numbers of subjects led to generally lower exponents than larger numbers.

Shape of target. The shape of the target significantly influenced judgments, $F(4, 38) = 4.51$, $p < .01$. In particular, Duncan follow up tests revealed that cubes led to significantly higher exponents than the other figures, but the other figures did not differ from each other. Individual studies that looked at this variable found small if any differences in judgments based on shape, and the shapes that produced the highest exponent varied across studies or conditions (Ekman & Junge, 1961; Ekman, Lindman, & William-Olsson, 1961; Frayman & Dawson, 1981; Sjoberg, 1960; Teghtsoonian, 1965).

Standard. The vast majority of studies of volume employed a standard. Using a standard led to significantly lower exponents and lower variability. While this tendency is still apparent when Frayman and Dawson's data are factored out, it is no longer significant.

No studies placed the standard at the top of the stimulus range, and only two placed it at the bottom of the range. Despite these small numbers, t-tests indicate that placing the standard in the middle of the range results in significantly lower exponents than placing it a the bottom. This significant difference disappears if Frayman & Dawson's data are eliminated.

Stimulus range. As with distance and area estimation, there is a significant negative correlation between the log stimulus range and the exponent, $r = -.64$, $p < .05$. Factoring out Frayman and Dawson, who used the same stimulus range to generate all 24 exponents, actually increases the significance level of this effect and produces a more linear function, $r = -.69$, $p < .001$. This data is consistent with Teghtsoonian (1965), who found volume estimation exponents for both cubes and octahedrons decreased significantly with increasing stimulus range.

Stimulus size. The correlation between the average stimulus size and the exponent were not significant for either data set, although their is a slight tendency for exponents to decrease with larger stimuli. Teghtsoonian (1965) also found that volume estimation exponents significantly declined with increasing average stimulus size, but this is probably an artifact resulting from increasing stimulus range.

Stimulus type. Slightly more than half of the volume estimates were based on drawn or photographed targets rather than actual physical objects. Actual physical stimuli produce slightly, but significantly higher volume exponents than drawn or photographed stimuli. This tendency shrinks to insignificance if Frayman and Dawson's data are factored out. Individual research studies on this variable also found significantly higher exponents with physically present stimuli than simulated ones (Ekman & Junge, 1961; Frayman & Dawson, 1981).

Multivariate analyses. As before, a series of linear multivariate regression analyses were done with the volume judgment data. The exponent was the outcome variable and all variables that displayed any significant univariate associations with the exponent served as predictor variables, except that I did eliminate categorical variables with fewer than four data points in a cell in order to have enough variation in the data values to make the regression possible. The predictor variables entered included age, instructions, stimulus type, number of subjects, and log stimulus range. Variables with no significant univariate association with the exponent were excluded to limit the multivariate model to a reasonable size. Even with these exceptions, fitting a regression equation to such a small number of data values proved problematic because instructions and log stimulus range happened to be very highly intercorrelated. To compensate for this, two regression analyses were performed, one including age, log stimulus range, stimulus type, and the number of subjects as predictor variables and the other involving age, instructions, stimulus type, and the number of subjects. In each case, three factors proved to be significantly related to the exponent in the simultaneous entry multiple regression. In the first case, the significant factors were average age, log stimulus ratio, and stimulus type. Once the significant variables were determined, a second regression analysis was performed employing only these significant variables to determine the best fitting equation to predict the exponent. This equation accounted for 46.75% of the variance in the exponent.

The results of this regression equation can be substituted into equation 5.1 to yield the following general equation to predict volume judgments:

$$J = \lambda V^{[-.062(\text{sim}) - .045 \log(\text{max/min}) + .008(\text{age}) + .615]} \qquad (5.10)$$

where "V" is the physical volume of a target and "sim" is coded "1" when judgments are based on a drawing or photograph and "0" if an actual physical object is used.

When the instructions take the place of the log stimulus range, three variables are once again significantly related to the exponent: age, instructions, and stimulus type. This equation accounted for 67.86% of the variance. Substituting this regression equation into equation 5.1 yields the following power function to predict volume judgments:

$$J = \lambda V^{[-.068(\text{sim}) - .163(\text{app}) + .004(\text{age}) + .719]} \qquad (5.11)$$

where "sim" is coded "1" when judgments are based on a drawing or photograph and "0" if an actual physical object is the target, and "app" is coded "1" when apparent volume instructions are employed and "0" if neutral instructions are used.

Angle Estimates

Although it was not the focus of my literature search, I did run across a two studies that asked subjects to judge the size of angles. Wagner (1985) had subjects estimate the size of angles formed by stakes pounded into a grass field using four methods, magnitude estimation, category estimation, mapping, and matching. In the matching task, subjects were given a set of cards that displayed angles ranging from 0° to 180° in 10° increments, and subjects were asked to match a target angle in the field to the card that most nearly matched it. Wagner and Feldman (1989) asked subjects in a large gymnasium to estimate the size of three-dimensional angles specified by points of light mounted on wooden dowels using magnitude estimation under both full-cue (lights on) and reduced-cue (lights off) conditions.

The average exponent across all six conditions was .76. Because this exponent reflects an average across a fairly wide range of conditions and methods, an exponent that is more comparable to most distance, area and volume estimates might by seen by looking at the average exponent using magnitude estimation under full-cue conditions, which was .84.

In terms of the effects of method, Wagner (1985) found the largest exponent using mapping (.97), the next largest with magnitude estimation (.81), the next largest with matching (.82), and the smallest with category estimation (.47). Wagner and Feldman (1989) found much smaller exponents under reduced-cue conditions (.61) than under full-cue conditions (.87).

Of course, one can argue that numeric psychophysical techniques are inappropriate for angle judgments. Unlike distance, area, and volume, which have a meaningful zero point, but no upper limit, and therefore represent ratio scales; angles are bounded on both ends between 0° and 180° (or 0° to 360° if one thinks of the full circle). Indeed, the average coefficient of determination reported across the four conditions in Wagner (1985) was only .625, and it was only slightly better for magnitude estimation alone at .689. Thus, angle judgments across all four methods did not conform to a power function formulation very well at all.

Actually, the primary discoveries of these two studies had little to do with the exponent or coefficient of determination. Both studies found the angles that were oriented so that they faced directly toward or directly away from the subject were judged to be much larger than angles seen from the side. Wagner felt this implied that visual space was compressed in the in-depth dimension relative to the frontal one. In effect angles facing toward or away from the subject are smashed open, while those seen from the side are squeezed closed.

Cross-metric Comparisons

Although it is important to know separately the effects of context on each of the metric dimensions reviewed here; looking at them together allows one to compare and contrast the effects of contextual variables across all three (or four if one includes angle judgments) dimensions. In this way, one can know which variables have little effect at all, which have unique effects across a single dimension, and which appear to have more universal significance.

Less powerful variables. Certain variables had inconsistent effects across dimensions. For example, it would appear that slightly higher exponents arose under full-cue rather than reduced cue conditions for distance estimates, but reduced-cue conditions had higher (although insignificantly so) exponents for area estimates. Of course, most of what I have classified as reduced-cue conditions here, might not be considered to be particularly reduced because many of the studies simply limited head motion or induced the subject to look at the target monocularly. Numerical estimation techniques have seldom been used with truly reduced-cue settings such as in almost total darkness. Under these conditions exponents may be much lower (Wagner & Feldman, 1989).

Although instructions had inconsistent effects on distance judgment exponents, it had more profound effects on area and volume judgments. For the latter dimensions it would appear that objective instructions lead to the highest exponents while apparent instructions lead to the lowest. Distance judgments using magnitude or ratio estimation and directly perceived stimuli showed the same pattern, but the inclusion of memory and inference conditions in the data set reversed this trend.

As for method, fractionation, triangulation, category estimation, and mapping produced lower exponents that magnitude estimation, ratio estimation, and magnitude production for distance estimation. However, the former methods were seldom used for area and volume judgments. A comparison of ratio and magnitude estimation exponents leads to contradictory results, where magnitude estimation produces higher exponents for distance estimation but lower exponents for area and volume. Use of a standard, standard position, and average stimulus size also had inconsistent or insignificant effects on the exponent.

More powerful variables. Other variables have more consistent effects across dimensions. For example, age had at least some effect across all three dimensions. Exponents tended to increase with age, while coefficients of determination appeared to decline. It is not clear why these effects occur, although one might speculate that exponent increases because the older populations tended to consist of more numerically and psychophysically trained individuals such as graduate students and psychology professors. Perhaps the decline in coefficients of determination might correspond to a decline in attentional or sensory abilities with increasing age.

Similarly, there was some tendency for small numbers of subjects to be associated with larger exponents with distance and volume judgments. Although this trend might be the result of artifactual factors such as large number of subjects being common in memory and inference studies, it may also be related to greater methodological precision when smaller numbers of subjects are focused on by the experimenter.

While the effects of age and the number of subjects are relatively small, immediacy has a much larger effect. Both distance and area judgments show the same basic pattern. Exponents are highest for perceptual conditions, lower for memory conditions, and lowest for inference conditions. The single study comparing perceptual and inference conditions in volume estimation was in line with this pattern.

Similarly, experimental setting has a consistent influence for both distance and area judgments. Exponents are highest when judgments are collected indoors rather than outdoors.

Finally, as stimulus range increased, the size of the exponent consistently declined for all three dimensions. As in Wiest and Bell (1985), stimulus range and immediacy proved to be the two most important contextual variable influencing psychophysical judgments.

Theories of Spatial Judgment

Teghtsoonian's Dynamic Range Theory. The last result, that the exponent consistently declines as a function of increasing stimulus range, provides dramatic support for Robert Teghtsoonian's Dynamic Range Theory (Teghtsoonian, 1971, 1973; Teghtsoonian & Teghtsoonian, 1978). According to this theory, the range of numbers used by subjects tends to be relatively constant regardless of the stimulus set; so, increasing the stimulus range has the effect of flattening the power function and decreasing the exponent. According to Teghtsoonian (1971), the exponent may be predicted by the following formula:

$$\gamma = \frac{\log R_\psi}{\log R_\phi} \tag{5.12}$$

where γ is the exponent, R_ψ is the ratio of the largest to the smallest number used by subjects (or the ratio of the largest to smallest sensory magnitude), and R_ϕ is the ratio of the largest to smallest stimulus used in the experiment. Because Teghtsoonian argues that R_ψ is relatively constant, it follows that the exponent should systematically decline with increasing stimulus range.

While this theory certainly accounts for one of the major results of this meta-analysis, it does not tell the whole story. Even after stimulus range is taken into account, other contextual variables still have a considerable influence on the exponent.

Precision, information, and the exponent. Wagner (1998) purposed that the exponent for the power function might be related to the concept of uncertainty reduction. One of the fundamental tenants of information theory is that having information reduces uncertainty. In terms of spatial perception, information rich environments, like a well-lit field, reduce uncertainty about spatial layout more that information poor environments, like a dark room. Cognitive maps and memory are incomplete compared to direct spatial perception, and this results in greater uncertainty about spatial layout. Uncertainty about spatial layout in turn should influence judgment precision. As a consequence, greater uncertainty should increase the size of JND's for distance, area, volume, and angle judgments. This will in turn increase the size of the Weber fraction under high uncertainty conditions. Recent empirical work supports this conclusion by finding that higher uncertainty conditions produce higher Weber fractions (Al-Zahrani, Ho, Al-Ruwaitea, & Bradshaw, 1997; Baranski & Petrusic, 1992).

The effect of information uncertainty is a general one that applies to all psychophysical judgments using numeric estimation techniques. Baird and Noma (1978), Murray (1993), and Wagner (1998) point out that it is possible to derive the power function from Weber's Law and Ekman's Law via Fechnerian Integration. Weber's Law states that $\Delta S = kS$, where S is the physical size of a stimulus, ΔS is the size of the just noticeable difference, and k is the Weber constant. Ekman's Law states that number usage in judgments follows an analog to Weber's Law, namely, $\Delta J = hJ$, where J is a judgment, ΔJ refers to likely variation in number usage, and h is the Ekman constant. If both of these laws hold

$$\frac{\Delta J}{\Delta S} = \frac{hJ}{kS} .$$ (5.13)

To perform Fechnerian Integration we assume that just noticeable differences can be written as differentials to yield

$$\frac{dJ}{dS} = \frac{hJ}{kS}$$ (5.14)

or

$$\frac{dJ}{hJ} = \frac{dS}{kS} .$$ (5.15)

Integrating both sides we obtain

$$\frac{1}{h}\int \frac{dJ}{J} = \frac{1}{k}\int \frac{dS}{S} .$$ (5.16)

After integrating we have

$$\ln(J) = \frac{h}{k}\ln(S) + C .$$ (5.17)

Which yields

$$J = C' S^{h/k} = \lambda S^{h/k}.$$ (5.18)

Thus, the exponent in a power function depends on how precisely subjects can differentiate between stimuli and how precisely they use numbers to make judgments. Conditions which make our knowledge of stimuli more precise or which require subjects to precisely focus will decrease the size of the Weber fraction, k, and Equation 5.18 implies that this will lead to an increase in the exponent. In summary, Equation 5.18 predicts lower exponents under all circumstances where information reduction results in poorer judgment precision.

This theory also implies that variations in number usage could also influence exponents. If the Ekman constant, h, increases more than the Weber constant, k, exponents could actually rise. (An increase in the Ekman constant essentially would mean that a small change in the stimulus would lead to a larger change in the numbers used to make judgments. Or another way to put it, the same increase in the number used would correspond to a smaller change in the stimulus. An increase in the Ekman constant could result from people striving to make finer differentiations between stimuli.) It is possible that judgment instructions could bring about this situation; however, Teghtsoonian (1971) argues that Ekman's constant is in fact constant across a wide variety of judgment conditions.

While this uncertainty reduction theory will go a long way to toward explaining the pattern of power function exponents displayed in the empirical literature, not every one is likely to embrace it. One weakness of this theory is that it has assumed that JND's can be rewritten as differentials. Luce and Edwards (1958) and Luce (1993) point out that this assumption may be questionable, and the derivation of Steven's Law based on Fechnerian integration may be invalid. Indeed, we had reason to question whether visual space is functionally continuous enough to justify the differential form earlier. At this point though, I would make several replies to these objections. First of all, most data tend to be rather well fit by the power function, but one seldom hears of anyone making use of Luce and Edwards's formulations. I don't think we should easily abandon an equation to seems to work so well under so many circumstances. Second, Equation 5.18 may be a useful theoretical construct for helping to explain the spatial literature even if one questions the derivation. One can choose to think of it as the starting point of a theory rather than the end product of Fechnerian integration.

Finally, one can come to similar conclusions about the effects of uncertainty reduction even if one does not assume that JND's can be written as differentials. Once again, credit for this alternative formulation goes to Teghtsoonian (1971). As before, we may write the power function as:

$$J = \lambda S^{\gamma}. \tag{5.19}$$

Teghtsoonian then assumed that if one increased the physical stimulus by one JND (ΔS), this would be experienced consciously as one perceptual JND (ΔJ) larger. Substituting this into Equation 5.19 yields

$$J + \Delta J = \lambda(S + \Delta S)^{\gamma}. \tag{5.20}$$

Dividing Equation 5.20 by Equation 5.19 gives

$$1 + \frac{\Delta J}{J} = (1 + \frac{\Delta S}{S})^{\gamma}. \tag{5.21}$$

Taking the logarithm of both sides and substituting in the symbols used previous for the Weber and Ekman constants produces

$$\ln(1 + h) = \gamma \ln(1 + k). \tag{5.22}$$

and therefore the exponent may be written

$$\gamma = \frac{\ln(1 + h)}{\ln(1 + k)}. \tag{5.23}$$

Thus, although the two different formulations based on different assumptions about writing the JND as a differential found in Equations 5.18 and 5.23 are not equivalent, they both lead to the same basic conclusion. Decreasing the Weber constant or increasing the Ekman constant should lead to larger exponents.

Applying theory to data. The foregoing theories can largely, but not entirely, account for the results of the meta-analysis presented here. For example, one would expect that perceptual conditions would result in more precise judgments (smaller Weber constants) than memory judgments, which would in turn be more precise that inference judgments, because the use of memory and inference should increase uncertainty about spatial layout. Consistent with this, exponents are highest for perceptual conditions and lower for memory and inference conditions. One would also expect based on this theory that full-cue settings should produce more precise judgments (and therefore higher exponents) than reduced-cue settings because uncertainty should be greater under when full information is not available to specify spatial layout. While individual research studies and the distance estimation data support this conclusion, the area estimation data do not.

One factor that might account for this discrepancy is experimental rigor. One would expect that well-controlled experimental settings should result in more precise judgments and higher exponents. For area judgments, most of what I have characterized as reduced-cue settings has involved laboratory studies that fix head position or otherwise rigidly control the information available to subjects. This attempt at experimental control may account for the higher exponents found under reduced cue settings in area estimation. Similarly, small numbers of subjects are often used when the amount of data collected is large or when the experimental control is so great that it is difficult to repeat over many individuals. If true, small numbers of subjects may be associated with greater experimental control, and therefore greater judgment precision and higher exponents. This prediction is consistent with the data presented earlier that found significant negative correlations between sample size and the exponent. By the same basic reasoning, one might expect that experiments conducted indoors would tend to simplify the judgment process and be conducive to experimental control compared to those conducted in the more variable outdoor environment. Hence, indoor judgments should be more precise than those collected outdoors, and theory would predict that the exponent should also be higher. Once again, the meta-analysis reported here is consistent with this conclusion.

Psychophysical training and numeric sophistication should also lead to more precise judgments. This greater precision should be associated with higher exponents and it is. The meta-analysis confirms that older, more sophisticated populations have higher exponents. Similarly, one would expect that objective instructions would require subjects to produce their judgments more carefully (because accuracy has been emphasized) than neutral instructions, and neutral instructions should produce more precise judgments than apparent instructions that provide the loosest judgment task for subjects. My theory would predict that objective instructions should produce the highest exponents and apparent instructions the lowest. This conclusion is consistent with most individual distance estimation studies on the issue and is consistent with the meta-analysis presented here for area and volume judgments; however, the overall analysis of the distance estimation data is inconsistent on this issue.

Conclusion

This chapter has reviewed the spatial estimation literature for three geometric properties (and to a lesser extent a fourth). One may conclude from this review that distance judgments are associated with exponents averaging close to one (1.02 for the perceptual data), area estimates have somewhat lower average exponents of about .8 (.84 for the perceptual data), angle estimates appear—based on preliminary information—to average about .76, and volume estimates average a bit more than .6 (.64 for the entire volume data set). These values are very similar to what Baird (1970) said 30 years ago. Similarly, the effects of memory and inference conditions are similar to those reported by Wiest and Bell (1985). For distance estimates, the average exponent for perceptual conditions was 1.02, for memory conditions it was .87, and for inference conditions it was .77. For area estimates, the average exponent was .84 for perception, .67 for memory, and .50 for inference.

It is also clear that contextual variables have significant effects on the judgments subjects produce. For five contextual variables (age, number of subjects, immediacy, experimental setting, and stimulus range), these effects are consistent across all three spatial properties, and in the case of several other variables (instructions, cue conditions, method, standard use, and standard position), effects are clearly apparent in one or two of the data sets but less clearly present in the third.

The present review also highlights certain gaps in the experimental literature that could be usefully investigated further. For example, there has been little systematic research on the effects of truly reduced-cue settings. This is odd because there has been considerable work on this issue in the related size constancy literature. Volume and angle estimation also appear to be orphan dimensions that have garnered little attention. Another missing piece of the puzzle concerns the effects of method on judgments. More work needs to be done using category estimation, mapping, and absolute judgment as well as the production methods. Future research will no doubt bring greater clarity on these issues.

6

Factors Affecting Size Constancy

Much of the spatial perception literature is not quantitative in a way that is detailed enough to really say much about the geometry of visual space. Many researchers and theorists seek to describe the cues used for depth perception or the internal mechanisms that underlie spatial representations using standard experimental techniques that vary conditions across groups (Gibson, 1950; Herschenson, 1999; Rock, 1983). These types of studies do not generate data that is sufficiently rich to support detailed mathematical modeling. Obviously, the last chapter, which looked at the direct estimation of spatial metrics, reported on one body of research that is an exception to this rule. Another area in space perception that has also yielded a numerically rich database is the size-constancy literature.

This chapter will discuss the size-constancy paradigm and lay out some of the factors that influence size constancy. Following this, I offer a review of the literature that presents major theoretical positions on size constancy in chronological order along with empirical work that bears on each theory (some of which may be of more recent origin). The chapter will then summarize the literature and present my own theory that can explain much of this literature in a way that is consistent with the direct estimation literature discussed in the previous chapter.

The Basic Paradigm

In the prototypical size constancy experiment, a comparison stimulus of adjustable size is located near the observer. A standard stimulus of constant size is located at various distances from the observer. In other studies, these roles are reversed with the standard located near the observer and the comparison placed at different distances away. The observer's task is to adjust the comparison stimulus until it's size appears to match each standard.

As one would expect, observers accurately reproduce the standard when it lies close to the observer (at the same distance away as the comparison). However, adjustments can become increasingly inaccurate as the standard grows more distance from the observer.

If the observer accurately adjusts the near comparison to match the standard at all distances, the observer is said to display *constancy*. On the other hand, if the observer sees distant standards as being smaller than they really are and adjusts the comparison to be physically smaller than the standard, the observer is said to show *underconstancy*. Conversely, if distant standards incline the observer to make the comparison too large, the observer is said to show *overconstancy*.

Factors Affecting Size Constancy

A number of variables control whether observers display constancy, underconstancy, or overconstancy including the nature of the standard stimulus used, the orientation of the standard relative to the observer, instructions, the availability of cues for depth, and the observer's age.

Standard stimulus. Standards vary from flat, two-dimensional figures such as circles and triangles to three-dimensional stimuli like cubes. The instructions given to observers vary in the meaning assigned to the word size, sometimes emphasizing adjustments in a single dimension, at other times directing the observer's attention to area or volume.

Stimulus orientation. Although one could present the standard at any of an infinite number of orientations relative to the observer, in practice only two orientations are typically looked at: frontal and flat (in-depth). Frontal objects are placed perpendicular to the ground so they directly face the observer. Flat objects lie on the ground or parallel to the ground so the observer sees them extend away from him/her in depth.

Instructions. Four types of instructions have been used in most experiments: objective, perspective, apparent, and projective. *Objective instructions* ask the observer to match the actual physical size of the standard. In other words, the observer is asked to adjust the comparison stimulus so that a ruler placed along side the comparison and the standard would measure exactly the same length. *Perspective instructions* explicitly train observers concerning the laws of perspective (e.g., by pointing out how railroad tracks appear to converge with increasing distance) and ask subjects to compensate for the apparent shrinkage of objects with distance in order to give accurate size judgments. *Apparent instructions* ask the observer to adjust the comparison so that it subjectively "looks," "seems," or "appears" to be the same size as the standard. These instructions emphasize the subjective or phenomenal experience of size. Finally, *projective instructions* attempt to incline the observer to report the perceived visual angle that a standard subtends. Usually this is done by referencing an analogy such asking the subject to pretend that their visual experience is painted onto a two-dimensional canvas and that they should adjust the comparison so that it takes up as much of the visual canvas as the standard. In other words, the observer is encouraged to take an artist's-eye view.

Depth cue availability. Stimulus cue conditions vary from rich naturalistic conditions with plenty of cues to depth available such as a grassy field or a hall with many scattered objects intervening between the observer and the target, to controlled laboratory settings with uniform surface conditions, viewing through artificial pupils, partially or totally darkened rooms with only the standard and comparison stimuli illuminated, and viewing stimuli against dark backgrounds through a darkened tunnel. Here, for example, the grassy field would be considered a highly full-cue condition, and the darkened tunnel would produce a very reduced-cue setting. Experiments also vary between binocular and monocular viewing conditions, with monocular viewing being considered as a reduced-cue setting.

Historical Review

According to Ross and Plug (1998), interest in the problem of size constancy dates back to ancient times. Ptolemy described the phenomenon in the second century A.D., as did Malebranche in the 17th century. Outlines of the basic theoretical explanations currently employed by modern researchers can also be traced to antiquity. Explanations based on the Size-Distance Invariance Hypothesis were proposed by Euclid (c. 300 B.C.), Iby al-Haytham (c. 1030), DesCartes (1637), and Helmholtz (1867, 1881). Relative-size related explanations were laid out by Plotinus (c. 300 A.D.), Leonardo da Vinci (c. 1500), and Hering in the 19th century.

The first modern experimental investigation of the topic may be attributed to Martius (1889). Using apparent size instructions, Martius asked observers to match a near standard rod by choosing among a set of distant comparison rods. He found that his subjects generally produced accurate matches at all distances, with a slight tendency toward underconstancy.

Brunswik and Thouless Ratios. Brunswik (1929) revived interest in the problem as part of a more general investigation of perceptual constancy. Brunswik (1929, 1933, 1956) believed that size judgments always represent a compromise of two perceptual attitudes. One can either think of size objectively, in which case observers will attempt to adjust the comparison to match the physical size of the standard (similar to the objective instructions reported above), or one can think of size subjectively, in which case the observer should attempt to adjust the visual angle of the comparison to match the visual angle of the standard (similar to the projective instructions). However, when Brunswik asked observers to view size subjectively by asking them to report how large the standards "looked" or "appeared" (similar to the apparent instructions) he found that observers never matched the visual angle of the stimulus, but always adjusted it to be too large, somewhere between an objective and a visual angle (or projective) match. Brunswik believed the subjective judgments demonstrated a "regression to the real."

According to Brunswik, an observer's judgment must always lie between the objective and visual angle size of a stimulus. Under differing experimental conditions, the judgment may be closer to one extreme or another, but it should never fall outside of the range defined by those two perceptual poles. Overconstancy, where the comparison is adjusted to be larger than the objective size of the standard, is not theoretically possible. Any data that shows overconstancy implies some sort of error in experimental procedure. As Koffka (1935) argued, the achieved cannot exceed the potentially achievable. Indeed as recently as Teghtsoonian (1974), some theorists have argued that overconstancy does not and cannot exist.

To measure the degree to which an observer's choice of comparison reflects a physical or visual angle match, Brunswik developed the following formula:

$$R = \frac{S' - P}{S - P} \qquad (6.1)$$

where R represents the Brunswik ratio, S' is the perceived size of the object as measured by the comparison stimulus selected by the observer, S is the physical size of the stimulus, and P is the comparison stimulus that would represent the correct projective or visual angle match. When this ratio is close to zero, observers are selecting a comparison approximating a projective match. When this ratio is close to one, the comparison chosen is physically the same as the standard.

The Brunswik ratio has several weaknesses that led Thouless (1931a) to propose an alternative formulation to measure the degree to which judgments reflect physical or visual angle matches. The Thouless Ratio can be expressed as follows:

$$T = \frac{\log S' - \log P}{\log S - \log P} \qquad (6.2)$$

Once again, a Thouless Ratio of zero indicates a projective match while a Thouless Ratio of one demonstrates a physical match. Another way of looking at this is that Thouless ratios of less than one show underconstancy, Thouless ratios of greater than one would show overconstancy, and Thouless ratios of one show constancy.

The Thouless Ratio has several advantages over the Brunswik ratio that led Brunswik himself to adopt Thouless's formulation. First of all, most experimenters of the time tended to think of the elements of the equation in subjective terms. According to Fechner's Law, $J = k \log S$, where J is the perceived stimulus magnitude and S is the physical magnitude of the stimulus. Equation 6.2 is produced by substituting perceived quantities for physical quantities in Equation 6.1 in terms of Fechner's Law. In addition, Sedgwick (1986) points out that the Thouless Ratio is unaffected by procedural issues such as whether the comparison stimulus is place nearer to the observer than the standard or farther away, while the Brunswik Ratio will change radically depending on the relative locations of the standard and the comparison. Finally, Myers (1980) has shown theoretically that the Thouless Ratio can be directly related to the power function. Thus, the Thouless Ratio may be more theoretically meaningful than the Brunswik Ratio.

By the end of the 1940's Brunswik and Thouless Ratios have tended to fall out of favor. There seem to be three reasons that these ratios are seldom used today. First, Joynson (1949) pointed out that the formulas conflate angular and linear measures and are therefore mathematically incoherent. Second, the ratios are based on a theoretical notion of perceptual compromise between objective and projective attitudes. When later theories moved beyond perceptual compromise, the Brunswick and Thouless Ratios were abandoned along with the theory. Finally, researchers developed simpler, less theoretically loaded ways to report data.

Early empirical research on size constancy. Early research on size-constancy used Brunswik and Thouless Ratios to express the effects of conditions on size judgments. Under Brunswik's supervision, Holaday (1933) systematically investigated variables that influence size constancy. Using cubes placed on the floor of a large, empty hall just below the subject's head for stimuli, Holaday varied instructions and cue conditions to produce 28 Thouless Ratios. In most cases, Thouless Ratios were less than one, indicating under-constancy. (There were a few exceptions, however, resulting in "theoretically impossible" ratios greater than one.) He also found that Thouless Ratios declined with increasing distance (once again consistent with underconstancy). He also found that instructions that emphasized the objective size of the target object produced higher Thouless Ratios than instructions that emphasized apparent or projective size. In addition, he discovered that successively eliminating cues to depth (ranging from having the lights on with the intervening space between the observer and the target filled with various objects to give a better impression of depth, to the lights on with an unfilled space, to the lights out, to the lights out with monocular viewing) decreased Thouless Ratios systematically, implying increasing underconstancy with reduced-cue settings. Monocular viewing produced more underconstancy than binocular viewing under the most reduced-cue settings, but did not affect judgments when other cues to depth were present. The superiority of binocular viewing was confirmed a few years later by Hermans (1937). Holaday also found that individual differences in visual acuity affected constancy judgments.

Other researchers from this period examined the child development of size constancy. Frank (1926; 1928), Burzlaff (1931), Beyrl (1926), and Brunswik and Cruikshank (1937) found size-constancy to be present as early as the first year of life. In fact, both Frank and Bruzlaff found that constancy is as strong for young children as it is for adults, while Beyrl and Brunswik and Cruikshank found some improvement in size constancy judgments over the course of the first ten years of life. In fact, Beyrl found a tendency toward underconstancy for young children (eight years old or less) and constancy for older children. However, Frank (1928) points out that this tendency toward underconstancy for the youngest subjects was not very strong; Brunswik ratios for the youngest children varied between .77 to .95—not far from the 1.0 ratio for perfect constancy.

Thouless (1931a, 1931b; 1932) published an influential series of articles on size constancy (using projective instructions, or at least intending to). In one study, Thouless (1931a) examined the subjective size of stimuli oriented in-depth by presenting circles and squares lying along the ground with respect to the observer and asking subjects to select among a set of frontally presented ellipses and rectangles the comparison which best matched the standard. He found that the in-depth dimension was perceptually smaller than the frontal dimension for each stimulus. This foreshortening increased with increasing distance from the observer. For circles 54.5 cm from the observer the in-depth dimension was perceived to be 77% of the size of the frontal dimension, at 109 cm it was 59% of the frontal size, and at 163.5 cm it was 49% of the frontal size. Thouless Ratios for the subjective size of in-depth stimuli were also low (ranging from .57 to .42 for circles, and .74 to .6 for squares) and they declined with increasing distance. These results are consistent with a strong tendency toward underconstancy for these in-depth stimuli.

Thouless (1931b) examined the effects of reducing cues to depth on size perception. He found that binocular viewing generally lead to greater Thouless Ratios (averaging .61) than monocular viewing (averaging .48). Eliminating depth cues almost entirely by having subjects look at the target monocularly through a tube or by using a pseudoscope reduced the Thouless Ratio (averaging .31) but did not reduce the value to zero as one might expect. However, in a second experiment in which he reduced depth cues even further and eliminated inferred knowledge of the stimulus size by presenting varying standard stimuli of differing sizes led to Thouless Ratios that were very close to zero (the projective value) under monocular conditions, but not under binocular conditions. In a third experiment, Thouless attempted to give feedback to his observer's by showing them what projective size means, but in the subsequent experiment, observers continued to show Thouless Ratios bigger than zero, demonstrating that subjects were not able to wholly adopt a projective attitude.

Thouless (1932) looked at the affect of individual differences on size constancy. He found that more intelligent subjects and men were more capable of taking on a projective attitude, yielding lower Thouless Ratios, than less intelligent subjects and women. Younger subjects assumed the projective attitude more easily than older ones. Trained artists were more able to assume the projective attitude, but even they did not display Thouless Ratios of zero. Personality (introversion vs. extraversion) had no affect on size judgment.

In another systematic study of size constancy, Sheehan (1938) set triangles, circles, and cubes on a table. The room was well lit, but the table was covered in black and surrounded by black curtains. The standard was placed either at 100 cm or 150 cm in front of the subject while a variable comparison was 300 cm away. Unlike previous studies that used a blend of apparent and projective instructions, Sheehan clearly used apparent instructions.

Sheehan found that subjects selected consistently smaller comparisons as being the same size as the standard when the distance between the standard and comparison increased. Another way of putting this is that the comparison seemed larger the further away it was from the standard. Sheehan recognized that this result implied overconstancy, but because this was theoretically impossible, she attributed her results to shrinkage in the nearer standard resulting from poorer accommodation. Sheehan also found relatively lower Thouless Ratios for cubes and circles compared to triangles.

After the 1930s, Brunswik and Thouless Ratios were used less often, as data reporting more akin to Holway and Boring (1941) took their place. However, these ratios still occasionally have their uses. For example, Battro, Reggini, and Karts (1978) used the Thouless Ratio to predict the shape of Hillebrand's (1902) parallel alleys without recourse to Luneburg's (1947, 1948, 1950) hyperbolic geometry model. More recently, in a study similar to Thouless (1931), Farrimond (1990) had observers judge the shape of rectangle placed flat on a table. Farrimond calculated Brunswik ratios as a function of alcohol consumption. In one experiment, observers who drank alcohol showed greater underconstancy (R = .26) than those who did not drink alcohol. In two other experiments, subjects showed increasing underconstancy (declining Brunswik ratios) as time passed since alcohol consumption. Brunswik ratios declined most rapidly after alcohol consumption when the observers did not ingest food before drinking than when food was consumed first.

Holway and Boring's paradigm. Subsequent size-constancy studies were more closely modeled after Holway and Boring (1941), who wrote a classic paper on size constancy that contained a set of data sufficiently rich to allow for detailed mathematical modeling. They had five observers judge the size of circular standards placed at various distances ranging from 10 to 120 ft. from the observer relative to an adjustable comparison located 10 ft. away using apparent size instructions. Since the standards subtended a constant visual angle, the physical size of each standard increased linearly with increasing distance. Judgments took place in a fairly reduced cue environment (a darkened room with illuminated objects and some reflection off floor surfaces) under four viewing conditions: binocular observation, monocular observation, monocular observation through an artificial pupil, and monocular observation through an artificial pupil and a dark tube. The observer was seated in a chair and the objects were placed on the floor.

Figure 6.1 shows the average results across observers as a function of distance to the target. The figure also shows curves that represent the best fits of a model that will be discussed toward the end of this chapter. Binocular viewing yielded a slight tendency toward overconstancy. In terms of individual subjects, four out of five showed overconstancy, and one showed underconstancy. Monocular viewing led to fairly good constancy on the average, with the results of individual subjects varying somewhat. Two of the five subjects showed a slight tendency toward underconstancy, two showed almost perfect constancy, and one showed slight overconstancy. Monocular viewing through an artificial pupil produced marked underconstancy by all five observers with judgments lying approximately halfway between an objective and a projective match. Only three observers participated in the fourth condition using monocular observation through a dark tube, eliminating almost all cues to depth. All three subjects showed a dramatic underconstancy, almost (but not quite) achieving a projective match.

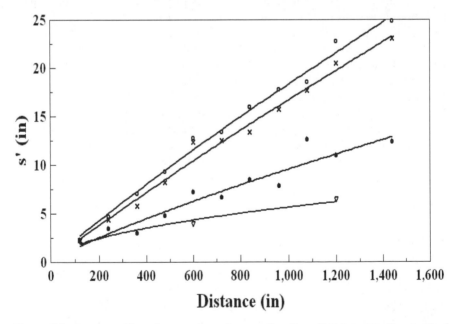

Figure 6.1. Average adjusted comparison size as a function of distance to the standard for Holway and Boring (1941) data. Open circles collected under binocular viewing conditions, xs under monocular viewing, filled circles under monocular viewing with an artificial pupil, and inverted triangles under monocular viewing with a reduction tunnel. Solid lines represent best fitting full model curves.

Later studies by Lichten and Lurie (1950) and Over (1960) took this reduction of cues one step further by eliminating residual light reflecting off of surrounding objects. Under these totally reduced conditions, perfect projective matches were obtained.

Gilinsky's theory of size constancy. In the 1950s, Gilinsky (1951) developed one of the first comprehensive theories for size constancy. She also published a number of empirical studies based on her theory. Gilinsky was influenced by Luneburg's (1947, 1948, 1950) theory of space perception that we discussed in Chapter 3, which posited that visual space is best conceived of as a hyperbolic geometry. One prediction of this theory is that visual space should be bounded; that is, there should be a maximum distance in visual space. Gilinsky used this concept of boundedness to construct the following formula relating perceived distance to physical distance:

$$\frac{d}{D} = \frac{A}{A + D} \tag{6.3}$$

where d is the perceived distance, D is the physical distance, A is the maximum limit of perceived distance under a given set of conditions. According to this theory, perceived distance is a decelerating function of physical distance under all conditions that gradually reaches an asymptote at A as physical distance increases. When A is infinitely large, distance perception is accurate, and distance perception is increasingly inaccurate, particularly for long physical distances, as A approaches zero.

Before going on to discuss how this distance formula ties in with her predictions concerning size constancy experiments, a few critique of this first formula should be mentioned. First of all, Fry (1952) argued that the formula was not actually consistent with Luneburg's theory, but covertly assumed that visual space is Euclidean as part of its derivation. Smith (1952) also questioned the derivation of Gilinsky's theory. More seriously, as Smith pointed out, the theory does not coincide with a host of data. In the previous chapter we found that perceived egocentric distance generally follows a power function with an exponent slightly greater than one. While no power function actually approaches an asymptote as Gilinsky predicts, one could make a case that Gilinsky's theory could approximately model distance judgments when exponents are less than one. What Gilinsky's theory could never predict would be distance judgments with exponents greater than one, because such judgments would not only never be bounded, but perceived distance follows an accelerating function as physical distance increases. In other words, Gilinsky's theory is not compatible with many of the egocentric distance estimation studies reviewed in the last chapter.

Gilinsky next derived a formula for perceived size based on her formula for perceived distance. This formula is

$$\frac{s}{S} = \frac{A + \delta}{A + D}$$
                                                                                      (6.4)

where s is perceived size, S is "subjective true size" by which she meant the size the standard is perceived to be when it is the same distance away as the comparison lying the "normal viewing distance," δ, away from the observer. This formula predicts that size judgments will vary between perfect constancy when A is infinity and projective match when A is zero. In other words, size judgments should always show increasing underconstancy with increasing distance from the observer except in the ideal case where visual space is unbounded (Euclidean). Once again, overconstancy is theoretically impossible. The fact that overconstancy is so regularly seen in the data cannot be accounted for by her theory.

Gilinsky conducted a number of classic experiments on size constancy to test her theory. In one experiment, Gilinsky (1951) had observers mark off equal distance intervals. The observers stood at one end of an 80 ft. long archery range while the experimenter moved a pointer stick away from the observer at a constant rate. The observer was asked to periodically stop the pointer to mark off successive increments of equal perceived length. While previous size constancy experiments tended to use frontally oriented stimuli, the effect of this procedure is to conduct a size constancy experiment that for the first time looks at equal perceived sizes for stimuli oriented in-depth. Gilinsky's data show underconstancy under these conditions.

Gilinsky (1955) looked at the affects of instructions on size judgments. In this experiment, Gilinsky brought observers to a level grassy area 5000 ft. long. Four frontally oriented standard triangles whose altitude and base measured between 42 and 78 in. were placed at six distances ranging from 100 to 4000 ft. from the observer. Observers adjusted a near comparison 100 ft. away to match the size of each standard using either objective or projective instructions. As seen in Figure 6.2, objective instructions were associated with overconstancy, while projective instructions were associated with strong underconstancy. Nevertheless, subjects did not produce a true projective match under projective instructions, Brunswik's "regression to the real" still obtained. There was also some tendency for the overconstancy of objective instructions and the underconstancy of projective instructions to be magnified for smaller standards relative to larger ones.

Other works from this era were generally consistent with Gilinsky's data. Chalmers (1952), Gibson (1947), Jenkin (1957, 1959), and Smith (1953) all found objective instructions led to overconstancy under binocular conditions, while Joynson (1949) and Singer (1952) found that projective instructions produced strong underconstancy.

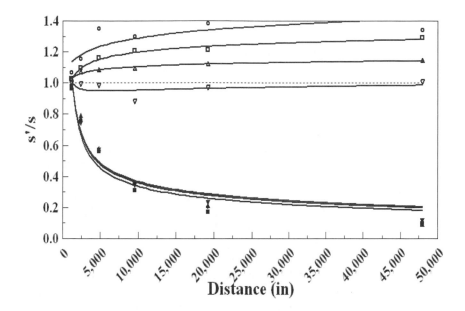

Figure 6.2. Average ratio of comparison to standard as a function of distance to the standard in Gilinsky's (1955) data. Objective data show overconstancy and are represented with open symbols. Projective data shows strong underconstancy and are represented by closed symbols. Circles collected with 42 in standard, squares with 55 in standard, upward pointing triangles with 66 in standard, and downward pointing triangles with 78 in standard. Solid lines represent best fitting full model curves. The dashed line represents perfect constancy.

Smith (1953) also showed that overconstancy still obtains for objective instructions regardless whether the comparison was placed at a near or far position. Overconstancy is not an artifact of comparison placement. Jenkin (1959) found that this overconstancy still obtained even when the target was a familiar object, although familiar size cues did reduce the extent of the overconstancy.

Early work was also consistent with the idea that apparent size instructions closely approximated true constancy or led to slight underconstancy (Gibson, 1950; Singer, 1952). In fact, Gibson believed that constancy is the rule across all distance ranges. In his words, "An object can apparently be seen with approximately its true size as long as it can be seen at all" (p. 186).

Carlson and the perspective-size hypothesis. In the following two decades, Carlson further studied the effects of instructions on size judgments. Carlson (1960) studied binocular size constancy under full-cue conditions (well-illuminated with a black felt background) by having observers adjust a near comparison triangle (10 ft. away) to match three standard triangles (40 ft. away) that ranged from 44 mm and 159 mm in altitude using either objective, apparent, or projective instructions. Carlson also looked at the effects of comparison placement and the order in which instructions were given to observers. He found that objective instructions gave rise to overconstancy in all conditions. On the average, the near comparison was adjusted to be 24% larger than the true size of the standard suggesting that more distant stimuli are seen as larger than nearer ones. Apparent instructions sometimes produced overconstancy and sometimes underconstancy. On the average, the near comparison was adjusted to be 3.4% larger than the standard's true size, which is only a small deviation from veridical perception in the direction of overconstancy. Carlson noted that more intelligent subjects had a greater tendency toward underconstancy using apparent instructions, perhaps because they more clearly saw the distinction between the objective and apparent attitudes. Finally, projective instructions yielded strong underconstancy, with the comparison adjusted to be 38% smaller than the true size of the standard. Larger separations between the standard and the comparison magnified these effects, while the size of the standard had little affect on judgments.

Carlson (1962) replicated this work and added a perspective instruction condition. The procedure was almost identical to his previous study, and he found similar results. Perspective instructions led to the greatest degree of overconstancy (the near comparison was adjusted to be 42% larger than the standard's true size), while objective instructions produced a somewhat smaller degree of overconstancy (20.5%). Apparent instructions gave rise to a slight tendency toward underconstancy (the comparison was set to be 9.5% smaller than physically accurate), while projective instructions showed stronger underconstancy (43% smaller than physically accurate). Similarly, Carlson and Tassone (1967) found that perceived size increased with increasing distance from the observer for objective instructions, but decreased slightly with increasing distance for apparent instructions, and decreased swiftly with increasing distance for projective instructions. Repeated practice magnified these trends.

Carlson (1977) felt the affects of instructions could be accounted for by the perspective-size hypothesis. According to this hypothesis, instructions influence an observer's belief about what happens to size as distance increases. Observers are aware that in a certain sense objects do appear smaller as they recede in distance just as railroad tracks appear to come together at the horizon, while in another sense, observers are aware that objects don't actually change size as they move away. Perspective and objective instructions can cause observers to overcompensate for these perspective changes, while some types of apparent instructions and all projective instructions ask observers embrace them and to ignore physical reality. I believe Carlson's theoretical approach is a reasonable one, bringing us closer to understanding what is really going on in a size-constancy experiment; however, the theory lacks a quantitative character that would allow precise modeling of experimental results.

In other instruction-related research, Leibowitz and Harvey (1967, 1969) studied size perception under naturalistic conditions, including a populated area, an athletic field, and along railroad tracks with standards located from 100 ft. to 1680 ft. away and an adjustable comparison 50 ft. away. Observers made judgments using objective, apparent, and projective instructions of the size of a wooden rod, an aluminum tube, and a strip of canvas. Concurrent with previous research, they found overconstancy with objective instructions, constancy at all distances for apparent instructions, and strong underconstancy for projective instructions. The results were reported in terms of Brunswik Ratios, and they found essentially constant R-values at all distances of 1.3 for objective instructions, 1.0 for apparent instructions, and .5 for projective instructions. However, Teghtsoonian (1974) pointed out that a constant R value of 1.3 might better be called overestimation rather than overconstancy, because a constant Brunswik ratio does not indicate that perceived size increases with increasing distance from the observer.

Epstein and the Size-Distance Invariance Hypothesis. Epstein (1963) was also interested in the affects of instructions on size perception. Similar to previous research, Epstein had observers judge the size of a far standard placed at one of five distances (from 10 ft. to 120 ft.) by adjusting a variable comparison placed 5 ft. away from the observer. Observers were given one of four instructions: perspective, objective, apparent, and projective. Unlike previous research, however, observers only made judgments for one standard and one instructions set. In other words, distance to the standard and instructions were between-subjects variables rather than within-subjects variables. Why use a between-subjects design? Epstein noted that Carlson (1962) suggested that overconstancy might result because judgments at different distances are not really independent, but rather are made in a sequence in which the most distance stimuli are typically much farther away from each other than nearer stimuli. Epstein wanted to see if truly independent judgments of size would show the same trend as previous research. In addition, Epstein had observers estimate the distance to the standard relative to the comparison using a magnitude production technique (similar to magnitude estimation). Observers adjusted a ruler relative to a standard distance and attempted to reproduce the ratio of the distances to the standard and the comparison.

Epstein's data are seen in Figure 6.3. Notice that perspective instructions give rise to strong overconstancy (on the average, the comparison is adjusted to be 70% bigger than the most distant standard's true size), as do objective instructions, although to a slightly lesser extent (the comparison averages 53% bigger than physically accurate). Apparent instructions yield the flat function of constancy with slight underconstancy (the comparison averages 5% smaller than physically accurate), and projective instructions result in strong underconstancy (the comparison averages 68% smaller than physically accurate). All of these results are consistent with past research. More interestingly, Epstein found that distance estimates mirrored size estimates. Overestimation of distance gave rise to underestimation of size, while underestimation of distance gave rise to overestimation of size.

This relationship between perceived size and perceived distance supported Epstein's own theory to account for size constancy data. Epstein, Park, and Casey (1961) believed that perceived size could be related to perceived distance as specified by the Size-Distance Invariance Hypothesis, which states that

$$d' = s' \tan\theta \qquad\qquad (6.5)$$

where d' is perceived distance, s' is perceived size, and θ is the visual angle subtended by a target. Overconstancy resulted from a misperception of distance.

According to this theory, if perceived distance is an accelerating function of physical distance under binocular conditions and objective instructions, perceived size should be overestimated as distance increases. (In truth, this theory is similar to one proposed Smith (1953).)

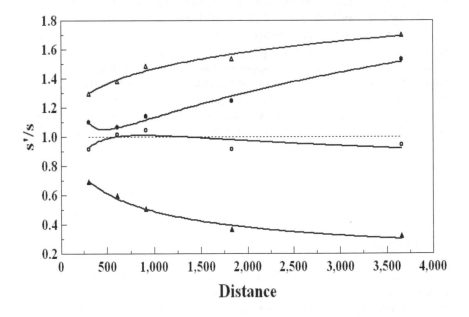

Figure 6.3. Average ratio of comparison to standard as a function of distance to the standard in Epstein's (1963) data. Perspective data are represented with open triangles, objective data with filled circles, apparent data with open circles and projective data with filled triangles. Solid lines represent best fitting full model curves. The dashed line represents perfect constancy.

Once more, both Epstein and Smith stated their theories in the most general of terms; neither stated their theories in a mathematical form that might allow more precise modeling of size constancy data. In addition, their approach has little to say as to why instructions, target orientation, and other factors might influence size judgments. As we will see, my own attempt to model the effects of these factors on size constancy data and to unify it with the direct estimation literature mentioned in the previous chapter will be very much in the spirit of Epstein and Smith, but more precisely stated. Therefore, Epstein's (1963) data also gives strong support to the theory I will present later.

Other evidence supports a systematic relationship between size and distance perception in accordance with the size-distance invariance hypothesis. For example, Epstein and Landauer (1969) had subjects make magnitude estimates of size and distance of a luminous disk under reduced cue conditions. The researchers systematically varied the physical size, distance to the target, and visual angle of the target, across three experimental conditions. In each condition one of the three target attributes was held constant while the other two varied. When varying, the diameter of the target disk varied from 5 mm to 82 mm, the distance to the target varied from 25 cm to 295 cm, and the visual angle of the target varied from .25° to 5.5°. In each case, size estimates, distance estimates, and target visual angle where directly related to each other in accordance with the predictions of the size-distance invariance hypothesis. As visual angle increased, distance estimates linearly decrease while size estimates linearly increased. A number of other studies from this era produced results consistent with the size-distance invariance hypothesis (Epstein, Park, & Casey, 1961; Künnapas, 1968; Landauer & Epstein, 1969; Wallach & McKenna, 1960).

Figure 6.4 shows the average ratio of comparison to standard as a function of distance to the standard in Epstein and Landauer's experiment for the experimental condition where standard size was held constant. (The experimental condition most equivalent to other size constancy data we have presented.) Note the strong tendency to underconstancy under these reduced-cue conditions.

Higashiyama (1977, 1979, 1983, 1984b) also conducted a series of studies examining the relationship between perceived size and perceived distance. In these experiments, the observer was shown squares of various sizes located at a constant distance away. Under full-cue conditions, observers accurately perceived size and knew that distance was constant. Under reduced-cue settings (limiting cues to accommodation and convergence or requiring observers to look through an artificial pupil), observers assumed that perceived size was constant and smaller squares were seen as farther away (Higashiyama, 1977).

Higashiyama (1983) had observers make magnitude estimates of perceived size and distance using both apparent and objective instructions and found that perceived distance was inversely related to perceived size in both cases.

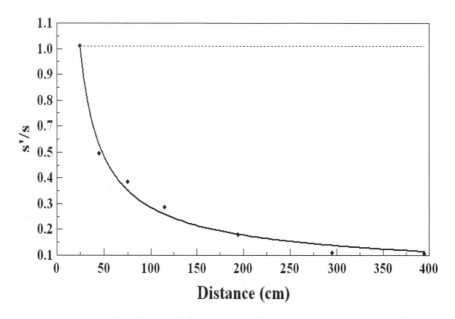

Figure 6.4. Average ratio of comparison to standard as a function of distance to the standard in Epstein & Landauer's (1969) data. Because judgments used magnitude estimation, perceived size has been normalized to make perceived size of the near standard equal to physical size in order to make the plot equivalent to other graphs. Data were collected under reduced-cue conditions. Solid lines represent best fitting full model curves. The dashed line represents perfect constancy.

His estimates of the exponent for the power function relating perceived distance and physical distance varied across instructions. The exponent was 1.0 for apparent instructions and 1.2 for objective instructions.

More recently, Brenner and van Damme (1999) have shown that errors in size judgments of a tennis ball were closely related to errors in estimating distance in a manner consistent with the Size Distance Invariance Hypothesis.

Gogel and familiar size cues. A number of researchers have examined the relationship between perceived size and perceived distance another way. Following Hastorf (1950) and Ittelson (1951), these researchers have noted that familiar or assumed size can influence perceived size and distance under reduce-cue settings. In other words, knowledge can influence perception. For example, Baird (1963) presented objects of varying sizes under reduced-cue conditions and told observers that the objects were of the same size as a familiar object. He then had the observers judge the distance to the objects. He found that the subjects' estimates of distance were consistent with the Size-Distance Invariance Hypothesis.

Estimated distance was proportional to the visual angle of the stimulus. Later research (Fitzpatrick, Pasnak, & Tyer, 1982; Gogel, 1968; Gogel & Mertens, 1967; Park & Michaelson, 1974) have supported Baird's conclusion. Off-sized familiar objects produce distance judgments that vary with the visual angle just as the Size-Distance Invariance Hypothesis would predict.

On the other side of the coin, Coltheart (1969) and Tyer, Allen, and Pasnak (1983) found that verbally telling subject the distance to an object presented under reduced-cue conditions allows subjects to make accurate size judgments, while subjects not given this distance information estimate size based on the visual angle of the stimulus. Tyer et al. also found that giving size information helped subjects make better distance estimates than when this information was not provided (although the effect was rather weak).

More recently, Higashiyama and Kitano (1991) had observers judge the size of and distance to a poster of a woman and an unfamiliar board located at different distances away under natural outdoor conditions. They found that size estimates for the woman showed constancy with increasing distance, while size estimates for the board showed increasing overconstancy. In a second experiment, they asked observer to judge the size of and distance to both targets when distance was held constant while the actual size of the target was manipulated. In this case, as the size-distance invariance hypothesis would predict, perceived size was inversely and linearly related to perceived distance in both cases. The familiar-sized woman tended to be seen as being closer to a constant size than was the unfamiliar-sized board, reflecting the effects of knowledge on size perception.

Gogel and DaSilva (1987a) had observers judge the perceived size and distance of a constant-sized blank rectangle or of a playing card of known size at three distances ranging from 56 cm to 149 cm away under reduced-cue conditions using both apparent and objective instructions. As in other cases, the distance estimates tended to be inversely related to size estimates. Perceived size declined with distance for apparent instructions for both stimuli. For objective instructions, perceived size was constant for the playing card of known size, while the blank rectangle decreased in size with increasing distance. As before, reduced-cue conditions are associated with underconstancy; however, it appears that a strong familiar-size cue can overcome this tendency.

One way to interpret these results is to conclude that familiar size influences perceived size and that this perceived size in turn affects perceived distance in accord with the size-distance invariance hypothesis. A number of researchers, most notably Gogel, question this interpretation (Gogel 1969, 1973, 1974, 1990, 1993, 1998; Gogel & DaSilva, 1987a, 1987b; Predebon 1987, 1990, 1992). According to Gogel's theory, familiar size does not influence perceived distance, but rather has an affect on cognitive factors associated with judgment. Based on his earlier work (Gogel, 1965), Gogel believes that under reduced-cue conditions objects are perceptually located approximately two meters away from the observer; a phenomenon commonly known as the specific distance (or equidistance) tendency. This distance corresponds to the resting state of accommodation and convergence (Leibowitz & Owens, 1977; Owens, 1986; Owens & Leibowitz, 1976). For unfamiliar objects this reference distance can determine perceived size in accordance with the Size-Distance Invariance Hypothesis. However, for familiar objects, a mismatch between perceived size and the familiar size of the object may occur. Under these conditions, distance judgments are based on cognitive processes that determine what distance would produce the presented visual angle for an object of that known size (according to the Size Distance Invariance Hypothesis). Thus, Gogel believes the perceived size may differ from size judgments because the later may be based on cognitive factors.

Higashiyama's (1984b) research supported Gogel's theory. He had observers judge the size of and distance to familiar objects like stamps and books using either apparent or assumptive instructions. With apparent instructions, observers were told to ignore their knowledge of familiar size when making judgments while observers given assumptive instructions were told to take this knowledge into account. Familiar size effects on size and distance estimates were greater under assumptive instructions than under apparent instructions, demonstrating the influence of cognition on judgments.

These cognitive effects can be strong enough to wholly override distance information. Haber and Levin (2001) had subjects estimate the size of and distance to familiar objects under full-cue conditions. They also had subject estimate the size of the objects from memory. They found that distance information had no impact on size judgments at all, while size judgments largely corresponded to judgments based on memory. Variation in size judgments corresponded to variation in memory judgments. The authors believed that their results demonstrated that the Size Distance Invariance Hypothesis cannot adequately account for size and distance judgments.

Predebon (1979, 1987, 1990, 1992b) also conducted a number of studies that seem to support Gogel's theory. For example, Predebon (1979) had subjects judge the size of normal and off-size familiar objects and adjacent unfamiliar objects under full-cue conditions. Although one might presume that the two objects are perceptually the same distance away from the observer, familiar size still affected judged size while the perceived size of the adjacent object was unaffected. If perceived size was determined according to the Size Distance Invariance Hypothesis without further cognitive analysis, one would not expect to see this difference. Similarly, Predebon (1987, 1990) found that familiar size influenced verbal estimates of distance in inches but did not influence judgments using a ratio scaling technique based on an unlabeled standard (a method which Predebon considered more indirect). If the indirect measure more closely corresponds to perception of distance, this would argue that familiar size affects occur due to cognitive factors involving verbal labeling.

Predebon (1992b) had subjects judge the size and distance of familiar and unfamiliar objects using both objective and apparent instructions under reduced-cue conditions. He found strong familiar size affects under objective instructions but not under apparent instructions.

This study and Gogel's recent theoretical work (1990, 1993) imply that space is actually only perceived one way, and that the affects of instructions or judgment method really only reflect cognitive influences that are added on subsequent to perception. According to this view, apparent instructions may reflect perceived space more veridically than objective, perspective, or projective instructions which all include a layer of cognitive influence.

In my view, the problem with this formulation is that it requires us to reach into the conscious mind and unambiguously know what real perception looks like as opposed to cognitively generated judgments. Gogel believes he has found a way to accomplish this through the use of a head motion technique that localizes objects in perceptual space via a triangulation of visual directions. Yet, one may wonder whether a description of visual space based on this method corresponds to our perceptual experience any better than judgments using other techniques. One may also wonder whether the metric properties of visual space (distance, angle, area, volume, etc.) are all derivable from simple visual direction. Does Gogel's measure really correspond to facts about visual direction of the dominant eye more than facts about our perception of space? At the root of this method is the assumption that visual space is simple, coherent, and Euclidean, assumptions we had reason to doubt in Chapter 4. If one is unwilling to assume that it is possible to objectively know what conscious experience is like, if one believes that spatial experience is already quite cognitive when perceived, or if one believes that the mind is flexible enough to truly see the world in more than one way, then it is impossible to know which data reflects "real perception" and which data arises from mere cognitive influence. Data based on many judgment techniques must be seen as equally valid, and one must accept that there may be many geometries of visual space instead of only one.

Baird and the butterfly model. Baird's influence on the size-constancy literature goes beyond the investigation of familiar size effects. Much of Baird's other early work concerned the effects of instructions on size-judgment. For example, Baird (1965) had observers judge the size of a standard triangle (12.75 in. in height) located 10 ft. away by adjusting a near comparison located 5 ft. away (under full-cue, binocular conditions). The procedure was sequential: observers first studied the standard after being given either objective, apparent, or projective instructions, and then matched the comparison to the standard from memory in terms of either objective or projective instructions. With objective instructions, observers adjusted the comparison to be 19% too large consistent with past findings of overconstancy. The surprising result obtained under projective instructions, where the comparison was adjusted to be 2% too large. Thus, Baird found overconstancy instead of the strong underconstancy normally associated with projective instructions. Clearly, the earlier study period altered the way subjects thought of the standard enough to influence their subsequent judgments.

In Baird and Biersdorf (1967), observers judged the length of an 8 in. paper strip located from 24 in. to 216 in. from the observer by selecting from a series of comparison strips using objective instructions. The comparison was either located near the observer at 24 in. or far from the observer at 216 in. Stimuli were presented in a well-lit room against a dark (photographer's cloth) surface, and observers rested their head in a chin rest 18 in. above the table surface. For both the near and the far comparison, length judgments increased with increasing distance to the standard, indicating overconstancy. The most distant standard was seen as 14% bigger than the nearest standard for the near comparison, and 37% bigger than the nearest standard for the far comparison.

Baird and Biersdorf then reoriented the standard. Instead of placing it frontally, as in the first part of the experiment, the standard was placed flat so that it was now oriented in-depth relative to the observer.

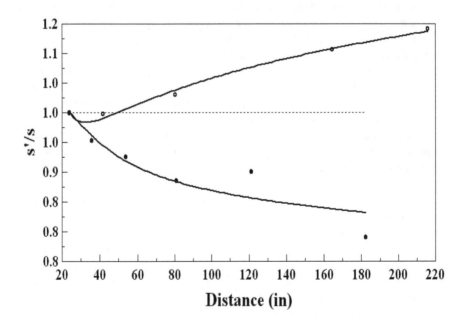

Figure 6.5. Average ratio of comparison to standard as a function of distance to the standard in Baird and Biersdorf's (1967) data. Open circles represent data for frontal standards while closed circles represent data from flat standards. Solid lines represent best fitting full model curves. The dashed line represents perfect constancy.

Under these conditions, underconstancy was obtained for both near and far comparisons. The most distant standard was seen as 21% smaller than the nearest standard for the near comparison, and 24% smaller than the nearest standard for the far comparison. This underconstancy for in-depth oriented stimuli is consistent with other past work (Gilinsky, 1951; Gogel, 1964; Harway, 1963). Baird and Biersdorf also had observers judge the egocentric distance to the various standards using magnitude estimation, but obtained inconsistent data depending on the reference standard used.

Figure 6.5 shows average ratio of the size of comparison to standard size as a function of distance to the standard for Baird and Biersdorf's data. Note that the frontally oriented standards show strong overconstancy while the flat standards show strong underconstancy.

Wagner, Kartzinel, and Baird (1988) also noted that most research on the affects of instructions on size-judgments used frontally oriented stimuli. Wagner et al. looked at the affects of instructions on stimuli oriented in-depth.

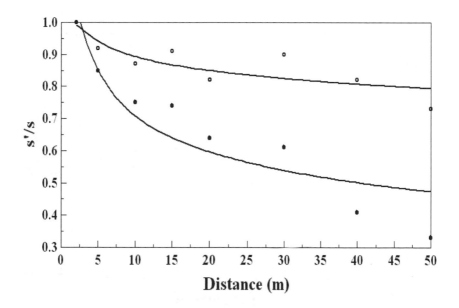

Figure 6.6. Average ratio of comparison to standard as a function of distance to the standard in Wagner, Kartzinel, & Baird's (1988) data. Open circles represent data for objective instructions while closed circles represent data for projective instructions using the method of adjustment. Solid lines represent best fitting full model curves. A constant value of 1.0 would represent perfect constancy.

The standard stimuli were one-meter long wooden dowels placed flat on the ground parallel to the subjects' line of sight at eight different distances ranging from 2m to 50 m away from the observer.

Subjects adjusted a comparison to match each standard using either objective or projective instructions. In addition, subjects made magnitude estimates of size using the same instruction type. Subjects in both conditions made magnitude estimates of distance to the standards using objective instructions.

Under objective instructions, subjects displayed underconstancy with both judgment methods; however, the underconstancy was more severe for magnitude estimation (-50% for the most distant standard) than for the adjustment method (-24%). Projective instructions yielded an even more extreme degree of under-constancy that was about the same for both methods (-70%). Figure 6.6 displays this data for the adjustment task, while Figure 6.7 shows this data for the magnitude estimation task. Distance judgments also displayed underestimation for far stimuli relative to near ones. The power function exponents were almost identical for subjects in both conditions, averaging .74.

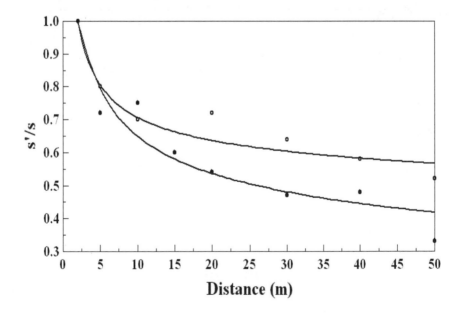

Distance (m)

Figure 6.7. Average ratio of comparison to standard as a function of distance to the standard in Wagner, Kartzinel, & Baird's (1988) data. Open circles represent data for objective instructions while closed circles represent data for projective instructions using magnitude estimation. Solid lines represent best fitting full model curves. A constant value of 1.0 would represent perfect constancy.

Baird (1968, 1970) explained size judgments in terms of a family of three models that taken as a whole were called the "butterfly model." In these models the ratio of the sizes of the comparison to the standard seen in an experiment is a power function of a theoretical ratio that should exist between them, where the nature of the theoretical ratio will vary with different judgment tasks. On one extreme observers produce a null match where the visual angle of the comparison is adjusted to match the visual angle of the standard (what we have called a visual angle or projective match); on the other extreme observers produce a ratio match in which the physical size of the comparison matches the physical size of the standard (an objective match). The great virtue of his model is that the exponent of the power function relates to a host of experimental variables, including instructions and cue conditions.

Although this theory can fit a considerable amount of data, it is not as simple, intuitive, and unitary as the theory Baird and I developed later which will be discussed (in a modified form) later in this chapter.

Child development and size constancy. A number of studies have looked at developmental trends in size perception. Zeigler and Leibowitz (1957) revived interest in the problem using a design closely modeled after Holway and Boring (1941). They had 7- to 9-year-old boys and a group of adults adjust a comparison to match a constant visual angle standard using apparent size instructions. Distance to the standard ranged from 10 to 100 feet. They found that the boys showed underconstancy, increasing underestimation of size with increasing distance, while adults showed only a slight tendency toward underconstancy. For the most distant stimulus boys underestimated stimulus size by 62% while adults underestimated by only 8.5%. Figure 6.8 shows the average adjusted comparison size a function of distance to the standard for both age groups.

In one of the most detailed studies on the development of size constancy, Harway (1963), using a procedure similar to Gilinsky (1951), asked five groups of standing observers (ages 5 1/2 yrs., 7 yrs., 10 yrs., 12 yrs., and adult) mark off successive 1 ft. intervals (with a one foot ruler placed on the ground beside them as a reference standard) in a level, grassy field. There were two series of judgments, one in which the observer's heights were equalized and one with no control for height. As in previous work with in-depth oriented stimuli, the results showed increasing underconstancy with distance for all five groups, with greater underconstancy for the younger groups (ages 5 1/2 yrs., 7 yrs., and 10 yrs.) than for older groups (12 yrs. and adult). Harway found little change in judgments when height was equalized compared to when height was not.

Rapoport (1967) found little difference in size estimates using objective and apparent instructions for children between 5 yrs. and 11 yrs. of age. Observers between 13 and 20 yrs of age showed increasingly more overconstancy with objective instructions compared to estimates using apparent instructions.

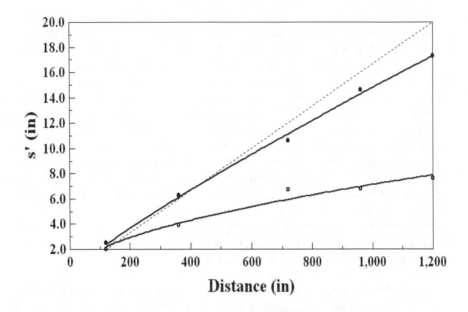

Figure 6.8. Average adjusted comparison size as a function of distance to the standard for Zeigler and Leibowitz's (1956) data. Open circles represent childrens' (7-9 yrs.) data, while filled circles represent adults' (18-24 yrs.) data. Solid lines represent best fitting distance model curves. The dashed line represents perfect constancy.

Similarly, Wohlwill (1963, 1970) found that young children's size judgments tended toward underconstancy with an increasing trend toward overconstancy as age increased. Jenkin and Feallock (1960) found constancy for age 8 and age 14, and overconstancy for adult subjects. Carlson and Tassone (1963) compared size judgments of college students to 61- to 80-year-old individuals. Both groups showed overconstancy for objective instructions and constancy for apparent in- structions, but the difference was less pronounced for older subjects.

Another factor that may influence the affects of development on size- constancy is distance to the standard. For example, Cohen, Hershkowitz, and Chodak (1958) and Rapoport (1967) both found that children displayed good con- stancy when standard stimuli were near at hand. However, Zeigler and Leibowitz (1957), Leibowitz, Pollard, and Dickson (1967) and Brislin and Leibowitz (1970) all showed that when presented with a wider range of stimuli under full-cue con- ditions, including some at greater distances (up to 61 m), children show pro- nounced underconstancy and that increasing age was associated with an increasing tendency toward constancy and overconstancy.

Teghtsoonian also looked at developmental influences on size perception. In Teghtsoonian and Teghtsoonian (1970b) observers judged the apparent area of irregular polygons using magnitude estimation. They found that apparent area grew with increasing distance to the target in their first study, which employed high school students of both sexes, but apparent area was approximately constant as a function of distance when college women were used as subjects. Finally, they also noted that perceived distance increased with physical distance according to a power function with an exponent of 1.2. Thus, overconstancy is once again associated with perceived distance being an accelerating function of physical distance. However, in the Teghtsoonian's case, increasing age led to a decline in overconstancy, although to a small degree.

Teghtsoonian and Beckwith (1976) asked observers to judge the apparent height of a rectangle using magnitude estimation. Their observers were 8, 10, 12, or 20 years of age. They found a slight tendency toward underconstancy for 8- and 10-year-olds, constancy for 12-year-olds, and a slight tendency toward overconstancy for 20-year-olds; however, these differences were not statistically reliable. They also asked subjects to estimate distance to the target using magnitude estimation. In this case, apparent distance increased with physical distance as a power function with an exponent of 1.1. Two possible reasons why Teghtsoonian did not find large age effects were that she used apparent size instructions, which generally do not produce strong overconstancy (restricting the range over which outcomes can vary), and the use of magnitude estimation, which may be a less precise method than magnitude production.

There is a great deal of evidence showing that some ability to correctly perceive size across changes in distance may be built into us a birth. Bower (1964, 1966) conditioned 8-week-old infants to turn their head to a 30 cm cube placed 1 m away. The infants showed greater conditioned responses to the same size cube placed 3 m away than to a cube that was the same visual angle 3 m away. Day and McKenzie (1981) and McKenzie, Tootell, and Day (1980) habituated 18-week-old children to the presence of an object. Children subsequently showed greater habituation to a same sized object placed further away than to an object of different size. In fact, Granrud (1987) and Slater, Mattock, and Brown (1990) found similar differential habituation based on the objective size of stimuli for newborn infants, indicating that even newborn children are able to determine that changing distance does not change the size of an object or alter the object's significance. (Although Slater et al. also found differential habituation resulting from changing the visual angle of the stimulus, indicating that infants are also detect changes in projective size.) Using Brunswik's terminology, it would seem that even the youngest children do not make projective matches, but display some "regression to the real."

In general, it would seem the youngest children show some underconstancy (although not to the point of a projective match) while increasing age is associated with increasing constancy or even over constancy. How can this trend be explained? Shallo and Rock (1988) presented a theory for this phenomenon that they supported with two experiments. Their first experiment was a traditional size-constancy experiment, modeled after Brislin and Leibowitz (1970), in which observers were asked to match standard stimuli presented at various distances away to a series of comparison stimuli that varied in size but were at a constant distance away. In this traditional approach the visual angles of the standard stimuli were proportionate to standard size and therefore it also varied. Under these conditions, both groups of children (average ages 5.2 and 8.3 years) showed a strong tendency toward underconstancy (-36.7% and -32.6% underestimation respectively for the most distant stimulus) while adults selected comparisons that were very close to accurate (very slight underconstancy of -5.2%). Shallo and Rock's second experiment changed the nature of the comparison. Here, elements of the comparison series varied in both size and distance from the observer such that each comparison stimulus subtended exactly the same visual angle. Under these conditions, all age groups produced matches that were fairly close to accurate. There was only the slightest and non-significant tendency for the youngest children to display underconstancy (-7.9%) while older children showed constancy (-2.0%) and adults produced over constancy (+12.5%).

Shallo and Rock used their results to explain why children often show greater underconstancy than adults. The authors believe that in the typical size-constancy experiment, children select comparison stimuli based largely on the visual angle they subtend rather than referencing the comparison's size, while adults ignore the visual angle and select comparison stimuli based on the comparisons size. Turning Brunswik's dictum on its head, children show a "regression to the projective" when confronted with this task. In Shallo and Rock's second experiment, this strategy was no longer available to the children (because all the comparisons had the same visual angle); so, they were forced to select comparison stimuli according to size.

Recent work on size constancy. The last decade and a half has seen continued work on size constancy. One recent trend in the study of size constancy is looking at the affects of motion on size perception (e.g., Gogel, 1998). For example, Whitaker, McGraw, and Pearson (1999) examined the perceived size of expanding and contracting stimuli. They found that perceived size at a given instant is biased in the direction of the size change. They also found that illusory expansion from a movement after-effect produced the same misperception of size.

Another variable that might influence size perception is whether the stimulus is at eye level or elsewhere in the field of vision. Bertamini, Yang, and Proffitt (1998) had subjects judge the size of frontally oriented objects located the same distance away from the observer that were placed both at eye level and below eye level under full-cue conditions. They found size perception was most accurate for eye-level stimuli. The authors believe that this indicates that perceived size must be influenced by factors other than perceived distance alone.

McKee and Smallman's dual calculation theory. One of the more recent theories for size-constancy phenomena was proposed by McKee and Smallman (1998). Based on prior research studies, the authors calculate Weber fractions for size and distance judgments. They found that the Weber fraction for size judgments is about .02-.04 (the just noticeable difference was 2% to 4% of the size of the standard); (Burbeck, 1987; Klein & Levi, 1987; McKee, Welch, Taylor, & Bowne, 1990). The Weber fraction for distance judgments was about .05-.06 (5-6%); (McKee, Levi, & Bowne, 1990; Norman, Todd, Perotti, & Tittle, 1996). McKee and Smallman reason that size judgments can be no more precise than the information from which they are derived. If size judgments were based exclusively on distance perceptions this would imply that they could at best produce Weber fractions equivalent to those of distance perception. The fact that the data shows size judgments to be more precise implies that size judgments are based, at least in part, on information other than distance.

McKee and Smallman believe this additional information comes from relative size cues such as surface texture and the presence of familiar size information. This proposal is similar in spirit to Gibson and other researchers emphasis on texture gradients as fundamental information present in the ambient optical array to afford size perception (Andrews, 1964; Gibson, 1950; Nakayama, 1994). In fact, Ross and Plug (1998) indicate that such relative-size explanations for size constancy date back to the time of Plotinus in the third century, Leonardo da Vinci in the 15th century and Castelli in the 17th.

Having said this, McKee and Smallman believe that relative-size cues are also not able to fully account for size judgments. They say that by themselves, only small changes in perceived size can be accounted for by relative-size cues, and there is a host of data showing that perceived distance does in fact influence perceived size. McKee and Smallman believe that the data is best accounted for by a dual calculation theory in which the human mind simultaneously calculates size using both relative size and distance based information. Normally, these two calculations agree with one another and serve to cross validate size estimates. Under special circumstances, such as in the laboratory, these two estimates may disagree. The estimate that dominates will depend on where attention is directed (and perhaps the instructions used); however, the authors do seem to feel that relative-size cues are somewhat more important. This theory can account for some of the studies reported earlier where distance and size judgments appeared to be somewhat uncoupled.

One recent study revisited instruction affects and seems to be consistent with McKee and Smallman's theory. Kaneko and Uchikawa (1997) asked subject to judge the size of stimuli using objective and projective instructions. Stimuli either had a blank surround or one that conveyed a sense of depth. Projective judgments were not influenced by the surrounding context while objective judgments were. The authors feel that this indicates that different perceptual mechanisms underlie the two types of judgments, just as McKee and Smallman might predict.

Summarizing the Size-Constancy Literature

A few lessons about size constancy can be learned from the foregoing review. While the shape of the standard stimulus has no apparent affect on size judgments, all of the other factors mentioned at the beginning of this chapter do have affects. For frontally oriented targets under full-cue conditions, all 19 studies employing objective instructions showed overconstancy ranging from +19 to +53% and averaging +28% for the most distant standard. For the two studies examining perspective instructions, this overconstancy was even more extreme, averaging +56%. On the other hand, of the 22 studies using apparent instructions under these conditions, 5 show marked underconstancy, 12 show close to constancy, and five show overconstancy. The judgments of the most distant stimuli ranged from an underconstancy of -10% to an overconstancy of 13%, with an average displaying a slight underconstancy of -2%. Projective instructions almost always (in 9 out of 10 cases) produce underconstancy with judgments of the most distant stimuli ranging from an underconstancy of -68% to a slight over constancy or +2% in one outlying study. The average degree of underconstancy for projective instructions for the most distant stimulus was -37%.

Frontally oriented stimuli under reduced conditions are associated with under constancy for both objective and apparent instruction sets. In terms of the individual studies reported earlier, reduced-cue conditions resulted in underconstancy in ten cases, constancy in two, and a very slight overconstancy in one. Stronger underconstancy occurred when more cues to depth are eliminated. Binocular conditions show little underconstancy, while monocular conditions show more, and the use of artificial pupils and tubes show even more. When cues to depth are completely eliminated by controlling for the illumination of nearby objects, judgments approach a projective match.

For flat stimuli under full-cue conditions, 18 of 19 studies show underconstancy for all types of instructions, with one study showing constancy using objective instructions. The underconstancy ranged from -21% to -50% for objective instructions, averaging -30%. For projective instructions, this overconstancy average -70% across two studies. None of the studies reviewed looked at size constancy for flat stimuli under reduced-cue conditions.

In short then, objective and perspective instructions tend to produce overconstancy under full cue conditions for frontal stimuli, apparent instructions produce constancy, and projective instructions produce underconstancy. Reduced cue conditions or reorienting the stimulus so that it is flat are almost always associated with underconstancy.

Another factor that appears to influence size judgments is age. Young children usually display underconstancy with an increasing tendency toward overconstancy with age. Eleven of 13 studies employing 5- to 11-year-olds showed underconstancy while the remaining two displaying constancy. For 12- to 16-year-olds, one study found underconstancy, three constancy, and two overconstancy. On the other hand, adults who took part in these developmental studies showed overconstancy in six cases and constancy in the remaining four.

A small number of studies suggest the possibility the intelligent subjects and trained artists are better able to assume a projective attitude. One study seems to indicate that alcohol use leads to strong underconstancy.

For unfamiliar stimuli, all 20 studies reported here found that size and distance judgments appear to be inversely related in a way that is consistent with the Size-Distance Invariance Hypothesis. For familiar stimuli, the picture is somewhat murkier, with 12 studies showing results consistent with the Size-Distance Invariance Hypothesis and 4 showing inconsistent results. Knowledge can sometimes override perceived distance when making size judgments leading to an uncoupling of size and distance estimates. This uncoupling of size and distance estimates seems to occur most commonly under full-cue conditions when subjects are give plenty of information on which to base distance judgments while they are simultaneously inclined through instructions to rely on memory or when experimental conditions give misleading relative size information on which to base size judgments. Objective instructions are more likely to incline the subject to make this mistake, while apparent and projective instructions do not.

Explaining Size-Constancy Data

There are a number of approaches one can take toward understanding this diverse size-constancy data. One way to simplify the problem is to embrace some of the data as reflecting perceptual experience while dismissing other data as representing the artificial product of experimental confounds. Brunswik, Thouless, and Gilinsky believed that overconstancy could only result from mistakes in procedure because size judgments represent a compromise between two perceptual attitudes. Gogel seems to believe that perceived experience can be measured using a triangulation method, and that data inconsistent with this method reflect cognitive factors rather than perceptual experience. In particular, apparent (or perhaps projective) size instructions appear to be more valid than objective instructions.

On the other hand, it is also possible that apparent size instructions render the more suspect data. Perhaps apparent size data could be just a statistical combination of some subjects interpreting apparent instructions to mean objective size instructions while others think they mean projective size instructions—the combination of data from these two interpretations yielding constancy on the average.

Other researchers such as Carlson, Epstein, Baird, and McKee accept size-constancy data at face value, attempting to find general perceptual principles or develop models that explain variations in the data. Of these theorists, only Baird (1970) attempted to develop precise mathematical models to predict size judgments as a function of instructions and experimental conditions.

The Transformation Theory of Size Judgment

I believe that most of the size constancy data can be accounted for by the transformation theory of size judgment that Jack Baird and I developed (Baird & Wagner, 1987, 1991; Wagner & Baird, 1987; Wagner, Baird, & Fuld, 1989). The purpose of the remainder of this chapter is to describe an updated form of this theory, show how well it models the size-constancy literature, and discuss how it largely unifies the size-constancy and direct perception literatures (discussed in the previous chapter).

According to the transformation theory, physical size translates into perceived size through a two-stage process. First, by the time stimulus information reaches the retina it has undergone a fundamental transformation. The eye does not represent the physical size of the object, but light bouncing off of the object describes a solid visual angle on the retina (Gibson, 1979). Second, an inverse transformation occurs when the mind translates this visual angle back into spatial form. In Brunswik's (1956) terminology, the first transformation converts the distal stimulus into the proximal stimulus while the second transformation converts the proximal stimulus into the percept. The first transformation is a physical process in which there is no room for error. The second, inverse transformation, however, is a psychological process. If the correct inverse transformation is applied to the proximal stimulus, the percept will be accurate, but if elements of the inverse transformation are incorrectly applied, the percept will be in error.

The first transformation. The mathematical form of the first transformation is rather straight-forward to determine, but more complex than many researchers realize. For a frontally oriented object whose bottom or top edge is aligned with the observer's eye-level, physical size, s, is translated into the visual angle at the retina, θ, according to the equation

$$\tan \theta = \frac{s}{d} \tag{6.6}$$

where d represents the physical distance from the observer's eye to the stimulus. As we noted earlier, this becomes the familiar form of the Size-Distance Invariance Hypothesis by substituting perceived size, s', and perceived distance, d', for physical size and distance in this equation (Epstein, 1963; Epstein, Park, & Casey, 1961; Künnapas, 1968; Landauer & Epstein, 1969).

When a frontally oriented object is not aligned with the observer's eye level, the visual angle is determined by a more complicated formula. (See Baird and Wagner (1991) for a derivation.)

$$\theta = \cos^{-1}\left(\frac{h^2 + d^2 + ds}{\sqrt{h^2 + d^2}\sqrt{h^2 + (d+s)^2}}\right) \tag{6.7}$$

Here, h represents the height of the observer above the surface on which the object lay.

Wagner, Baird, and Barbaresi (1981) showed that flat objects, which extend in-depth away from the observer, transform into the visual angle at the retina according to a different equation:

$$\theta = \cos^{-1}\left(\frac{h^2 + d^2 - hs}{\sqrt{h^2 + d^2}\sqrt{d^2 + (h-s)^2}}\right) \tag{6.8}$$

One implication of these equations is that for an object of the constant physical size, the relationship between the visual angle and physical distance changes depending on the orientation of the stimulus. Figure 6.9 shows the visual angle of an object of a given physical size as a function of distance to the object and stimulus orientation. While the visual angle decreases with distance for both stimulus orientations, this decrease occurs more rapidly for a flat stimulus. Another implication of these formulas is that the height of the observer plays a critical role in the perception of flat objects. In fact, as the height of the observer approaches zero, the visual angle impinging on the retina also approaches zero regardless of the distance to the object.

If an object's orientation lies outside of these two extremes, the visual angle is determined by an even more general formula derived in Baird and Wagner (1989, 1991). The formulas for frontal and flat stimuli are simply special cases of this more general formula:

$$\theta = \cos^{-1}\left(\frac{d^2 + ds\cos\phi - hs\sin\phi + h^2}{\sqrt{(d + s\cos\phi)^2 + (h - s\sin\phi)^2}\sqrt{h^2 + d^2}}\right) \tag{6.9}$$

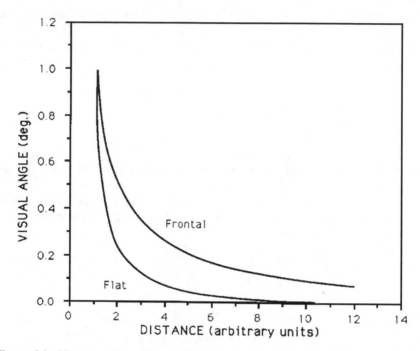

Figure 6.9. Visual angle as a function of distance for frontal and flat targets. From Baird and Wagner 1991. Copyright 1991 by the American Psychological Association. Reprinted with permission.

The elements of this formula are graphically depicted in Figure 6.10. In the formula, θ is the visual angle of the stimulus, s is the target object's size, d is the distance along the ground from the observer to the object, h is the height of the observer above the ground, and ϕ is the orientation of the object relative to the ground.

The inverse transformation. In order to achieve constancy and recover the original size of the stimulus, the visual system must perform the appropriate inverse transformation on the visual angle impinging on the retina. Physically, the correct inverse transformation to determine size based on the visual angle, distance to the object, height of the observer, and orientation of the stimulus is (see Baird & Wagner, 1991 for a derivation):

$$s = \frac{\sin(\theta)\sqrt{h^2 + d^2}}{\sin(\phi - \theta + \delta)} \qquad (6.10)$$

where $\delta = \tan^{-1}(h/d)$.

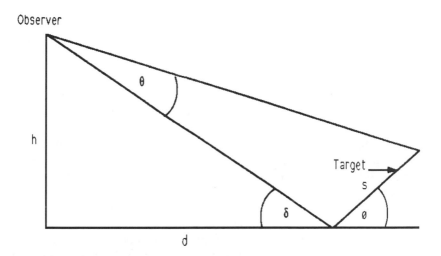

Figure 6.10. Schematic diagram of an observer of height h viewing a target of size s at orientation ϕ located a distance d away from him/her. From Baird and Wagner 1991. Copyright 1991 by the American Psychological Association. Reprinted with permission.

When attempting to determine perceived size, the visual system does not have direct knowledge of physical distance, target orientation, or observer height, but must rely on its perceptions of these quantities. In fact, McCready (1985, 1986) and Baird, Wagner, and Fuld (1990) have suggested that even the visual angle in this equation is best thought of as a perceived quantity. In fact, many paradoxes associated with the moon illusion can be simply accounted for by assuming that observers are really reporting on the perceived visual angle when talking about the size of the moon. Similarly, although you would think that someone would know their own height very well, prisms and new glasses can sometimes temporarily alter our height perception resulting in size and distance estimation errors.

While each of these quantities might actually be consciously misperceived, it is also possible that although we correctly perceive each of these quantities consciously, the visual system might mistakenly apply the wrong quantity when transforming the visual angle in perceived size. For example, we may consciously perceive that a stimulus is flat, but not sufficiently compensate for its orientation when applying the inverse transformation to determine perceived size.

Equation 6.10 can be rewritten to take into account these perceived or applied quantities to yield

$$s' = \frac{\sin(\theta') \sqrt{h'^2 + d'^2}}{\sin\left(\phi' - \theta' + \delta\right)} \qquad (6.11)$$

where s' is perceived size, d' is perceived (or applied) distance to the object, h' is perceived or applied height of the observer, ϕ' is the perceived or applied orientation of the stimulus, and θ' is the perceived or applied visual angle of the proximal stimulus. Misperceiving or misapplying any of these quantities could lead to misperceptions of size.

To simplify matters, let us assume that observers correctly perceive the visual angle and are familiar with their own height. I believe that misperception of the remaining two factors, distance to the target stimulus and target orientation, can account for much of the size constancy data reported in the present chapter in a way that is largely consistent with the direct estimation literature reported in the previous chapter. In particular, I believe that instructions and cue conditions can alter the way distance is used to determine perceived size. In addition, I believe that subjects may not fully take into account changes in stimulus orientation for flat stimuli, and that this can account for the consistent underconstancy seen in size judgments for flat stimuli.

Fitting the Model to the Data

To apply this model to past size constancy data, I would like to introduce three variations of the above model. In the *distance model*, I assume that perceived distance is a power function of physical distance. This model has two parameters, the exponent, γ, and a scaling constant, κ. In this model, Equation 6.11 is rewritten to read:

$$s' = \kappa \frac{\sin(\theta) \sqrt{h^2 + d^{\gamma^2}}}{\sin\left(\phi - \theta + \delta\right)} \qquad (6.12)$$

where

$$\delta = \arctan\left(\frac{h}{d^\gamma}\right).$$

In the *orientation model*, I assume that the visual system applies an inverse transformation that would be appropriate for a different stimulus orientation. For example, the visual system might try to apply an inverse transformation for a frontal stimulus to a physically flat stimulus. This model also has two parameters, the applied orientation, ϕ*, and a scaling constant, κ. In this case, Equation 6.11 will now look like:

$$s' = \kappa \, \frac{\sin(\theta) \, \sqrt{h^2 + d^2}}{\sin\!\left(\phi^* - \theta + \delta\right)}.$$ (6.13)

Finally, data can also be fit to a *full model*, in which both distance and orientation can be misperceived. This model has three parameters, the exponent, γ, applied orientation, ϕ*, and a scaling constant, κ. The inverse transformation for this model looks like:

$$s' = \kappa \, \frac{\sin(\theta) \, \sqrt{h^2 + d^{\gamma^2}}}{\sin\!\left(\phi^* - \theta + \delta\right)}$$ (6.14)

where

$$\delta = \arctan\left(\frac{h}{d^\gamma}\right).$$

Equations 6.12, 6.13, and 6.14 can easily be fit to many of the classic data sets reported earlier in this chapter. In some cases, when the standard varies as a function of distance as in Holway and Boring (1941) these models were directly fit to the data. For most of the data fit to the models, the standard has a constant size and the comparison is adjusted to appear equal to the standard. In this case, I calculated the ratio of the near comparison to the far standard, s'/s. Equations 6.12, 6.13, and 6.14 can then be applied to the data by dividing both sides of the equations by the size of the standard.

I should note that the approach taken here differs from Baird and Wagner (1991) in a number of ways. First, although Baird and Wagner introduced Equation 6.11, it didn't apply it to any data. Instead, we introduced a number of simplifying assumptions to make fitting the models easier. In addition, to make plotting easier, logarithms were applied to the equations, which given the simplifying assumptions used, converted the models into straight-line fits. In this chapter, I directly fit the models to the data, as expressed in Equations 6.12, 6.13, 6.14, without simplification or processing. This allows me to display the data in a more accessible and meaningful fashion and to more clearly show the forms of the relationships predicted by the models. Second, the approach taken by Baird and Wagner separated distance and orientation models. The approach taken here allows me to fit a combined model that allows for misperception or misapplication of both distance and orientation at the same time, what I have called the "full model." Comparing the full model to fits based on each factor independently can give a sense of the relative power of each factor under different experimental conditions.

Table 6.1 shows the best-fitting parameter values and correlations between model predictions and data when the three models were fit to the data from a number of classic size constancy experiments. Most size constancy experiments compare perceived size across a small number of experimental conditions.

The selected experiments had rich data sets that allowed for detailed modeling; in particular, these experiments collected size judgments at multiple distances from the subject. Note that orientation angles in the table are expressed in terms of degrees. Full-model could not be fit to the Holway and Boring's Reduction Tunnel condition because data were only collected for three distances; so, the number of degrees of freedom of the model would equal the number of data points.

Model parameters for the exponent for distance can be compared to the trends seen in distance and area estimation discussed in Chapter 5. (Because most size-constancy studies involve adjusting the area of a two-dimensional comparison until it equals a standard, area estimation exponents may be more relevant than they might first seem. The visual system might attune itself more in line with the task at hand—which is area estimation.) In addition, the relative importance of applied distance and orientation can be evaluated for each experimental variable.

Instructions. Gilinsky (1955), Epstein (1963), and Wagner et al. (1988) looked at size constancy as a function of instructions. Best fits of the full model are shown in Figures 6.2 (Gilinsky), 6.3 (Epstein), 6.6 and 6.7 (Wagner et al.). In general, the full model fits the data very well, although there are a few exceptions. (Average comparison sizes in Gilinsky's objective instruction data for the 78-inch standard were quite variable, as were those based on Epstein's apparent instruction data.) Overall, the distance model explains more of the variance than the orientation model, although there are a few exceptions.

This is consistent with the idea that instructions may incline observers to redefine distance. In Chapter 2 we discussed how distance can be defined in different ways through the use of different metric functions. I believe that the different instruction sets ask subjects to define the concepts of size and distance differently. Projective instructions, in particular, ask observers to deemphasize distance and treat all objects as if they were the same distance away. This should incline observers to use a small exponent for distance in equations 6.12 and 6.14. Instructions that emphasize accurate size and distance, such as objective and perspective instructions, should lead to higher exponents for distance in keeping with the precision theory introduced in the previous chapter. In keeping with these predictions, Table 6.1 shows the model produces higher exponents for perspective and objective instructions, moderate exponents for apparent instructions, and low exponents for projective instructions.

Table 6.1

Theoretical Fits of the Distance, Orientation, and Full Models to Classic Size Constancy Data

Key Variable Article Experimental Condition	Full Model				Distance Model			Orientation Model		
	κ	γ	φ*	r	κ	γ	r	κ	φ*	r
Instructions										
Gilinsky (1955)										
42-Inch Standard										
Objective	0.103	0.974	3.261	0.949	0.748	1.059	0.819	0.067	2.796	0.943
Projective	11.86	0.617	71.60	0.973	9.514	0.642	0.972	0.008	178.7	0.835
54-Inch Standard										
Objective	0.042	1.032	177.3	0.990	0.700	1.057	0.973	0.025	1.168	0.959
Projective	12.30	0.606	72.51	0.968	9.933	0.629	0.967	-.002	-.425	0.831
66-Inch Standard										
Objective	0.329	1.020	159.1	0.987	0.858	1.027	0.979	0.055	177.2	0.934
Projective	11.57	0.623	73.50	0.965	9.547	0.644	0.964	0.003	0.442	0.815
78-Inch Standard										
Objective	0.134	1.030	10.88	0.503	1.005	0.996	0.113	0.338	20.68	0.322
Projective	11.53	0.622	74.60	0.978	9.645	0.641	0.978	-.008	1813	0.848
Epstein (1963)										
8-Inch Standard										
Perspective	0.146	1.031	174.2	0.977	0.791	1.104	0.949	0.130	176.0	0.965
Objective	0.013	1.269	4.550	0.987	0.451	1.147	0.917	0.085	176.7	0.760
Apparent	0.201	0.770	178.1	0.746	1.169	0.972	0.309	0.880	66.64	0.047
Projective	0.887	0.601	173.8	0.991	4.157	0.688	0.987	-0.02	183.2	0.883
16-Inch Standard										
Perspective	0.066	1.199	12.72	0.997	0.608	1.112	0.946	0.245	170.5	0.790
Objective	0.015	1.308	7.787	0.996	0.402	1.153	0.899	0.158	173.4	0.714
Apparent	0.330	0.931	169.0	0.710	0.878	1.015	0.104	0.626	141.1	0.523
Projective	2.177	0.568	167.9	0.991	5.010	0.660	0.988	-0.04	186.3	0.884
Combined										
Perspective	0.624	1.112	68.21	0.988	0.701	1.107	0.988	0.191	173.5	0.924
Objective	0.015	1.288	6.335	0.993	0.426	1.150	0.913	0.123	175.0	0.739
Apparent	0.253	0.853	175.5	0.726	1.014	0.993	0.108	0.822	122.7	0.149
Projective	1.490	0.585	170.7	0.991	4.564	0.674	0.988	0.032	4.740	0.884
Wagner et al. (1988)										
Objective(adj)	1.059	0.923	79.66	0.840	0.541	0.600	0.195	0.709	121.2	0.752
Projective(adj)	1.102	0.703	42.25	0.925	0.603	0.523	0.827	0.321	146.1	0.741
Objective(me)	0.739	0.895	118.5	0.954	0.545	0.554	0.926	0.368	143.0	0.908
Projective(me)	1.082	0.687	44.79	0.957	0.577	0.515	0.913	0.265	149.9	0.849
Orientation										
Baird & Biersdorf (1967)										
Frontal	0.473	1.105	132.5	0.996	0.276	1.036	0.893	1.051	69.29	0.833
Flat	1.290	0.902	62.62	0.922	0.320	0.952	0.912	0.764	113.2	0.871
Age										
Zeigler & Leibowitz (1957)										
Children	2.230	0.547	14.26	0.983	9.691	0.547	0.983	0.326	49.25	0.846
Adult	1.318	0.863	36.40	0.998	2.273	0.863	0.998	0.843	72.77	0.994
Cue Conditions										
Epstein & Landauer (1969)										
Reduced Cue	2.006	0.334	19.10	0.996	14.04	0.172	0.994	0.028	7.068	0.938
Holway & Boring (1941)										
Full Cue	1.274	0.901	38.71	0.995	2.082	0.900	0.994	0.929	63.60	0.991
Monocular	1.166	0.918	4.503	0.993	1.677	0.918	0.993	0.881	68.41	0.991
Artificial Pupil	1.174	0.822	39.93	0.956	1.868	0.822	0.956	0.533	103.8	0.944
Reduction Tunnel*					9.357	0.513	0.982	0.387	91.00	0.676

Exponents for distance and area estimation reported in the meta-analysis of the previous chapter give mixed support to these predictions and to the exponents generated by the model. Exponents for distance judgments show little difference between objective instructions and apparent instructions for all perceptual data, but they do show somewhat higher exponents for objective instructions over apparent instructions for magnitude estimation data. Unfortunately, no past research has looked at exponents for distance estimation for perspective and projective instructions. Exponents for area estimation are quite consistent with the above predictions and with the model. Exponents for area estimates are much higher with objective instructions than with projective instructions.

Orientation. Baird and Biersdorf (1967) explicitly examined the affects of target orientation. (See Figure 6.5.) In addition, fits to Wagner et al. (1988) who examined size perception of flat targets can be compared to the Gilinsky (1955) and Epstein (1963) who looked at frontally oriented targets. Once again, the full model fits Baird and Biersdorf's data quite well. Based on the model fits, exponents for frontal targets appear to be slightly higher than for flat targets. Similarly, exponents for fits of the model to Wagner et al.'s objective instruction data are lower than exponents for fits to Gilinsky and Epstein's objective instruction data. As one might suspect, the most dramatic affect of target orientation was on the orientation parameter. Best-fitting orientation parameters for flat targets deviated greatly from the 0° physical orientation of the target. This suggests that observers may not adequately adjust for the flat orientation of the stimulus when applying the inverse transformation to flat targets. Further support for this possibility will be reported in the next chapter that looks at multidimensional research studies which actually compares perception across these two dimensions.

Comparing these results to exponents found in the meta-analysis reported in the previous chapter shows mixed results. Distance estimation exponents, once again, show little effect for target orientation. However, the meta-analysis showed that area estimation exponents for frontal targets are much larger on average than exponents for flat targets.

Age. Zeigler and Leibowitz (1957) compared size estimates of 7- to 9-year-old children to those of young adults ranging from 18- to 24-years-old. (See Figure 6.8.) Model fits (which were very good) show much lower exponents for children than for adults. Orientation parameters also deviated from the 90° physical target orientation more for children than for adults. These parameter values are in accord with both the distance and area exponents found in the meta-analysis, which showed lower exponents for young people than for adults.

Cue conditions. Holway and Boring (1941) compared size constancy across four conditions that presented increasing degrees of cue reduction. (See Figure

6.1.) In addition, Epstein and Landauer (1969) examined size constancy under highly reduce-cue conditions. (See Figure 6.4.) Epstein and Landauer's data can be compared to other studies such as Gilinsky (1955) and Epstein (1963) who looked at size constancy under full-cue conditions. According to the model applied to Holway and Boring's data, exponents are very similar between full-cue and monocular condition, lower when observers viewed the target through an artificial pupil and lower still when viewers looked through a reduction tunnel. Exponents for fits to Epstein and Landauer's experiment were very low. These results make perfect sense, because reduction in depth cues should result in small distance estimation exponents. Under totally reduced settings, distance estimation exponents would fall to zero and all targets would seem to be the same distance away.

Unfortunately, the meta-analysis presented in the previous chapter found little difference between distance estimation exponents under full-cue and reduced-cue conditions. As noted in the previous chapter, however, almost all of the studies classified as "reduced-cue" in the meta-analysis simply limited subjects to monocular viewing. According to the fits of the model to the Holway and Boring data, monocular viewing leads to little change in the distance estimation exponent (or the exponent might even see a slight increase under these conditions). Virtually no research has looked at distance estimation exponents under truly reduced-cue settings such as in a darkened room.

The moon illusion as a special case. Wagner, Baird, and Fuld (1989) point out that the moon illusion may actually represent a special case of size constancy and that the apparent size of the moon may be well predicted by a variant of the above model. The moon at the horizon is seen in the context of many cues to depth. The exponent for the power function for distance should be relatively high under these circumstances. By Equation 16.12 or 16.14 this should lead to constancy and the distant moon should be see as large. On the other hand, when the moon is seen high in the sky, there are few intervening cues to depth, and the exponent for the power function for distance should be small. Under these circumstances, strong underconstancy should be observed and a distant moon will be perceived as very small.

Other evidence supports this model. If cues to depth are eliminated, such as by having people look at the moon through a tube or over a wall, the horizon moon no longer looks large (Kaufman & Rock, 1962). The tube or wall should have the effect of reducing the exponent for distance estimation close to the value used for the moon at higher elevations. Another bit of evidence that supports the model is that if visual terrain is present, the greater the perceived distance to the moon the larger the difference in perceived size between zenith and horizon moons (Kaufman & Rock, 1962). This also make sense, because if constancy obtains, as it would with distance exponents close to one, then the greater the perceived distance to the moon, the larger the moon should appear given that it subtends the same visual angle at all perceived distances away. The zenith moon will seem increasingly smaller relative to this expanding horizon moon.

The one phenomenon that cannot be accounted for by Wagner et al.'s (1989) model is that as the elevation to the moon increases, people report that it seems further away (McCready, 1986). Neither Wagner et al. nor the standard Rock and Kaufman (1962) flattened-dome model can account for this paradox. Both require that the zenith moon seem closer to the person. The only way I know of to account for this "size-distance paradox" is to reconceptualize what is meant by the term perceived size when speaking of the moon. Baird, Wagner, and Fuld (1990) and McCready (1986) point out that the size-distance paradox disappears and that all major phenomena surround the moon illusion can be accounted for by assuming that observers are really reporting on the perceived visual angle when they speak of the size of the moon. In other words, subjects are assuming a projective attitude under these circumstances. If the moon has a constant perceived size, a shrinking perceived visual angle for the zenith moon will make it seem further away than a horizon moon with a large perceived visual angle.

Summary of the Size-Constancy Literature

Researchers have studied size-constancy phenomena for over a century. Over this time period, a number of factors have been found to influence perceived size. Overconstancy typically occurs when objective or perspective instructions are used under full-cue conditions with binocular viewing of frontally oriented objects. Constancy is usually found when apparent instructions are used. Underconstancy is associated with the use of projective instructions (particularly with intelligent or artistic subjects), reduced-cue conditions, flat target orientations, child subjects, and possibly the use of alcohol. For unfamiliar stimuli, distance judgments appear to be closely related to size judgments in accordance with the Size-Distance Invariance Hypothesis. Familiar size information can sometimes decouple this relationship.

A number of theorists have attempted to explain these relationships. Most of these models are qualitative or only focus on a limited range of size constancy phenomena. Some of the past models cannot account for the often-reported phenomena of overconstancy. The primary virtues of the Transformation Theory presented at the end of this chapter is that it is comprehensive, can make precise quantitative predictions concerning size judgments, and links the size-constancy literature to the literature employing direct estimation of distance and area reported in Chapter 5.

7

The Metrics of Visual Space: Multidimensional Approaches to Space Perception

The previous chapters should give a sense of how venerable and vast the space perception literature is—venerable because its roots can be traced back to the beginnings of scientific psychology and beyond and vast because of the sheer bulk of intellectual effort and empirical research directed at the problem. Having said this, I think it is also fitting to make a few critical comments about the deficiencies of most of this work, particularly if one's goal is to discover the geometry or geometries of visual space.

First and foremost, the great majority of empirical research on space perception is unidimensional. Some studies look at size and distance judgments in response to frontally oriented targets, while others look at size and distance judgments for flat targets oriented in-depth. However, few researchers have focused on size and distance judgments for frontal and flat targets simultaneously within a single study. Research on targets oriented between these two extremes is rare indeed.

If one wishes to discover the geometry of visual space, the unidimensional character of this research is disappointing. Our visual perceptions of the world have at least three dimensions; thus, the geometry of visual space under a given set of conditions must be defined over at least three dimensions as well. Any less could not fully capture the richness of our experience.

For example, based on unidimensional work alone, one cannot determine whether frontal targets are somehow perceived differently than flat targets, nor how perception changes as target location changes from one point in space to another. The idea that such variations might make a difference is not far fetched. Frontal and in-depth judgments may depend on somewhat different mechanisms and the visual system might use different cues at different locations in space. For example, convergence and accommodation are most useful within two meters from the observer; outside of that range, the visual system depends more heavily on monocular cues (Cutting & Vishton, 1995; Liebowitz, Shina, & Hennessy, 1972).

In addition, the geometry of a space concerns more that distance relations. Area, volume, and angle are also important geometric properties. The perception of angles, in particular, is especially fundamental when considering the geometric character of visual space, but studies that examine angle perception as a function of stimulus conditions, angle location, and angle orientation are few and far between. Studies on the perception of large-scale angles under natural viewing conditions are virtually nonexistent.

The present chapter concerns those rare studies that take a multidimensional approach to space perception. In particular, I will discuss in some detail two of my own studies that I believe are particularly noteworthy in this regard. These studies look at spatial judgments in two and three dimensions, and data from these studies are rich enough to make it possible to model the structure of visual space. Following this discussion, the remainder of the chapter will consider research studies by other authors that take multi-dimensional approaches to space perception of their own.

The Metric of Visual Space

Wagner (1982, 1985) looked at the effects of target location and orientation on distance and angle judgments using four judgment methods. The experiment took place outdoors in a large, flat, grassy field on a series of 16 sunny (but hot) summer days. There were plenty of textural cues to depth, but few known-size cues.

Locations in the field were delineated by a set of ten randomly placed stakes. Observers used magnitude and category estimation to judge the distance between pairs of stakes in the field. Observers made similar judgments for the angles formed by triplets of stakes in the field. Here, one stake served as the vertex and the other two stakes defined the legs of the angle. Physically, distances ranged from 7 m to 72 m and angles ranged from 1° to 179°.

In addition, observers were given a sheet of paper and a set of pins with letters attached that corresponded to each stake in the field. Observers stuck pins in the paper to create a map that described their perceptions of the stake layout. I subsequently determined distance and angle judgments by reading them off of the map.

Finally, in the perceptual matching phase, observers were given a set of 19 cards with the angles between 0° and 180° in 10° increments drawn on them. The observer was asked to match angles formed by stakes in the field to the angle drawn on a card most closely equal to it.

What I found. As noted in Chapter 5, length and area judgments generally fit a power function very well. The first step of the analysis was to fit power functions to each observer's data for each metric property. As Stevens (1975) would predict, magnitude estimation exponents (averaging .99 for distance estimation and .81 for angles) were always higher than category estimation exponents (averaging .90 for distance and .47 for angles). Because mapping constrains judgments to fit onto a Euclidean plane, exponents found with this method cannot deviate from one by much (averaging .96 for distance estimation and .97 for angles). Actually, the use of paper alone doesn't force the space to be Euclidean, but when you combine this with my decision to collect data by measuring distances and angles on the plane with rulers and protractors, it forces the judgments derived to take on a Euclidean character.

Perceptual matching yielded similar exponents to magnitude estimation (averaging .82). This is a little surprising because perceptual matching would appear to be more similar to category estimation that magnitude estimation because each angle is assigned to one of 19 categories. Perhaps the large number of categories changed the character of the task to allow observer's to make fine distinctions similar to magnitude estimation. Note that, distance estimation exponents generally were consistent with those reported in Chapter 5. The exponent for distance estimation was close to one both here and in the meta-analysis reported earlier.

To perform more detailed analyses, I needed to describe the position of individual stimuli. Chapter 4 describes a coordinate system for visual space that attempted to describe distance judgments in a natural way consistent with previous empirical work. For distance judgments, stimulus location was defined in terms of the distance from the observer to the nearest stake, R, the angular direction to the nearer stake relative to the observer (the polar angle), θ, and the orientation of the point with respect to the observer's frontal plane, ϕ, which ranged from $0°$ (frontal—with the farther point to the observer's right), to $90°$ (in-depth), to $180°$ (frontal—with the farther point to the observer's left). For angle judgments, orientation (ϕ) was defined by the ray that bisected each angle. For orientations of $0°$, the angle was pointing to the observers right, $90°$ meant the angle was pointing away from the observer, $180°$ (or $-180°$) meant that the angle was pointing to the observer's left, and $-90°$ meant that the angle directly facing the observer. (See Figures 4.1 and 4.2 for a more detailed account of the variables analyzed.)

To estimate the affects of each of these variables on distance and angle estimates, judgments were divided by the corresponding physical distance or angle and plotted as a function of R, θ, and ϕ. This analysis shows if the relative sizes of judgments at certain locations are larger than equivalent stimuli at other locations.

I analyzed the affects of each of these variables across each combination of observer, judgment method, and metric property using both analysis methods. The only variable that consistently influenced judgments was stimulus orientation (ϕ). For distance judgments, distances seen in-depth (one stake behind the other from the observer's point of view) appeared to be perceptually compressed relative to frontally oriented stimuli (one stake beside the other). Although I will speak in terms of a compression of the in-depth dimension of visual space, an equivalent formulation would be describing the effect as an expansion of visual space in the frontal dimension.

Figure 7.1 shows two graphs depicting distance judgments divided by the physical distance corresponding to each judgment as a function of stimulus orientation for two observers. The top figure represents the strongest degree of relative compression of the in-depth dimension while the bottom figure shows the weak compression observed. The basic pattern seen is typical of all observers and judgment methods. On the average, the same physical distance is seen as slightly more than twice as large in frontal orientations as it is in in-depth orientations for all judgment methods.

The extent of this illusion is dramatic. Contrast the 100% change in perceived size as a function of orientation to other commonly reported illusions. For example, in the moon illusion, the horizon moon is typically reported to be 30% larger than the zenith moon (Baird, Wagner, & Fuld, 1990). In the Müller-Lyer illusion, lines flanked by inward pointing arrows are normally seen as 10% to 30% larger than lines flanked by outward pointing arrows (Goldstein, 2002). In addition, this stimulus orientation illusion occurs under the most natural and generally experienced sort of conditions.

Angle judgments were also affected by stimulus orientation. Figure 7.2 shows a typical graph for a single subject of angle judgments divided by the corresponding physical angle size as a function of stimulus orientation. This graph (which reflects a pattern which occurred for all subjects and all judgment methods) shows that angles are seen as relatively larger when they are facing either directly toward or directly away from the observer ($\phi = 90°$ or $\phi = -90°$) and relatively smaller when the angle was facing either to the observers left or right ($\phi = 180°$, $0°$, or $-180°$).

The angle data is also consistent with the idea that visual space is perceptually contracted in the in-depth dimension relative to the frontal dimension as compared to physical space. The legs of an angle facing either toward or away from the observer are perceptually "squeezed apart" in the in-depth dimension causing the legs of the angle to expand perceptually. The legs of an angle facing either to the left or right of the observer are squeezed together causing the angle to be seen as smaller.

This perceptual compression of the in-depth dimension can be seen directly in the mapping data. Figure 7.3 shows a typical map produced by observers. The squares represent the physical location of the stakes in the field while the map made by the observer is shown using diamonds. To make the two plots comparable, the left-right (x) dimensions of the two plots have been scaled such that the minimum and maximum x-coordinates of each plot are aligned with each other. In physical terms, the stakes were actually widely scattered along the in-depth dimension, but the maps observers produced showed much less variation in this dimension. Once again, the in-depth dimension appears to be perceptually compressed relative to the frontal dimension as compared to physical space.

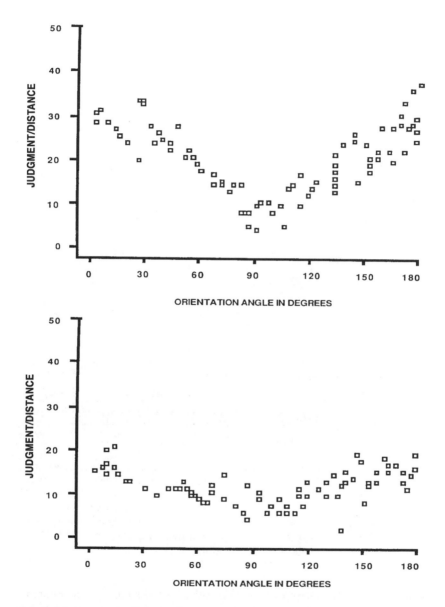

Figure 7.1. Two examples of the ratio of judgment to distance as a function of stimulus orientation for distance estimation. The top panel shows one of the greatest degrees of relative compression of in-depth judgments, while the bottom panel shows one of the smallest degrees of compression. Each graph shows data from one observer and one judgment method (magnitude estimation). Based on a figure from Wagner, 1985. Copyright 1985 by the Psychonomic Society, Inc. Reprinted by permission.

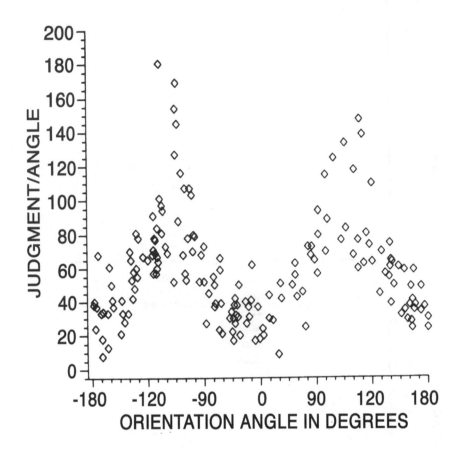

Figure 7.2. A typical example of the ratio of judgment to physical angle as a function of stimulus orientation for angle estimation. Here 0° indicates that the angle is facing toward the observer's right; 180° and −180° indicate it is facing toward the observer's left; -90° indicates it is facing toward the observer, and 90 indicates it is facing away from the observer. While the data are from one observer using one judgment method (mapping), they are typical of all observers and methods. Based on a figure from Wagner, 1985. Copyright 1985 by the Psychonomic Society, Inc. Reprinted by permission.

Modeling metric functions. In Chapter 3, we noted that past researchers have proposed a variety of models for visual space including Euclidean, hyperbolic, and spherical geometries. These researchers generally employed indirect methods to support their synthetic theories. The foregoing data allows for a more direct approach to the problem. Candidate metric functions for distance (including those based on the best know synthetic geometries) can be applied to the data to determine how well each function fits the data.

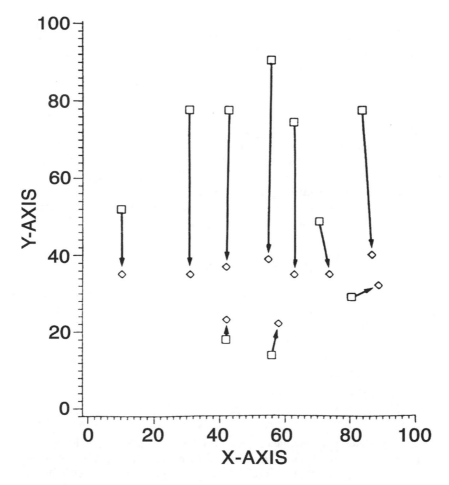

Figure 7.3. A typical example of a direct comparison of physical and estimated stake location using the mapping technique. Squares represent the physical locations of the stakes. Diamonds represent the judged location. The arrows display the correspondence between points on the two maps. The data are from one observer, but are typical of all observers. Based on a figure from Wagner, 1985. Copyright 1985 by the Psychonomic Society, Inc. Reprinted by permission.

Four models will be discussed here. (I actually looked at 12 candidate functions, but most of them didn't fit very well.) The first two models concern Affine transformations on Euclidean space. The third and forth models examine spherical and hyperbolic metric functions.

The Affine contraction model. Visual space appears to be compressed in the in-depth dimension relative to the frontal dimension compared to physical space.

One simple model for this phenomenon is to think of visual space as representing an Affine transformation of physical layout. That is, if the observer is placed at the origin of a Cartesian coordinate plane with the x-axis corresponding to the observer's frontal dimension and the y-axis corresponding to the observer's in-depth dimension, this model would propose that frontal dimension is accurately perceived, that is x' = x (where x' is perceived distance while x is physical distance along the frontal dimension), while the in-depth dimension is perceptually compressed, that is y' = cy (where y' is the perceived distance along the in-depth dimension, y is the corresponding physical distance, and c is a parameter reflecting the degree of compression). After this Affine transformation, the geometry of visual space is still Euclidean, but distances and angles will be systematically distorted relative to physical space.

Because the geometry is still Euclidean, the perceived distance (J) between two points P_1 and P_2 can be expressed by Equation 7.1

$$J = \sqrt{(x_1'-x_2')^2+(y_1'-y_2')^2}. \tag{7.1}$$

Here (x_1',y_1') and (x_x',y_x') correspond to the coordinates of P_1 and P_2 in visual space. This equation can be re-expressed in physical terms by substituting the above transformations into the equation

$$J = \sqrt{(x_1-x_2)^2+(cy_1-cy_2)^2}$$

$$J = \sqrt{(x_1-x_2)^2+c^2(y_1-y_2)^2}. \tag{7.2}$$

where (x_1,y_1) and (x_2,y_x) are the physical coordinates of points P_1 and P_2.

To make this model more general and to provide a stronger test if visual space really is Euclidean, this model can be re-expressed as an Affinely transformed Minkowski metric:

$$J = \sqrt[R]{|x_1-x_2|^R+(c\,|y_1-y_2|)^R}. \tag{7.3}$$

where R is the Minkowski parameter. When the Minkowski parameter is two, the space is Euclidean.

Finally, as seen in Chapter 5, distance judgments are well-fit by a power function. The power function scaling constant and exponent take into account changes in scale between visual space and physical space, the affects of experimental conditions, and the affects of judgment method. To take this into account, Equation 7.3 can be rewritten in an even more general form

$$J = k\left\{\sqrt[R]{|x_1-x_2|^R+(c\,|y_1-y_2|)^R}\right\}^n. \tag{7.4}$$

Table 7.1 shows the best fitting parameters and correlation coefficients between the best fitting model and the data when applied to the distance judgments. The first column of r values represent the model's fit when a single function is applied to all observers combined, while the second column of r values represent the model's fit when parameters are estimated separately for each observer.

Overall, the fits of the model are quite good. Statistical tests were preformed to determine if each of the model parameters is statistically necessary. For example, the exponent, n, differs significantly from 1.0 only for category estimation. More interestingly, setting the Minkowski parameter to 2.0, the Euclidean value, results in no statistically significant reduction in variance accounted for. The coefficient of determination is identical to that reported in the table to three decimal points. Thus, the data is perfectly consistent with a Euclidean model for visual space.

The contraction parameter, c, however, is statistically and conceptually important. Setting the contraction parameter to 1.0 results in large and highly significant reductions in variance accounted for. This parameter, which is relatively consistent across judgment methods, indicates that physical distances oriented in-depth are seen as about half as large as when the same physical distance is frontally oriented. (The average compression parameter across the three methods was .47.)

Table 7.1

Best-Fitting Parameter Values and Correlation Coefficients for Fits of the Affine Contraction Model to Distance Judgments Employing Magnitude Estimation (ME), Category Estimation (CE), and Mapping (MA). The First Column of r Values are Based on a Single Fit of the Model to the Combined Data, while the Second Column of r Values are Based on Separate Fits of the Model Parameters to Each Observer's Data

Method			*Parameter*			
	k	n	R	c	r(single)	r(individual)
ME	26.10	0.97	2.22	0.49	0.861	0.932
CE	3.32	0.91	1.67	0.53	0.899	0.981
MA	5.93	0.95	1.65	0.38	0.891	0.964

The vector contraction model. While the Affine contraction model fits the data quite well, one aspect of it seems unrealistic. Any eye, head, or body reorientation would change would change the way Cartesian coordinates are assigned and thus should change perceived size. An example may make this clearer. Figure 7.4 shows two stake pairs that have the same orientation with respect to x-axis. One stake pair is directly in front of the observer while the other is somewhat off to the right. For the first pair, one stake is behind the other with respect to the observer; however, if the observer merely turns his or her head to look at the second pair of stakes, they would appear to be somewhat frontally oriented. The Affine contraction model would predict that both of these distances would undergo the same degree of compression and be perceived as the same length. What is more, the degree of compression should lessen with a mere turn of the head. It seems likely that these two stimuli should be perceived differently because one is truly oriented in-depth relative to the observer and the other is not.

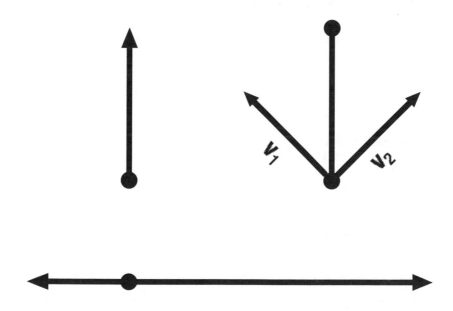

Figure 7.4. Diagram displaying two pairs of stakes with different orientations with respect to the observer but identical orientations with respect to the x-axis. The vectors v_1 and v_2 are the components into which the distance defined by the pair of stakes on the right are divided in the vector contraction model. Based on a figure from Wagner, 1985. Copyright 1985 by the Psychonomic Society, Inc. Reprinted by permission.

A second model refines the Affine contraction model to correct for this problem. According to this model, the distance between two points may be thought of as being a vector originating at the nearer point which has a frontally-oriented component, V_1, and an in-depth oriented component, V_2. The length of these component vectors will depend on the stimulus orientation (ϕ) of the extent with respect to the observer. That is,

$$V_1 = D\cos\phi$$
$$V_2 = D\sin\phi \qquad (7.5)$$

Where D is the Euclidean distance between the two points. In the vector contraction model, the perceived size of the frontal component of visual space is unchanged compared to physical space, $V_1' = V_1$, but the perceived in-depth component of the space is compressed compared to physical space, $V_2' = cV_2$. Where c is a parameter expressing the degree of compression. Perceived distance, J, is the norm (or length) of this two-component visual vector. Mathematically, this can be expressed as:

$$J = \sqrt{V_1'^2 + V_2'^2}$$

$$J = \sqrt{V_1^2 + (cV_2)^2}$$

$$J = \sqrt{(D\cos\phi)^2 + (cD\sin\phi)^2}$$

$$J = D\sqrt{(\cos\phi)^2 + (c\sin\phi)^2}. \qquad (7.6)$$

Generalizing this equation to the form of a power function yields:

$$J = k\left\{D\sqrt{(\cos\phi)^2 + (c\sin\phi)^2}\right\}^n. \qquad (7.7)$$

Table 7.2 shows the best fitting parameters and correlation coefficients between the best fitting model and the data when applied to the distance judgments. As before, the first column of r values represent the model's fit when a single function is applied to all observers combined, while the second column of r values represent the model's fit when parameters are estimated separately for each observer.

Table 7.2

Best-Fitting Parameter Values and Correlation Coefficients for Fits of the Vector Contraction Model to Distance Judgments Employing Magnitude Estimation (ME), Category Estimation (CE), and Mapping (MA). The First Column of r Values are Based on a Single Fit of the Model to the Combined Data, while the Second Column of r Values are Based on Separate Fits of the Model Parameters to Each Observer's Data

	Parameter				
Method	k	n	c	r(single)	r(individual)
ME	27.60	0.93	0.46	0.868	0.938
CE	0.33	0.88	0.49	0.913	0.936
MA	6.08	0.93	0.40	0.896	0.967

This model accounts for a slightly higher percentage of the variance in the data than the Affine contraction model. Setting either the exponent or the compression parameter to 1.0 both lead to statistically significant declines in the percentage of variance accounted for. However, the exponent is close to 1.0, while the average compression parameter is .45. This indicates once again that a frontally oriented extent seems more than twice as large as the same physical extent oriented in-depth. This implies an impressive degree of compression in the in-depth dimension of visual space.

The vector contraction model is similar in spirit to Yamazaki (1987) who believed that visual space is a composite of a connected set of Affine-transformed local regions whose degree and direction of compression can vary with position in space.

The spherical geometry model. As discussed in Chapter 2, a common view among many philosophers and phenomenologists is that visual space is best described as a spherical geometry (Angell, 1974; Ben-Zeev, 1989, 1990; Daniel, 1974; French, 1987; Husserl, 1910; Reid, 1764/1813; Scheerer, 1986). According to this model, the distance between two points is the length of the arc of a great circle passing through the two points. If the observer is at the center of the circle, and all past spherical models make this assumption, the length of arc is proportional to the visual angle between the two points.

Wagner (1982, 1985) derived a formula that allows one to determine the visual angle (ε) in terms of the distance to the nearest point of the visual extent (R), the physical distance between the two points that define the extent (D), the height of the observer (h), and stimulus orientation with respect to the observer (ϕ). The formula is

$$\varepsilon = \text{Arccos} \left[\frac{h^2 + R^2 + RD \sin\phi}{\sqrt{R^2+h^2}\sqrt{R^2+D^2+h^2+2RD \sin\phi}} \right]. \tag{7.8}$$

The complete spherical model then takes a power function form, namely

$$J = k(\varepsilon)^n \tag{7.9}$$

Unfortunately, this model does not work as well as the previous two. Table 7.3 shows best fitting parameter values and correlation coefficients between the best fitting model and the data for the spherical model. Note that the estimated height of the observer is much too high. Setting h to a more reasonable value of 2.0 m results in large decrements in variance accounted for. Because of this failure and because the correlation coefficients are smaller, the spherical model can be largely rejected. I only say largely rejected, because the height parameter can be reinterpreted in a way that might make it more acceptable. When one looks from a great distance at a very localized section of a very large sphere, that little section appears almost flat and Euclidean. Mathematicians say that geometries of constant curvature are locally Euclidean. What the height parameter may really be saying is that the curvature of visual space is very close to zero, the Euclidean value. In this sense, the "spherical model" generates a result that is consistent with the Affine contraction model, namely that visual space under these conditions behaves in a very Euclidean fashion.

Table 7.3

Best-Fitting Parameter Values and Correlation Coefficients for Fits of the Spherical Geometry Model to Distance Judgments Employing Magnitude Estimation (ME), Category Estimation (CE), and Mapping (MA).

	Parameter			
Method	k	n	h	r
ME	2203.5	1.00	108.5m	0.777
CE	17.4	0.91	92.5m	0.843
MA	276.2	0.92	53.0m	0.812

The hyperbolic geometry model. As seen in Chapter 3, many psychologists have suggested that visual space can best be described as a hyperbolic geometry (Aczel, Boros, Heller, & Ng, 1999; Blank, 1953, 1957, 1958, 1959; Heller, 1997a, 1997b; Indow, 1967, 1974, 1990, 1995; Luneburg, 1947, 1948, 1950). In the hyperbolic model, distance between points can be expressed in terms of physical coordinates with a mapping function. Distance judgments can be predicted based on Indow's (1974, 1990, 1995) hyperbolic geometry mapping function, which when put in a power function form for modeling purposes is

$$J = k \left\{ T \ \text{arcsinh}\left[\sqrt{\left(\frac{1+K(q_1)}{4}\right)\left(\frac{1+K(q_2)}{r}\right)}\left(\frac{1}{T}\right)D \right] \right\}^n . \tag{7.10}$$

where $q_i = 2 \exp(-R_i)$ and $T = 2/\text{sqr}(-K)$, J is the observer's judgment, R_i is the distance from the observer to the points, D is the physical distance between the points that define the visual extent, and K is the Riemannian curvature of the space. If $K > 0$, the space is spherical, if $K < 0$ the space is hyperbolic and if $K = 0$ the space is Euclidean. In terms of computer modeling, Equation 7.10 really only works in the hyperbolic case because values of K greater than or equal to zero result in either imaginary square roots or division by zero.

For this reason, attempts at fitting the hyperbolic model to visual space proved to be frustrating. The curvature parameter inevitably approached zero at which point the curve fitting routine "crashed." In general, the hyperbolic model was not supported. Once again, the fact that the curvature parameter inevitably approached zero can be seen as support for a Euclidean (or perhaps mildly spherical) model of visual space.

Applying the Affine contraction model to the angle data. As seen in Figure 7.2, stimulus orientation systematically affected angle judgments as well as distance judgments. These judgments are also consistent with the idea that visual space might be compressed in the in-depth dimension relative to physical space. For distance judgments, this conception was formalized in the Affine contraction model. Fortunately, it is possible to apply this same model to the angle data. For any Riemannian geometry (including an Affine transformed Euclidean one), an angle is related to its component vectors by the following formula:

$$\text{Cos}(A') = (v' \cdot w')/(\|v'\| \|w'\|) \tag{7.11}$$

For the Affine contraction model, the power function form of the model is

$$A' = k \left\{ \text{arccos}\left| \left[\frac{(v' \cdot w')}{(\|v'\| \|w'\|)} \right] \right| \right\}^n . \tag{7.12}$$

where

$$\left(v'.w'\right) = v_1 w_1 + c^2 v_2 w_2$$

$$\|v'\| = \sqrt{v_1^2 + (cv_2)^2}$$

$$\|w'\| = \sqrt{w_1^2 + (cw_2)^2}.$$

Here, k is a scaling factor, n is an exponent, v_1 and v_2 are the x- and y-components of the vector v that forms one of the legs of the angle, w_1 and w_2 are the x- and y-components of the vector w that forms the other leg of the angle, and c is the contraction parameter of the Affine contraction model.

Table 7.4 shows the best-fitting parameter values and correlation coefficients between the best fitting model and the data when applied to the four sets of angle data. The exponent and contraction parameter are both significantly smaller than 1.0, because setting either to parameter to 1.0 leads to large decrements in variance accounted for. Note that the contraction parameters (which average .48) are very consistent with those reported for distance estimates. In fact, fixing the contraction parameter to the values reported earlier does not lead to a significant decline in variance accounted for. In other words, the Affine contraction model data from two different sets of judgments are internally consistent, and both sets of data support a strong compression in the in-depth dimension of visual space relative to physical space.

Table 7.4

Best-Fitting Parameter Values and Correlation Coefficients for Fits of the Affine Contraction Model to Angle Judgments Employing Magnitude Estimation (ME), Category Estimation (CE), Mapping (MA), and Perceptual Matching (PM).

	Parameter			
Method	k	n	c	r
ME	71.90	0.79	0.63	0.837
CE	3.31	0.46	0.52	0.838
MA	55.30	0.86	0.39	0.851
PM	5.60	0.72	0.39	0.864

Applying the vector contraction model to the angle data. The same formula from Riemannian geometry makes it possible to apply the vector contraction model to the angle data. The power function form of this model is

$$A' = k \left\{ \arccos \left[\frac{(v'.w')}{[(\|v'\| \ \|w'\|)]} \right] \right\}^n.$$
(7.13)

where

$$v'.w' = \left[D(v)\cos\phi(v) \right] \left[D(w)\cos\phi(w) \right] + \left[cD(v)\sin\phi(v) \right] \left[cD(w)\sin\phi(w) \right]$$

$$\|v'\| = \sqrt{ \left[D(v)\cos\phi(v) \right]^2 + \left[cD(v)\sin\phi(v) \right]^2 }$$

$$\|w'\| = \sqrt{ \left[D(w)\cos\phi(w) \right]^2 + \left[cD(w)\sin\phi(w) \right]^2 }.$$

Here, A' is the perceived angle, k is a scaling factor, n is the exponent, c is the contraction parameter, v' and w' are the two perceived vectors making up the two legs of the vector, D(v) and D(w) are the physical lengths of the two legs of the angle, $\phi(v)$ and $\phi(w)$ are the orientations of the two legs with respect to the observer.

Table 7.5 shows the best-fitting parameter values and correlation coefficients between the best fitting model and the data when applied to all four sets of angle judgments. Note that the vector contraction model fits the data either as well or better than the Affine contraction model. Once again, the model shows about same degree of compression in the in-depth component of visual space as with the distance data. (The contraction parameter averages .45.) Once again, the vector contraction model presents an internally consistent view of visual space that indicates a large degree of compression in the in-depth dimension of visual space.

Table 7.5

Best-Fitting Parameter Values and Correlation Coefficients for Fits of the Vector Contraction Model to Angle Judgments Employing Magnitude Estimation (ME), Category Estimation (CE), Mapping (MA), and Perceptual Matching (PM).

	Parameter			
Method	k	n	c	r
ME	71.40	0.81	0.65	0.836
CE	3.30	0.45	0.47	0.848
MA	56.00	0.85	0.38	0.853
PM	5.90	0.67	0.30	0.891

The Metrics of Visual Space in Three Dimensions

Like any study, the foregoing one had a number of limitations. In particular, the stimuli were bound to the ground; whereas, normal vision is three-dimensional in character. Objects have heights as well as widths and depths. In addition, the work might imply that it has somehow specified *the* geometry of visual space. Yet, one of the most enduring themes of this book is that there is no single geometry that describes visual space, but its geometric character actually varies as a function of experimental conditions.

The second study I would like to talk about (Wagner & Feldman, 1989), which has never been published outside of a conference proceedings paper until now, is a follow up to Wagner (1982, 1985). This study extended the first one by responding to the objections just raised. First of all, stimulus locations varied across three dimensions instead of only two. Secondly, the judgments were carried out under both well-lit, full-cue conditions and darkened, reduced-cue conditions.

The experiment took place in a large gymnasium that was almost totally dark when the lights were turned off. The stimuli were 10 four-watt light bulbs placed on top of unpainted wooden dowels (2.7 cm in diameter). To minimize light from reflecting off the dowels, walls, and floors, the lights were shielded by film canisters on all sides except the one pointed toward the observer. Lights were left off unless they formed part of the stimulus currently being judged on a given trial. To allow the experimenter to point out specific lights to the observer, lights could be made to temporarily blink. The position of each light was randomly determined according to a uniform distribution within the testing space that was 15m wide by 30m deep by 5m tall. The observer sat on a chair at the edge of the testing area and was allowed free head and body movement provided he or she did not attempt to leave the chair. The floor was covered with a vinyl covering with simulated wood grain texture that provided ample textual cues to depth when the room light was on but no definable reference points. Two lights (1m apart) were placed on top of 1.2m high dowels 2m off to the observer's right to serves as a reference standard. Figure 7.5 shows a diagram of the experimental layout.

Six undergraduates participated in all three phases of the study during each experimental session. Each observer participated in a total of four sessions, two in the light and two in the dark. In the first phase of each session, subjects were asked to make magnitude estimates of the distance between each possible pair of stimuli where the distance between the two standard lights served as a reference standard and was assigned a value of 10 units. In the second phase, observers were asked to judge the size of angles formed by one light that served as the vertex and two other lights that defined the legs of the angle. Observers were given a set of cards on which angles varying from 0° to 180° in 10° increments were drawn.

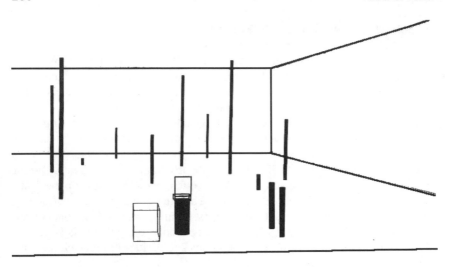

Figure 7.5. Schematic diagram displaying the experimental layout for Wagner and Feldman's experiment. The observer sat in the chair seen in the foreground and judged distance and angles formed by lights atop randomly place wooden dowels. Distance judgments were made relative to a standard defined by lights atop two wooden dowels placed to the observer's right.

The observer's task was to find the angle on the cards that most closely matched the angle formed by the specified lights. In the third phase of the session, observers were asked to magnitude estimates of the distance from themselves to each of the lights using the same reference standard as in the first phase.

Data analysis. Overall, observers were better at making their judgments in the light than in the dark. The median power function exponent for the egocentric distance judgments was .99 in the light but only .70 in the dark. The former exponent is identical to the average egocentric distance exponent for all data combined of .99 reported in Chapter 5. It is only slightly smaller that the average exponent of 1.06 for egocentric judgments using magnitude estimation reported in that chapter. The median exponent for angle judgments was .87 in the light but only .61 in the dark. Observers were very poor at making exocentric distance judgments regardless of the stimulus condition; the median exponent in the light was .67, while in the dark it was .61. This is much lower than the average exponent of .95 for exocentric distance judgments based on all data combined or of 1.01 for exocentric distance judgments using magnitude estimation reported in Chapter 5. Of course, the typical exocentric distance estimation task involves stimuli directly attached to the ground or table. In the current experiment, stimuli were often widely separated from the ground, making localization more difficult.

More detailed analyses require looking at variations in judgment ability corresponding to the position of the stimulus in space. Given that the stimuli are now three dimensional, there are a few more dimensions of the stimulus to look at to see if they influence the judgments people give. We can look at judgments of distance as a function of the direction the nearest point lay from the observer (both in-depth vs. frontal and horizontal vs. vertical), the distance the nearest point lay from the observer, and the orientation of the points with respect to the observer's line of sight toward the nearest point (both to the left and right of this line of sight and above and below it). A similar coordinatization was made with respect to the vertex of the angle where the orientation of the angle was defined by the direction of its bisector. In other words, a generalization of the "natural coordinates" described in Chapter 4 was used to break down the data.

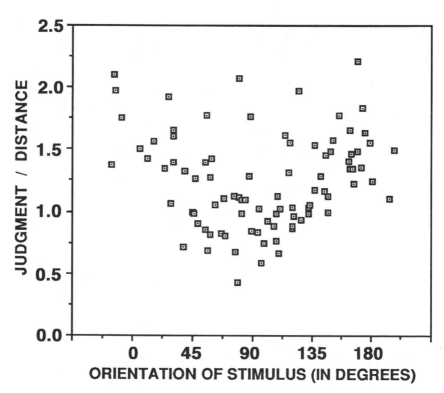

Figure 7.6. The ratio of distance judgments to physical distance as a function of stimulus orientation (in degrees) relative to the observer's line of sight under full-cue conditions. Data are from a single observer, but are typical of other observers.

DARK

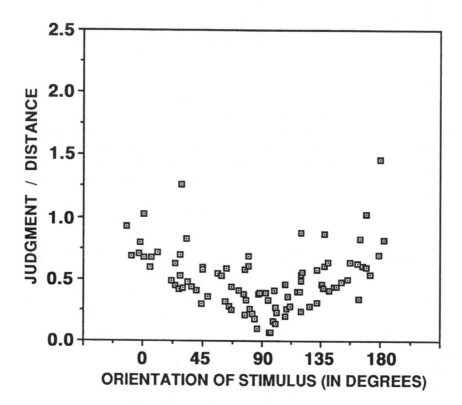

Figure 7.7. The ratio of distance judgments to physical distance as a function of stimulus orientation (in degrees) relative to the observer's line of sight under reduced-cue conditions. Data are from a single observer, but are typical of other observers.

Once again, the only variable that influenced judgments was the orientation of the stimuli. In particular, the in-depth vs. frontal orientation produced a very consistent pattern of results for both distance and angle judgments. (The horizontal–vertical orientation of the stimulus produced no consistent pattern of results.) What is more, the pattern depended on the cue conditions—whether it was light or dark in the room.

Figure 7.6 shows a typical example of the pattern seen for all subjects for egocentric distance judgments under full-cue conditions. The figure shows the ratio of judged distance to physical distance for each judgment as a function of the orientation of the stimulus with respect to the observer's line of sight. Note that observers tend to estimate the size of the stimulus to be relatively larger at frontal orientations of 0° and 180° than at the in-depth orientation of 90°. The average relative size of in-depth oriented distance judgments is 53% of the average relative size of frontally oriented distance judgments. As in Wagner (1985), there appears to be a strong compression in the in-depth dimension of visual space. Once again, the same physical stimulus appears to be about half as large when oriented in-depth as when oriented frontally.

This compression of the in-depth dimension of visual space is even more pronounced for exocentric distances judgments made under reduced-cue, darkened conditions. Figure 7.7 shows a typical example of the pattern seen for all subjects. In the dark, in-depth oriented stimuli are only seen as 43% as large as frontally oriented stimuli on the average.

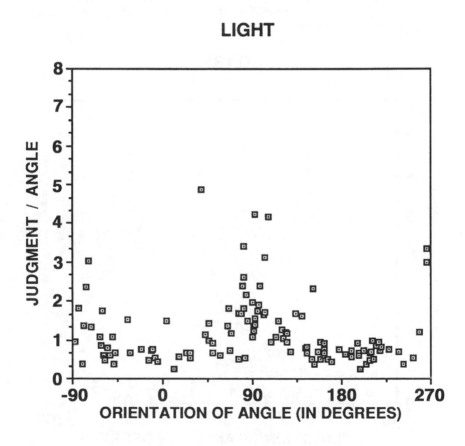

Figure 7.8. The ratio of angle judgments to physical angle as a function of stimulus orientation (in degrees) relative to the observer's line of sight under full-cue conditions. Data are from a single observer, but are typical of other observers.

Angle judgments also produce a pattern similar to that seen in Wagner (1985). Figure 7.8 shows a typical example of the pattern seen for all subjects under full-cue conditions. The figure shows the ratio of angle judgments to the physical size of the angle as a function of stimulus orientation of the angle with respect to the observer's line of sight. Note that the observers tend to estimate the size of the angle to be relatively larger when the angle is facing either directly toward (-90° or 270°) or directly away from (90°) the observer than when angles face either to the right or left (0° or 180°) respectively.   On the average, angles facing toward the right or left are seen as 50% as large as those facing directly toward or away from the observer when seen in the light. Once again, this is consistent with the idea that visual space is compressed in the in-depth dimension. Angles facing directly toward or away from the observer are expanded by this compression, while those facing to the left or right are perceptually squeezed by the same compression.

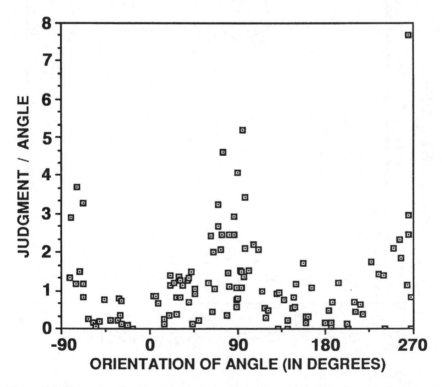

Figure 7.9. The ratio of angle judgments to physical angle as a function of stimulus orientation (in degrees) relative to the observer's line of sight under reduced-cue conditions. Data are from a single observer, but are typical of other observers.

Reduced-cue, darkened conditions magnify this effect. Figure 7.9 shows a typical example of the pattern seen for all observers. In the dark, angles facing toward the side (right or left) are seen as only 35% as large as those facing either directly toward or directly away from the observer. Thus, both the distance and angle judgments indicated that reduced-cue conditions increase the compression of visual space in the in-depth dimension as compared to physical space.

Modeling the metric of visual space in three dimensions. Three models were applied to the data: the hyperbolic geometry model, the Affine contraction model, and the vector contraction model. As before, the hyperbolic model produced very poor fits to the data. Once again, the curvature constant, K, always approached the Euclidean value of zero at which point the curve fitting routine "crashed."

To take into account the three-dimensional character of the stimuli, the Affine contraction model was generalized to include a third dimension (z). For modeling purposes, this general model was put in the form of a Minkowski metric as

$$J = \sqrt[R]{|x_1 - x_2|^R + c_1|y_1 - y_2|^R + c_2|z_1 - z_2|^R}. \tag{7.14}$$

To take into account the fact that magnitude estimates take the form of a power function, the final form of the Affine contraction model used in curve fitting was

$$J = k \left\{ \sqrt[R]{|x_1 - x_2|^R + c_1|y_1 - y_2|^R + c_2|z_1 - z_2|^R} \right\}^n. \tag{7.15}$$

where k is a scaling constant, n is the exponent, c_1 in the degree of compression in the in-depth dimension, and c_2 is the degree of compression–expansion in the horizontal dimension.

Once again, the model fit the data quite well. Table 7.6 shows best fitting parameter values for the model along with the average standard error of the estimate for the overall fit of the Affine contraction model to the data. For distance judgments collected under full-cue conditions, the in-depth compression parameter, c_1, had a value of about .52; which is very close to the contraction parameter value of .49 found in the previously discussed study with magnitude estimation. Setting the Minkowski parameter to the Euclidean value of 2.0 did not lead to significant decline in the variance accounted for. According to the horizontal–vertical illusion, a vertically oriented stimulus should seem slightly larger than a horizontally oriented stimulus of the same physical size (cf. Masin & Vidotto, 1983; von Collani, 1985). However, in the present study, the horizontal compression parameter, c_2, proved to be quite variable across subjects, and setting the parameter to 1.0 did not significantly reduce the variance accounted for. In general, compression in-depth appears to have a much stronger and reliable affect on perceived size than does horizontal vs. vertical orientation in the frontal plane.

In the dark, the Affine contraction model showed an even stronger affect of in-depth vs. frontal orientation on distance judgments. Table 7.6 also shows the best fitting parameter values for the Affine contraction model on distance judgments under reduced-cue conditions. Once again, setting either the Minkowski parameter to the Euclidean value of 2.0 or the horizontal-vertical parameter value to 1.0 did not significantly change the fit of the model. The in-depth contraction parameter, c_1, of .35 showed a much stronger degree of compression than in the light.

As in Wagner (1985), the Affine contraction model can also be applied to the angle estimation data. As before, the power function formulation of the Affine contraction model is

$$A' = k \left\{ \arccos \left[\frac{(v'.w')}{(\|v'\| \ \|w'\|)} \right] \right\}^n . \tag{7.16}$$

where

$$(v'.w') = v_1 w_1 + c_1^2 v_2 w_2 + c_2^2 v_3 w_3$$

$$\|v'\| = \sqrt{v_1^2 + (c_1 v_2)^2 + (c_2 v_3)^2}$$

$$\|w'\| = \sqrt{w_1^2 + (c_1 w_2)^2 + (c_2 w_3)^2}$$

Table 7.6

Best-Fitting Parameter Values and Overall Standard Error of the Estimate for Fits of the Affine Contraction Model to Distance and Angle Judgments under Reduced and Full-Cue Conditions.

			Parameter			
Method	k	n	R	c_1	c_2	SE
Distance						
Light	15.40	0.805	1.684	0.520	0.948	0.527
Dark	14.04	0.893	1.848	0.349	1.512	0.569
Angle						
Light	0.846	1.062		0.617	0.987	0.455
Dark	5.393	0.829		0.322	1.249	0.510

Table 7.6 shows the best fitting parameters when applying this equation to the angle judgments under full-cue conditions. The in-depth contraction parameter value of .62 is somewhat consistent with the .52 value found with distance estimation.

Also as with distance estimation, reduced-cue conditions magnified this compression in-depth. Table 7.6 shows the best fitting parameters for the Affine contraction model for angle judgments made in the dark. Here, the in-depth contraction parameter value of .32 is very similar to the .35 value for distance estimates. Once again, the in-depth dimension is even more squeezed when judgments are made in the dark.

This makes sense because reduced-cue conditions should eliminate cues to depth, making objects in different depth planes seem closer to each other. Our attempt at eliminating cues to depth in the present experiment was not perfect because some light bounced off walls to give a shadowy impression of some beams in the room. In all likelihood, if depth cues were completely eliminated under more controlled conditions, all objects might appear to be at the same distance away, as in Gogel's (1965) specific distance tendency. Under these conditions, the contraction parameter of the Affine models would likely approach zero. In effect, complete reduction of cues might make visual stimuli appear to be projected on the surface of a sphere. Hence a more complete model of visual space might describe the geometry of the space as systematically varying with stimulus conditions along a dimension with Euclidean and spherical poles. Under the best of conditions, visual space is clearly Euclidean with relatively modest compression in-depth. As depth cues are eliminated, compression in-depth increases. In the limiting case, the compression is complete and visual space would be most akin to a two-dimensional spherical geometry, where the physical world is mapped on to a sphere with a radius corresponding to the default specified by an individual's specific distance tendency.

The vector contraction model in three dimensions. The vector contraction model can also be generalized from two to three dimensions and applied to the present data set. Figure 7.10 shows how a visual extent can be broken down into vector components in three dimensions. The distance is broken down into a frontal horizontally oriented component, V_1, an in-depth oriented component, V_2, and a vertically oriented component. In the three dimensional vector contraction model, the physical in-depth and horizontal components can each be compressed (or expanded) by constant amounts to yield visual in-depth and vertical components, V_2' and V_3', while the visual horizontal component V_1' is unchanged. Perceived distance (J) is the norm (or length) of this three-component visual vector. This may be written as

$$J = \sqrt{V_1'^2 + V_2'^2 + V_3'^2}$$

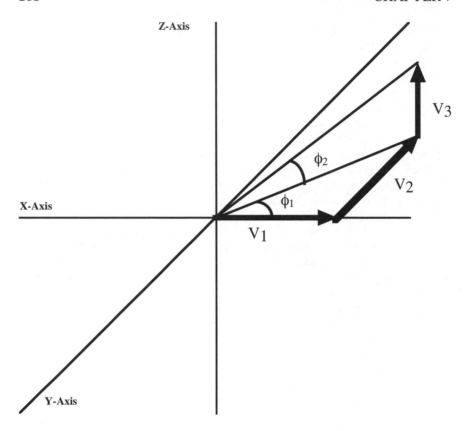

Figure 7.10. Diagram displaying how a distance can be broken into three vector components. The vectors v_1, v_2, and v_3 are the x-, y-, and z-components into which the distance is divided in the vector contraction model.

$$J = \sqrt{V_1^2 + (c_1 V_2)^2 + (c_2 V_3)^2}$$

where

$$V_1 = D^* \cos \phi_1$$

$$V_2 = D^* \sin \phi_1$$

$$V_3 = D \sin \phi_2$$

and

$$D^* = \sqrt{(x_1-x_2)^2 - (y_1-y_2)^2}.$$

Therefore,

$$J = \sqrt{(D^*\cos \phi_1)^2 + (c_1 D^* \sin \phi_1)^2 + (c_2 D \sin \phi_2)^2}. \qquad (7.17)$$

Here, D is the length of the stimulus, D^* is the projection of the stimulus onto the onto the x-y (median) plane, ϕ_1 is the orientation angle with respect to the frontal plane, and ϕ_2 is the orientation angle with respect to the median plane. (Note that ϕ_2 is defined slightly differently than in the data breakdown reported earlier in order to assure that the three visual vectors represent a complete orthogonal breakdown of the stimulus.) This equation can be generalized to the form of a power function

$$J = k\left\{ \sqrt{(D^*\cos \phi_1)^2 + (c_1 D^* \sin \phi_1)^2 + (c_2 D \sin \phi_2)^2} \right\}^n. \qquad (7.18)$$

Table 7.7 shows the best fitting parameter values and average standard errors of the estimate when this model is fit to the distance data under full-cue conditions. Once again, the in-depth contraction parameter of .61 is significantly less than 1.0 and is somewhat higher than the contraction parameter of .46 found when the vector contraction model was applied to the magnitude estimation distance data in Wagner (1985). However, a value of .61 still represents a considerable degree of compression in the in-depth dimension of visual space.

Table 7.7

Best-Fitting Parameter Values and Overall Standard Error of the Estimate for Fits of the Vector Contraction Model to Distance and Angle Judgments under Reduced and Full-Cue Conditions.

			Parameter		
Method	k	n	c_1	c_2	SE
Distance					
Light	19.05	0.770	0.606	0.854	0.547
Dark	18.94	0.737	0.379	1.215	0.549
Angle					
Light	0.962	1.024	0.581	1.013	0.508
Dark	1.219	0.975	0.338	1.445	0.493

The second contraction parameter, c_2, for the vertical dimension of visual space varied quite a bit from observer to observer; however, in this case, setting the parameter to 1.0 did result in a significant decline in variance accounted for. Another unusual aspect of this data is that the vector contraction model accounted for slightly less of the variation in the data than did the Affine contraction model. Typically the vector contraction model accounts for slightly more of the variance.

Table 7.7 also shows the best fitting parameter values and average standard errors of the estimate when the vector contraction model is applied to the distance data collected under reduced-cue conditions. In this case, the vector contraction model fits the data slightly better than the Affine contraction model. Note the in-depth compression parameter, c_1, shows a stronger and highly significant degree of compression of .38. Once again, visual space shows more compression under reduced-cue conditions than under full-cue conditions. The vertical compression parameter, c_2, did not significantly differ from 1.0.

As before, the vector contraction model can also be applied to the angle data. Table 7.7 shows the best fitting parameter values when the vector contraction model is applied to angle judgments under full-cue conditions. The in-depth compression parameter of .58 significantly differs from 1.0 and is very close to the .61value found under the same conditions for distance judgments. This value is also in the same range as those found with the vector contraction model for angle judgments in Wagner (1985). The model appears to account for slightly less of the variation in the data than the Affine contraction model.

Under reduced cue conditions, the degree of compression in the in-depth dimension is even more extreme. The average in-depth contraction parameter, c_1, was .34. This value is very close to the .38 value found with distance judgments. The vertical contraction parameter, although large, does not significantly differ from 1.0. Once again, the vector contraction model accounts for slightly more of the variance for reduced-cue judgments than did the Affine contraction model.

Other Evidence for Compression of the In-Depth Dimension

Other recent studies have confirmed the conclusion that visual space is compressed in the in-depth dimension relative to physical space. For example, Toye (1986) performed a study similar in many ways to those reported above. (Also see Haber (1985) for a preliminary report of this research.) Toye randomly placed 13 metal stakes in a 21m diameter round area of a flat grassy field. Eight observers were asked to judge the distance (in feet) between each pair of stakes. Observers were also asked to draw a map of stake positions. All eight observers participated in two experimental sessions. Half of the observers made their judgments from the same position both sessions, while the other half shifted positions. The latter subjects moved 90° along the edge of the circle; so that, any pairs of stakes that were oriented in-depth relative to the subject in the first position were now frontally oriented and visa versa.

Toye performed non-metric multidimensional scaling (assuming a Euclidean metric) on the pairwise distance judgments to generate a Euclidean map reflecting the observer's perception of the scene. He then statistically compared the discrepancy between the coordinates of the points according to the MDS solution and the maps observers produced on one hand with the physical coordinates of the points on the other.

Toye's main result was that the distance between pairs of points oriented in-depth relative to the observer were closer together on both perceptual maps than were frontally oriented pairs of points when compared to the physical layout of the points. In other words, the in-depth dimension of visual space was contracted relative to the frontal dimension just as Wagner (1982, 1985) found. When observers shifted positions by 90° around the edge of the field, this compression traveled with them. Frontally oriented distances in the original orientation grew smaller on their perceptual maps as they were now oriented in-depth relative to the observer from the new position. Similarly, originally in-depth oriented extents expanded in size on their perceptual maps when the observer moved to the new position from which they viewed the points frontally.

Toye found the average ratio of in-depth to frontal judgments when observers shifted positions was .85 (c = .85). That is, the same distances when oriented in-depth were judged to be 85% as large as when those distances are oriented frontally. Although Toye's data does show significant compression in the in-depth dimension of visual space, this ratio is considerably larger than that found in either of my studies reported earlier in this chapter. One possible explanation for this discrepancy lies in the instructions used. Both of my studies clearly used apparent size instructions, while Toye used objective size instructions. Objective size instructions may incline the observer to compensate somewhat to bring judgments more in line with physical reality.

Using a procedure similar to Wagner (1985) and Toye (1986), Haber, Haber, Levin, and Hollyfield (1993) asked 17 sighted and 7 blind observers to judge the distance between objects in an information rich, indoor office environment using objective instructions. They found that both sighted and blind observers produced judgments that were linearly related to physical distance with a true zero point. Haber et al. also found a significant tendency for frontally oriented distances to be perceived as longer than equivalent distances oriented in-depth. Although it is difficult to translate their findings into percentage of compression in the in-depth dimension, it appears that the degree of compression is smaller under the information-rich, indoor, objective-instruction conditions used in this experiment.

In a literature review, Todd, Tittle, and Norman (1995) reported evidence from multiple sources revealing a consistent pattern of results that indicates that perception of distances in-depth is different from perception of vertical or horizontal distances. Once again, they conclude that visual space is best described as an affine transformed space.

Based on the work of Foley (1972) and Wagner (1985), Suppes (1995) agreed that visual space appears to follow an affine transformation. Following a careful, axiomatic, foundational analysis, Suppes also proved that the compression or expansion of visual space must be aligned with the depth-axis.

Like my own study reported earlier in this chapter, Higashiyama (1996) compared distance perception across all three dimensions of visual space. He had observers adjust the longitudinal distance from themselves to a building to appear equal to standard vertical or horizontal distances on a wall. Consistent with the idea that visual space is compressed in the in-depth dimension, observers adjusted the longitudinal distance to be physically larger than either horizontal or vertical standards. Thus, in-depth oriented distances needed to be much larger than horizontal or vertical distances in order to seem to be the same size.

Is the compression constant? Loomis, Da Silva, Fujita, and Fukusima (1992) had observer's adjust the length of an in-depth oriented comparison until it appeared to equal a 1.0 m, 1.5 m, or 2.0 m frontally oriented standard using objective instructions. The standards were placed between 4m and 12 m from the observer. In all cases, observers adjusted the in-depth comparison to be much larger than the frontal standard. For the nearest standards, the comparison was made 37% larger than a physical match on the average; while for the most distant standards, the comparison was made 77% too large on the average. Once again, these data are consistent with a compression of in-depth oriented distances relative to frontally oriented ones because observers needed to magnify in-depth distances in order to make them appear equal to a frontal distance. Putting these results in the same terms as those that reported earlier, the compression parameter ranged from .56 to .73; that is, in-depth oriented stimuli were judged to be 56% to 73% as large as they would be if they were oriented frontally.

Loomis et al. replicated this experiment as part of another study. In the replication, the in-depth comparison was made 37% larger on the average than a physical match to the frontal standard, while the comparison was made 67% too large for the most distant standard. In other words, compression parameters ranged from .60 to .73.

While all three of the previous studies by Wagner or Toye assumed a constant degree of compression in the in-depth dimension of visual space, Loomis et al. (1992) indicates that this compression may not be constant. Instead near in-depth stimuli appear to be less visually compressed than ones further away. However, their data also showed that this change in compression was rapid for nearer stimuli, and the compression appeared to reach an asymptote for the more distant stimuli. Because all of the stimuli for both Wagner and Toye were relatively distant, this may explain why the degree of compression seemed almost constant in these studies. Perhaps visual space is less compressed in-depth for near stimuli because binocular and oculomotor cues to depth are still effective for near stimuli and become increasingly less useful as stimuli recede from the observer.

Loomis, Philbeck, and Zahorik (2002) performed two experiments which looked at the relationship of perceived depth to perceived frontal extent using both monocular and binocular judgments. In the first experiment observers adjusted a depth interval until it was perceptually equal to a frontal interval. (Once again, I will express their data in terms of compression of the in-depth dimension their results showed.) For near stimuli (20 to 50 cm from the observer) they found in-depth stimuli to be perceived to be 91% (c = .91) as big as the same frontal stimulus, showing a compression in the in-depth dimension. However, under binocular conditions, in-depth stimuli were seen as between 2 and 5% larger than frontal stimuli, indicating an expansion in the in-depth dimension (c = 1.02 to 1.05). At greater distances from the observer, the in-depth dimension was always compressed. In depth stimuli were seen as 93% (c = .93) as large as frontal stimuli two meters from the observer and 83% (c = .83) as large four meters from the target. Under monocular conditions, the compression parameters ranged from .86 for targets two meters away to .78 for targets four meters away. In the second experiment they presented various depth and frontal interval combinations and had observers judge the ratio of depth to frontal extent. Under monocular conditions, in-depth stimuli were seen as 80% (c = .80) as large as frontal stimuli when the target was one meter from the observer, and 65% (c = .65) as large for stimuli 1.5 or 2 m away. Under binocular conditions, the compression was smaller, ranging from .87 for stimuli 1 m away to .80 for stimuli 1.5 or 2 m from the observer.

Levin and Haber (1993) reanalyzed Toye's (1986) data and performed two new experiments requiring observers to estimate the distance between stakes in a field using objective instructions. Once again, they found that frontally oriented distances were overestimated relative to in-depth distances. Levin and Haber believed that they could explain this phenomenon. They note that the visual angles of frontally oriented stimuli are larger than the visual angles for in-depth oriented stimuli the same distance from the observer. Their experiments showed that size estimates were generally larger for stimuli subtending larger visual angles when physical distance was held constant. This correlation between perceived size and visual angle held true regardless of the reason for changes in the visual angle (orientation, distance from the observer, or changes in physical distance between stakes). If distance estimates are a linear combination of physical size and visual angle, frontally oriented stimuli should be perceived as larger. This theory might also provide an alternative account for why Loomis et al. (1992) found less compression for nearer stimuli, because in-depth oriented stimuli will have increasingly larger visual angles as they draw nearer to the observer. In fact, in-depth stimuli will be increasingly seen from above as they grow closer to the observer. In effect, both "frontal" and "in-depth" stimuli are seen frontally when they are at your feet, and in this limiting case, both would have the same visual angle.

Tittle, Todd, Perotti, and Norman (1995) describe the types of Klein transformations that could exist when physical space is mapped onto visual space. (In Chapter 2, we discussed Klein's Euclidean, similarity, conformal, affine, and topological transformations.) Tittle et al used random-dot CRT displays to convey stereoscopic and motion-based depth information to observers. In one experiment observers, who sat from 75 cm to 175 cm from the screen, were asked to adjust display parameters until they saw a half-cylinder. Overall, the results indicated that the in-depth dimension of visual space was expanded when the display was closer than 1 m from the observer, while the in-depth dimension was compressed for more distant displays.

In a second experiment, observers were shown an angle facing toward them that they were asked to adjust to equal 90°. When observers sat closer than 1m from the screen, the observers tended to adjust the angle to be slightly larger than 90°, a result which would be consistent with an expansion of the in-depth dimension which would make angles facing the observer stretch to appear smaller. However, when observers sat more than 1 m from the screen, observers adjusted the angle to be smaller than 90°, indicating that angles are perceptually expanded—which is consistent with visual space being compressed at distances greater than 1 m from the observer.

In two other experiments, they tested whether visual space was affine. The authors reasoned if visual space is affine, a plane should look flat instead of curved. They allowed observers to adjust two intersecting planes to see if they would align them at an 180° angle. They found that adjustments were very near to 180° when observers relied on motion cues alone or when observers were more than 1m from the display. At nearer distances, observers who had binocular disparity information adjusted the planes to intersect at a bit more than 178°, indicating a modest departure from the predictions of an affine transformation model for very near stimuli.

Of course, one question mark that always applied to random-dot stereogram studies is that such stimulus presentations may not provide all of the rich stimulus information normally available to our visual system. In this case, however, the data appear to be consistent with those found under more natural conditions.

Sipes (1997) confirmed that visual space is compressed in the in-depth dimension. Similar to Loomis et al. (1992), Sipes found that the degree of compression varied with viewing distance to the targets with more compression found as viewing distance increased. Sipes believed that the compression is lessened at near distances because stereoscopic cues to distance are most effective near to the observer. To prove this point, Sipes used a system of mirrors to effectively increase interocular distance and to boost stereoscopic cues to depth. As hypothesized, this hyperstereopsis greatly reduced perceived compression in the in-depth dimension of visual space.

Loomis and Philbeck (1999) provide further evidence of the influence of stereopsis on depth compression. They had subjects monocularly and binocularly view L-shaped configurations in which one part of the L was a rod oriented in depth while the other was a rod oriented frontally. Subjects judged the ratio of the depth and width for two different configurations that differed in scale. Loomis and Philbeck found that the ratio of in-depth to frontal size was constant under monocular viewing conditions, but not constant under binocular conditions.

Cuijpers, Kappers, and Koenderink (2000) took a different tack to investigate the compression of visual space. They placed pointers and targets at various positions in front of observers and asked them to adjust the pointer so that it seemed to point at the target. Target positions ranged from 1 m to 5 m from the observer. Errors in pointer position that are nearer to the frontal plane than the true direction would indicate visual space is perceptually squeezed in the in-depth dimension, while errors that deviate more from the frontal plane would indicate an expansion of the in-depth dimension. Like Tittle, Todd, Perotti, and Norman (1995), they found an expansion of the in-depth dimension of visual space for targets very near the observer, but a compression for targets further from the observer. The degree of compression or expansion was symmetrical about the median plane. Binocular viewing produced very different and more consistent (but not necessarily more accurate) results than monocular viewing. Sikl and Simecek (2004) confirmed that visual space is compressed in depth for all but very near stimuli. Sikl and Simecek showed observers one-meter standard intervals defined by rods pounded into a dirt field that varied in orientation and were placed either 2, 5, or 10 meters from the observer. Observers were asked to locate a third rod such that the new rod would be collinear with the first two rods and the distance between the new rod and the one of the standard rods would match the standard. Observers adjusted in-depth oriented intervals to be larger than frontal intervals for comparisons except those nearest the observer (the center of this interval would be about 1 m from the observer) where the opposite occurred.

The most interesting aspect of this data concerned the precision or variability of judgments. The author found a trade off between the accuracy and reliability of the angular alignment of the rods and the accuracy and reliability of size estimates. The authors found that angular alignment of the rods was most accurate and least variable for in-depth oriented configurations while size estimates were least accurate and more variable for these configurations. Frontal configurations showed the opposite pattern, with the least accurate and most variable angular alignments but the most accurate and least variable size estimates.

**Perspectives on the Vertical Dimension:
Taking Space Perception to New Heights**

Gaze elevation. Anyone who has hiked up a mountain knows that 100m above you looks further away than 100m along a flat plane. Similarly, it certainly looks further down from the top of a high-dive board than it does when looking at the same distance when standing on the side of the pool. One possible explanation of these observations is that emotion, in particular, fear, can influence distance perception. Another possibility is that distances may generally be perceived differently when looking up or down as opposed to straight ahead.

While no one that I know of has looked at the affects of emotion on distance perception, a number of researchers have looked at the affects of gaze elevation under less threatening circumstances. Typically, such studies can either have observers "look at" edges or extents which are horizontal or vertical with respect to gravity by standing off to the side, "look down" at those same distances by peering over an edge, or "look up" at edges or extents by standing or lying at the bottom of a bridge, hill, or wall. As a general rule distances that are vertical with respect to gravity are seen as longer than physically identical horizontal distances.

For example, Morinaga (1935) found that a horizontal comparison needed to be made 4 to 14% too large to appear to match a vertical standard. Similarly, Makishita (1947) found that when looking up, a horizontal comparison needed to be made larger than a vertical standard in order to make them appear equal in size. Osaka (1947) also showed that subjects who were looking up needed to make a horizontal comparison 12% to 21% too large to match a vertical standard. For physically equal sized stimuli, Ohno (1951, 1972) showed that vertical distance appears longer than when horizontal for standing observers, but found the opposite trend if the observer was lying on the ground. Okabe, Aoki, and Hamamoto (1986) found observers overestimated the length of both uphill and downhill trails compared to trails along a flat surface.

Baird and Wagner (1982) asked observers to estimate the distance to the night sky. We generally found that observers estimated the distance to be greater when looking up to the zenith than when asked to estimate the distance to the sky above the horizon. However, individual observers varied considerably from one another, including some observers who reported the opposite pattern. Of course, such data may say more about the perceived shape of the night sky (or lack of definite shape) than they do about the affects of gaze elevation on distance perception.

In one of the most complete studies on the topic, Higashiyama and Ueyama (1988) had observers adjust a horizontal comparison to match five vertical standards in four conditions. Observers either looked down the side of the vertical surface over an edge, looked at the vertical surface from the side, looked up at the vertical surface while standing or looked up at the vertical surface while lying on the ground. They found that in all cases the horizontal comparison needed to be made too large to match the vertical extent. Looking up or looking down produced similar 16% to 26% over adjustments. The fact that there was little difference between lying down and standing up indicated that head orientation per se is not responsible for this effect. Looking at the vertical extent resulted in an even bigger over adjustment of the horizontal comparison of 67%.

Yang, Dixon, and Proffitt (1999) present evidence that the horizontal–vertical illusion is larger for real objects than it is for objects represented in pictures and line drawings. Vertical sizes were seen as larger than equivalent horizontal sizes and this effect was twice as large for natural stimuli than pictorial stimuli.

Living in a Distorted World

Much of the preceding work indicates that visual space is very different from physical space under quite ordinary conditions. Given that our perceptual world is so distorted, how can we survive? It would seem that such massive distortions would make interacting with the physical world difficult. Any answer to this question can only be speculation. Nevertheless, there may be a number of good reasons why humans are reasonably competent at interacting with their misperceived environment.

First of all, it may be true that people tend to either engage in frontally oriented activity or in–depth oriented activity, but seldom activity that requires accuracy in both dimensions at once. Within either dimension, judgment may be very good. It is only between dimensions that distortion arises. Activities that demand both frontal and in-depth responses might themselves be broken down into independent frontal and in-depth motor responses.

Second, for many activities, the most critical issue may be to decide what the geodesic (or shortest path) connecting points in the environment is. The absolute length of the geodesic may be irrelevant. For the Affine contraction model, at least, moving from one place to another should be error free. The geodesic of an Affine transformed visual space is identical to the geodesic for physical space.

Third, humans do make errors when embarking on a new activity. Novice fencers seldom lunge far enough. New pilots often think the ground is too close. (Some accidents are caused by cutting the engines too soon.) When placing stakes in the field during data collection for Wagner (1985), I often seemed to undershoot when I estimated the in-depth component of stake placement (prior to actual physical measurement). Since completing my own research on this issue, I have sometimes noted that parking spaces that seem too small (when oriented in-depth) are often more than large enough. (A bit of knowledge that has come in handy on more than one occasion.) With repeated experience or practice, people are able to compensate to overcome these sorts of errors.

Fourth, when interacting with an environment repeatedly, we may see the environment from many different perspectives. Over time, something akin to non-metric multidimensional scaling may occur. Distortions and contradictions arising from multiple perspectives may be resolved to yield a single coherent cognitive map or model for the environment that might be identical to physical space. It is entirely possible that once we are completely familiar with an environment we interact with it more in keeping with our model of it than in keeping with our direct perceptions. Indeed, Vishton and Cutting (1995) conclude that wayfinding is probably a combination of continuously noting the displacements of objects in comparison to a rough mental map of environmental layout. Yates (1985) proposes an extreme version of this concept; saying that our awareness is never direct, but that we are always interacting with a model of the world.

Fifth, with experience we may come to associate definite distances and angles with commonly encountered objects. Walls meet at right angles. People are a bit less than two meters tall. Known size cues like these may aid us in interacting with the environment. In fact, the distorted nature of our perceptual experience may be why known size cues are so powerful. In judging sizes and angles we may come to trust our knowledge over our direct experience.

Stevens (1995) proposed that perception of layout may be represented independently of shape perception and that these two sorts of representations may be derived from different perceptual cues. In particular, Stevens believes that shape perception is largely learned through associating particular stimulus patterns with known extrinsic shapes without needing to perceive all of the spatial information necessary to construct a complete spatial representation of a scene. If true, observers would be able to recognize objects and interact with them without accurately perceiving the spatial layout of a scene as a whole. The Loomis and Philbeck study (1999), which we talked about earlier, empirically confirmed that shape can be determined independently of perceived size.

In fact, a number of recent studies have suggested a sixth alternative: Perhaps we have two visual systems: One that creates the model of the world that we consciously experience, and one that allows us to interact with the world. We may have one visual system for seeing (of which we are conscious), and a second visual system that guides action. (Cf., Grossberg, 1991, for a complete exposition of this sort of theory.) While the visual system that informs conscious experience may be quite inaccurate (as has been demonstrated countless times throughout this book), the visual system that guides action can be quite accurate.

For example, Solomon and Turvey (1988) conducted nine experiments to examine the accuracy of egocentric length perception based exclusively on haptic cues. In their experiments observers were given rods of varying lengths that they could move but could not see. Observers sat on the left side of a screen while their right arm held the rod on the unseen right side of the screen. They were asked to touch the unseen side of a screen with the rod and then adjusted a comparison (which they could see but not directly touch) until it seemed to be the same distance away from them as the point of the rod touching the screen. In all nine experiments, these haptic estimates of perceived length were quite accurate. Perceived length was an almost prefect linear function of physical length with coefficients of determination ranging from .94 to 1.00.

On the other hand, Eby and Loomis (1987) asked observers to throw a ball at targets located one of five distances away. The observers were visually shown each target and then blinders were place in front of their eyes before they actually threw the ball. Unlike Solomon and Turvey, the relationship between haptically produced distance estimates and physical distance was not linear. Eby and Loomis found that subjects were most accurate for short distances and that they increasingly undershot the target as distance to the target increased. The relationship between thrown distance and physical distance was fit to a power function with exponents averaging .79 for both overhand and underhand throwing conditions. However, coefficients of determination were very poor, averaging .36 for underhand throwing and .64 for overhand throwing. Excluding the data for one clumsy observer raised these coefficients of determination to .81 and .87, respectively.

Loomis, Da Silva, Fujita, and Fukusima (1992) directly compared visual and motoric perceptions of space. As reported earlier, they asked observers to adjust an in-depth comparison until it appeared to equal a frontally oriented standard using objective size instructions. For this visually directed task, in-depth stimuli appeared 56% to 73% smaller than they would have if oriented frontally. The researchers also asked observers to judge distance motorically by showing the observers a target (ranging from 4m to 12m from the observer) and then asking the observer to walk to the target. The results showed that observers walked distance matched physical distance to a high degree of accuracy. Loomis et al. (1992) point out that at least four previous experiments have reported the same degree of walking accuracy for targets ranging from 2 m to 22 m from the observer (Elliott, 1986, 1987; Rieser, Ashmead, Talor, & Youngquist, 1990; Steenhuis & Goodale, 1988).

Of course, walking to a target is not equivalent to adjusting an in-depth oriented comparison to match a frontal standard because both the initial view of the target and the walking task are in-depth oriented tasks. To make the walking task more equivalent to the visual one, Loomis et al. (1992) showed observers two targets, in some cases aligned frontally with respect to the observer and in some cases aligned in-depth relative to the observer. Observers were then asked to walk with their eyes closed to one of the targets and then walk to the second target without opening their eyes. In this case, neither distance to the first target, nor orientation of the two targets with respect to the observer affected the length walked between targets. In other words, while in-depth oriented stimuli were perceptually compressed relative to the same frontal stimuli when judged visually, in-depth and frontal stimuli were experienced as being the same when judged motorically. A subsequent pointing task confirmed the accuracy of motoric judgments. Loomis et al. (1992) conclude that we may have two ways of representing space – one that informs conscious experience and one that guides action.

A number of researchers have shown that many behavioral tasks, from avoiding collisions with incoming objects to running to intercept a flying projectile can be accomplished without relying on any knowledge of distance information whatsoever (Lee, 1976; Regan et al., 1994; Todd, 1981; Todd, Tittle, & Norman, 1995). For example, McBeath, Shaffer, and Kaiser (1995) believe that baseball players can catch fly balls by following a "linear optical trajectory" that does not require the observer to take into account acceleration, velocity, and the moment to moment position of the flying ball. The authors feel that an outfielder only needs to depend on a projection of their visual world or what perceptual psychologists refer to as the visual field to guide motion. According to their theory, outfielders are running the proper path when the ball follows a straight-line in the visual field that converges on their direction of motion. (See Dannemiller, Babler, and Babler, 1996; Jacobs, Lawrence, Hong, and Giordano, 1996; and McBeath, Shaffer, and Kaiser, 1996, for a debate on this issue.) Most recently, Shaffer, Krauchunas, Eddy, and McBeath (2004) have shown (using cameras attached to their heads) that dogs use a similar strategy when catching Frisbees.

Indeed, Oudejans, Michaels, Bakker, and Dolne (1996) have shown that stationary observers are very poor at predicting the catchableness of a ball. Yet, moving subjects can go to the right place. The authors conclude that ball players rely on kinematic information rather than relying on their perceived visual geometry.

Pagano and Bingham (1998) present further evidence for the independence of visual and motoric representations of distance. The authors had subjects verbally judge the visually perceived distance to objects both before and after reaching for the targets. They found that verbal and reaching errors were uncorrelated and that verbal judgments did not improve after allowing subjects to reach for the targets. Similarly, Goodale and Milner (1992) also found no correlation between perceptual judgments and visually guided action.

Clinical evidence also supports the possibility of parallel spatial systems. Carey, Dijkerman, and Miller (1998) presented the case of a female with visual-form agnosia whose ability to reach for blocks was very similar to control subjects while her ability to verbally estimate distance to objects was very poor. This study bolsters the idea the separate pathways might exist in the brain for different forms of spatial information.

Schwartz (1999) asked blindfolded participants to walk until stopped and then asked them to return to their starting point. Even though subjects were prevented from counting steps and gate was varied, subjects performed the task remarkably well.

Philbeck (2000) presented two experiments in which observers matched a depth interval to be perceptually equal to a frontal interval (located 3 m to 5 m from the observer). Subjects adjusted the depth interval to be 25% larger than the true physical size of the frontal interval, once again demonstrating compression in the in-depth dimension of visual space. However, when subjects were asked to walk this interval even after very brief visual exposures (150 ms), subjects could accurately walk the distance.

On the other hand, Seizova-Calic (1998) and Armstrong and Marks (1999) have shown that haptic space, like visual space, shows some anisotropy; that is, the in-depth dimension is perceived differently than the frontal dimension. In both studies, the same distance was perceived to be longer when oriented in-depth as opposed to frontally. This would indicated that haptic space is expanded in the in-depth dimension just as some researchers have shown the in-depth dimension of visual space is expanded for stimuli within arm's reach.

Does Visual Space Exist?

Perception in context: Another challenge. Much of the preceding work implicitly assumes that visual space exists in the abstract and that our perceptions neatly fit into that abstract structure. Admittedly, the structure of visual space is likely to be very complex with perceived distance depending on stimulus orientation, distance from the observer, cue conditions, the meaning given to distance through instructions, and other factors; however, once one knows the metric formulas that apply to perception, it should be possible to predict a subject's judgments for any stimulus. The shape of the stimulus or the presence of other stimuli should not fundamentally alter the judgments that subjects produce.

Unfortunately, this simple picture is unlikely to be wholly true. Recent studies have shown that the perception of the position of an object in space can be shaped by the presence of other stimuli. For example, Thorndyke (1981) found that empty intervals typically appear shorter than intervals containing intervening elements; a phenomenon Thordyke labeled the filled-space illusion. Schoumans, Koenderink, and Kappers (2000) found that observers perceived the orientation of a target differently if the target was seen in front of two intersecting planes than if the target was seen without this context. While Schoumans et al. (2000) used computer-generated stimuli, Schoumans, Kapers, and Koenderink (2002) replicated these results using physical stimuli instead. Kappers and Pas (2001) observed a phenomenon consistent with these results under natural conditions by having observers judge the perceived orientation of parallel ceiling lights in a large room.

Similarly, Cuijpers, Kappers, and Koenderink (2001) presented reference targets at various orientations and locations relative to the observer. Observers were asked to rotate a comparison target until it appeared parallel to the reference target. Contrary to the Luneberg's predictions (or that of any geometry of constant curvature), the comparison's orientation systematically deviated from the reference orientation and that the degree of deviation varied as a function of relative location of the stimuli in space. (Consistent with previous work showing compression in visual space in the in-depth dimension.) More interestingly, they also found that the degree of deviation was influenced by how the stimuli were oriented compared to the walls of the room in which the experiment was conducted. Thus, the angular judgments not only varied with position in space, but also were influenced by the presence of reference stimuli.

Cuijpers, Kappers, and Koenderink (2002) looked at the special case of collinearity, where the comparison was rotated to form a straight line with the reference target. Once again, the authors found deviations from correct alignment up to 22°, although the overall degree of deviation from physically appropriate was smaller than it was in the previous studies. The authors argue that this once again shows an inconsistency in visual space, collinearity should simply be a special case of parallelism in a Riemannian geometry. They argue that the geometry of visual space may differ as a function of experimental task. Obviously, I agree with this point, because I too think the geometry of visual space varies as a function of method and stimulus conditions.

Norman, Lappin, and Norman (2000) presented another challenge to the simple view of visual space. They found that lengths oriented along the curved dimension of a cylinder were generally perceived to be longer than physically equivalent lengths along a flat surface. The factors that influenced errors in perceptions of curved lengths seemed to vary from individual to individual, with some people being influenced by distance to the cylinder while others were influenced by the target's orientation. They conclude that the types of distortions seen with curved surfaces are of a different character than the compression in the in-depth dimension reported previously.

Does visual space exist at all? If the shape of a stimulus can alter our spatial perceptions in fundamental ways or if perceptions of stimuli change along with the presence of contextual objects, then this adds complicating factors to modeling spatial perception that must be accounted for by future models. Kappers and Koenderink argue that these phenomena indicate that visual space cannot be thought of in metric terms because distance relations change based on the presence of reference stimuli such as right angle corners.

Indeed, one early reader of this work felt that I should join Kappers and Koenderink and end my book at this point. He felt that this book as a whole nearly constituted a proof that visual space does not exist and that visual perception cannot be described in geometric terms. He felt this conclusion would help break perceptual psychology out of a conceptual spiral of seeking answers that can never be found. Presumably, this would then free the rest of perception to focus on questions like form perception and cues to depth that are more easily addressed without resorting to arcane mathematics.

This position has some justification. In Chapter 3, we showed that visual space does not satisfy the axioms of any of the geometries of constant curvature, whether it be hyperbolic, spherical, or Euclidean. In Chapter 4, we noted that visual space didn't even satisfy the axioms of very general geometries like metric, Banach, or Riemannian spaces. Obviously, the studies reported in the present section of this chapter help bolster this claim. In Chapter 5, we found that estimates of size, distance, area, volume, and angle are influenced by other contextual variables, like age, judgment method, stimulus range, and whether the experiment was conducted indoors or outdoors. The later contextual factor might reflect the presence of a reference framework formed by the walls of a room similar to Kappers and Koenderink. In Chapter 6, we noted that size judgments change along with still more contextual variables such as instructions, cue conditions, the presence of known-size cues, and stimulus orientation. The present chapter has once again shown that judgments depend on stimulus orientation, cue conditions, and gaze elevation. The present chapter (along with some elements of Chapters 4 and 9) also shows that our experience of space changes from one modality to another. In particular, space revealed to us through touch is experienced differently than our visual perceptions of that space. Chapters 5 and 8 also point out that our memory of metric properties such as size, distance, area, and angle are different from our direct perceptions of them. In fact, memories that develop across time as in "inference conditions" vary even further from direct perception. If visual space is conceived of as a simple, unitary framework into which perceptual objects neatly fit and distance, area, angular, and volume relations are immutable constants uninfluenced by contextual variables, then this book clearly does represent a definitive proof that no such space exists.

The question of whether visual space exists or not is actually a semantic one. What does one mean by a geometry of visual space? If one believes that visual geometry must conform to the axioms of one of the better-known synthetic geometries in order to qualify as a geometry, then visual space doesn't really exist. However, if one defines a geometry as I do, then visual space certainly does exist. I believe as long as it is possible to assign coordinates to locations in visual space and as long as it is possible to systematically predict metric judgments as functions of these coordinates, then these coordinates and metric functions define the geometry of the space. The fact that these equations might change along with contextual variables such as reference stimuli does rule out a Kantian view that visual space is a single conceptual framework that the human mind employs to make sense of the world. The truth is more complicated than this. Visual geometry is a shifting, changing thing that is not defined by a single geometry; rather it is best thought of a as a family of geometries. The specific geometry experienced at a given moment will vary along with changes in mental set and stimulus conditions.

Throughout this book, we have seen that the geometry of visual space, and metric relationships in particular, changes along with instructions and experimental conditions. The impact of reference stimuli on perception (as in Kappers and Koenderink) is just another factor that must be accounted for in developing metric equations that predict judgments. This situation in some ways reminds me of the General Theory of Relativity in which the presence of massive objects warps the fabric of space in the region surrounding such objects. Perhaps the presence of objects or structural patterns in stimuli can alter spatial perception in local regions in a similar way. In addition, the reference stimulus that appears to most influence directional perception in Kappers and Koenderink's works are right angle corners. This may simply be another example of "known shape" cues influencing perception.

Of course, the idea that size and angle perception might change depending on the local context in which a target appears greatly complicates the structure of visual spaces. If true, it might be difficult to create a coherent model of visual space as a whole. Visual space might consist of a set of local regions loosely patched together to make a rough quilt at higher levels of scale. This viewpoint is particularly descriptive of cognitive maps as will be seen in the next chapter.

Understanding Higher Dimensional Research

Summary of the multidimensional literature. Earlier in this chapter, we found that three-dimensional visual space can be thought of as an Affine transformation of physical space. A slightly better form of this model expressed visual space in terms of vectors. According to Equation 7.18, distance judgments can be predicted by the equation

$$J = k \left\{ \sqrt{\left(D^* \cos \phi_1\right)^2 + \left(c_1 D^* \sin \phi_1\right)^2 + \left(c_2 D \sin \phi_2\right)^2} \right\}^n . \tag{7.19}$$

where J is the observer's distance judgment, D is the physical length of the stimulus, D^* is the projection of the stimulus onto the onto the x-y (median) plane, ϕ_1 is the orientation angle of the stimulus with respect to the frontal plane, ϕ_2 is the orientation angle with respect to the median plane, k is a scaling constant, and n is the power function exponent. In this equation, c_1 is a compression parameter representing the relative size of in-depth stimuli compared to frontal ones, while c_2 is a second parameter representing the relative size of vertical objects compared to horizontal ones.

The main conclusion that can be reached from the data reported in this chapter is that the in-depth dimension of visual space is perceived differently from the frontal dimension. In particular, the in-depth dimension of visual space appears to be strongly compressed relative to the frontal dimension for stimuli more than one or two meters from the observer. In terms of Equation 7.19, this means that c_1 tends to have values smaller than one. In fact, for distant stimuli, the value of the compression parameter approaches .5. Beyond about 7 m from the observer, this compression appears to be almost constant, while the degree of compression lessens greatly for stimuli close to the observer. For very near stimuli, there are even reports that the in-depth dimension sometimes expands relative to the frontal dimension. It appears that the degree of expansion/compression changes very rapidly in the area of space within arms reach of the observer. Therefore, the "compression" parameter, c_1, should not be thought of as a constant but as a function of distance from the observer.

The compression of the in-depth dimension of visual space is more extreme under reduced-cue conditions than under full-cue conditions. Under reduced cue conditions, c_1 appears to approximately equal .35. Visual space appears to exhibit greater in-depth compression than haptic space. That is, c_1 appears to be much closer to 1.0 for spatial experience based on touch and motor behavior than it is for visual experience. In addition, preliminary evidence suggest that the compression of the in-depth dimension is less extreme for experiments employing objective instructions than it is for apparent or projective instructions. The compression parameter, c_1, appears to be closer to .8 for objective instructions. Thus, the compression parameter should be thought of as a function of not only distance, but of modality and experimental conditions.

Although my research with Evan Feldman on three-dimensional space perception reported earlier in the chapter did not show any consistent pattern in the vertical-horizontal parameter, c_2; research reported later in this chapter implied that gaze elevation and vertical stimulus orientation does affect perceived size. Based on the research reported earlier, vertical stimuli appear to be seen as being about 15% larger than horizontal stimuli of the same physical size on the average. That is, we would expect c_2 to have a value of about 1.15.

None of these conclusions could be reached based on the unidimensional work reported in Chapters 5 and 6. In addition, much of the literature reported in the present chapter is very recent. However, I feel compelled to mention that many of these findings were anticipated by the classic work of Thouless (1931a). Thouless examined the subjective size of stimuli oriented in-depth by presenting circles and squares lying along the ground with respect to the observer and asking subjects to select among a set of ellipses and rectangles the comparison which best matched the standard. He found that the in-depth dimension was perceptually smaller than the frontal dimension for each stimulus. This foreshortening increased with increasing distance from the observer. For circles 54.5 cm from the observer the in-depth dimension was perceived to be 77% of the size of the frontal dimension, at 109 cm it was 59% of the frontal size, and at 163.5 cm it was 49% of the frontal size. These results are consistent with a strong compression of in-depth orient stimuli. In fact, the compression parameters for the distant stimuli in Thouless's work are very similar to those reported earlier in the chapter.

Modeling the multidimensional literature. In any case, how can one account for the variable degree of compression seen in visual space? I believe that the model presented in the previous chapter goes some way to explain this phenomenon. It is possible that the observer does not completely take into account the orientation of the stimulus when transforming the visual angle of a stimulus into perceived size. In general, if the same inverse transformation were used to convert a frontally oriented visual angle and a in-depth oriented visual angle into perceived size, the in-depth stimulus would be perceived as much smaller than the frontally oriented stimulus because the visual angle for in-depth oriented targets are generally (but not always) smaller than the visual angle for frontally oriented targets the same distance away from the observer.

An example will help show how in-depth and frontal visual angles compare. In Chapter 6, formulas were presented to show how frontally oriented stimuli (Equation 6.6) and in-depth oriented stimuli (Equation 6.7) are converted into visual angles as a function of observer height, target size, and distance to the target. I used these formulas to calculate visual angles as a function of distance to the target for a number of combinations of target sizes and observer heights. Figure 7.11 shows the ratio of the in-depth to frontal visual angles as a function of distance to the target for each combination of target size and observer height.

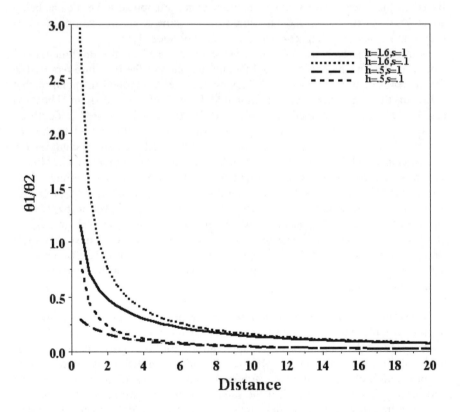

Figure 7.11. The ratio of in-depth to frontal visual angles as a function of distance to the target for four combinations of target size and observer height.

A few points may be noted about this figure. First, in-depth oriented stimuli subtend much smaller visual angles than frontally oriented stimuli for distant targets. If observers did not sufficiently take into account this change, this would lead them to perceive in-depth oriented intervals as being smaller than physically equivalent frontal targets the same distance away. Second, this relative shrinkage of in-depth targets reaches something of an asymptote for targets more than six to eight meters from the observer. Third, the relative sizes of in-depth to frontal visual angles changes rapidly near the observer, and this would lead to much less shrinkage in the perception of in-depth targets near to the observer. Fourth, there are circumstances when in-depth visual angles are actually larger than frontal angles when stimuli are very near the observer; circumstances which would lead to in-depth stimuli being perceived as larger than equivalent frontal targets. In this case, the in-depth dimension of visual space would seem to expand rather than contract relative to the frontal dimension. In other words, Figure 7.11 captures many of the key features of that the experimental data show.

While this observation might move us toward understanding why visual space follows the pattern of compression in the in-depth dimension found in the data, there are a number of factors that lead me to believe that it is not the whole explanation. First, even under the most extreme circumstances (under reduced conditions) compression parameters have never been found to be smaller than .3, while the relative compression displayed in Figure 7.11 is sometimes much more extreme than this. Clearly, observers must at least partially adjust for the orientation of the target or else in-depth targets would often look tiny compared to equivalent frontal targets. Second, research reported earlier pointed to the importance of stereopsis in reducing the degree of compression. A simple model based exclusively on visual angles could not explain this phenomenon. Third, some studies that have looked at the effect of observer height on size judgments (e.g., Harway, 1963) have found little effect. On the other hand, Ooi, Wu, and He (2001) and Philbeck and Loomis (1997) found height to be an important predictor of size judgments. Yet, according to Equations 6.6 and 6.7, observer height should have a major effect on judgments. Figure 7.11 also displays how strongly observer size affects the ratio of in-depth and frontal visual angles. Clearly, the observer must also be able to take into account their elevation relative to the target when perceiving size.

A more complete account of the perceptual compression of the in-depth dimension of visual space could involve the "full model" describe by Equation 6.14. This model predicts size judgments based on perceived distance to the stimulus as well as applied stimulus orientation. The parameters of this equation (the exponent of the power function for perceived distance and the applied orientation) change as a function of instructions and experimental conditions. If $s_d(d,\alpha,\beta,\delta, ...)$ represents the perceived size predicted by the Equation for an in-depth interval at a certain distance away under experimental conditions α, β, and δ, and if $s_f(d,\alpha,\beta,\delta, ...)$ represents the perceived size predicted by the

Equation for a frontally oriented interval at the same distance away and under the same conditions, then perhaps $c_1(d,\alpha,\beta,\delta, ...)$ might be found by Equation 7.20

$$c_1\left(d,\alpha,\beta,\delta,... \ \right) = \frac{s_d\left(d,\alpha,\beta,\delta,... \ \right)}{s_f\left(d,\alpha,\beta,\delta,... \ \right)}.$$
(7.20)

If Equation 7.20 or something like it can predict the compression of the in-depth dimension of visual space noted in this chapter, then such an equation would serve to unify the three main types of spatial perception research reported in this book. Because Equation 7.20 is derived from Equation 6.14, which predicts judgments in the size constancy literature, Equation 7.20 would link the multidimensional literature to the size-constancy literature. In addition, because fits of Equation 6.14 to the size constancy literature results in exponents that are consistent with exponents found in the direct estimation literature reported in Chapter 5, Equation 7.20 in turn would link the multidimensional and size-constancy literature to data found in the direct estimation literature.

In conclusion. Research on multidimensional approaches to space perception have shown once more that visual space is often very different than physical space. This research also brings home the point that the geometry of visual space often changes radically as a function of experimental conditions. Finally, the data shows that metric relations change as objects reorient or move from one position in visual space to another.

8

Cognitive Maps, Memory, and Space Perception

Most people take for granted our ability to move around in the everyday environment. Yet, considering how complex the environment is and how often our starting points and destinations change according to our circumstances and needs, the human ability to get from one place to another in unique and creative ways is truly amazing. This movement would be impossible without a detailed understanding of the spatial layout of our familiar environment. This knowledge of spatial layout, which develops across time, is known as a cognitive map.

Cognitive maps help us get around our environment efficiently, so that we can quickly acquire food, clothing, and other necessities of life. Without them, we would be reduced to the level of primitive robots that move about at random, searching until they find what they need or, in more advanced cases, mindlessly retracing old routes until helplessly confronted by change.

In light of this evolutionary importance, it is not surprising that a considerable literature developed devoted to the study of cognitive maps. Much of this work grows out of environmental and applied psychology, although mainstream cognitive and perceptual psychologists and professional geographers often make forays into the field. In my experience, many researchers in this area do not appear to be familiar with work done by others with different orientations. For example, environmental researchers are sometimes not familiar with work done by cognitive psychologists or cognitive geographers.

Relationship to other spatial literature. Cognitive mapping is not the only area of psychology concerned with human spatial abilities. As we have seen in the previous chapters of this book, mainstream perceptual psychologists have been studying spatial perception and the geometry of visual space since the foundation of the discipline (e.g., Helmholtz, 1867; Luneburg, 1947; Martius, 1889; Thouless, 1931a 1931b, 1932). In addition, intelligence testing researchers and cognitive psychologists are also interested in human spatial abilities as measured by psychological tests (e.g., Halpern, 2004; Voyer, Voyer, & Bryden, 1995) and mental rotation tasks (Shepard, 1988; Shepard & Metzler, 1971).

In fact, some readers may wonder why I have elected to include a chapter on memory and cognitive maps in a book on the geometries of visual space. I do so because I believe that memorial space and cognitive maps are extensions of visual space perception. I believe that memorial space and cognitive maps originally derive from direct visual experience and that they represent a generalization

189

of visual space across time. Having said this, there are also many differences between cognitive maps and the literature reported earlier.

What is it that separates cognitive mapping from other spatial literatures? The following list identifies some of the more important features of the cognitive mapping literature. Although some of the items on the list may also be true of other spatial literatures, the combination of the following features is unique to cognitive mapping.

(1) Cognitive mapping has an environmental emphasis. Cognitive mapping fits comfortably into environmental psychology for a number of good reasons. Most cognitive mapping studies take place in natural, everyday settings. Unlike much of the space perception research which seeks to limit the information available to subjects by doing experiments in the dark, having subjects look through artificial pupils or distorting lenses, or limiting head motion; cognitive mapping utilizes information rich, "ecologically valid" settings (Gibson, 1979). Also unlike other spatial literatures, the nature and structure of the natural environment are critically important variables for cognitive mapping researchers. For example, the existence of "edges" like streams or railroads have a major impact on the structure of cognitive maps.

(2) Similarly, cognitive mapping studies are often concerned with where the subjects *are*, while spatial perception research usually asks subjects to describe what they see. Subjects are often asked to make judgments concerning the orientation or location of places relative to themselves. The location of a subject is an important variable in an ecological setting, unlike laboratories, where the location of the laboratory relative to the rest of the environment is seldom at issue.

(3) Cognitive mapping also focuses on a different level scale for spatial knowledge. The literature on spatial abilities seldom uses stimuli that can't fit on a piece of paper. Space perception studies are limited to stimuli that are close enough for the subject to see. Cognitive mapping, on the other hand, is concerned with the layout of environments that range from buildings on the small end of the scale to campuses, cities, states, and even nations on the high end of the scale.

(4) Cognitive maps develop gradually across time through daily experience with the environment. Although other spatial literatures occasionally focus on spatial memory, cognitive mapping is by its nature concerned with processes related to memory. Thus, unlike other spatial literatures, cognitive mapping is concerned with knowledge accumulated across time. Because of this, cognitive mapping studies often use longitudinal designs. If researchers use cross-sectional designs, they will often examine the effects of years of exposure to an environment. In other words, cognitive mapping studies possess the "time orientation" that Proshansky (1976) listed in his early paradigm-defining article as one of the essential features of environmental psychology (a principle which few other subareas of environmental live up to in spite of Proshanky's hopes).

One element not included on this list is a statement that cognitive maps seek to determine the cognitive representation of spatial knowledge. I've left this off of the list for two reasons. First, other spatial literatures often use cognitive explanations too. Secondly, as I will point out later in this chapter, it may be difficult or impossible to make sensible statements about the precise cognitive representation of spatial knowledge. Because I believe that references to cognitive representations are dubious and unnecessary, it wouldn't make sense to list these representations as defining features of the cognitive mapping literature.

Chapter outline. The purpose of this chapter is to describe recent research in the cognitive mapping literature. In particular, we will begin by examining the structure of cognitive maps and how cognitive maps are acquired across time. Then we will turn to the influence of individual differences on cognitive map formation. Following this, we will examine methods for studying cognitive maps and their interrelation, inaccuracies in cognitive maps, the psychophysics of cognitive mapping, and whether cognitive maps are Euclidean or non-Euclidean spaces. We will also touch on several models for psychophysical judgments of cognitive maps. Finally, we will discuss why cognitive maps do not require reference to cognitive representations.

Structural Elements of Cognitive Maps

The legacy of Kevin Lynch. The original impetus for cognitive mapping research was Lynch's (1960) influential book, *The image of the city*, although some interest in the subject dates back as far as Towbridge (1913). Lynch was a city planner who hoped to improve the livability of cities through active urban planning. (An effort that began in England as evidenced by the "New London Satellite Towns" of the 19th century.) As part of this effort, Lynch determined that some cities were more "imageable" or "legible" than others. *Imageable* cities evoke clear images, associations, and emotions in an observer. Legible cities produce high levels of agreement among its citizens concerning what the major, distinctive features of the city are. *Legible* cities are not only more pleasing overall to their residents, but they are also easier to find ones way about in, because legible cities more naturally give rise to memorable images that help organize our spatial knowledge.

According to Haken and Portugali (2003), the legibility and imageability of cities can be related Shannon's information theory. Bland cities with indistinguishable buildings and streets have lower information content than cities with unique structures and distinct districts. People prefer cities with high information content because they aid in our natural tendencies to categorize and organize our experiences.

Lynch believed that five structural features of a city determine its imageability and legibility: paths, landmarks, nodes, edges, and districts. *Paths* are defined as a connected series of images or impressions that a person has. In effect, paths consist of familiar routes that subjects have traveled during their exploration of a new environment. *Landmarks* are locations that come to gain special significance to the person. While landmarks may refer to officially designated landmarks like

Mount Rushmore or the Statue of Liberty, they are more likely to consist of slightly more mundane reference points like the old church or the grocery store. In Lynch's terms, landmarks serve as "familiar kernels" around which spatial knowledge is organized. *Nodes* refer to focal points where paths come together. Not surprisingly, nodes are often associated with landmarks that are located at the node. After all, the fact that paths come together at a node may be why the landmark gains significance in the first place. *Edges* are things that limit travel like rivers, seashores, railroads, and walls. Edges make it difficult to integrate cognitive maps. Finally, *districts* are areas of common character that serve as major units in one's cognitive map.

Despite of all the research that has been conducted on cognitive maps, Lynch's taxonomy still works fairly well as a conceptual scheme to organize the literature (c.f., Coucleis, Golledge, Gale & Tobler, 1987; Giraudo & Péruch, 1988). In particular, Aragones and Arredondo (1985) and Magaña (1978) used cluster and correspondence analysis to empirically confirm that people do indeed think of their environments in terms similar to those Lynch proposed, although they did find that landmarks and nodes were not very distinct from each other. (A finding that would not have surprised or disappointed Lynch for reasons just mentioned.) They also noted that the word "edge" may actually have two subtly different meanings. In one sense it may refer to structures within a city that set off districts from one another. It may also refer to the edge or periphery of the city.

Other structural taxonomies. Others such as Kuipers (1982), Krupat (1985), and Teske and Balser (1986) have proposed their own taxonomies. These researchers speak of "higher-order environmental relations" that include simple, lower-order structural features similar to those Lynch mentioned—places (which include buildings and landmarks), paths, and nodes—along with functional and cognitive features of the cognitive map. These higher-order features include *destinations*, which are defined as collections of paths and nodes converging on a functionally significant place and *itineraries*, which refer to destinations connected by a travel strategy that orders them. This viewpoint proposes that static structural features of cognitive maps should not be studied independently of the functional purposes that these maps serve. While many agree with this functional viewpoint, reminiscent of Dewey (1896) and Wagner and Owens (1992), in practice, most cognitive mapping research deals exclusively with "lower-order" physical features of the environment.

Similarly, Gärling, Böök and Lindberg (1984, 1986) feel that Lynch's basic outline is valid, but is only a subset of the meaningful elements of a cognitive map. They point out that cognitive maps exist on many levels of scale, from maps of buildings to maps of buildings within districts, districts within towns, and towns within nations. The basic elements making up cognitive maps for each of these levels of scale might be slightly different. In addition, cognitive maps probably also contain some non-spatial associations with places. Places have names, functions, degrees of attractiveness, and affective tones for each individual.

Gärling et al., like Kuipers (1982) and Teske and Balser (1986), emphasize the functional components of cognitive maps. To Gärling et al., the main elements of a cognitive map are knowledge of places, the spatial relationships between them, and travel plans. The formation of travel plans is described in terms of four stages: (1) Individuals need to know the location of each place they are likely to visit. (2) They must develop an itinerary, the places they want to go. (3) They then must determine the order of the visits. (4) Finally, they need to consider how they should travel in order to travel from each location to the next. The development of travel plans requires individuals to pay careful attention to landmarks, nodes, and traffic signs (e.g., one-way signs often change the best route to travel).

Kaplan's SESAME theory is a truly cognitive approach to cognitive maps (Kaplan, 1973, 1976; Kaplan & Kaplan, 1982/1989; Kearney & Kaplan, 1997). SESAME is an acronym for the Seminar on Environmental Sensitive Adaptive Mechanisms, which worked on models of cognition. The basic elements of this theory are mental objects, which are internal representations derived from perceptions of the world, and associations, which are perceptual features linked to mental objects or relationships between mental objects. In terms of Lynch's taxonomy, landmarks and nodes are types of mental objects, while paths are a set of associations. General as it is, Kaplan's model is significantly less abstract than most cognitive models because he believes that the origins of mental objects are firmly linked to our perceptions of features of the world. According to SESAME, cognitive knowledge develops over time and people have a sense of ownership of knowledge firmly implanted across time in their cognitive map from multiple perceptual experiences. Kaplan believes that people have little awareness of the structure of their cognitive maps and that they use them unconsciously with little awareness of the structure of the map and how solutions to wayfinding problems are arrived at. Kaplan's theory is successful at understanding semantic priming data and categorization of non-metric information associated with places. Kaplan's theory seems somewhat less successful in making concrete predictions about perceptions of spatial layout and wayfinding tasks.

The anchor point theory. Golledge and his colleagues believe that the key structural element of a cognitive map is what they call an anchor point (Golledge, 1991, 1992a, 1992b; Golledge & Stimson, 1997). Anchor points are locations of particular cognitive salience that serve as the kernels around which cognitive maps develop. Although anchor points would superficially appear to be identical to the landmarks of Lynch's taxonomy, there are a number of important differences. First of all, landmarks are typically associated with locations that citizens of a city would collectively agree are of special significance, while anchor points are individually defined. The key anchor points for most individuals are the home, the workplace, or the school, places that are likely to be significant to only to a given individual. Second, landmarks are largely thought of as simply being reference locations, while anchor points serve as organizational elements around which knowledge of local regions develop. A concept somewhat anticipated by Sadalla, Burroughs, and Staplin (1980) in their discussion of reference points. Couclelis, Golledge, Gale, and Tobler (1987) say anchor points help perform cognitive functions such as organizing spatial knowledge, guiding navigation, and forming the basis of estimates of distance and direction. Third, anchor points are hierarchically organized with some locations having more cognitive salience than others. In fact, the elements that have the most cognitive salience are personally significant places like the home or the workplace while public landmarks are likely to be of lesser import. These salient points serve as anchors for organizing our knowledge of features of secondary importance. As cognitive maps develop, features of secondary import then serve as anchors for localizing features of tertiary import and so on. Fourth, anchor points are also organized hierarchically in terms of level of scale, with anchor point systems developing at international, national, regional, urban, neighborhood, and single route levels. Fifth, the linkages between anchor points provide a skeletal structure for representing and organizing cognitive maps. Eventually, anchor point regions (like Lynch's districts) are integrated as this skeletal structure is fleshed out.

Like Lynch, Golledge believes nodes or choice points are of special importance. Golledge, Smith, Pellegrino, Doherty, and Marshall (1985) found that the overall salience of an anchor point is related to the number of alternative actions associated with that location and that the salience of locations declines as distance from choice points increases. They also found that choice points serve as a natural way for individuals to segment routes between locations. Golledge (1992b) proposed that more activities than traditional wayfinding are part of and involved in the development of cognitive maps. Thus, it is not surprising that locations like the home, where many activities take place, are likely to serve as the best anchor points.

Although Golledge's terminology presents a number of subtle advances, Lynch's terminology has become part of the technical vocabulary of the cognitive mapping literature. I will tend to use Lynch's and Golledge's terminology somewhat interchangeably in the rest of this chapter.

Acquisition of Cognitive Maps

Prerequisites for acquisition. A person's first impressions of a new environment are often ones of confusion, disorientation, feeling overwhelmed, feeling like ones memories are jumbled, and feeling excited or uncomfortable. These reactions are typical for good reasons. The person doesn't have any organization to fit impressions and experiences into. With no organization, it is not surprising that people should feel some adverse reactions to all of the new information that bombards them (Cohen, 1978; Lazarus & Cohen, 1977; Milgram, 1970).

Although a small number of researchers such as Hasher and Zacks (1979) feel that subsequent acquisition proceeds automatically by way of unconscious inference, most researchers in cognitive mapping support the contention that the acquisition of cognitive maps is an active process. Random or passively incorporated experiences seldom lead to learning (Moore, 1979). In truth, this issue has not been fully resolved because the evidence on these issues is somewhat mixed.

First of all, learning cognitive maps seems to be largely an intentional act. Desiring to know how an environment is laid out helps in learning about it. For example, Moeser (1988) studied cognitive map learning in a hospital where rooms and corridors had irregular sizes and failed to follow any set pattern. Moeser found that nurses who had worked in this environment for more than two years had poorer knowledge of its spatial layout than did naive subjects who were merely asked to learn the buildings layout after a half-hour experience studying maps of the building. Ellen (1980) also showed that locomotion without engagement of higher mental processes leads to little learning.

Secondly, it appears that people learn best when they develop their own "action plans" (Gärling, Böök, & Lindberg, 1984; Moore, 1979), that is they must be involved in actively planning and physically executing a strategy for getting from one place to another. They must be both active pilots and navigators through their familiar world. For example, Hazen (1982) had 64 2- to 4-year-old children either passively or actively explore a museum, and then asked them to reverse the route traveled. Active explorers displayed more accurate knowledge of spatial layout and could better trace the route back. Using cats as subjects, Poucet (1985) indicated that passive locomotion could only lead to the simplest cognitive maps. In contrast, Wilson (1999) found little difference in spatial memory between passive and active observers when exploring a computer generated virtual environment.

On the other hand, observers that focus exclusively on getting from one place to another without specific interest in learning about spatial layout tend to perform more poorly than those who are also interested in learning about layout (Rossano & Reardon, 1999; Sweller & Chandler, 1994; Sweller & Levine, 1982). Sweller (1994) believes this "goal-specificity" phenomenon can be accounted for in terms of cognitive load. When observers are focused on a specific wayfinding task, they direct their attention to solving that task leaving few resources available for irrelevant information, such as learning about spatial layout.

Indeed, acquiring cognitive maps is said to be effortful and requires active attention. The more one concentrates on the environment, the better one should learn it. Consistent with this contention, Cohen, Cohen, and Cohen (1988) found that children who performed activities at different locations that were functionally related to each other and required mental effort learned locations along a path better than those who merely walked along the path or performed unrelated activities. Allen and Willenborg (1998) asked some subjects to repeat strings of random digits during a simulated route-learning task. Subjects who engaged in the cognitively demanding task performed more poorly on scene recognition and distance estimation measures than control subjects. Böök and Gärling (1980) asked some observers to count backwards while walking. Other observers were not given this cognitively demanding task. They found that distance and direction estimates were less accurate in the counting condition. Lindberg and Gärling (1982, 1983) also found that a concurrent task tended to decrease the accuracy of estimates based on path knowledge. On the other hand, Lindberg and Gärling (1981a, 1981b) found that concurrent cognitive tasks did not prevent acquisition of path knowledge although it did impair orientation performance and increase latency for responding.

Paths and landmarks. According to Lynch (1960) and Appleyard (1970, 1976) the first bit of organization that we acquire are paths. That is, we remember how to get from one place to another. A number of other factors influence the speed and accuracy with which path knowledge is acquired. Time and mobility, two factors that define how much experience we have with an environment, are probably the two most important factors that influence the acquisition of cognitive maps. Hourihan and Jones (1979), for example, found that these two factors account for about two-thirds of the variance in interpoint distance estimates. Teske and Balser (1986) also found that more mobile subjects had superior cognitive maps. Evans, Marrero, and Butler (1981) found that the number of paths that subjects knew in Irvin, California, and Bordeaux, France, grew dramatically over the course of a year.

Early works also stressed that paths are learned before two- or three-dimensional spatial structures (Lynch, 1960). For example, Appleyard (1970, 1976) examined sketch maps produced by residents of an urban area and noted that short-term residents who had lived in the area less than one year produced more sequentially dominant maps characterized by more path usage as compared to long-term residents whose maps were more spatially dominant. Devlin (1976) noted that the sketch maps of short-term residents maintained the same path structure at two weeks as at two months, but that their placement of landmarks showed greater variability. Gärling, Böök, Lindberg, and Nilsson (1981) found that rudimentary acquisition of a single path was very quick; after only one trial subjects were able to correctly report the order in which various landmarks were passed. Memory for the location of landmarks developed slightly slower (by the second trial it pretty good). Lindberg and Gärling (1982, 1983) conclude that learning paths requires less information processing capacity than learning the distances between and directions to landmarks because the later types of judgments produced longer reaction times and lower accuracy than judgments related to path knowledge. Tani (1980) and Waller (1986) showed that cognitive maps in young children consist of only partially integrated route knowledge. The development of spatial knowledge such as the location of landmarks is a secondary process that develops with age.

More recently, however, most theory has emphasized the importance of landmarks or anchor points to map acquisition. In fact, some research supports the hypothesis that landmarks are learned first and that paths are learned subsequently. For example, Magliano, Cohen, Allen, and Rodrigue (1995) showed slides mimicking a walk through a small town and gave subjects instructions emphasizing that they remember either landmarks, paths, or spatial configurations. All subjects remembered landmarks, but route and configuration knowledge were only learned well when subjects were instructed to learn these elements. Their results suggest that landmarks are the primary elements of cognitive map acquisition. In addition, Evans, Marerro, and Butler (1981) determined from sketch maps drawn shortly after coming to a new city that subjects drew fewer paths (defined as continuous lines on the figure) than landmarks and that the number of paths subjects knew increased significantly across time (2 weeks vs. 10 months) whereas the number of landmarks did not. Gärling, Böök, and Ergezen (1982) found that subjects living in Umea, Sweden, less than four months could give fairly good estimates of directions to different landmarks, but could not remember which places they would pass along the most direct path between two places. They also found this ordering ability improved significantly after subjects had lived in the area more than a year.

Several comments may be made about data concerning the order in which paths and landmarks are learned. First, it is not surprising that the number of paths known should increase with time more than the number of landmarks. It is also not surprising that subjects might not know the most direct paths between landmarks selected by the experimenter very well. Even if there were only one path connecting N landmarks, simple mathematics tells us that there must be $N(N-1)/2$ paths connecting each possible pair of landmarks. In addition, there are an infinite number of possible paths connecting each pair of landmarks. No wonder the number of paths known increases with time, there are so many more to learn. One need not know all possible paths between landmarks to make true the statement that "some paths are known before the spatial layout of landmarks is." Second, sketch maps possess certain demand characteristics; namely, they ask subjects to draw maps like those seen in an atlas—ones that primarily list places and only list a few of the more prominent paths. After all, it would be an impossible task to list all possible paths between places. Third, there is one logical sense in which landmarks must be known before its possible to know paths because knowing a path involves knowing locations along the way, including landmarks. Anooshian, Pascal, and McCreath (1984) found that children learn to identify landmarks before they learn the route-order in which landmarks are passed, and that they learn route-order before they learn route-shape and route-length. This is a much weaker statement concerning the priority of landmarks, however, than the dubious idea that people learn the spatial location of landmarks before they learn the paths between them.

It is fair to say that landmarks and paths are both learned early in the processes of acquiring cognitive maps. It is also fair to say that the presence of salient landmarks help subjects develop their path structure. For example, Rowen and Hardwick (1983) found that children were significantly more accurate in reporting spatial locations that are clearly marked with landmarks and that accuracy is greatest when the landmarks are salient. Hardwick, Woolridge, and Rinalducel (1983) examined individual differences in landmark selection when subjects learned unfamiliar routes. They found that people with poor spatial ability tended to base their cognitive maps on less spatially informative landmarks than those with better spatial ability. Gärling, Lindberg, Carreiras, and Böök (1986) showed that distance estimates between familiar landmarks or anchor point were significantly more accurate than estimates of distances between less familiar places.

Integration of paths and the role of landmarks. As time passes, the cognitive maps of an individual include more landmarks and more paths. Starting with regions surrounding anchor points, the details of small districts are learned and knowledge of separate districts are integrated. For example, Schouela, Steinberg, Leveton, and Wapner (1980) followed the development of college students' cognitive maps of their campus over a period of six months. They found that their subjects' sketch maps improved in differentiation, articulation, and integration across time. The mean number of buildings correctly located and streets included increased with time while the mean number of distortions decreased. Early maps included only the most salient anchor points, while subsequent maps include more places of increasingly secondary import. When drawing maps, subjects tended to place salient anchor points on the map first and then fill in details surrounding them. Evans, Marrero, and Butler (1981) also found a corresponding progression in maps of Irvine, California, and Bordeaux, France.

Similarly, Devlin (1976) asked the wives of Navy officers to draw maps of a small town both 2-1/2 weeks and three months after moving to the area. She found that the first maps showed the major arteries of the town along with a bit more detail concerning paths surrounding their homes. Subsequent maps featured the home area less prominently and included more streets and landmarks. The downtown area gained greater prominence.

Thus, as time passes, the details of a cognitive map are filled in. The process begins with a sketchy understanding of small areas surrounding salient anchor points. As the individual explores the region, more details are filled in and the small areas gradually expand.

Putting the parts together. How are anchor point regions and the myriad of paths between them integrated into a complete two- or three-dimensional spatial structure? Baird and Wagner (1983) proposed a triangulation method by which path knowledge may be integrated to yield the two- or three-dimensional cognitive maps. According to this theory, early path-knowledge can give a new resident to a city a rudimentary idea of how far apart various landmarks are from one another. This knowledge of pair-wise distance in turn places constraints on the possible spatial layout of landmarks. For example, if a person wanted to position Point B relative to Point A and he/she only knew that the distance between Points A and B was d_1, then the Point B could be located at any point along a circle of radius d_1 centered around A. If the observer now wanted to position a third point, C, relative to A and B, and if he/she also knew that the distance between A and C was d_2, and the distance between B and C was d_3, Point C would lie at the one of the two intersections between a circle of radius d_2 centered at Point A, and a circle of radius d_3 centered at Point B. If the observer now positioned a fourth point based on knowledge of the distance from first three, the position of the new point could be unambiguously determined by the positions of the first three points. (Distance-based circles centered at each of the three known points should meet at a single point.) Subsequently placed points could also be unambiguously positioned on the person's cognitive map.

Unfortunately, this simple theory is unlikely to fully explain the development of spatial structure because a number of factors complicate the triangulation process. First of all, inter-point distance estimates are likely to be very imprecise, because they must be based on path knowledge and the path traveled from one location to another is seldom straight. For example, Péruch, Giraudo, and Gärling (1989) found that estimated inter-point distances were more in line with path lengths than as-the-crow-flies, straight-line distance. So, really precise localization of places is likely to involve combining information from many inter-point distance estimates to achieve a converging sense of a locations position.

In addition, map construction is complicated by the fact that exponents for distance estimation for cognitive maps are generally much less than 1.0 (as noted in Chapter 5). As discussed in Chapter 4, this should lead to large distortions in the placement of locations on the map (if the map fits together at all). In addition, because power functions with exponents less than one will shrink long inter-point distance more than short distances, the positions assigned to points by a triangulation process are not likely to be unique, but will change for different combinations of landmarks used in locating a place (assuming the distance-based circles intersect at one point at all).

There is evidence that such distortions do occur and that they really reflect observers' perceptions. Baird and Merrill (1979) asked a group of observers to draw sketch maps of a small community. They then gave observers a choice between a real map of the town and observer-generated ones, and observers believed the distorted, observer-generated ones better reflected their perceptions of the layout of the town.

These difficulties could be overcome if people used something akin to non-metric multidimensional scaling to determine spatial structure. With non-metric MDS, any monotonic transformation of distance applied to the original inter-point distances will yield the same solution. Regardless of the distances that enter the process, a Euclidean non-metric MDS will always yield a unique solution that correctly recovers object locations, and inter-point distance exponents (comparing original, physical distances to perceived distance) will always equal to 1.0. (Assuming physical space is Euclidean, the perceptual transformation applied to distances is monotonic, and a Euclidean MDS solution is generated.)

In practice, individuals probably employ something of a combination of metric and non-metric procedures. After all, sketch maps and distance estimates do show considerable distortions in cognitive maps; so, perceptions of distance must influence judgments to some extent. In addition, MDS requires an intact data matrix (all possible inter-point distance estimates are available) in order to work. In the real world, people probably haven't traveled all combinations of paths between all places in their cognitive maps. Something like triangulation is probably used at least to fill in these gaps.

In any case, as observers learn more about their environments, distance estimates should grow more accurate, and multiple sources of information should allow ever more accurate placement of locations. Eventually, people develop a true spatial representation. In consequence, they can use their knowledge to get from one place to another in unique ways. The will use paths they have never used before, creating "short cuts," and in the process gather new knowledge to further refine their maps.

As time passes people tend to think less in terms of paths and images of past experiences, and start to think in a more abstract way (Foley & Cohen, 1984a, 1984b). After a number of years, the image can be examined and used from many starting points and perspectives, both real and imagined (Kirasic, Allen, & Siegel, 1984). Also, with time, the representation becomes more like a 3-D sculpture in a person's mind.

Gärling, Böök, Lindberg, and Arce (1990) demonstrated this by looking at the development of elevation knowledge across time. They had two groups of subjects, one who lived in Umeå, Sweden, for 2 months, and the other group had lived there about 26 months. They found that the newer residents tended to exaggerate differences in elevation, while the older residents had more realistic impressions.

Individual Differences in Cognitive Maps

Age and cognitive mapping ability. The ability to acquire cognitive maps varies along with personal characteristics of individuals. One of the most commonly studied factors which influences cognitive mapping ability is age. As a general rule, a child's spatial competency increases along with their age and experience. In one early study on this topic, Herman and Siegel (1978) had kindergarten, Grade 2, and Grade 5 students walk through a simulated town and then asked them to construct a model of the town. Construction accuracy increased as a function of both age and the number of times they walked through the town. Similarly, Allen, Kirasic, and Beard (1989) found improvement in maze learning ability across age for 6- to 12-year-old children. In addition, Lehnung, Leplow, Haaland, Mehdorn, and Ferstl (2003) showed that fifth and sixth graders were significantly more accurate at drawing a pointer on a piece of paper directed toward local landmarks than were first graders. However, Lehnung, Haaland, Pohl, and Leplow (2001) found that even 5-year-olds can make accurate bearing estimates if they use their fingers to specify direction instead of a pointer.

Younger children appear to use a path-based organization for their maps while the ability to use a more abstract, spatial organization increases with age. In effect, young children can only accomplish the first stages of acquisition process discussed above, while increasing age allows the child to move further along in the process. In one demonstration of this, Biel (1979) asked 6- and 10-year-old children to draw maps of their home neighborhood. Biel found that the young children drew maps one path at a time, indicating that they lacked an overall frame of reference when drawing maps. Older children seemed to be positioning paths and landmarks within a spatial framework. Tani (1980) believed that the transition from path-based to spatial representations occurs around Grade 2, with younger children using a path-based representation and older children using a spatial representation. Second graders used a hybrid of the two representations in her study. On the other hand, even some adults appear to still use a path-based representation of their environment and never achieve a fully spatial representation (Aginsky, Harris, Rensink, & Beusmans, 1997).

The presence of salient landmarks or anchor points is particularly important to young children (Devlin, 2001). For example, Siegel and Schadler (1977) asked kindergartners to construct scale models of their classroom. The authors found that the availability of salient landmarks improved the children's performance. Cohen and Schuepfer (1980) found that Grade 2 children could only remember the configuration of a series of hallways if prominent landmarks were present along the route. Sixth graders and adults were less affected by this manipulation.

Likewise, Bell (2002) found that children made many more errors in placing an object in the absence of prominent landmarks while the presence or absence of landmarks made less difference to adults. Plester, Richards, Blades and Spencer (2002) showed that 4- and 5-year-old children are much better able to find objects located close to distinctive landmarks than near less distinctive features.

Children's maps appear to be egocentrically organized, and they use their home as their most important anchor point. For example, Biel (1982) found distance estimates from a child's home to other places tended to be more accurate than distance estimates between other landmarks. Also consistent with the idea of egocentrism, Waller (1986) found that five-year old children had a tendency to describe routes in terms of their own behaviors they engage in to get to a goal, while eight-year old children describe external landmarks along the route of travel. Similarly, Biel (1986) interviewed 6- and 10-year-old children while drawing sketch maps, and he found that 6-year olds seemed to be recalling their own movements when engaging in the task, while 10-year-olds appeared to use a general frame of reference.

Children also seem to be less capable of integrating disparate districts or compensating for the presence of edges that block their view. For example, Anooshian and Wilson (1977) asked kindergartners and adults to walk a number of routes through an outdoor environment and then engage in a mapping task. They found that children's maps were particularly affected by the presence of barriers to sight and that distance estimates derived from the maps were particularly poor when edges were present.

At the other end of the developmental process, Kirasic's (1985) literature review concludes that elderly adults have difficulty learning new routes in unfamiliar areas. The ability to remember new landmarks and locations correctly appears to be much poorer in elderly adults (60 to 80 yrs.) compared to young (17 to 25 yrs.) and middle (39 to 50 yrs.) adults (Thomas, 1987). However, Ohta and Kirasic (1983) have shown that, while the elderly may not perform well at tradition map construction and map reading tasks, they seem to perform perfectly well in real-world wayfinding in a familiar environment.

Mode of travel and cultural effects. Children (and adults as well) vary greatly in the quality and extent of their geographical experience. Individuals who walk from home to school are likely to have a far different experience of it than those who drive. Walkers have the time to notice small details like the beauty of a flower and the feistiness of a dog, while drivers are likely to know about a larger geographical range (Lynch & Rivkin, 1959). For example, Gärling, Böök, Lindberg, and Nilsson (1981) found that acquisition was somewhat faster for subjects who learned a path while driven in a car as compared to subjects who walked the same path.

Individuals who navigate will have a different experience than someone who is merely along for the ride. In one of my favorite studies, Carr and Schissler (1969) recorded the eye movements of drivers and passengers traveling along the Northeast Expressway of Boston. As one would expect, the passengers' eyes wandered more freely from the road, and the direction of gaze shaped what each remembered about the trip. In this study, passengers made a more complete and more detailed description of the route than drivers. Although passengers might be able to report on more detail, Appleyard (1970) found that drivers have more complete mental maps about landmark locations than passengers. In general, drivers seem to know an environment in an abstract, spatial sense, while passengers know it more in terms of detailed images.

The degree of navigational experience greatly affects the accuracy of children's cognitive maps. Rissotto and Tonucci (2002) studied the spatial knowledge of children who either walked to school on their own, walked to school in the company of an adult, or were driven to school by an adult. They found that children who walked by themselves drew better sketch maps of the area, were better at reading maps of the area, and were better able to recall details of their route than the other two groups. Similarly, Cornell, Hadley, Sterling, Chan, and Boechler (2001) demonstrated that children who engage in adventure exploration of their neighborhoods, particularly those who often led the way, were better able to select and use good landmarks, particularly landmarks at strategic locations like on the skyline and at intersections. Explorers also used better wayfinding strategies in general. (Not surprisingly, Cornell et al. also found that 12-year-olds had more navigational experience and used better navigational strategies than 8-year-olds.)

Differences in cognitive abilities from navigational experience may reflect the influence of socioeconomic status and culture. In general, higher social class children tend to include a larger swath of a city in their maps, and they are better able to describe the spatial layout of the entire city, while poorer children know their neighborhoods well, but have little sense of the city as a whole (Goodchild, 1974; Karan, Bladen, & Singh, 1980; Orleans, 1973). Similarly, Parameswaran (2003) asked Indian and American children to draw sketch maps of their neighborhood and school. Parameswaran found that Indian children drew more detailed maps of a smaller region, while American children drew less detailed, but better coordinated maps of the overall spatial structure of the region and they included a larger geographical area. In general it would appear that children with fewer opportunities to travel by car know their own neighborhoods very well, but have less knowledge of surrounding regions than those who have the ability to travel widely. Cognitive maps appear to mirror the nature of a child's experience.

Sex differences. Several meta-analyses have concluded that clear sex differences exist in spatial and cognitive mapping abilities with men performing better than women overall; however, the magnitude of sex effects varies as a function of the spatial ability measured. Men are much better than women at mental rotation tasks, but differences in performance on other spatial visualization tasks such as the embedded figure task are small but significant (Halpern, 2004; Linn & Petersen, 1985; Voyer, Voyer & Bryden, 1995).

On real world cognitive mapping tasks, the picture is more mixed, but generally support the conclusion that men show better spatial skills. For example, Allen (1974) found males to be superior to females on six tests of spatial ability. Siegel and Schadler (1977) showed that males were better at constructing models of schoolrooms. McGuinness and Sparks (1983) found that males drew more accurate sketch maps and include more detail on those maps. Webley and

Whalley (1987) also showed boys to have superior cognitive mapping skills to females. Everitt and Cawallader (1972) and Orleans and Schmit (1972) discovered that husband drew more complete and comprehensive maps of their neighborhoods than their wives. They also found that wives used the home as an anchor point while their husbands used more abstract coordinates.

At least 14 studies have shown that men are better able to point accurately toward landmarks than women largely in familiar (and sometime newly learned) environments (Conning & Byrne, 1984; Cornell, Heth, & Boechler, 1999; Curtis, Siegel, & Furlong, 1981; Gale, Golledge, Pellegrino, & Doherty, 1990; Golledge, Ruggles, Pellegrino, & Gale, 1993; Golledge, Smith, Pellegrino, Doherty, & Marshall, 1985; Holding & Holding, 1989; Hollyfield, & Foulke, 1983; Kirasic, Allen, & Siegel, 1984; Lawton, Charleston, & Zieles, 1996; Lehnung et al., 2003; Matthews, 1992; Montello, 1991; Neidhardt & Schmitz, 2001). On the other hand, several other studies found no gender differences when men and women learn the layout of new environments (Herman, Blomquist, & Klein, 1987; Herman, Cachuela, & Heins, 1987; Montello & Pick, 1993). A couple of the studies that found superior directional abilities among men, however, also found that women performed equally well at learning new paths from one place to another in an unfamiliar environment (Lawton et al., 1996; Holding & Holding, 1989).

How can one explain sex differences in localization of places? One explanation that naturally follows from these data is that men may engage in more geographical exploration than women. Consistent with this idea, Beatty and Bruellman (1987) found that men had more geographical knowledge than women, but there were no gender differences in the acquisition or retention of locations on unfamiliar maps of simulated towns. Other researchers believe that males perform better at wayfinding in part because they have been culturally conditioned to believe they are better able to navigate, and they suffer less anxiety when doing so than females (Lawton, 1994, 1996; Lawton, Charlseton, & Zieles, 1996; Schmitz, 1997).

Other possible explanations for sex differences posit that women and men use different cognitive mapping strategies. Some researchers have suggested that women are good at remembering paths, while men use a more abstract spatial structure (Cornell et al., 1999; Everitt & Cadwallader, 1972; Lawton, 1994, 1996; Orleans & Schmidt, 1972). Others have suggested females organize their spatial knowledge around landmarks or anchor points and are poor at integrating these local regions or placing them into a larger spatial structure (Holding, 1992; Sandstrom, Kaufman, & Huettel; 1998). Some researchers believe that the cognitive mapping advantage of men arises as a consequence of their superior mathematical abilities (Pearson & Ferguson, 1989).

In an article that can only be described as relentless, Malinowski and Gillespie (2001) examined a number of these explanations of sex differences. The authors studied 978 students at the United States Military Academy who engaged in a wayfinding task as a requirement for graduation. Malinowski and Gillespie found that males made significantly fewer errors and completed the task in less time than females. The authors then used multiple regression analysis to show that a number of alternative explanations for sex differences could not fully account for these differences. The authors showed that sex differences still remained even after taking into account differences in mathematical ability, athletic ability, anxiety, self-confidence, previous experience, and motivation. In addition, the multiple regression analysis showed that mathematical ability and previous experience were also significant predictors (above and beyond the affects of gender) of wayfinding skill.

Cognitive mapping in the blind. Studies on the effects of visual impairment on spatial ability often compare performance between sighted subjects, blindfolded subjects with normal vision, adventitiously blind individuals who lost their sight after the first few years in life, and congenitally blind individuals who were born blind or lost their sight very early in life. Studies in this area are often very inconsistent, in part because most of them rely on very small numbers of blind subjects (Loomis et al., 1993). In some cases, the performance of a single blind individual is compared to sighted subjects. Given this lack of statistical power, it is not surprising that some studies find significant differences in performance between blind and sighted subjects while others do not.

Early work on the blind proposed that they were incapable of spatial thinking and could not form cognitive maps (Van Senden, 1932/1960). More recently, Dodds, Howarth, and Carter (1982) led congenitally and adventitiously blind 11-year-old children along a series of routes over repeated trials. They found that congenitally blind children showed "a complete lack of spatial understanding" as they performed much more poorly at pointing, map drawing, and spatial reasoning tasks that adventitiously blind children.

Other researchers have found that the spatial skills of congenitally blind individuals are no worse than adventitiously blind and blindfolded individuals. For example, Landau, Gleitman, and Spelke (1981) compared spatial performance of a 2-1/2-year-old blind child to blindfolded children with normal vision. They found that the blind subject could chose the proper route from one location to another as well as the blindfolded children. Passini, Proulx, and Rainville (1990) asked congenitally blind, adventitiously blind, blindfolded, sighted, and poor vision subjects to learn their way through a maze. Sighted and poor vision subject made the fewest errors, followed by the congenitally blind, with blindfolded and adventitiously blind subject performing the worst. Loomis et al. (1993) found that congenitally blind subjects performed as well at a pointing task as adventitiously blind subjects and blindfolded subjects with normal vision.

In all likelihood, the truth about spatial abilities of the blind falls between these two extremes. Blind individuals do have a spatial sense, but the way they understand spatial layout is probably different from sighted people. For one thing, spatial navigation is probably a more cognitively demanding task for the blind. Passini, Delisle, Langlois, and Proulx (1988) showed that when asked to engage in a wayfinding task in a complex building, congenitally blind subjects performed as well as sighted controls, but they needed to plan their route in more detail, they needed to stop more often to consider were to go next, and they needed to gather and use significantly more bits of information.

Other researchers suggest that the blind are more likely to use a path-based organization for their cognitive maps rather than an abstract, Euclidean one. For example Rieser, Lockman, and Pick (1980) asked congenitally blind, adventitiously blind, and sighted individuals to estimate straight line distance and walking distance between landmarks. They found no significant difference between groups on the walking-distance measure, but found congenitally blind individuals performed worse than the adventitiously blind who performed worse than sighted subjects on the straight line, Euclidean distance estimation task. Similarly, Bigelow (1996) found that congenitally blind children (8 to 12 years of age) took longer to learn and made more errors on a distance estimation tasks. Blind subject particularly had more trouble with a straight line distance estimation task than with a route-learning task.

Others researchers believe that the blind use a more egocentric organization for spatial information. Brambring (1982) and Dodds, Howarth, and Carter (1982) said that congenitally blind individuals described the route from one location to another in self-referential terms, while adventitiously blind individuals described a route in terms of external referents. Consistent with an egocentric organization, Byrne and Salter (1983) showed that the home is a particularly important anchor point for the blind. They found that the blind made more accurate direction estimates from their home than from other locations.

Other individual difference factors. A number of other individual-difference factors appear to be related to cognitive mapping ability. First of all, some researchers have found that high mathematical ability (as measured by performance on the quantitative section of the SATs) leads to better performance on spatial tasks (Malinowski & Gillespie, 2001; Pearson & Ferguson, 1989). Malinowski and Gillespie (2001) also show that previous experience with outdoor activities like camping, hunting, and hiking is associated with better wayfinding performance. Rovine and Weisman (1989) established that Embedded Figure Task performance significantly predicted their subjects' ability to select the best route on a wayfinding task, estimate distance traveled, and estimate the number of turns made.

Personality and emotional factors may also be related to cognitive mapping ability. Bryant (1982) gave the California Personality Inventory to 85 undergraduates and then asked them to point at various campus landmarks. She found the pointing task errors were significantly negatively correlated with Capacity for Status, Sociability, Social Presence, and Self-Acceptance scores. Herman, Miller, and Shiraki (1987) noted that freshmen underestimated distances to locations they liked more than to distances they disliked. This effect of affect was not present in seniors.

Distortions in Cognitive Maps

Neither direct space perception nor cognitive maps accurately reflect physical layout. Despite the complexities discussed in previous chapters, the geometry of directly perceived environments is relatively simple compared to that of cognitive maps. In Chapter 4, I pointed out that distance estimation power functions with exponents different from one distort visual space such that it no longer satisfies the axioms of a metric space. This problem is even more acute for cognitive maps because distance estimation power function exponents for cognitive maps deviate even further from unity than for direct perception.

In addition, cognitive maps show new types of distortions not seen in spatial perception. In general, I would characterize many of these distortions as arising from insufficient information or from information reduction on the part of the mind. For example, cognitive maps are often incomplete. Unexplored areas form blank spots in our understanding of which we are surprisingly unaware. Because we are unlikely to want to go or even think of going to places that don't exist in our map, these blank spots often stubbornly persist (Krupat, 1985).

Good form, I say. One way we reduce information in cognitive maps is through a tendency toward "good form" (Byrne, 1979). Non-parallel paths are remembered as parallel, non-perpendicular intersections are remembered as perpendicular, curved paths are remembered as straight. For example, most people would be surprised to learn that Miami is actually west of Quito, Ecuador, because they think of the Americas as lying along a straight line (Tversky, 1981). In addition, people tend to idealize the orientation of frames of reference to simplify the task of remembering. For example, the San Francisco Bay actually runs from southeast at San Jose to northwest at San Francisco, although most people seem to think the bay is aligned in a north-south orientation (Tversky, 1981).

Such simplifications ease the burden on memory, while violations of simplifying heuristics make spatial layout difficult to remember. For example, Sadalla and Montello (1989) asked subjects to walk along pathways that had turns in them ranging from 0° to 180° in 15° increments. Subjects were then asked to estimate the turn angle and to point toward the start of the pathway. Subjects made the fewest errors on both tasks for 0°, 90°, and 180° turns. All angles were estimated as being closer to 90° than they actually were. Montello (1991) found similar results using naturally occurring locations in an urban setting. On the other hand, Herman, Blomquist, and Klein (1987) found no difference in pointing accuracy between two naturally occurring locations: one located in an area with straight streets arranged in a regular grid and the other with curved streets that did not intersect at right angles.

Howard and Kerst (1981) provide another example of tendency toward good form. They used multidimensional scaling to form maps of a college campus either based on long-term experience or based on studying a map. In the long-term experience condition, observers tended to "square up" their maps by judging the width and the depth of the campus to be nearly the same when they actually differed markedly. Direct perception of maps did not produce these distortions, although some tendency to "square up" was found among subjects who relied on their memories of map study. There was also a propensity to break the campus into three clusters of buildings. Distances within a cluster were underestimated while distances between clusters were overestimated compared to physical reality.

Thinking in categories. This last finding is an example of another way in which information reduction occurs in cognitive mapping. The complex details of a map are often summarized into more general categories (Stevens & Coupe, 1978). Once again, most people would be surprised to learn that Reno, Nevada, is west of San Diego, California, because they know that California is generally west of Nevada and all parts of the state are assumed to follow this general rule. Similarly, we tend to group North America with South America and Europe with Africa; so, people expect that North America should be aligned with Europe. Most people are surprised to find out that Madrid is north of Washington, DC, and Paris is north of Toronto (Tversky, 1981).

Integration errors. The structural details of cognitive maps often don't fit together into coherent wholes. Brysch and Dickinson (1996) had subjects learn two pathways. They then made orientation and distance judgments either between points that were along the same pathway or between points that were on different pathways. Directly experienced within-pathway judgments were more accurate than inferred between-pathway judgments.

Integration between districts is difficult. For example, distance estimates across edges are often much worse than judgments within a district or on the same side of an edge (Canter & Tagg, 1975). On a smaller scale, the presence of barriers that block sight of previously walked areas or make travel difficult worsens distance and orientation judgments (Belingard & Péruch, 2000; Cohen, Baldwin, & Sherman, 1978; Cohen & Weatherford, 1980; Herman, Miller, & Heins, 1987; Sherman, Croxton, & Giovantto, 1979). Even when physical barriers are not present, people learn maps in terms of hierarchically connected categories that still negatively affect distance estimates when subjects are asked to make judgments across category groupings (McNamara, Hardy, & Hirtle, 1989).

Number of intersections. Paths through information rich environments with many nodes and landmarks tend to be seen as longer than those through information poor environments (Brennan, 1948; Downs & Stea, 1973; Lee, 1970). In fact, when asked to draw maps people have a tendency to draw familiar elements of their environment as disproportionately large. For example, New Yorkers seldom comprehend how much of the country lies beyond the Hudson River.

Sadalla demonstrated this phenomenon, which he called "the angularity effect," in two studies. In the first study, Sadalla and Staplin (1980) tested Downs and Stea's (1973) "route segmentation hypothesis" which proposed that the presence of environmental features like landmarks and nodes would cause a route to be mentally segmented compared to a route without these features. Down and Stea's predicted that the increased information density would cause segmented routes to seem longer. To test this hypothesis, Sadalla and Staplin asked observers to walk straight paths containing one, four, or seven intersections. The intersections also varied in the number of route choices presented. Sadalla and Staplin found that walking-distance estimates increased as the number of intersections increased. However, inconsistent with Downs and Stea's information density concept, the number of alternative paths at each intersection did not influence judgments. I will present a psychophysical explanation of the angularity effect that does not suffer from this weakness later in the chapter.

In the second study, Sadalla and Magel (1980) asked subjects to walk one of two paths: one had two 90° turns along it, and the other had seven 90° turns. Although both paths were physically the same length, subjects consistently estimated walking distance to be longer when they made more turns. On the other hand, Herman, Norton, and Klein (1986) did not find that the number of turns had any affect on walking distance judgments in four experiments employing children of 7- to 11-years-old. In a critique of Herman et al., Heft (1988) notes that Herman et al. controlled for route segmentation, and this equalization of segments may account for not replicating Sadalla and Magel (1980). (See Herman (1988) for a reply.) Turns per se might not influence walking distance judgments, but, consistent with Downs and Stea (1973) and Sadalla and Staplin (1980), route segmentation may be the more important factor. Thus, the same path from one location to another can change perceived length depending on whether it has landmarks and nodes along its length.

Distance asymmetry. Cognitive maps violate metric axioms in yet another way. Distance estimates are often not symmetric or commutative. That is, the perceived distance from Point A to Point B can be different from the perceived distance from Point B to Point A. For example, Lee (1970) asked people to estimate the inward distance from points outside the city to the city center or in the opposite direction from the city center to outside the city. Lee found that inward distances were underestimated while outward distances were overestimated. This may be an example of "time flies when you are having fun." Perhaps, people who live in Dundee, Scotland, (where the study was performed) look forward to a trip downtown, but are less enthused by the trip back.

To add to the confusion, Briggs (1973) and Golledge and Zannaras (1973) found the opposite. Specifically, Golledge and Zannaras found that inward distances (from the subjects' Ohio State campus to the downtown) were judge to be longer than outward distances returning home. The authors proposed that students would encounter more traffic as they approached downtown and that this perceived increase in hassle would lead to negative affect. They also proposed that the heavy traffic would lead people to mentally break the trip into short travel segments, which according to the angularity effect should lengthen perceived driving distance.

Burroughs and Sadalla (1979) and Sadalla, Burroughs, and Staplin (1980) discovered another sort of distance asymmetry. In the later study, subjects were asked to judge the distance from reference points (highly salient landmark or anchor points that help guide navigation) to non-reference locations. They also asked subjects to start with non-reference location and judge the distance to reference points. They found that the perceived distance from a reference point to a non-reference location was significantly smaller than the perceived distance from a non-reference location to a reference point. Foley and Cohen (1984a) also found asymmetries in judgments toward and away from a salient anchor point.

Cadwallader (1979) looked at violations of metric axioms for cognitive mapping distance judgments in another way. He had subjects make 3000 judgments of inter-point distance. He compared pairs of judgments between the same locations to see if they violated commutativity. He found that 66% of the pairs showed judgments differing from each other by more than 10%, 42% differed more than 20%, 22% differed more than 30%, and 11% differed more than 40%. He also found that distance judgments were sometimes intransitive. That is if the distance A is judged greater than B, and distance B is judged greater than distance C; we would expect that distance A would be judged greater than distance C, but Cadwallader found this was not always the case. Cadwallader also found that distance judgments violated the triangle inequality, another basic assumption of a metric space.

Other cognitive mapping errors. Carreiras and Gärling (1990) discuss another odd fact about cognitive maps. People seem to have more difficulty keeping the East-West dimension of their maps straight, while they have little difficulty with the North-South dimension. Perhaps this has something to do with experience with cartographic maps, where East–West is associated with right–left body positions and North–South is associated with up and down. People seem to find the right–left distinction more confusing than the up–down one, probably because gravity resolves any doubt about the later distinction.

Elevation also influences distance judgments. For example, Hanyu and Itsukushima (1995) had subject s walk paths that either included a stairway or a flat path. Subjects then estimated the distance and time to walk each path. Time and distance were overestimated for the path including the stairway while the flat path led to accurate estimation.

The Psychophysics of Spatial Memory

While many researchers have studied cognitive maps, a relatively small number have attempted to specify psychophysical functions relating perceived distance to physical distance. Most studies on distance perception in this area merely statistically compare distance estimates across conditions and never bother to look at the functional form these judgments take.

Memory and the exponent. Nevertheless, some researchers have looked at the affects of memory on distance judgments. For example, Wiest and Bell (1985) reviewed 70 studies on distance perception and classified judgments in three ways: based on direct perception of distance, based on memory following direct perceptual experience, or based on general geographic knowledge (their "inference" judgment condition). Weist and Bell found that the average power function exponents for direct viewing, memory, and inference were 1.08, .91, and .75, respectively. This decline in exponents from perception to memory is consistent with most other research in memory psychophysics (cf. Algom, 1992 for an excellent review).

Chapter 5 of this book contains a much more extensive meta-analysis based on over seven times as many studies and exponents. My meta-analysis found that the average power function exponents for direct viewing, memory, and inference were 1.02, .87, and .77, respectively, for data derived from all judgment methods and 1.04, .90, and .81 for magnitude estimation data. These numbers are fairly consistent with those of Weist and Bell, and show a decrease in exponents associated with memory and the lowest exponents associated with inference conditions. My meta-analysis also showed that average coefficients of determination (based on magnitude estimation data) are highest for direct perception ($R^2 = 0.96$), lower for memory judgments ($R^2 = 0.85$), and lowest for inference conditions ($R^2 = 0.81$). Thus, cognitive maps do not follow a power function form as well as direct perception judgments. This is not surprising given all of the unique sources of error associated with cognitive maps just discussed.

One should note that, in both of these meta-analyses, inference judgments were often based on knowledge of macro geographical features such as the distances between cities and the size of countries that must have been learned originally from maps. This sort of knowledge differs from true cognitive maps based on the accumulation of individual experiences across time. The following comments will largely focus on cognitive mapping studies.

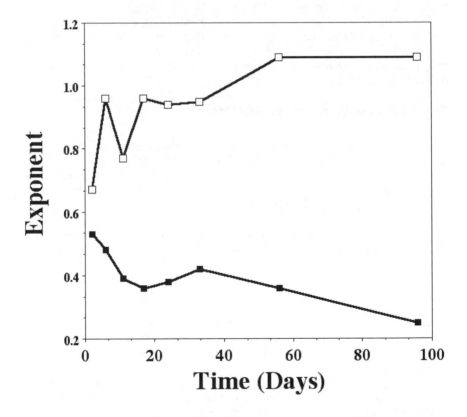

Figure 8.1. The top curve (open squares) shows the mean power function exponent for distance judgments between campus locations as a function of acquisition time (in days) since first moving to Lancaster, PA. The bottom curve (closed squares) shows the standard deviation of distance judgment exponents as a function of time.

Distance functions across acquisition. While cognitive mapping distance estimation exponents tend to be lower than those for direct perception, mapping exponents increase with time and experience. Wagner and Feldman (1990) performed a longitudinal study in which college freshmen, who were originally unfamiliar with the layout of the campus and the city (Lancaster, Pennsylvania), were asked to make distance judgments between various locations on campus over the course of 13 weeks. Subjects employed magnitude estimation relative to a standard distance from the subject to a building that could be directly seen through a window. Figure 8.1 shows the mean power function exponent for their distance judgments as a function of time and experience with the environment. The figure also displays the variability of these exponents. Notice that the power function exponent increases significantly with time and experience with the environment until it approaches about 1.1, values similar to those Wiest and Bell and I found for direct perception. Also, notice that the variability in responding decreases with time.

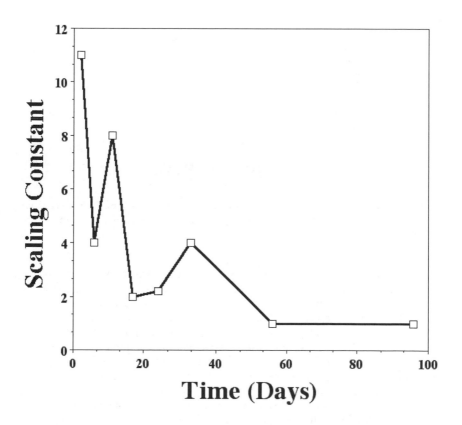

Figure 8.2. The mean power function scaling constant for campus distance judgments as a function of acquisition time (in days) since first moving to Lancaster, PA.

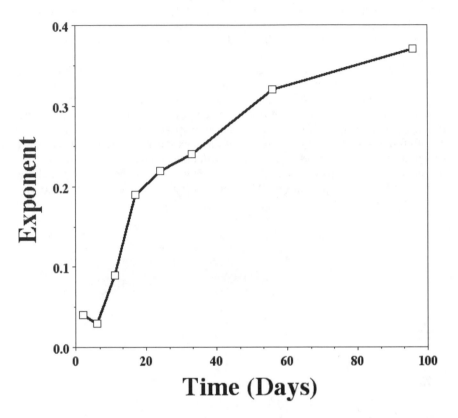

Figure 8.3. The mean power function exponent for distance judgments between various city locations as a function of acquisition time (in days) since first moving to Lancaster, PA.

The scaling constant for the power function also changed with time. Figure 8.2 shows the average scaling constant for the best fitting power functions for distance estimates as a function of time. The scaling constant has been normalized so that accurate reporting of the standard distance results in a value of 1.0. Note that the scaling constant shows a significant decline with time until it reaches 1.0, which shows accurate use of the standard. The large size of the scaling constant during the first few weeks can be attributed to one of three factors. First, the standard may have been used improperly. Second, if the standard is properly used, the scaling constant, which is the y-intercept on a plot of log-judgment vs. log-distance, will shift with changes in the exponent, which is the slope of the best fitting line on such a plot. Third, observers may actually perceive partially familiar distances in their cognitive maps as being larger than perceptually present distances like the standard.

Observers were also asked to judge the distance between various locations in the wider community. Average exponents as a function of time are shown in Figure 8.3. Note that the exponent once again increases as a function of time. However, the exponent reported here are much lower than those for campus locations and the exponent has yet to achieve an asymptote even after 13 weeks. This trend probably arises because student geographical knowledge of the wider community was still poor at the end of the term. I should also mention that the variability of the exponent and the size of the scaling constant declined significantly across time just as with campus judgments (although these trends showed great variability than before).

Finally, observers also judged familiarity with locations, the strength of their emotional reaction to locations, and the difficulty of going from one location to another on a 7-point scale. Familiarity and emotional reactions increased significantly with time, while travel difficulty ratings decreased significantly with time.

Other research on distance estimation exponents. Other researchers have also looked at how power function exponents change as a function of acquisition. For example, Foley and Cohen (1984a) had different groups of subjects estimate distance between locations in a major building on the University of Toronto campus. Some subjects rated distance prior to being given a tour of the building, others after being given a tour, others after one year on campus, and a last group after four years on campus. Pre-tour power function exponents averaged about 0.2, while post-tour exponents average about 0.7. Both 1- and 4-year resident exponents averaged about 0.9. In a second study, Foley and Cohen (1984b) compared performance of first year and fourth year students on distance estimates within the same building. The power function exponent for first year students was 0.83, while the exponent for fourth year students was 0.93. In both cases, cognitive map distance estimation exponent increased along with acquisition, approaching direct perception exponents after acquisition is complete.

In a comparable study, Kirasic, Allen, and Siegel (1984) asked college freshmen (more than 6 months on campus) and upper classmen (more than one year on campus) to rate distances between different campus buildings. Distance estimation exponents for freshmen averaged .56, while exponents for upper classmen averaged .63.

Allen, Siegel, and Rosinski (1978) showed slides taken at 3 m increments along a 645 m path through a commercial and residential neighborhood in Pittsburgh. In one study, slides were either presented in a random order or in sequence and observers were asked to estimate distances between locations. Power function exponents for the distance estimates were 0.43 following the random presentation and 0.74 for the sequential presentation. In a second study, observers were given either one or two presentations of the slide sequence and once again asked to make distance judgments. The exponent for a single presentation was 0.63, but rose to 0.98 following a second presentation. Once again, this study shows that the better one knows an environment, the higher the exponent.

Individual differences in cognitive mapping. Acquisition is not the only factor that influences distance judgments. A small number of studies have suggested that individual differences can affect judgments. For example, Lowrey (1970, 1973) asked observers to use complete ratio estimation to judge the distance between various landmarks. He found that driving experience, which largely covaried with the observer's SES, significantly influenced power function exponents (Lowrey, 1973). The average power function exponent for drivers was 0.56 while the average for non-drivers was 0.38. On the other hand, the average exponent for males (0.48) did not differ significantly from the average exponent for females (0.50). The fact that drivers have higher exponents makes sense because drivers have greater opportunities to explore their environment than non-drivers. As with the acquisition data, the better an individual knows the layout of their environment, the higher the power function exponent.

Canter and Tagg (1975) reported on 11 distance estimation experiments in cities around the world. Ten of these studies employed undergraduates, and the mean power function exponent for these studies ranged from 0.87 to 0.97, averaging .93. On the other hand, when pedestrians in central Glasgow were randomly recruited as subjects from off the street, the mean power function exponent was only 0.52. This suggests that undergraduates may not be representative of the population as a whole. Perhaps undergraduates (contrary to what you would expect from faculty grousing) have superior quantitative or spatial skills than the general population.

Different method, different maps? As with direct perception, different judgment methods can lead to different pictures of cognitive maps. In fact, in some studies, different methods have produced flatly contradictory results. For example, Briggs (1973) asked college students to estimate the distance from the college to various locations. The locations were either further away from the downtown area than the campus ("Away Judgments") or they were closer to downtown than the college campus ("Toward Judgments"). Some of the locations were chosen to be along a straight major artery that passed by campus ("Straight Judgments"), while others were located along winding secondary roads ("Bends Judgments"). Subjects were asked to judge road length both in terms of miles to the target or using magnitude estimation relative to a standard distance. Analysis of exponents showed the two judgment methods produced contradictory results. For mileage estimates, the average exponent for Away Judgments ($\gamma = .61$) was larger than for Towards Judgments ($\gamma = .55$), and the average exponent for Bends Judgments ($\gamma = .76$) was larger than for Straight Judgments ($\gamma = .48$). Magnitude estimation judgments showed the opposite trends with Away Judgments showing a smaller exponent ($\gamma = .66$) that Toward Judgments ($\gamma = .97$), and Bends Judgments showed a smaller exponent ($\gamma = .74$) than Straight Judgments ($\gamma = .80$).

Other studies have contrasted the two main methods of investigating cognitive maps: direct estimation of inter-point distance and sketch mapping (Baird & Wagner, 1983). For example, Sherman, Croxton, and Giovanatto (1979) asked 62 undergraduates to judge distance between all possible pairs of 10 locations on the Miami University campus using magnitude estimation. Observers were also asked to construct a map of the campus using ten wooden blocks, and distance judgments were derive from measurements taken from their model. Power functions were applied to both sets of data. Magnitude estimation produced an average exponent of 1.05, while the average exponent for the mapping condition was 0.89.

Similarly, Baird, Merrill, and Tennenbaum (1979) asked ten undergraduates to use magnitude estimation to make pair-wise distance estimates between various Dartmouth campus buildings and compared these judgments to those derived from maps subjects drew on a computer screen. The average magnitude estimation exponent was 0.97 while the average mapping exponent was 0.92.

Finally, Kerst, Howard, and Gugerty (1987) had subjects study a map of a fictitious college campus. Subjects then either made direct magnitude estimates between locations while looking at the map, made magnitude estimates from memory immediately after looking at the map, made magnitude estimates from memory 24 hours later, made a sketch map from memory immediately after looking at the map, or made a sketch map 24 hours later. The mean power function exponents for magnitude estimation were 1.09 for direct perception, 0.77 for immediate memory, and 0.66 24 hours later. For mapping, the mean exponent was 0.86 for immediate memory, and 0.83 24 hours later.

Taken together, these studies imply that direct perception exponents vary quite a bit, but mapping exponents are always near to, but slightly below 1.0, averaging about 0.9. Second, while power function exponents increase with increasing experience with an environment, simple memory delay leads to a decline in exponents.

Logically, mapping exponents cannot differ from 1.0 very much due to the constraints that mapping places on judgments. As a consequence of the distortions reported earlier, distance relationships in cognitive maps must be non-Euclidean; however, the physical constraints of mapping together with the measurement techniques used by the researchers investigating mapping force these non-Euclidean judgments back into a Euclidean form. As I pointed out in Chapter 4, power functions distort angular relations between the parts of a figure. Exponents that greatly deviate from 1.0 would not be able to fit on the Euclidean map. Most particularly, Chapter 4 pointed out that while exponents less than one will result in distorted angles on the new map, they can at least be represented there. When distance judgments are transformed by power functions with exponents greater than 1.0, angles in physical space often simply cannot be represented at all on the new map. Therefore, it should be impossible for power function exponents based on maps to be greater than 1.0.

Summary of the psychophysics of cognitive maps. The most important conclusion that can be derived from this review of psychophysical studies is that judgment accuracy and power function exponents for cognitive maps are greatly influenced by the quality and quantify of information available to specify distance and the extent to which this information has been acquired. When more information is available and subjects have learned this information well, judgments tend to be more accurate and power function exponents tend to be higher.

Theories to Account for Memory and Cognitive-Mapping Data

A precision theory for acquisition and forgetting. As in other areas of memory psychophysics, power function exponents for distance judgments tend to be lower for memory and inference conditions than they are for direct perception. This pattern of results is inconsistent with one of the most widely known theories concerning the affects of memory on psychophysical judgment: the reperception hypothesis (Kerst & Howard, 1978; Moyer et al., 1978). According to this theory, memory involves going through the same perceptual process a second time. So, if perceived size is a power function of physical size with a given exponent, memory judgments would involve transforming perceived size once more by the same power function used to determine perceived size in the first place. In terms of physical size, this would mean that the power function is applied twice, and the exponent for memory judgments should be the square of the exponent for perceptual judgments. That is,

$$J = \lambda \left(S^{\gamma} \right)^{\gamma} = \lambda S^{\gamma^2} \qquad (8.1)$$

Unfortunately, the distance estimation data don't support the predictions of the reperception hypothesis. If Wiest and Bell (1985) are correct and direct perception produces an average exponent of 1.08, the reperception hypothesis would predict that the exponent under memory conditions would increase to 1.17. This is very different from the average exponents of 0.91 for memory and 0.75 for inference that Weist and Bell reported. The meta-analysis reported in Chapter 5 of this book, is also inconsistent with the reperception hypothesis. According to the meta-analysis, the average exponent for direct distance estimation was 1.02 for all data and 1.04 for magnitude estimation. Based on these data, the reperception hypothesis would predict memory exponents of 1.04 and 1.08, respectively. These are very different from memory exponents of 0.87 for all data and 0.90 for magnitude estimation in the meta-analysis. Average inference exponents of 0.77 and 0.81, respectively, deviate even further from the reperception hypothesis's predictions.

Distance judgments are more consistent with a class of theories based on the concept of uncertainty. One version of this uncertainty theory (Kerst & Howard, 1978; Moyer et al., 1978) attributes memory exponent declines to response constriction. Another version of this theory (Algom, Wolf, & Bergman, 1985) attributes them to an overall change in dynamic response range.

Chapter 5 presented another theory to account for a wide variety of psychophysical effects using the uncertainty concept. In this approach, memory psychophysics effects derive from the most basic of all psychophysical laws, Weber's Law.

According to information theory, information acquisition reduces uncertainty, while information loss should increase uncertainty. In terms of spatial perception, memory results in a loss of information, which increases uncertainty about spatial layout compared to direct perception. As we have seen, cognitive maps (at least initially) are very incomplete compared to direct spatial perception, and this also results in greater uncertainty about spatial layout. On the other hand, acquisition of cognitive maps across time results in an increase in information and decreases in uncertainty about spatial layout. Over very long periods of time, observers may develop cognitive maps that are accurate enough that localization certainty may rival direct perception.

Uncertainty about spatial layout should affect judgment precision. As a result, greater uncertainty should increase the size of JND's for distance judgments. This will, in turn, increase the size of the Weber Fraction under high uncertainty conditions.

To be more specific, I propose that the primary effect of memory on psychophysical judgments is to reduce judgment precision. And thus, we would expect Weber Fractions for memory and inference conditions to be higher than in direct perception conditions. Recent empirical work supports this conclusion by finding that memory conditions produce higher Weber Fractions (Al-Zahrani et al., 1997; Baranski & Petrusic, 1992).

In Chapter 5, we used Fechnerian Integration to derive the power function based on this theory. This derivation produced the following equation:

$$J = \lambda S^{h/k} \qquad\qquad (8.2)$$

where J is a judgment, S is the physical size of a stimulus, λ is the scaling constant, k is the Weber Fraction, and h is the Ekman constant (which is related to number usage).

Thus, the exponent in a power function depends on how precisely subjects can differentiate between stimuli and how precisely they use numbers to make judgments. If memory conditions make our knowledge of stimuli less precise and this increases the size of the Weber fraction, k, Equation 8.2 implies that this will lead to a decline in the exponent—just as memory psychophysics and cognitive mapping data typically shows.

On the other hand, acquisition of cognitive maps implies a gain in information across time. As a result, judgment precision should increase and the Weber Fraction should decrease as time passes and as observers come to know their environment better. According to this scenario, Equation 8.2 would predict that the exponent should increase with time during acquisition, just as the data shows.

Explaining the angularity effect. A second cognitive-mapping phenomenon that is easy to explain mathematically is the "angularity effect." Segmented routes, with many turns and intersections, are often perceived as being longer than physically equivalent routes that are not segmented (Brennan, 1948; Downs & Stea, 1973; Lee, 1970; Sadalla & Magel, 1980; Sadalla & Staplin, 1980). However, some researchers have not been able to replicate this effect (Herman, Norton, & Klein, 1986).

Downs and Stea (1973) proposed that segmented routes contained greater information density, and that information rich routes seem longer. However, Sadalla and Staplin found that increasing information density by presenting more alternative paths at each intersection did not affect distance judgments. Thus, Downs and Stea's information density concept cannot account for the angularity effect. I believe a simpler, psychophysical explanation can explain the angularity effect and also suggest why this phenomenon does not always occur.

In Chapter 4, while discussing the fact that distance judgments often fail to satisfy the axioms of a metric space, particularly the triangle inequality, we mentioned the following inequality holds (See Baird, Wagner, and Noma, 1982, for a proof):

$$a^{\gamma} + b^{\gamma} > (a+b)^{\gamma} \text{ if } a,b > 0, \gamma < 1 \qquad (8.3)$$
$$a^{\gamma} + b^{\gamma} < (a+b)^{\gamma} \text{ if } a,b > 0, \gamma > 1.$$

Because cognitive mapping distance functions are fairly well described by a power function and because the exponent of this power function is generally considerably less than 1.0, Equation 8.3 implies that the sum of the perceived lengths of the two route segments should be longer than the perceived length of the unsegmented route. In other words, the low exponents that are typically found with cognitive mapping distance estimation should lead to a strong angularity effect. On the other hand, if the observer knows the spatial layout so well that the exponent is close to 1.0, no angularity effect would occur, and the sum of the two segments would equal the unsegmented route under these circumstances. It is possible that Herman et al. could not replicate that angularity effect because their subjects' distance functions had exponents near 1.0.

How Cognitive are Cognitive Maps?

Since the fall of Behaviorism in the late 1960's or early 1970's, psychology has been dominated by the cognitive science paradigm. In so doing, psychology has returned to its Structuralist and Psychoanalytic roots after a half-century hiatus in which consideration of the problems of mind was temporarily suppressed. It is no accident that the cognitive mapping literature began in earnest at about the same time that cognitive psychology rose to prominence. The cognitive revolution provided much of the impetus that motivated the development of cognitive mapping research and many of the theoretical approaches and concepts used by cognitive mapping researchers are explicitly cognitive in nature. Even the name "cognitive mapping" implies that cognitive maps are inherently cognitive entities that must be understood in those terms. However, I believe that the cognitive science paradigm has left much of psychology, and cognitive mapping in particular, entangled in a theoretical morass that can only be escaped by leaving behind the cognitive science paradigm altogether.

So, what's the problem? In my view, human conceptions vary in the degree to which they are tied to reality. Some conceptions are directly tied to observables. For example, statements about the physical layout of an environment can be confirmed by some set of operations. For small environments, distances between locations and the direction from one location to another can be directly measured using tape measures and protractors. For larger-scale environments, measurements can be made off maps or aerial photographs. Similarly, human wayfinding behavior can be observed and operationalized. Individuals can also report on their own conscious images and perceptions of spatial layout using words or numeric estimates. Admittedly, we cannot know how accurately words and estimates reflect experience, and no one can examine another's experience and confirm such observations. Yet, at least, we firmly know that conscious experience exists, and introspection is a form of observation that references something real. If introspective reports deviate too much from a person's experience, we expect the person to say "No, I had that wrong; here is what I really perceived." In addition, introspection has the virtue of consensual validation. Multiple individuals can compare their introspective reports, achieving a measure of confidence in reports that reflect a commonality of experience.

Unfortunately, the conceptions of cognitive psychology do not have the same level of reality found in physical, behavioral, and introspective data. The theoretical entities of cognitive psychology exist in an ephemeral land of representations. No set of operations exists to test the validity of representations. They cannot be measured directly like physical layout; they cannot be observed like behavior; and they are not open to introspection like conscious experience. No matter how advanced our knowledge of brain physiology becomes, no one will ever stumble across a representation when looking at the brain. Complex patterns of neural firing and chemical changes in neurons will be found in plenty, but representations will not be found among the thicket. Cognitive entities exist nowhere other than the imagination of the cognitive psychologist. Borrowing a concept from Gould (1996), cognitive psychology reifies concepts, ascribing reality to something that actually exists only in thought.

This is why I referred to cognitive science as a return to our Psychoanalytic roots. The realm of representations differs little from Freud's Unconscious mind. Only the style of furniture has changed in the black box, but the same objection can be made to both representations and the unconscious. They are both imaginary territories filled with imaginary conceptions that are only loosely tied to data.

Working with a black box has its advantages. The cognitive theorist has literally infinite degrees of freedom for their modeling, limited only by the bounds of the human imagination. As Wilcox (1992) points out, such modeling can never truly be predictive. As Wilcox says, "We cannot, by definition, know about unconscious events except by inferring them from the very things we are trying to predict, if we cannot predict from the environment, we cannot predict at all" (p. 44.). Because we know that there are an infinite number of concepts waiting on the bench, cognitive theories (like those of psychoanalysis) can't really be falsified. In the face of contrary data, one merely modifies the theory, presenting it again after a quick fix.

The best that cognitive psychology can offer are descriptive theories that model past data. However, even at the inception of cognitive psychology, Chomsky (1968) was aware that creating a successful descriptive model doesn't necessarily mean that people actually do something in the same fashion as the model. Countless models can describe the same data; models that may have very little to do with the way humans actually operate.

In psychoanalysis, Freud was fond of not only proposing unconscious entities and their dynamics, but he also allowed for these entities to be transformed before their conscious expression. He would speak of a chain of associations, symbolic reinterpretation, and conversion into the opposite. In this way his model could be made to fit any set of data. I remember one paragraph in his "Wolfman" case study in which no fewer than four transformations occur in succession (Freud, 1918). Similarly, a cognitive system consists of a whole set of fabrications. A cognitive model has the freedom to suggest a wide range of representation types, relationships between representations, chains of events that the elements follow through time, and transformations that occur as the entities are realized in experience and behavior.

The real danger here is that the cognitive approach often drives researchers to waste effort to resolve false controversies. I am old enough to remember the great Analog vs. Propositional Debate. The propositional side of this debate asserted that memory was like language and that all memories were stored in terms of sentence like structures. The analog side was willing to admit that memory contained propositions, but they felt that in addition to this, memory also contain continuous representations akin to images. For years, untold effort was directed at supporting one side of this debate while attacking the other. Study after study was performed designed to resolve the debate, but every time a critical study appeared to decide the issue in favor of one side in the debate, the other side was able to show that its theory could also account for the new data after all. Finally, after years of research, Anderson (1978) wrote a famous *Psychological Review* article that mathematically proved that for every propositional model there exists an equivalent analog model that can generate the same predictions and visa versa. Since Anderson convincingly demonstrated that no data could ever differentiate between the theories, cognitive researchers quietly dropped the problem and moved on to argue about other equally irresolvable issues.

So, what is the alternative? Ben-Zeev (1986) believed that memory can be thought of in two ways. In the substantive approach, the mind is thought to be a set of entities along with a storage place for them. Cognitive psychology follows the substantive approach. Representations are stored in the unconscious mind. The other way to think of memory is the relational approach. Here, the mind consists of a set of capacities and a set of actualized states. Memory is a process that leads to behavior and conscious experience as end products. Ryle (1949) would say that memory is best thought of as a mental achievement.

Applying this to the problem at hand, the substantive approach would think of cognitive maps as being a mental map that exists in the head somewhere that is recalled at need. According to this approach, the goal of research should be to describe this unconscious entity. In the relational approach, cognitive maps are the end product of a reconstructive process. While one could study changes in neural structure and the sequence of neural activity that accomplish this process, no map-in-the-head exists.

If one takes the relational approach seriously, cognitive mapping research has a different purpose. The goal of research is now to describe the relationship between knowable entities and to make sense of that relationship. The new question research must address is simply "How does the layout of the physical environment and characteristics of observer relate to our experience and to wayfinding behavior?" In truth, little is lost by abandoning the map-in-the-head concept, because the most memorable and important contributions of past mapping research were already directed at this question.

My view is somewhat reminiscent of Skinner (1985) who accused cognitive psychologists of misusing the metaphor of storage and retrieval and speculating about inaccessible internal processes. However, unlike Skinner, I believe that conscious experience also constitutes a type of datum that is legitimately an object of study. To me, experience is also an observable.

Others, such as Wilcox (1992), make argument similar to my own to argue for adopting a Gibsonian paradigm in the place of cognitive science. However, contrary to the doctrine of Naive Realism, our perceptions do not always accurately reflect the world. As we have seen time after time in this book, our perceptions and the actions we take based on them are sometimes greatly in error. For psychology to be complete, we cannot simply dismiss pervasive and systematic distortions in perception. We must study and explain the process that leads us to sometimes get things wrong as much as we must study and explain how we sometimes get things right.

Rejecting a representational or structural view of cognitive maps in favor of a functional or relational view would seem to imply rejecting the existence of any geometry of cognitive maps. If the unconscious picture in the head does not exist, hasn't the geometry we might attempt to model also disappeared?

While one might not be able to model cognitive representations, one can model people's experience of spatial layout that arises at the end of the reconstructive process. As I have said many times before, as long as coordinates can be assigned to locations (based on physical coordinates) and as long as we can systematically predict judgments of metric properties like size, distance, area, angle, and direction taking into account location of places and contextual variables, then a geometry for cognitive maps still exists. This cognitive map geometry is likely to be more complex than the geometry of visual space arising from direct perception, and it is likely to deviate even further from Euclidean or even Riemannian ideals, but it still should be possible to make progress investigating these experiential spaces that develop across time.

The Geometry of Cognitive Maps

Having said this, the geometry of cognitive maps is very strange indeed. Cognitive mapping geometry violates many of the axioms that traditional geometries assume. For example, the structural elements of cognitive maps differ from direct perception. Paths, the lines that make up cognitive maps, are seldom straight. Unlike traditional geometry, some locations in cognitive maps are more significant than others such as landmarks, destinations, and anchor points. The regions that make up cognitive maps are seldom fully integrated, resulting in a patchwork of mini-maps or districts that define regions that are in turn organized around anchor points. These mini-maps are often bounded by edges that often make cross mini-map integration incomplete. In addition, these mini-maps are linked together hierarchically to form structures that cover larger areas, but in less detail.

The structure of cognitive maps differs from person to person, with some individuals relying on a path-based organization (the young, females, the less mobile, the blind, and those with poor mathematical or spatial skills), while others develop more abstract, global organizations (the old, males, the well-traveled, the sighted, and those with good mathematical and spatial skills). Although it is tempting to think of these representations as being two-dimensional like most maps, our cognitive maps eventually take on a three-dimensional character, although elevation judgments are often in error.

Cognitive maps are distorted in still other ways that are different from traditional geometries. For example, cognitive maps have many holes in them in which whole regions of physical space are undefined in the cognitive map. Cognitive maps show evidence of mental simplification in that cognitive maps are perceived as containing straighter, more parallel, and more perpendicular elements than physical reality. Cognitive maps are also incorrectly reoriented to align themselves with cardinal directions of a compass. In addition, the details of cognitive maps are often summarized into categories, and inter-location judgments are often more based on these categories than on the inter-location relationships that truly exist in the real world. In addition, cognitive map distance is influence by information density, unlike traditional geometries.

Cognitive maps violate many of the axioms of metric or Riemannian spaces. For example, distance estimates are often asymmetrical and do not show transitivity. Distance judgments also often do not conform to the triangle inequality. The lack of smooth transitions across gaps and edges indicate that cognitive maps do not constitute a Riemannian manifold, nor do they constitute a topologically valid transformation of physical space. In Chapter 4, we pointed out that distance estimation exponents that differ from 1.0 yield distortions in angular judgments and the inability of the parts of these geometries to fit into coherent wholes. Because cognitive mapping exponents tend to differ from 1.0 even more than direct estimation exponents, these problems apply even more strongly to cognitive maps. All of these distortions are particularly extreme when a person first begins developing a cognitive map, and they become less profound as the person comes to know the area better. Thus, the geometry of cognitive maps is not constant, but it is a shifting, changing entity that adjusts to experience.

Therefore, it would appear that cognitive maps do not conform to any traditional geometric model. While I do believe that geometries for cognitive maps exist, the problem of determining the exact nature of these geometries is difficult and challenging.

9

The Geometries of Visual Space Conclusion

This chapter has two purposes. First, it attempts to distill the conclusions that can be drawn based on evidence presented in the foregoing chapters. Secondly, it looks to the future, expanding the concept of experiential space to modalities other than vision and suggesting research opportunities that past research has not fully explored.

Lessons Learned

The first conclusion that presents itself from the data discussed in this book is that visual space is not the same as physical space. Despite of the claims of Gibsonian Naïve Realism (Gibson, 1979), our perceptions often do not match physical reality under very ordinary circumstances. Even under full-cue, naturalistic conditions, distance, area, angle, and volume judgments are transformed by power functions that generally do not have exponents precisely equal to 1.0. In addition, the in-depth dimension of visual space typically evinces an affine transformation relative to the frontal dimension. Under reduced-cue settings (which generally occur at least once a day in the natural world), these distortions are even more pronounced.

Secondly, the human mind is flexible enough and the world provides enough variation that no single geometry can fully encompass human visual experience. We can think of distance as the crow flies, as route distance, and as an artist would paint it. We can take into account the laws of perspective or ignore them. We can apply city-block metrics, time metrics, and effort metrics. We can measure visual space using different psychophysical techniques, and each leads to a different metric on the space. Even if the physical world produced a single image in the mind, the geometry of that image changes when people place a different metric on it. Even looked at physically, a flat piece of paper can host an infinite set of geometries; it is only forced to be Euclidean when distance is defined in a Euclidean way. The human mind can quickly shift from one metric to another just as we can shift the forward face of a Necker Cube with a small mental effort, and with each shift in metric, a new geometry applies to visual space.

In addition, physical context and stimulus conditions can shape the geometry of experience. Full-cue and reduced-cue conditions alter our experience of depth, from an expansive dimension under well-lit, natural settings to one in which the dimension almost vanishes altogether and the world seems to lie on the surface of a sphere surrounding the person under completely reduced circumstances. The geometry of the space changes when we view a scene from different perspectives, shifting with the orientation of the stimulus relative to our position. The presence or absence of reference frames can alter our perceptions of the world. Allowing people to move their heads or bodies produces different metric functions than highly controlled conditions with bite-bars and monocular vision.

One could limit discussion by saying that only a single mental metric, only a single method of measurement, only a single experimental layout, and only a single set of stimulus conditions legitimately describe visual space. Yet, any attempt to do this inevitably throws away large amounts of data. I believe our field is better off accepting that a multiplicity of geometries exist and attempting to develop meta-theories that show how the geometries change as a function of mental set and circumstances.

I draw another conclusion from the foregoing chapters that might be controversial to some. I feel the analytic approach to geometry, in which one defines a geometry by developing coordinate equations describing the metric properties of a space, is generally more useful to psychologists than the synthetic approach, in which one defines a geometry through listing global postulates.

Although past attempts at specifying visual space synthetically have been sophisticated and often seductively beautiful (for one who has the eye to see this sort of beauty), empirical evidence has not been kind to these theories. For example, not one of the six axioms of Luneburg's hyperbolic geometry model has been supported by research, nor have predictions derived from Luneburg's model been supported, such as those concerning visual space being bounded, visual space having constant negative curvature, the sum of the angles of a triangle being perceptually less than 180°, and the surface of Vieth-Müller circles as being perceptually at a constant distance from the observer. In addition, the Blumenfeld visual-alley experiment that Luneburg's model was created to explain can be accounted for in more conventional ways which are more closely aligned to past size-constancy research. Luneburg's model appears to only work under a very narrow set of conditions in which no head or body motion is allowed and monocular cues to depth are absent. Most damning to me, Luneburg's (1948) report that observers do not perceive the distance alleys as being parallel or even forming straight lines calls into question whether Blumenfeld visual alleys really violate Euclid's parallel postulate at all. No second parallel to a line through a given point appears to truly exist.

Yet, other proposed synthetic geometries such as the Euclidean and spherical geometries, have not faired much better. Most of Luneburg's axioms are equally essential to these other geometries constant curvature as they are to a hyperbolic account. Empirical rejection of these axioms not only disconfirms the hyperbolic model, but it disconfirms Euclidean and spherical models as well.

The analytic approach proves far more flexible and general than the synthetic approach, and it is much easier to develop models analytically for the affects of context, instructions, and judgment method. Rather than ignoring the bulk of the space perception literature, the analytic approach can incorporate these data into its models.

By the way, a distinction should be made between the analytic approach and specific examples of analytically defined spaces like metric spaces, Banach spaces, and Riemannian geometries. We have shown that visual space sometimes violates the basic assumptions of all three of these specific sorts of analytic geometries. (And one should note that this failure is also a challenge to most synthetic geometries, because they are simply special cases of these more general spatial structures.) Nevertheless, we can still use the analytic approach to model data that is so poorly behaved that it does not satisfy these very general assumptions. We can develop quasi-metrics that describe judgments analytically even though we recognize that the equations we produce do not fall within any common mathematical class. The analytic approach is more general than any of its subtypes.

This book also justifies a number of conclusions concerning the psychophysics of metric judgments. First of all, the power function appears to fit these judgments very well, particularly for direct perception. Coefficients of determination average about .95 for perceptual distance, area and volume judgments. Although most previous work has focused on the exponent of this function, a few studies have found that the scaling constant of this equation is also meaningful. Compared across conditions, variations in the scaling constant indicate a general tendency to report larger numbers in one condition compared to the other.

On the average, people are quite good at judging distance. The average power function exponent for distance judgments was 1.02, very close to the linear exponent of 1.0. Exponents for area and volume judgments were lower, averaging 0.84 and 0.64 respectively. However, averages can be deceiving. After all, I have heard it said that the average household with children has two-and-a-half kids, and I have yet to see a half child. Around these averages, exponents show a great deal of variation attributable to contextual conditions.

A number of factors significantly affect the size of the exponent. As Teghtsoonian's Dynamic Range Theory (1971) predicted, stimulus range had a strong influence on judgments for all metric dimensions. Larger stimulus ranges produce smaller exponents. Judgment method also affected exponents, with power function exponents being generally higher for magnitude estimation. Direct perception typically leads to higher exponents that memory, and memory leads to higher exponents than inference conditions in which knowledge is accumulated across time. Exponents appear to increase with age, and exponents are higher for indoor rather than outdoor settings. For distance estimation, the presence of a standard leads to lower exponents. For area and volume judgments, objective instructions give rise to higher exponents than apparent instructions.

These results are largely consistent with the idea that greater uncertainty leads to poorer judgment precision, and poorer judgment precision leads to lower exponents. A combination of this precision theory and Teghtsoonian's Dynamic Range Theory would seem to account for the great majority of the direct perception data.

This book also leads to a number of conclusions about the size-constancy literature. For example, instructions have a powerful affect on size judgments. Under full-cue conditions, objective and perspective instructions typically are associated with overconstancy, apparent instructions approximately show constancy, and projective instructions lead to strong underconstancy. One largely sees constancy or overconstancy for full-cue settings, but strong underconstancy results from highly reduced-cue conditions. Frontally oriented stimuli are more likely to produce constancy or overconstancy, while flat stimuli are likely to show underconstancy. Judgment ability also develops across time. Young children almost always display underconstancy, and as children grow older, we see more constancy and overconstancy. Judgments become similar to those of adults about the point that children enter Piaget's Formal Operations period. Early research also suggests that more intelligent and artistic subjects are better able to assume projective attitudes.

Although a small number of studies that manipulate "known-size" have produced inconsistent data, the vast majority of size-constancy research appears to validate the Size-Distance Invariance Hypothesis. My version of this model, which avoids many of the simplifying assumptions most past researchers have applied, does a credible job of mathematically modeling the form of past size-constancy research. This model also attempts to unify the direct estimation and size-constancy literatures. In particular, power function exponents derived from the model tend to show similar affects of context as those seen in the direct estimation data. The model also does a credible job of explaining the moon illusion, although a more complete explanation of this phenomenon probably requires thinking of moon size as being a perceived visual angle.

This book has also discussed research that looks at more than one dimension of visual space at one time. Two of my own studies lead to the clear conclusion that for relatively distant stimuli, the in-depth dimension of visual space is severely compressed relative to the frontal dimension when compared to physical space. This compression becomes even more pronounced under reduced-cue conditions. These studies tested a number of candidate models for visual space and found little support for the hyperbolic or spherical models. On the other hand, the data were consistent with visual space being an affine transformed version of physical space. A slightly better model conceived of visual size in terms of vectors in which the in-depth vector component shrinks compared to physical space.

A large number of other studies have found similar compression in the in-depth dimension of visual space for distant stimuli. However, recent work shows that when stimuli approach the resting state of accommodation and convergence at about two meters from the observer, the degree of compression changes rapidly. For near stimuli, the compression goes away, and for stimuli closer than one meter from the observer some studies have even found an expansion in the in-depth dimension relative to the frontal one. I have suggested that this change in the compression parameter may have something to do with the relative rate of change in the sizes of visual angles of frontal and flat stimuli as they approach the observer.

One factor which may complicate modeling of metric functions is recent work indicating that perceived size may be influenced by the shape of the stimulus or the presence of reference frames. In addition, other work implies the existence of a least two semi-independent spatial systems, one that guides action and a second that corresponds to our conscious perceptions of spatial layout.

Finally, this book has also considered cognitive mapping and the affects of memory on spatial judgment. Cognitive maps include non-spatial elements like feelings, memory associations, and functional meaning. The basic taxonomy Lynch proposed in 1960 still seems to describe the spatial elements of cognitive maps. Cognitive maps are still thought to be composed of paths, landmarks, nodes, edges, and districts, although the meaning of some of these terms have evolved. For example, Golledge's anchor point concept which is defined by the salience of a location to an individual seem more precise and relevant than Lynch's publicly defined landmarks.

Research has shown that learning cognitive maps is an active process that best occurs when a person intentionally focuses on the layout of an environment, develops action plans to explore it, and devotes attention to the process. People seem to learn paths and landmarks first, and then integrate their path knowledge relative to salient anchor points, perhaps by a multidimensional scaling like process. They then add details within each district and develop links between them. Only after considerable time, do people develop a true three-dimensional image of their environment.

A number of individual differences affect cognitive map acquisition. Young children appear to use a path based representation of their environment while older children and adults achieve a true spatial map. Free exploration and navigational responsibility improve children's mapping ability. Men appear to have better spatial abilities than women, and the blind appear to have cognitive maps similar to those of young children. High mathematical ability and extensive outdoor activity experience improve cognitive mapping ability.

Cognitive maps are subject to error. There tend to be many blank spots, a tendency to good form, integration errors, categorical thinking, and asymmetrical distance estimation. Judgments often show an angularity effect in which a path with many intersections or turns is seen as longer as a physically equivalent continuous path.

Psychophysically, cognitive mapping distance estimation exponents tend to be lower than those for direct perception. However, cognitive mapping exponents increase along with experience during acquisition. Judgment method strongly influences distance estimates in cognitive maps. In general, sketch maps produce exponent that are slightly less than 1.0, while magnitude estimation exponents can deviate widely from this ideal value.

Once again, the cognitive mapping data can be explained by the concept of uncertainty. Memory exponents tend to be less than perceptual exponents because forgetting introduces an element of uncertainty into knowledge of spatial layout. Similarly, exponents increase across acquisition, because knowledge of spatial layout improves as people learn about their environment.

Finally, I argue that the whole concept of a map-in-the head is questionable, as is all theorizing in terms of representations. A better way to think of memory is a relational model, in which memory is thought of as a mental achievement and the goal of theory is to relate known quantities of physical layout, wayfinding behavior, and conscious experience.

Future Research Directions

Experiential space. Most of this book has focused on vision for the very simple reason that most past work on space perception has looked at this sense. However, I believe that visual space is only one member of a larger class, that of experiential space. Humans are able to make judgments about the location of objects based on their other senses as well.

One sense that we have discussed at various places in this book is touch. We discussed the origin of haptic space in Chapter 4 and compared visual perception to haptic perception in Chapter 7. It's hard to say how purely haptic most of these studies are, because most of the studies involved having people look visually at a target and then reach for or walk to the target without vision. In this sense, much of the past work on haptic space has really concerned a blend of vision and touch. However, a few researchers, such as Solomon and Turvey (1988), Armstrong and Marks (1999), and Schwartz (1999), have truly separated the two dimensions. Haptic space was also discussed in Chapter 8 when we talked about cognitive map acquisition in blindfolded and blind subject.

Another sense that we have spent very little time on thus far is audition. Although poorer than vision, people do have some capacity to localize objects using their hearing. Auditory localization is complicated by the presence of echoes, which most researchers attempt to control. As such, it is difficult to know how much of this research truly describes auditory localization under ordinary, natural conditions (Zahorik, 1999).

Let me briefly describe a few studies on auditory space. Unfortunately, the number of studies is too small to allow for any firm conclusions to be reached about the geometry of auditory space.

As one example, Cochran, Throop, and Simpson (1968) asked observers to judge the distance from themselves to speech sounds originating either 1 to 29 m away in an open field. They found that errors increased sharply as distance increased, and that the data fit a power function with a low exponent (although the exact exponent was not reported). When observers stood in an elliptical room, judgments were much worse and did not fit a power function very well.

Mershon, Desaulniers, Amerson, and Kiefer (1980) showed that people had a tendency to localize a sound source as coming from a visually obvious source even when this source was not the true one unless the two differed by a very large amount. This suggests that our perception of auditory space is often captured by our visual experience.

Ashmead, Davis, and Northington (1995) showed that people were better able to walk to a sound source if they could listen to the sound as they moved. Thus, observers are able to use what might be called auditory motion parallax (what the authors called acoustic tau) to aid in distance estimation.

Loomis, Klatzky, Philbeck, and Golledge (1998) had observers walk blindfolded to a target that they had either seen or heard previously. Visually guided walking was much more accurate than auditorially guided walking.

Brungart, Durlach, and Rabinowitz (1999) asked subjects to point at sound sources generated in random locations within 1.5 m from the subjects. Localization was better for more distant stimuli and for stimuli located further off of the median plane; that is, observers could better determine the location of sound sources off to the side rather than located straight ahead. On the other hand, Simpson and Nation (1997) found little change in overall accuracy in distance estimates to sound sources for faced and side sources, although there was a tendency for observers to overestimate distance to faced sources and underestimate distance to side sources.

One sense that has received very little attention is olfaction. Anyone who has needed to hunt down the origin of an offensive odor knows that one can follow one's nose to some extent. This implies that in a world of odors we are to some extent aware of the spatial layout of their sources. This olfactory geometry is no doubt very imprecise, and yet imprecise of not, the geometry of smell deserves to be studied.

Trillo (1985) conducted the only study that I know of concerning olfactory space. She tested whether or not distance estimates based on smell showed transitivity, commutativity, and a true zero point (Do subjects perceive zero distance when they are located at the source of the smell?). She found that olfactory space did not show any of these features. She concluded that olfactory space is not Euclidean. I might add, that olfactory space is not a metric or Banach space either.

Suggestions for future research. My review of the direct estimation research in Chapter 5 revealed a number of potential research opportunities. Very little direct estimation research has been done under truly reduced-cue, night-like settings. This is surprising given the degree to which this variable has been studied in the size-constancy literature. Similarly, very few direct estimation studies have given projective instructions to their subjects in spite of the importance of these instructions to size-constancy researchers. In addition, the great majority of this research has employed magnitude estimation; this is particularly true of area, volume, and angle estimation. Surprisingly few direct estimation studies employ category estimation, despite of the general impression that perception texts give that category estimation is a major psychophysical technique.

Area, volume, and angle estimation have more unexplored territory that future researchers could explore. For example, few studies look at area judgments in natural outdoor settings and few have looked at the affects of stimulus orientation on area judgments. Volume judgment under natural outdoor settings has also not been examined. Indeed, there have been relatively few studies that look at the direct estimation of volume at all. The direct estimation of angles is virtually a virgin field begging for research.

On the other hand, the size-constancy work could benefit from looking at some of the variables that have proven important in the direct estimation literature. Size-constancy techniques could look at the affects of stimulus range, memory, age, and indoor vs. outdoor conditions.

Visual space perception, like physics, should generalize into the fourth dimension: time. Because the metric functions that describe visual space depend on factors such as perspective, visual geometry should change as a function of time for a moving observer. Yet, these motions also acts a cue to depth; so, one might expect that the change in metric might not be a simple one, and rate and direction of motion might influence our perception of spatial layout. In addition to looking at the affects of self-motion on visual space perception, the motions of the external objects are likely to influence our perceptions. Both self-motion and object motion are in need of further study.

Another area that needs further attention is the application of our knowledge of spatial perception to practical concerns. Although past researchers have applied spatial perception to driving, flying, map reading, sports performance, surgical accuracy, and the plight of special populations (Gillan, Schmidt, & Hanowski, 1999; Hiro, 1997; Kong, Zhang, Ding, & Huikun, 1995; Lapa & Lemeshchenko; 1982; McBeath, Shaffer, & Kaiser, 1995; Moore, 1907; Oudejans, Michaels, Bakker, & Dolne, 1996; Reinhard & Anthony, 1996; Roscoe, 1979, 1982, 1985; Turano & Schuchard, 1991; Westra, Simon, Collyer, & Chambers, 1982; Zhang, Huang, Liu, & Hou, 1995), more work is needed. As Dewey would say, a science best justifies itself when it helps improve the lives of our fellow humans. More work must be done.

In Conclusion

Space perception has a rich history. Too often, psychologists chase the latest fashion and ignore the historical and philosophical context from which their work arises. Some might feel that only current research is relevant because our instrumentation and our knowledge of methodology are superior to that which came before. I reject this notion. The great majority of researchers throughout the last century and beyond have been careful thinkers who have often employed clever and precise methods. The test of a good theory should be if it is able to explain a century's worth of data. Research that responds to only the most recent conceptions and data is likely to be redundant and add less to our knowledge than the researchers believe. History can, and often does, repeat itself in our field.

I believe that this book convincingly demonstrates that introspective reports can lead to a rich and sophisticated science. In answer to Watson's behavioristic challenge, progress is possible in the study of conscious experience. In addition, this book also answers Lockhead's (1992) charge that psychophysics is a sterile discipline that has failed to adequately incorporate the affects of context on judgments. When taken together the space perception literature really can be thought of as a thorough examination of precisely this issue.

However, taking context into account requires flexibility on the part of the theorist. No single geometry can account for the wide variety of research findings that psychologists have uncovered. The quest to determine *the* geometry of visual space is hopeless. Instead we must embrace the complexity of human perception and try to see how visual geometry varies as a function of instructions, method, and experimental conditions. Our goal should be to find not *the* geometry of visual space, but the *geometries* of visual space.

References

Abbott, E. A. (1884/1984). *Flatland: A romance of many dimensions*. NY: Signet Classics.

Aczél, J., Boros, Z., Heller, J., & Ng, C. T. (1999). Functional equations in binocular space perception. *Journal of Mathematical Psychology, 43*, 71–101.

Aginsky, V., Harris, C., Rensink, R., & Beusmans, J. (1997). Two strategies for learning a route in a driving simulator. *Journal of Environmental Psychology, 17*, 317–331.

Algom, D. (1992). Memory psychophysics: An examination of its perceptual and cognitive prospects. In D. Algom (Ed.), *Psychophysical approaches to cognition* (ch. 8, pp. 441–513). NY: North–Holland Press.

Algom, D., Wolf, Y., & Bergman, B. (1985). Integration of stimulus dimensions in perception and memory: Composition rules and psychophysical relations. *Journal of Experimental Psychology: General, 114*, 451–471.

Allen, G. L., Kirasic, K. C., & Beard, R. L. (1989). Children's expressions of spatial knowledge. *Journal of Experimental Child Psychology, 48*, 114–130.

Allen, G. L., Siegel, A. W., & Rosinski, R. R. (1978). *Journal of Experimental Psychology: Human Learning and Memory, 4*, 617–630.

Allen, G. L., & Willenborg, L. J. (1998). The need for controlled information processing in the visual acquisition of route knowledge. *Journal of Environmental Psychology, 18*, 419–427.

Al–Zahrani, S. S. A., Ho, M. Y., Al–Ruwaitea, A. S. A., & Bradshaw, C. M. (1997).Effect of destruction of the 5–hydroxytryptaminergic pathways on temporal memory. *Psychopharmacology, 129*, 48–55.

Anderson, J. R. (1978). Arguments concerning representations for mental imagery. *Psychological Review, 85*, 249–277.

Andrews, D. P. (1964). Error–correcting perceptual mechanisms. *Quarterly Journal of Experimental Psychology, 17*, 102–115.

Angell, R. B. (1974). The geometry of visibles. *Nous, 8*, 87–117.

Anooshian, L. J., Pascal, V. U., & McCreath, H. (1984). Problem mapping before problem solving: Young children's cognitive maps and search strategies in large–scale environments. *Child Development, 55*, 1820–1834.

Anooshian, L. J., & Wilson, K. L. (1977). Distance distortions in memory for spatial locations. *Child Development, 48*, 1704–1707.

Appleyard, D. (1970). Styles and methods of structuring a city. *Environment and Behavior, 2*, 100–117.

Appleyard, D. (1976). *Planning a pluralist city: Conflicting realities in Ciudad Guayana*. Cambridge, MA: MIT Press.

Aragones, J. I., & Arredondo, J. M. (1985). Structure of urban cognitive maps. *Journal of Environmental Psychology, 5*, 197–212.

Armstrong, L., & Marks, L. E. (1999). Haptic perception of linear extent. *Perception & Psychophysics, 61*, 1211–1226.

Ashmead, D. H., Davis, D. L., & Northinton, A. (1995). Contribution of listeners' approaching motion to auditory distance perception. *Journal of Experimental Psychology: Human Perception and Performance, 21*, 239–256.

Bailenson, J. N., Shum, M. S., & Uttal, D. H. (1998). Road climbing: Principles governing asymmetric route choices on maps. *Journal of Environmental Psychology, 18*, 251–264.

Baird, J. C. (1963). Retinal and assumed sized cues as determinants of size and distance perception. *Journal of Experimental Psychology, 66*, 155–162.

Baird, J. C. (1964). Size and distance estimates of triangles, lines, and dots. Unpublished manuscript referenced in Baird (1970).

Baird, J. C. (1965). Stimulus and response factors in size instruction effects. *Perceptual and Motor Skills, 21*, 915–924.

Baird, J. C. (1968). Toward a theory of frontal–size judgments. *Perception & Psychophysics, 4*, 49–53.

Baird, J. C. (1970). *Psychophysical analysis of visual space.* Oxford: Pergamon.

Baird, J. C., & Biersdorf, W. R. (1967). *Perception & Psychophysics, 2*, 161–166.

Baird, J. C., Merrill, A. A., & Tannenbaum, J. (1979). Cognitive representation of spatial relations. II. A familiar environment. *Journal of Experimental Psychology: General, 108*, 92–98.

Baird, J. C., & Noma, E. (1978). *Fundamentals of scaling and psychophysics.* NY: John Wiley & Sons.

Baird, J. C., Romer, D., & Stein, T. (1970). *Perceptual and Motor Skills, 30*, 495–501.

Baird, J. C., & Wagner, M. (1982). The moon illusion: I. How high is the sky? *Journal of Experimental Psychology: General, 111*, 296–303.

Baird, J. C., & Wagner, M. (1983). Modeling the creation of cognitive maps. In H. Pick & L. Acredolo (Eds.), *Spatial orientation.* New York: Plenum Press.

Baird, J. C., & Wagner, M. (1987). Growing a sizeable family of functions. In M. Teghtsoonian & R. Teghtsoonian (Eds.), *International Society for Psychophysics Annual* (Vol. 3, pp. 37–42). Durham, NH: International Society for Psychophysics.

Baird, J. C., & Wagner, M. (1991). Transformation theory of size judgment. *Journal of Experimental Psychology: Human Perception and Performance, 17*, 852–864.

Baird, J. C., Wagner, M., & Fuld, K. (1990). A simple but powerful theory of the moon illusion. *Journal of Experimental Psychology: Human Perception and Performance, 16*, 675–677.

Baird, J.C., Wagner, M., & Noma, E. (1982). Impossible cognitive spaces. *Geographical Analysis, 14*, 204–216.

Baranski, J. V., & Petrusic, W. M. (1992). The discriminability of remembered magnitudes. *Memory & Cognition, 20*, 254–270.

Barbeito, R. (1981). Sighting dominance: An explanation based on the processing of visual direction in tests of sighting dominance. *Vision Research, 21*, 855–860.

Barbeito, R., & Ono, H. (1979). Four methods of locating the egocenter: A comparison of their predictive validities and reliabilities. *Behavior Research Methods & Instrumentation, 11*, 31–36.

Battro, A. M., di Pierro Netto, S., & Rozenstrafen, R. J. A. (1976). Riemannian geometries of variable curvature in visual space: Visual alleys, horopters, and triangles in big open fields. *Perception, 5*, 9–23.

Battro, A. M., Reggini, H. C., & Karts, C. (1978). Perspectives in open spaces: A geometrical application of the Thouless index. *Perception, 7*, 583–588.

Beatty, W. W., & Bruellman, J. A. (1987). Absence of gender differences in memory for map learning. *Bulletin of the Psychonomic Society, 25*, 238–239.

Belingard, L., & Péruch, P. (2000). Mental representations and the spatial structure of virtual environments. *Environment and Behavior, 32*, 427–442.

Bell, S. (2002). Spatial cognition and scale: A child's perspective. *Journal of Environmental Psychology, 22*, 9–27.

Ben–Zeev, A. (1986). Two approaches to memory. *Philosophical Investigations, 9*, 288–301.

Ben–Zeev, A. (1989). Reid's opposition to the theory of ideas. In M. Dalgarno & E. Matthews (Eds.), *The Philosophy of Thomas Reid* (pp. 91–101). Dordrecht, Holland: D. Reidel.

Ben–Zeev, A. (1990). Reid and the Cartesian framework. *Journal of the History of the Behavioral Sciences, 26*, 38–47.

Berkeley, G. (1910). *Theory of vision and other writings.* New York: E. P. Dutton & Co.

Bertamini, M., Yang, T. L., & Proffitt, D. R. (1998). Relative size perception at a distance is best at eye level. *Perception & Psychophysics, 60*, 673–682.

Beyrl, F. (1926). Über die Grössenauffassung bei Kindern. *Zeitschrift für Psychologie, 100*, 344–371.

Biel, A. (1979). Accuracy and stability in children's representation of the large–scale environment. *Psychological Reports, 9*, 1–15.

Biel, A. (1982). Children's spatial representation of their neighborhood: A step towards a general spatial competence. *Göteborg Psychological Reports, 12*, 1–11.

Biel, A. (1986). Children's spatial knowledge of their home environment. *Children's Environments Quarterly, 3*, 2–9.

Bigelow, A. E. (1996). Blind and sighted children's spatial knowledge of their home environments. *International Journal of Behavioral Development, 19*, 797–816.

Björkman, M., Lundberg, I., & Tärnblom, S. (1960). On the relationship between percept and memory: A psychophysical approach. *Scandinavian Journal of Psychology, 1*, 136–144.

Björkman, M., & Strangert, B. (1960). The relationship between ratio estimates and stimulus dispersion. *Reports of the Psychological Laboratories: University of Stockholm*, No. 81.

Blank, A. A. (1953). The Luneberg theory of binocular visual space. *Journal of the Optical Society of America, 43*, 717–727.

Blank, A. A. (1957). The geometry of vision. *British Journal of Physiological Optics, 14*, 1–30.

Blank, A. A. (1958). Axiomatics of binocular vision. (The foundation of metric geometry in relation to space perception). *Journal of the Optical Society of America, 48*, 911–925.

Blank, A. A. (1959). The Luneburg theory of binocular space perception. In S. Koch (Ed.), *Psychology: A study of a science* (Vol. 1, pp. 395–426). New York: Mcgraw–Hill.

Blank, A. A. (1978). Metric geometry in human binocular perception: Theory and fact. In E. L. J. Leeuwenberg & H. F. J. M. Buffart (Eds.), *Formal theories of visual perception* (pp. 83–102). New York: Wiley.

Blumenfeld, W. (1913). Untersuchungen über die scheinbare Grösse in Sehraume. *Zeitshrift zür Psychologie, 65*, 241–404.

Böök, A., & Gärling, T. (1980). Processing information about location during locomotion: Effects of a concurrent task and locomotion patterns. *Scandinavian Journal of Psychology, 21*, 185–192.

Borg, G., & Borg, E. (1990). Psychophysical judgments of size and their use to test rating behaviour. *Reports from the Department of Psychology, Stockholm University, No. 717*, 1–25.

Borg, G., & Borg, E. (1992). Intelligence and rating behaviour in a psychophysical study of size. *Reports from the Department of Psychology, Stockholm University, No. 758*, 1–8.

Borg, G., & Marks, L. E. (1983). Twelve meanings of the measure constant in psychophysical power functions. *Bulletin of the Psychonomic Society, 21*, 73–75.

Boring, E. G. (1950/1988). *A history of experimental psychology* (2nd ed.). New York: Appleton–Century–Crofts.

Bower, T. G. R. (1964). Discrimination of depth in premotor infants. *Psychonomic Science, 1*, 368.

Bower, T. G. R. (1966). The visual world of infants. *Scientific American, 215*(6), 80–92.

Bradley, D. R., & Vido, D. (1984). Psychophysical functions for perceived and remembered distance. *Perception, 13*, 315–320.

Brambring, M. (1982). Language and geographic orientation in the blind. In R. J. Jarvella & W. Klein (Eds.), *Speech, place, and action: Studies in deixis and related topics* (pp. 203–218). New York: Wiley.

Bratfisch, O. (1969). A further study of the relation between subjective distance and emotional involvement. *Acta Psychologica, 29*, 244–255.

Bratfisch, O., & Lundberg, U. (1971). Subjective distance and emotional involvement: Experimental validation of the inverse squareroot law. *Report from the Psychological Laboratories, University of Stockholm, No. 332*, 1–15.

Brennan, T. (1948). *Midland city*. London: Dobson.

Brenner, E., & van Damme, W. J. M. (1999). Perceived distance, shape, and size. *Vision Research, 39*, 975–986.

Briggs, R. (1973). Urban cognitive distance. In R. M. Downs & D. Stea (Eds.), *Image and environment: Cognitive mapping and spatial behavior* (ch. 19). Chicago: Aldine.

Brislin, R. W., & Leibowitz, H. W. (1970). The effect of separation between test and comparison objects on size constancy at various age levels. *American Journal of Psychology, 83*, 373–376.

Brungart, D. S., Durlach, N. I., & Rabinowitz, W. M. (1999). Auditory localization of nearby sources: II. Localization of a broadband source. *Journal of the Acoustical Society of America, 106*, 1956–1968.

Bruno, N., & Cutting, J. E. (1988). Minimodularity and the perception of layout. *Journal of Experimental Psychology: General, 117*, 161–170.

Brunswik, E. (1929). Zur Entwicklung der Albedowahrnehmung. *Zeitschrift für Psychologie, 109*, 40–115.

Brunswik, E. (1933). Die Zugänglichkeit von Gegenständen für die Wahrnehmung und deren quantitative Bestimmung. *Archiv für die Gesamte Psychologie, 88*, 357–418.

Brunswik, E. (1956). *Perception and the representative design of psychological experiments* (2nd ed.). Berkeley: University of California Press.

Brunswik, E., & Cruikshank, R. M. (1937). Perceptual size–constancy in early infancy. *Psychological Bulletin, 34*, 713–714.

Bryant, K. J. (1982). Personality correlates of sense and direction and geographical orientation. *Journal of Personality and Social Psychology, 43*, 1318–1324.

Brysch, K. A., & Dickinson, J. (1996). Studies in cognitive maps: The euiavailability principle and symmetry. *Environment and Behavior, 28*, 185–203.

Burbeck, C. A. (1987). Position and spatial frequency in large–scale localization judgments. *Vision Research, 27*, 417–427.

Burroughs, W. J., & Sadalla, E. K. (1979). Asymmetries in distance cognition. *Geographical Analysis, 11*, 414–421.

Burzlaff, W. (1931). Methodologische Beiträge zum Problem der Farbenkonstanz. *Zeitschrift für Psychologie, 119*, 177–235.

Butler, D. L. (1983a). Influence of line context on power function parameters. *Perceptual and Motor Skills, 57*, 67–70.

Butler, D. L. (1983b). Effect of orientation on judgments of line length. *Perceptual and Motor Skills, 57*, 1015–1020.

Butler, D. L., & Overshiner, C. (1983). The role of mental computations in judgments of area and volume. *Perception & Psychophysics, 34*, 593–598.

Byrne, R. W. (1979). Memory for urban geography. *Quarterly Journal of Experimental Psychology, 31*, 147–154.

Byrne, R. W., & Salter, E. (1983). Distances and directions in the cognitive maps of the blind. *Canadian Journal of Psychology, 37*, 293–299.

Cadwallader, M. (1979). Problems in cognitive distance: Implications for cognitive mapping. *Environment and Behavior, 11*, 559–576.

Canter, D., & Tagg, S. K. (1975). Distance estimation in cities. *Environment and Behavior, 7*, 59–80.

Carey, D. P., Dijkerman, H. C., & Milner, A. D. (1998). Perception and action in depth. *Consciousness and cognition: An International Journal, 7*, 438–453.

Carlson, V. R. (1960). Overestimation in size–constancy judgments. *American Journal of Psychology, 73,* 199–213.

Carlson, V. R. (1962). Size–constancy judgments and perceptual compromise. *Journal of Experimental Psychology. 63,* 68–73.

Carlson, V. R. (1977). Instructions and perceptual constancy judgments. In W. Epstein (Ed.), *Stability and constancy in visual perception: Mechanisms and processes* (pp. 217–254). New York: Wiley–Interscience.

Carlson, V. R., & Tassone, E. P. (1963). Size–constancy and visual acuity. *Perceptual and Motor Skills, 16,* 223–228.

Carlson, V. R., & Tassone, E. P. (1967). Independent size judgments at different distances. *Journal of Experimental Psychology, 73,* 491–497.

Carr, H. A. (1925). *Psychology: A study of mental activity.* New York: Longmans, Green, and Co.

Carr, H. A. (1935). *An introduction to space perception.* New York: Longmans, Green, and Company.

Carr, S., & Schissler, D. (1969). The city as a trip: Perceptual selection and memory in the view from the road. *Environment and Behavior, 1,* 7–35.

Carreiras, M., & Gärling, T. (1990). Discrimination of cardinal compass directions. *Acta Psychologica, 73,* 3–11.

Chalmers, E. L. (1952). Monocular and binocular cues in the perception of size and distance. *American Journal of Psychology, 65,* 415–423.

Chew, E. I., & Richardson, J. T. E. (1980). The relationship between perceptual and memorial psychophysics. *Bulletin of the Psychonomic Society, 16,* 25–26.

Chomsky, N. (1968). *Language and mind.* Niles, IL: Harcourt, Brace, & World.

Cochran, P., Throop, J., & Simpson, W. E. (1968). Estimation of distance of a source of sound. *American Journal of Psychology, 81,* 198–206.

Clocksin, W. F. (1980). Perception of surface slant and edge lables from optical flow: A computational approach. *Perception, 9,* 253–269.

Codol, J. P. (1985). The estimation of physical distance between people: Am I as far from you as you are from me? *Année Psychologique, 85,* 517–534.

Cohen, R., Baldwin, L. M., & Sherman, R. C. (1978). Cognitive maps of a naturalistic setting. *Child Development, 49,* 1216–1218.

Cohen, R., Cohen, S. L., & Cohen, B. (1988). The role of functional activity for children's spatial representations of large–scale environments with barriers. *Merrill–Palmer Quarterly, 34,* 115–129.

Cohen, R., & Schuepfer, T. (1980). The representation of landmarks and routes. *Child Development, 51,* 1065–1071.

Cohen, R., & Weatherford, D. L. (1980). Effects of route traveled on the distance estimates of children and adults. *Journal of Experimental Child Psychology, 29,* 403–412.

Cohen, S. (1978). Environmental load and the allocation of attention. In A. Baum, J. Singer & S. Valins (Eds.), *Advances in environmental psychology* (Vol. 1, pp. 1–29). Hillsdale, NJ: Lawrence Erlbaum Associates.

Cohen, W., Hershkowitz, A., & Chodack, H. (1958). Size judgment at different distances as a function of age level. *Child Development, 29,* 473–479.

Collins, J. R. (1976). Distance perception as a function of age. *Australian Journal of Psychology, 28*, 85–90.

Coltheart, M. (1969). The effect of verbal size information on visual judgments of absolute distance. *Nature, 221*, 388.

Cook, M. (1978). The judgment of distance on a plane surface. *Perception & Psychophysics, 23*, 85–90.

Conning, A. M., & Byrne. R. W. (1984). Pointing to preschool children's spatial competence: A study in natural settings. *Journal of Environmental Psychology, 4*, 165–175.

Cornell, E. H., Hadley, D. C., Sterling, T. M., Chan, M. A., & Boechler, P. (2001). Adventure as a stimulus for cognitive development. *Journal of Environmental Psychology, 21*, 219–231.

Cornell, E. H., Heth, C. D., & Boechler, P. M. (1999). Home range and the development of wayfinding strategies. Paper presented at the *Society for Research in Child Development Biennial Meeting*, Albuquerque, NM.

Couclelis, H., Golledge, R. G., Gale, N., & Tobler, W. (1987). Exploring the anchor–point hypothesis of spatial cognition. *Journal of Environmental Psychology, 7*, 99–122.

Cuijpers, R. H., Kappers, A. M. L., & Koenderink, J. J. (2000). Investigation of visual space using an exocentric pointing task. *Perception & Psychophysics, 62*, 1556–1571.

Cuijpers, R. H., Kappers, A. M. L., & Koenderink, J. J. (2001). On the role of external reference frames on visual judgments of parallelity. *Acta Psychologica, 108*, 283–302.

Cuijpers, R. H., Kappers, A. M. L., & Koenderink, J. J. (2002). Visual perception of collinearity. *Perception & Psychophysics, 64*, 392–404.

Cuijpers, R. H., Kappers, A. M. L., & Koenderink, J. J. (2003). The metrics of visual and haptic space based on parallelity judgments. *Journal of Mathematical Psychology, 47*, 278–291.

Curtis, L. E., Siegel, A. W., & Furlong, N. E. (1981). Developmental differences in cognitive mapping: Configurational knowledge of familiar large–scale environments. *Journal of Experimental Child Psychology, 31*, 456–469.

Cutting, J. E. (1993). Perceptual artifacts and phenomena: Gibson's role in the 20th century. In S. C. Masin (Ed.), *Foundations of perceptual theory* (pp. 231–260). New York: Elsevier.

Cutting, J. E., & Vishton, P. M. (1995). Perceiving layout and knowing distances: The integration, relative potency, and contextual use of different information about depth. In W. Epstein & S. Rogers (Eds.), *Handbook of perception and cognition: Perception of space and motion* (pp. 69–117). New York: Academic.

Da Silva, J. A. (1982). Scales for subjective distance in a large open field from the fractionation method: Effects of type of judgment and distance range. *Perceptual and Motor Skills, 55*, 283–288.

Da Silva, J. A. (1983a). Ratio estimation of distance in a large open field. *Scandinavian Journal of Psychology, 24*, 343–345.

Da Silva, J. A. (1983b). Scales for measuring subjective distance in children and adults in a large open field. *The Journal of Psychology, 113*, 221–230.

Da Silva, J. A. (1985). Scales for perceived egocentric distance in a large open field: Comparison of three psychophysical methods. *American Journal of Psychology, 98*, 119–144.

Da Silva, J. A., & Da Silva, C. B. (1983). Scaling apparent distance in a large open field: Some new data. *Perceptual and Motor Skills, 56*, 135–138.

Da Silva, J. A., & Dos Santos, R. A. (1982). Scaling apparent distance in a large open field: Presence of a standard does not increase the exponent of the power function. *Perceptual and Motor Skills, 55*, 267–274.

Da Silva, J. A., & Dos Santos, R. A. (1984). The effects of instructions on scales for perceived egocentric distance in a large open field. *Bulletin of the Psychonomic Society, 22*, 189–192.

Da Silva, J. A., & Fukusima, S. S. (1986). Stability of individual psychophysical functions for perceived distance in natural indoor and outdoor settings. *Perceptual and Motor Skills, 63*, 891–902.

Da Silva, J. A., Marques, S. L., & Ruiz, E. M. (1987). *Bulletin of the Psychonomic Society, 25*, 191–194.

Da Silva, J. A., & Rozenstraten, R. J. A. (1979). Construção de uma escala subjetiva de distância pelo método de fracionamento *Psicologica, 5*, 45–58.

Da Silva, J. A., Ruiz, E. M., & Marques, S. L. (1987). Individual differences in magnitude estimates of inferred, remembered, and perceived geographical distance. *Bulletin of the Psychonomic Society, 25*, 240–243.

Daniels, N. (1974). *Thomas Reid's inquiry.* New York: Burt Franklin & Company.

Dannemiller, J. L., Babler, T. G., & Babler, B. L. (1996). On catching fly balls. *Science, 273*, 256–257.

Day, R. H., & McKenzie, B. E. (1981). Infant perception of the invariant size of approaching and receding objects. *Developmental Psychology, 17*, 670–677.

DesCartes, R. (1637/1956). *La dioptrique.* In C. Adam & P. Tannery (Eds.), *Oeuvres de Descartes* (Vol. 6). Paris: Librairie Philosophique J. Vrin.

Devlin, A. S. (1976). The "small town" cognitive map: Adjusting to a new environment. In G. T. Moore & R. G. Golledge (Eds.), *Environmental knowing: Theories, research, and methods* (pp. 58–66). Stroudsburg, PA: Dowden, Hutchinson, & Ross.

Devlin, A. S. (2001). *Mind and maze: Spatial cognition and environmental behavior.* Westport, CT: Praeger.

Dewey, J. (1896). The reflex arc concept in psychology. *Psychological Review, 3*, 357–370.

Dodds, A. G., Howarth, C. I., & Carter, D. C. (1982). The mental maps of the blind: The role of previous visual experience. *Journal of Visual Impairment & Blindness. 76*, 5–12.

Domimi, F., & Braunstein, M. L. (1998). Recovery of 3–D structure from motion is neither Euclidean nor affine. *Journal of Experimental Psychology: Human Perception and Performance, 24*, 1273–1295.

Dornic, S. (1967). Subjective distance and emotional involvement: A verification of the exponent invariance. *Report from the Psychological Laboratories, University of Stockholm, No. 237*, 1–15.

Downs, R., & Stea, D. (Eds.). (1973). *Image and environment*. New York: Aldine.

Drösler, J. (1979). Foundations of multi–dimensional metric scaling in Cayley–Klein geometries. *British Journal of Mathematical & Statistical Psychology, 19*, 185–211.

Drösler, J. (1988). The psychophysical function of binocular space perception. *Journal of Mathematical Psychology, 32*, 285–297.

Drösler, J. (1995). The invariances of Weber's and other laws as determinants of psychophysical structures. In R. D. Luce, M. D'Zmura, D. Hoffman, G. J. Iverson, & A. K. Romney (Eds.), *Geometric representations of perceptual phenomena* (pp. 69–93). Mahwah, NJ: Lawrence Erlbaum Associates.

Dzhafarov, E. N., & Colonius, H. (1999). Fechnerian metrics in unidimensional and multidimensional spaces. *Psychonomic Bulletin and Review, 6*, 239–268.

Eby, D. W., & Loomis, J. M. (1987). A study of visually directed throwing in the presence of multiple distance cues. *Perception & Psychophysics, 41*, 308–312.

Einstein, A. (1922). *The meaning of relativity*. Princeton, NJ: Princeton University Press.

Eisenhart, L. P. (1925). *Riemannian geometry*. Princeton, NJ: Princeton University Press.

Ekman, G., & Bratfisch, O. (1965). Subjective distance and emotional involvement: A psychological mechanism. *Acta Psychologica, 24*, 430–437.

Ekman, G., & Junge, K. (1961). Psychophysical relations in visual perception of length, area, and volume. *Scandinavian Journal of Psychology, 2*, 1–10.

Ekman, G., Lindman, R., & William–Olsson, W. (1961). A psychophysical study of cartographic symbols. *Perceptual and Motor Skills, 13*, 355–368.

Ellen, P. (1980). Cognitive maps and the hippocampus. *Physiological Psychology, 8*, 168–174.

Elliott, D. (1986). Continuous visual information may be important after all: A failure to replicate Thompson (1983). *Journal of Experimental Psychology: Human Perception and Performance, 12*, 388–391.

Elliott, D. (1987). The influence of walking speed and prior practice on locomotor distance estimation. *Journal of Motor Behavior, 19*, 476–485.

Epstein, W. (1963). Attitudes of judgment and the size–distance invariance hypothesis. *Journal of Experimental Psychology, 66*, 78–83.

Epstein, W., & Landauer, A. A. (1969). Size and distance judgments under reduce conditions of viewing. *Perception & Psychophysics, 6*, 269–272.

Epstein, W., Park, J., & Casey, A. (1961). The current status of the size–distance hypothesis. *Psychological Bulletin, 58*, 491–514.

Evans, G. W., Marrero, D. G., & Butler, P. A. (1981). Environmental learning and cognitive mapping. *Environment and Behavior, 13*, 83–104.

Everitt, J., & Cadwallader, M. (1972). The home area concept in urban analysis. In W. J. Mitchell (Ed.), *Environmental design: Research and practice*. Los Angeles: University of California Press.

Ewing, A. C. (1974). *A short commentary on Kant's Critique of Pure Reason*. Chicago: University of Chicago Press.

Farrimond, T. (1990). Effects of alcohol on visual constancy values and possible relation to driving performance. *Perceptual and Motor Skills, 70*, 291–295.

Fechner, G. T. (1860). *Element der Psychophysik*. Leipzig: Breitkopf & Härterl.

Feldman, J. A. (1985). Four frames suffice: A provisional model of vision and space. *Behavioral & Brain Sciences, 8*, 265–313.

Ferris, S. H. (1972a). Improvement of absolute distance estimation underwater. *Perceptual and Motor Skills, 35*, 299–305.

Ferris, S. H. (1972b). Magnitude estimation of absolute distance underwater. *Perceptual and Motor Skills, 35*, 963–971.

Fitzpatrick, V., Pasnak, R., & Tyer, Z. E. (1982). The effect of familiar size at familiar distances. *Perception, 11*, 85–91.

Foley, J. E., & Cohen, A. J. (1984a). Metal mapping of a megastructure. *Canadian Journal of Psychology, 38*, 440–453.

Foley, J. E., & Cohen, A. J. (1984b). Working mental representations of the environment. *Environment and Behavior, 16*, 713–729.

Foley, J. M. (1964a). Desarguesian property in visual space. *Journal of the Optical Society of America, 54*, 684–692.

Foley, J. M. (1964b). Visual space: A test of the constnat curvature hypothesis. *Psychonomic Science, 1*, 9–10.

Foley, J. M. (1966). Locus of perceived equidistance as a function of viewing distance. *Journal of the Optical Society of America, 56*, 822–827.

Foley, J. M. (1972). The size–distance relation and intrinsic geometry of visual space: Implications for processing. *Vision Research, 13*, 323–332.

Foley, J. M. (1980). Binocular distance perception. *Psychological Review, 87*, 411–434.

Frank, H. (1926). Untersuchung über Sehgrössenkanstanz bei Kindern. *Psychologische Forschung, 7*, 137.

Frank, H. (1928). Die Sehgrössenkanstanz bei Kindern. *Psychologische Forschung, 10*, 102–106.

Frayman, B. J., & Dawson, W. E. (1981). The effect of object shape and mode of presentation on judgments of apparent volume. *Perception & Psychophysics, 29*, 56–62.

French, R. E. (1987). *The geometry of vision and the mind body problem*. New York: Peter Lang.

Freud, S. (1918). An infantile neurosis. In J. Strachey & A. Freud (Eds. & Trans.), *The standard edition of the complete psychological works of Sigmund Freud* (Vol. 17). NY: Vintage.

Fry, G. A. (1950). Visual perception of space. *American Journal of Optometry, 27*, 531–553.

Fry, G. A. (1952). Gilinsky's equations for perceived size and distance. *Psychological Review, 59*, 244–245.

Fukusima, S. S., Loomis, J. M., & Da Silva, J. A. (1997). Visual perception of egocentric distances as assessed by triangulation. *Journal of Experimental Psychology: Human Perception and Performance, 23*, 86–100.

Funaishi, S. (1926). Weiteres über das Zentrum der Sehrichtungen. *Albrecht von Graefes Archiv für Ophthalmologie, 117*, 296–303.

Galanter, E. (1962). Contemporary psychophysics. In T. M. Newcomb (Ed.), *New directions in psychology* (Ch. 2, pp. 87–156). New York: Holt, Rinehart & Winston.

Galanter, E., & Galanter, P. (1973). Range estimates of distant visual stimuli. *Perception & Psychophysics, 14*, 301–306.

Gale, N., Golledge, R. G., Pellegrino, J. W., & Doherty, S. (1990). The acquisition and integration of route knowledge in an unfamiliar neighborhood. *Journal of Environmental Psychology, 10*, 3–25.

Gärling, T. (1970). Studies in visual perception of architectural spaces and rooms: IV. The relation of judged depth to judged size of space under different viewing conditions, *Scandinavian Journal of Psychology, 11*, 133-145.

Gärling, T., Böök, A., & Ergezen, N. (1982). Memory for the spatial layout of the everyday physical environment: Differential rates of acquisition of different types of information. *Scandinavian Journal of Psychology, 23*, 23–35.

Gärling, T., Böök, A., & Lindberg, E. (1984). Cognitive mapping of large–scale environments: The interrelationship of action plans, acquisition, and orientation. *Environment and Behavior, 16*, 3–34.

Gärling, T., Böök, A., & Lindberg, E. (1986). Spatial orientation and wayfinding in the designed environment. *Journal of Architectural Planning Research, 3*, 55–64.

Gärling, T., Böök, A., Lindberg, E., & Arce, C. (1990). Is elevation encoded in cognitive maps? *Journal of Environmental Psychology, 10*, 341–351.

Gärling, T., Böök, A., Lindberg, E., & Nilsson, T. (1981). Memory for the spatial layout of the everyday physical environment: Factors affecting rate of acquisition. *Journal of Environmental Psychology, 1*, 263–277.

Gärling, T., & Dalkvist, J. (1977). Psychophysical functions in visual size perception. *Umea Psychological Reports, 116*, 1–15.

Gärling, T., Lindberg, E., Carreiras, M., & Böök, A. (1986). Reference systems in cognitive maps. *Journal of Environmental Psychology, 6*, 1–18.

Gehringer, W. L., & Engel, E. (1986). Effect of ecological viewing conditions on the Ames' distorted room illusion. *Journal of Experimental Psychology: Human Perception and Performance, 12*, 181–185.

Gibson, J. J. (1933). Adaptation, after–effects, and contrast in the perception of curved lines. *Journal of Experimental Psychology, 16*, 1–31.

Gibson, J. J. (1947). *Motion picture testing and research* (report No. 7, AAF Aviation Psychology Research Reports). Washington: U. S. Government Printing Office.

Gibson, J. J. (1950). *The perception of the visual world.* Boston: Houghton Mifflin.

Gibson, J. J. (1959). Perception as a function of stimulation. In S. Koch (Ed.), *Psychology: A study of a science* (Vol. 1, pp. 456–501). New York: McGraw–Hill.

Gibson, J. J. (1966). *The senses considered as perceptual systems.* Boston: Houghton Mifflin.

Gibson, J. J. (1977). The theory of affordances. In R. Shaw & J. Bransford (Eds.), *Perceiving, acting, and knowing* (ch. 3). Hillsdale, NJ: Lawrence Erlbaum Associates.

Gibson, J. J. (1979). *The ecological approach to visual perception.* Boston: Houghton Mifflin.

Gibson, J. J., & Bergman, R. (1954). The effect of training on absolut estimation of distance over the ground. *Journal of Experimental Psychology, 48,* 473–482.

Gibson, J. J., Bergman, R., & Purdy, J. (1955). The effect of prior training with a scale of distance on absolute and relative judgments of distance over the ground. *Journal of Experimental Psychology, 50,* 97–105.

Gilinsky, A. S. (1951). Perceived size and distance in visual space. *Psychological Review, 58,* 460–482.

Gilinsky, A. S. (1955). The effect of attitude on the perception of size. *Journal of Psychology, 68,* 173–192.

Gillan, D. J., Schmidt, W., & Hanowski, R. J. (1999). The effect of the Müller–Lyer illusion on map reading. *Perception and Psychophysics, 61,* 1154–1167.

Giraudo, M. D., & Péruch, P. (1988). Spatio–temporal aspects of the mental representation of urban space. *Journal of Environmental Psychology, 8,* 9–17.

Gogel, W. C. (1964). Visual perception of spatial extent. *Journal of the Optical Society of America, 54,* 411–416.

Gogel, W. C. (1965). Equidistance tendency and its consequences. *Psychological Bulletin, 64,* 153–163.

Gogel, W. C. (1968). The affect of set on perceived egocentric distance. *Acta Psychologia, 28,* 283–292.

Gogel, W. C. (1969). The effect of object familiarity on the perception of size and distance. *Quarterly Journal of Experimental Psychology, 21,* 239–247.

Gogel, W. C. (1973). The organization of perceived space: II. Consequences of perceptual interactions. *Psychologische Forshung, 36,* 223–247.

Gogel, W. C. (1974). Cognitive factors in spatial responses. *Psychologia, 17,* 213–225.

Gogel, W. C. (1976). An indirect method of measuring perceived distance from familiar size. *Perception & Psychophysics, 20,* 419–429.

Gogel, W. C. (1981). The role of suggested size in distance responses. *Perception & Psychophysics, 30,* 149–155.

Gogel, W. C. (1990). A theory of phenomenal geometry and its applications. *Perception & Psychophysics, 48,* 104–123.

Gogel, W. C. (1993). The analysis of perceived space. In S. C. Masin (Ed.), *Foundations of perceptual theory* (pp. 113–182). New York: Elsevier.

Gogel, W. C. (1998). An analysis of perceptions from changes in optical size. *Perception & Psychophysics, 60,* 805–820.

Gogel, W. C., & Da Silva, J. A. (1987a). Familiar size and the theory of off–sized perceptions. *Perception & Psychophysics, 41,* 318–328.

Gogel, W. C., & Da Silva, J. A. (1987b). A two–process theory of the response to size and distance. *Perception & Psychophysics, 41*, 220–238.

Gogel, W. C., Loomis, J. M., Newman, N. J., & Sharkey, T. J. (1985). Agreement between indirect measures of percieved distance. *Perception & Psychophysics, 37*, 17–27.

Gogel, W. C., & Mertens, H. W. (1967). Perceived size and distance of familiar objects. *Perceptual and Motor Skills, 25*, 213–225.

Gogel, W. C., & Tietz, J. D. (1973). Absolute motion parallax and the specific distance tendency. *Perception & Psychophysics, 13*, 284–292.

Gogel, W. C., & Tietz, J. D. (1974). The effect of percieved distance on perceived movement. *Perception & Psychophysics, 16*, 70–78.

Gogel, W. C., & Tietz, J. D. (1979). A comparison of oculomotor and motion parallax cues of egocentric distance. *Vision Research, 19*, 1161–1170.

Gogel, W. C., & Tietz, J. D. (1980). Relative cues and absolute distance perception. *Perception & Psychophysics, 28*, 321–328.

Goldstein, E. B. (2002). *Sensation and perception* (6th Edition). Pacific Grove, CA: Wadsworth Thompson Learning.

Golledge, R. G. (1991). Cognition of physical and built environments. In T. Gärling & G. W. Evans (Eds.), *Environment, cognition, and action: An integrated approach* (pp. 35–62). New York: Oxford University Press.

Golledge, R. G. (1992a). Place recognition and wayfinding: Making sense of space. *Geoforum, 23*, 199–214.

Golledge, R. G. (1992b). The case of first–order primitives. In A. U. Frank, I. Campari & U. Formentini (Eds.), *Theories and methods of spatio–temporal reasoning in geographic space* (pp. 1–21). New York: Springer–Verlag.

Golledge, R. G., Ruggles, A. J., Pellegrino, J. W., & Gale, N. D. (1993). Integrating route knowledge in an unfamiliar neighborhood: Along and across route experiments. *Journal of Environmental Psychology, 13*, 293–307.

Golledge, R. G., Smith, T. R., Pellegrino, J. W., Doherty, S., & Marshall, S. P. (1985). A conceptual model and empirical analysis of children's acquisition of spatial knowledge. *Journal of Environmental Psychology, 5*, 125–152.

Golledge, R. G., & Stimson, R. J. (1997). *Spatial behavior: A geographic perspective*. New York: Guilford.

Golledge, R. G., & Zannaras, G. (1973). Cognitive approaches to the analysis of human spatial behavior. In W. H. Ittelson (Ed.), *Environment and Cognition*. New York: Seminar.

Goodale, M. A., & Milner, A. D. (1992). Separate visual pathways for perception and action. *Trends in Neuroscience, 15*, 20–25.

Goodchild, B. (1974). Class differences in environmental perception. *Urban Studies, 11*, 59–79.

Gould, S. J. (1996). *The mismeasure of man*. New York: W. W. Norton & Company.

Granrud, C. E. (1987). Size constancy in newborn infants. *Investigative Ophthalmology and Visual Science, 28* (Suppl.), 5.

Grossberg, S. (1991). Why do parallel cortical systems exists for the perception of static form and moving form? *Perception & Psychophysics, 49*, 117–141.

Haber, R. N. (1985). Toward a theory of the perceived spatial layout of scenes. *Computer Vision, Graphics, and Image Processing, 31*, 282–321.

Haber, R. N., Haber, L. R., Levin, C. A., & Hollyfield, R. (1993). Properties of spatial representations: Data from sighted and blind subjects. *Perception & Psychophysics, 54*, 1–13.

Haber, R. N., & Levin, C. A. (2001). The independence of size perception and distance perception. *Perception & Psychophysics, 63*, 1140–1152.

Hagen, M. A., & Teghtsoonian, M. (1981). The effects of binocular and motion–generated information on the perception of depth and height. *Perception & Psychophysics, 30*, 257–265.

Hagino, G., & Yoshioka, I. (1976). A new method for determining the personal constants in the Luneburg theory of binocular space. *Perception & Psychophysics, 19*, 499–509.

Haken, H., & Portugali, J. (2003). The face of the city is its information. *Journal of Environmental Psychology, 23*, 385–408.

Halpern, D. F. (2004). A cognitive–process taxonomy for sex differences in cognitive abilities. *Current Directions in Psychological Science, 13*, 135–139.

Handel, S. (1988). Space is to time as vision is to audition: Seductive but misleading. *Journal of Experimental Psychology: Human Perception & Performance, 14*, 315–317.

Hanyu, K., & Itsukushima, Y. (1995). Cognitive distance of stairways: Distance, traversal time, and mental walking time estimations. *Environment and Behavior, 27*, 579–591.

Hardwick, D. A., Woolridge, S. C., & Rinalducel, E. J. (1983). Selection of landmarks as a correlate of cognitive map organization. *Psychological Reports, 53*, 807–813.

Hardy, L. H., Rand, G., & Rittler, A. C. (1951). Investigation of visual space: The Blumenfeld alley. *Archives of Ophthalmology, 45*, 53–63.

Hardy, L. H., Rand, G., Rittler, M. C., Blank, A. A., & Boeder, P. (1953). *The geometry of binocular space perception.* Elizabeth, NJ: J. Schiller.

Harker, G. S., & Jones, P. D. (1980). Depth perception in visual stimulation. *US AFHRL Technical Report*, No. 80–19.

Hartley, A. A. (1977). Mental measurement in the magnitude estimation of length. *Journal of Experimental Psychology: Human Perception & Performance, 3*, 622–628.

Harway, N. I. (1963). Judgment of distance in children and adults. *Journal of Experimental Psychology, 65*, 385–390.

Hasher, L., & Zacks, R. T. (1979). Automatic and effortful processes in memory. *Journal of Experimental Psychology: General, 108*, 356–388.

Hastorf, A. H. (1950). The influence of suggestion on the relationship between stimulus size and perceived distance. *Journal of Psychology, 29*, 195–217.

Hazen, N. L. (1982). Spatial exploration and spatial knowledge: Individual and developmental differences in very young children. *Child Development, 53*, 826–833.

Heft, H. (1988). The vicissitudes of ecological phenomena in environment–behavior research: On the failure to replicate the "angularity effect." *Environment and Behavior, 20*, 92–99.

Heidegger, M. (1953/1959) *An introduction to metaphysics*. Garden City, NY: Anchor.

Heller, J. (1997a). On the psychophysics of binocular space perception. *Journal of Mathematical Psychology, 41*, 29–43.

Heller, J. (1997b). Psychophysical invariances in binocular space perception. *Zietschrift für Psychologie, 205*, 297–318.

Helmholtz, H. L. F. (1867). *Handbuch der physiologischen Optik* (1st ed.). Leipzing: Voss.

Helmholtz, H. L. F. (1867/1925). *Physiological Optics* (J. P. C. Southhall, trans.). Rochester, NY: Optical Society of America.

Helmholtz, H. L. F. (1868/1921). *Epistemological writings* (M. F. Lowe, trans.). Dordrecht, Holland: D. Reidel.

Helmholtz, H. L. F. (1881/1968). On the relation of optics to painting. In R. M. Warren & R. P. Warren (Eds.), *Helmholtz on perception: Its physiology and development* (p. 160). New York: Wiley.

Henle, M. (1974). On naive realism. In R. B. MacLeod & H. L. Pick, Jr. (Ed.), *Perception: Essays in honor of James J. Gibson* (ch. 2, pp. 40–56). Ithaca, NY: Cornell University Press.

Hering, E. (1879/1942). *Spatial sense and movements of the eye* (C. A. Radde, trans.). Baltimore: American Academy of Optometry.

Herman, J. F. (1988). On the failure to replicate the "angularity effect:" Reply to Heft. *Environment and Behavior, 20*, 100–102.

Herman, J. F., Blomquist, S. L., & Klein, C. A. (1987). Children's and adults' cognitive maps of very large unfamiliar environments. *British Journal of Developmental Psychology, 5*, 61–72.

Herman, J. F., Cachuela, G. M., & Heins, J. A. (1987). Children's and adults' long–term memory for spatial locations over an extended time period. *Developmental Psychology, 23*, 509–513.

Herman, J. F., Miller, B. S., & Heins, J. A. (1987). Barriers and spatial representation: Evidence from children and adults in a large environment. *Merrill–Palmer Quarterly, 33*, 53–68.

Herman, J. F., Norton, L. M., & Klein, C. A. (1986). Children's distance estimates in a large–scale environment: A search for the route angularity effect. *Environment and Behavior, 18*, 533–558.

Herman, J. F., & Siegel, A. W. (1978). The development of cognitive mapping of the large–scale environment. *Journal of Experimental Child Psychology, 26*, 389–406.

Hermans, T. G. (1937). Visual size constancy as a function kinesthetic cues in binocular and monocular accommodation and fixation. *Journal of Experimental Psychology, 21*, 145.

Hershenson, M. (1999). *Visual space perception: A primer*. Cambridge, MA: MIT Press.

Higashiyama, A. (1976). The 3– and 4–point experiments and a test of homogeneity in binocular visual space. *Japanese Journal of Psychology, 47*, 149–157.

Higashiyama, A. (1977). Perceived size and distance as a perceptual conflict between two processing modes. *Perception & Psychophysics, 22*, 206–211.

Higashiyama, A. (1979). The perception of size and distance under monocular observation. *Perception & Psychophysics, 26*, 230–234.

Higashiyama, A. (1981). Variation of curvature in binocular visual space estimated by the triangle method. *Vision Research, 21*, 925–933.

Higashiyama, A. (1983). A variety of size and distance judgments under monocular observation: Instructions and individual differences. *Perception & Psychophysics, 33*, 91–112.

Higashiyama, A. (1984a). Curvature of binocular visual space: A modified method of right triangle. *Vision Research, 24*, 1713–1718.

Higashiyama, A. (1984b). The effects of familiar size on judgments of size and distance: An interaction of viewing attitude with spatial cues. *Perception & Psychophysics, 35*, 305–312.

Higashiyama, A. (1996). Horizontal and vertical distance perception: The discorded–orientation theory. *Perception & Psychophysics, 58*, 259–270.

Higashiyama, A., Ishikawa, T., & Tanaka, K. (1990). Visual alleys as a function of instructions under informative and reduced conditions of viewing. *Perception & Psychophysics, 47*, 468–476.

Higashiyama, A., & Kitano, S. (1991). Perceived size and distance of persons in natural outdoor settings: The effects of familiar size. *Psychologia, 34*, 188–199.

Higashiyama, A., & Shimono, K. (1994). How accurate is size and distance perception for very far terrestrial objects? Function and causality. *Perception & Psychophysics, 55*, 429–442.

Higashiyama, A., & Ueyama, E. (1988). The perception of vertical and horizontal distances in outdoor settings. *Perception & Psychophysics, 44*, 151–156.

Hillebrand, F. (1902). Theorie der scheinbaren Grösse beim binokularen Schen. *Denkschrift der kaiserlichen Akademie der Wissenschaften Wien mathematisch–naturwissenschaftliche Classe, 72*, 255–307.

Hiro, O. (1997). Distance perception in driving. *Tohoku Psychologica Folia, 55*, 92–100.

Hoffman, E. R., & MacDonald, W. A. (1978). Scaling perceived distance along a road. *Scandinavian Journal of Psychology, 30*, 69–77.

Hoffman, W. C. (1966). The Lie algebra of visual perception. *Journal of Mathematical Psychology, 3*, 65–98.

Hoffman, W. C., & Dodwell, P. C. (1985). Geometric psychology generates the visual Gestalt. *Canadian Journal of Psychology, 39*, 491–528.

Holaday, B. E. (1933). Die Grössenkonstanz der Sehdinge bei Variation der inneren und äusseren Wahrnehmungsbedingungen. *Archiv für die Gesamte Psychologie, 88*, 419–486.

Holding, C. S. (1992). Clusters and reference points in cognitive representations of the environment. *Journal of Environmental Psychology, 12*, 45–55.

Holding, C. S., & Holding, D. H. (1989). Acquisition of route network knowledge by males and females. *The Journal of General Psychology, 116*, 29–41.

Hollyfield, R. L., & Foulke, E. (1983). The spatial cognition of blind pedestrians. *Journal of Visual Impairment and Blindness, 5*, 204–209.

Holway, A. H., & Boring, E. G. (1941). Determinants of apparent visual size with distance variant. *American Journal of Psychology, 54*, 21–37.

Hourihan, J. K., & Jones, L. E. (1979). Distance estimation and cognitive mapping: A multidimensional scaling analysis. *Irish Journal of Psychology, 4*, 79–94.

Howard, I. P., & Templeton, W. B. (1966). *Human spatial orientation.* New York: Wiley.

Howard, J. H., & Kerst, S. M. (1981). Memory and perception of catographic information for familiar and unfamiliar environments. *Human Factors, 23*, 495–503.

Howard, J. P., & Rogers, B. J. (1995). *Binocular vision and stereopsis.* New York: Oxford University Press.

Hume, D. (1739/1896). *A treatise of human nature.* L. A. Selby–Bigge (Ed.). Oxford: Clarendon Press.

Husserl, E. (1910). Phiosophie als strenge Wissenschaft. *Logcs, 1*, 289–341.

Idhe, D. (1986). *Experimental phenomenology.* Albany: State University of New York Press.

Indow, T. (1967). Two interpretations of binocular visual space: Hyperbolic and Euclidean. *Annual of the Japanese Association for Philosophy and Science, 3*, 51–64.

Indow, T. (1974). On geometry of frameless binocular perceptual space. *Psychologia, 17*, 50–63.

Indow, T. (1979). Alleys in visual space. *Journal of Mathematical Psychology, 19*, 221–258.

Indow, T. (1988). Alleys on an apparent frontoparallel plane. *Journal of Mathematical Psychology, 32*, 259–284.

Indow, T. (1990). On geometrical analysis of global structure of visual space. In H. G. Geissler (Eds.), *Psychological explorations of mental structures* (pp. 172–180). Toronto: Hogrefe & Huber.

Indow, T. (1995). Psychophysical scaling: Scientific and practical applications. In R. D. Luce, M. D'Zmura, D. Hoffman, G. J. Iverson, & A. K. Romney (Eds.), *Geometric representations of perceptual phenomena* (pp. 1–34). Mahwah, NJ: Lawrence Erlbaum Associates.

Indow, T., Inoue, E., & Matsushima, K. (1962a). An experimental study of the Luneburg theory of binocular space perception. I. The 3– and 4–point experiments. *Japanese Psychological Research, 4*, 6–16.

Indow, T., Inoue, E., & Matsushima, K. (1962b). An experimental study of the Luneburg theory of binocular space perception. II. The alley experiments. *Japanese Psychological Research, 4*, 17–24.

Indow, T., Inoue, E., & Matsushima, K. (1963). An experimental study of the Luneburg theory of binocular space perception. III. The experiments in a spacious field. *Japanese Psychological Research, 5*, 1–27.

Indow, T., & Watanabe, T. (1984a). Parallel–alleys and distance alleys on horopter plane in the dark. *Perception, 13*, 165–182.

Indow, T., & Watanabe, T. (1984b). Parallel– and distance–alleys with moving points in the horizontal plane. *Perception & Psychophysics, 35*, 144–154.

Irvin, G., & Verrillo, R. T. (1979). Absolute estimation of line length and afterimage as a function of viewing distance. *Sensory Processes, 3*, 275–285.

Ishii, K. (1972). Studies on the correlations among various kinds of constancy. In Y. Akishige (Ed.), *Constancies of perceptual world: Epistemological psychology* (Vol. 4). Tokyo: Ibunsha.

Issacs, L. D. (1981). Relationship between depth perception and basketball–shooting performance over a competitive season. *Perceptual & Motor Skills, 53*, 554.

Ittelson, W. H. (1951). Size as a cue to distance: Static localization. *American Journal of Psychology, 53*, 54–67.

Ivry, R. B., & Cohen, A. (1987). The perception of doubly curved surfaces from intersecting contours. *Perception & Psychophysics, 41*, 293–302.

Jacobs, T. M., Lawrence, M. D., Hong, K., & Giordano, N., Jr. (1996). On catching fly balls. *Science, 273*, 27–258.

James, W. (1890). *The principles of psychology* (Vol. 2). New York: Macmillan.

James, W. (1907/1964). *Pragmatism.* R. B. Perry (Ed.). Cleveland: World Press.

Jenkin, N. (1957). Effects of varied distance on short–range size judgments. *Journal of Experimental Psychology, 54*, 327–331.

Jenkin, N. (1959). A relationship between increments of distance and estimates of objective size. *American Journal of Psychology, 72*, 345–363.

Jenkin, N., & Feallock, S. M. (1960). Developmental and intellectual processes in size–distance judgment. *American Journal of Psychology, 73*, 268–273.

Johansson, G. (1986). Relational invariance and visual space perception: On perceptual vector analysis of the optic flow. *Acta Psychologica, 63*, 89–101.

Johansson, G., von Hofsten, C., & Jansson, G. (1980). Event perception. *Annual Review of Psychology, 31*, 27–63.

Jones, B. (1983). Psychological analyses of haptic and haptic–visual judgements of extent. *Quarterly Journal of Experimental Psychology, 35A*, 597–606.

Joynson, R. B. (1949). The problem of size and distance. *Quarterly Journal of Experimental Psychology, 1*, 119–135.

Kaneko, H., & Uchikawa, K. (1997). Perceived angular and linear size: The role of binocular disparity and visual surround. *Perception, 26*, 17–27.

Kant, I. (1923). *The philosophy of Kant.* Glasgow: Maclehose, Jackson, and Company.

Kant, I. (1781/1929). *Critique of pure reason.* N. Kemp Smith (trans.). London: Macmillan.

Kaplan, S. (1973). Cognitive maps in perception and thought. In R. M. Downs & D. Stea (Eds.), *Image and environment.* New York: Aldine.

Kaplan, S. (1976). Adaptation, structure, and knowledge. In G. Moore & R. Golledge (Eds.), *Environmental knowing.* Strondesberg, PA: Dowden, Hutchinson, and Ross.

Kaplan, S., & Kaplan, R. (1982/1989). *Cognition and environment: Functioning in an uncertain world.* Ann Arbor, MI: Ulrich's.

Kappers, A. M. L., & Te Pas, S. F. (2001). Deformation of visual space at the ECVP in Groningen. *Perception, 30*, 1275–1276.

Karan, P. P., Bladen, W. A., & Singh, G. (1980). Slum dwellers' and squatters' images of the city. *Environment and Behavior, 12*, 81–100.

Kaufman, L., & Rock, I. (1962). The moon illusion: 1. *Science, 136*, 93–961.

Kearney, A. R., & Kaplan, S. (1997). Toward a methodology for the measurement of knowledge structures of ordinary people. *Environment and Behavior, 29*, 579–617.

Kemp, S. (1988). Memorial psychophysics for visual area: The effect of retention interval. *Memory & Cognition, 16*, 431–436.

Kerst, S. M., & Howard, J. H. (1978). Memory psychophysics for visual area and length. *Memory & Cognition, 6*, 327–335.

Kerst, S. M., Howard, J. H. Jr., & Gugerty, L. J. (1987). Judgment accuracy in pair–distance estimation and map scetching. *Perception & Psychophysics, 25*, 185–188.

Kirasic, K. C. (1985). A road map to research for spatial cognition in the elderly adult. In R. Cohen (Ed.), *The development of spatial cognition* (pp. 185–198). Hillsdale, NJ: Lawrence Erlbaum Associates.

Kirasic, K. C., Allen, G. L., & Siegel, A. W. (1984). Expression of configurational knowledge of large–scale environments: Students' performance of cognitive tasks. *Environment and Behavior, 16*, 687–712.

Klein, S. A., & Levi, D. M. (1987). Position sense of the peripheral retina. *Journal of the Optical Society of America, 4*, 1543–1553.

Kline, M. (1972). *Mathematical thought from ancient to modern times*. New York: Oxford University Press.

Koenderink, J. J., van Doorn, A. J., Kappers, A. M. L., & Lappin, J. S. (2002). Large–scale visual frontoparallels under full–cue conditions. *Perception, 31*, 1467–1475.

Koenderink, J. J., van Doorn, A. J., & Lappin, J. S. (2000). Direct measurement of the curvature of visual space. *Perception, 29*, 69–79.

Koenderink, J. J., van Doorn, A. J., & Lappin, J. S. (2003). Exocentric pointing to opposite targets. *Acta Psychologica, 112*, 71–87.

Koffka, K. (1935). *Principles of Gestalt Psychology*. New York: Harcourt Brace.

Kong, Q., Zhang, T., Ding, B., & Ge, H. (1995). Psychological measurements of railroad drivers. *Chinese Mental Health Journal, 9*, 213–214.

Kowal, K. H. (1993). The range effect as a function of stimulus set, presence of a standard, and modulus. *Perception & Psychophysics, 54*, 555–561.

Krueger, L. E. (1989). Reconciling Fechner and Stevens: Toward a unified psychophysical law. *Behavioral and Brain Sciences, 12*, 251–320.

Krupat, E. (1985). *People in cities: The urban environment and its effects*. Cambridge: Cambridge University Press.

Kuipers, B. (1982). The "map in the head" metaphor. *Environment & Behavior, 14*, 203–220.

Künnapas, T. M. (1958). Measurements of subjective length in the vertical–horizontal illusion. *Acta Psychologica, 14*, 371–374.

Künnapas, T. M. (1960). Scales for subjective distance. *Scandinavian Journal of Psychology, 1*, 187–192.

Künnapas, T. M. (1968). Distance perception as a function of available visual cues. *Journal of Experimental Psychology, 77*, 523–529.

Landau, B., Gleitman, H., & Spelke, E. (1981). Spatial knowledge and geometric representation in a childe blind from birth. *Science, 213*, 1275–1278.

Landauer, A. A., & Epstein, W. (1969). Does retinal size have a unique correlate in perceived size? *Perception & Psychophysics, 6*, 273–275.

Lapa, V. V., & Lemeshchenko, N. A. (1982). Effect of the orientation method on the efficiency of pilot's spatial orientation. *Komicheskaya Biologiya i Aviakosmicheskaya Meditsina, 16*, 45–49.

Lawton, C. A. (1994). Gender differences in way–finding strategies: Relationship to spatial ability and spatial anxiety. *Sex Roles, 30*, 765–779.

Lawton, C. A. (1996). Strategies for indoor wayfinding: The role of orientation. *Journal of Environmental Psychology, 16*, 137–145.

Lawton, C. A., Charleston, S. I., & Zieles, A. S. (1996). Individual– and gender–related differences in indoor wayfinding. *Environment and Behavior, 28*, 204–219.

Lazarus, R. S., & Cohen, J. (1977). Environmental stress. In J. Wohlwill & I. Altman (Eds.), *Human behavior and environment* (pp. 90–127). New York: Plenum Press.

Lee, D. N. (1976). A theory of visual control of braking based on information about time to collision. *Perception, 5*, 437–459.

Lee, T. (1970). Perceived distance as a function of direction in a city. *Environment and Behavior, 2*, 40–51.

Lehnung, M., Haaland, V. O., Pohl, J., & Leplow, B. (2001). Compass–versus finger–pointing tasks: The influences of different methods of assessment on age–related orientation performance in children. *Journal of Environmental Psychology, 21*, 283–289.

Lehnung, M., Leplow, B., Haaland, V. O., Mehdorn, M., & Ferstl, R. (2003). Pointing accuracy in children is dependent on age, sex, and experience. *Journal of Environmental Psychology, 23*, 419–425.

Leibowitz, H. W., & Harvey, L. O., Jr. (1967). Size matching as a function of instructions in a naturalistic environment. *Journal of Experimental Psychology, 74*, 378–382.

Leibowitz, H. W., & Harvey, L. O., Jr (1969). Effect of instructions, environment, and type of test object on matching size. *Journal of Experimental Psychology, 81*, 36–43.

Leibowitz, H. W., & Owens, D. A. (1977). Oculomotor adjustments and space perception. In G. Oleron (Ed.), *Psychologie Experimentale et Comparee.* Paris: Presses Universitaires de France.

Leibowitz, H. W., Pollard, S. W., & Dickson, D. (1967). Monocular and binoculare size matching as a function of distance at various age levels. *American Journal of Psychology, 80*, 263–268.

Leibowitz, H. W., Shina, K., & Hennessy, H. R. (1972). Oculomotor adjustments and size constancy. *Perception & Psychophysics, 12*, 497–500.

Levin, C. A., & Haber, R. N. (1993). Visual angle as a determinant of perceived interobject distance. *Perception & Psychophysics, 54*, 250–259.

Lichten, W., & Lurie, S. (1950). A new technique for the study of perceived size. *American Journal of Psychology, 63*, 380–282.

Lindberg, E., & Gärling, T. (1981a). Acquisition of locational information about reference points during blindfolded and sighted locomotion: Effects of a concurrent task and locomotion paths. *Scandinavian Journal of Psychology, 22*, 101–108.

Lindberg, E., & Gärling, T. (1981b). Acquisition of locational information about reference points during locomotion with and without a concurrent task: Effects of number of reference points. *Scandinavian Journal of Psychology, 22*, 109–115.

Lindberg, E., & Gärling, T. (1982). Acquisition of locational information about reference points during locomotion: The role of central information processing. *Scandinavian Journal of Psychology, 23*, 207–218.

Lindberg, E., & Gärling, T. (1983). Acquisition of different types of locational information in cognitive maps: Automatic of effortful processing? *Psychological Research, 45*, 19–38.

Link, S. W. (1994). Rediscovering the past: Gustav Fechner and signal detection theory. *Psychological Science, 5*, 335-340.

Link, S. W. (2002). Fechner, Gustav Theodor. In E. Erwin (Ed.), *The Freud encyclopedia: Theory, therapy, and culture* (pp. 192-195). NY: Routledge.

Linn, M. C., & Petersen, A. C. (1985). Emergence and characterization of sex differences in spatial ability: A meta–analysis. *Child Development, 56*, 1479–1498.

Lockhead, G. R. (1992). Psychophysical scaling: Judgments of attributes or objects? *The Behavioral and Brain Sciences, 15*, 565–586.

Loomis, J. M., & Beall, A. C. (1998). Visually controlled locomotion: Its dependence on optic flow, three–dimensional space perception, and cognition. *Ecological Psychology, 10*, 271–285.

Loomis, J. M., Da Silva, J. A., Fujita, N., & Fukusima, S. S. (1992). Visual space perception and visually directed action. *Journal of Experimental Psychology: Human Perception and Performance, 18*, 906–921.

Loomis, J. M., Klatzky, R. L., Golledge, R. G., Cicinelli, J. G., Pellegrino, J. W., & Fry, P. A. (1993). Nonvisual navigation by blind and sighted: Assessment of path integration ability. *Journal of Experimental Psychology: General, 122*, 73–91.

Loomis, J. M., Klatzky, R. L., Philbeck, J. W., & Golledge, R. G. (1998). Assessing auditory distance perception using perceptually directed action. *Perception & Psychophysics, 60*, 966–980.

Loomis, J. M., & Philbeck, J. W. (1999). Is the anisotropy of perceived 3–D shape invariant across scale? *Perception & Psychophysics, 61*, 397–402.

Loomis, J. M., Philbeck, J. W., & Zahorik, P. (2002). Dissociation between location and shape in visual space. *Journal of Experimental Psychology: Human Perception and Performance, 28*, 1202–1212.

Lowrey, R. A. (1970). Distance concepts of urban residents. *Environment and Behavior, 2*, 52–73.

Lowrey, R. A. (1973). A method for analyzing distance concepts of urban residents. In R. M. Downs & D. Stea (Eds.), *Image and environment: Cognitive mapping and spatial behavior* (ch. 18). Chicago: Aldine Publishing Co.

Lucas, J. R. (1969). Euclides ab Omni Naevo Vindictas. *British Journal of the Philosophy of Science, 20*, 1–11.

Luce, R. D. (1993). Let's not promulgate either Fechner's erroneous algorithm or his unidimensional approach. *Behavioral and Brain Sciences, 16*, 155–156.

Luce, R. D., & Edwards, W. (1958). The derivation of subjective scales from just noticeable differences. *Psychological Review, 65*, 222–237.

Luneburg, R. K. (1947). *Mathematical analysis of binocular vision.* New York: Oxford University Press.

Luneburg, R. K. (1948). Metric methods in binocular visual perception. *Courant Anniversary Volume* (pp. 215–240). New York: Interscience.

Luneburg, R. K. (1950). The metric of binocular visual space. *Journal of the Optical Society of America, 40*, 637–642.

Lynch, K. (1960). *The image of the city.* Cambridge, MA: MIT Press.

Lynch, K., & Rivkin, M. (1959). A walk around the block. *Landscape, 8*, 24–24.

MacLeod, D. I. A., & Willen, J. D. (1995). *Is there a visual space?* In R. D. Luce, M. D'Zmura, D. Hoffman, G. J. Iverson, & A. K. Romney (Eds.), *Geometric representations of perceptual phenomena* (ch. 3, pp. 47-60.) Mahwah, NJ: Lawrence Erlbaum Associates.

MacMillan, N. A., Moschetto, C. F., Bialostozky, F. M., & Engel, L. (1974). Size judgment: The presence of a standard increases the exponent of the power law. *Perception & Psychophysics, 16*, 340–346.

Magaña, J. Z. (1978). An empirical and interdisciplinary test of a theory of urban perception. (Doctoral Dissertation, University of California , Irvine.) *Dissertation Abstracts International, 39*, 1460B (University Microfilms, No. 78–15, 840).

Magliano, J. P., Cohen, R., Allen, G. L., & Rodrigue, J. R. (1995). The impact of a wayfinder's goal on learning a new environment: Different types of spatial knowledge as goals. *Journal of Environmental Psychology, 15*, 65–75.

Makishita, S. (1947). Experiments on apparent equidistances. *Shinri, 1*, 62–64.

Malinowski, J. C., & Gillespie, W. T. (2001). Individual differences in performance on a large–scale real–world wayfinding task. *Journal of Environmental Psychology, 21*, 73–82.

Mapp, A. P., & Ono, H. (1999). Wondering about the wandering cyclopean eye. *Vision Research, 39*, 2381–2386.

Markley, R. P. (1971). Magnitude estimation: Range of response and the exponent. *Psychonomic Science, 22*, 71–72.

Martius, G. (1889). Über die scheinbare Grösse der Gegenstände und ihre Beziehung zur Grösse der Netzhautbilder, *Philosophische Studien, 5*, 601–617.

Mashhour, M., & Hosman, J. (1968). On the new "psychophysical law": A validation study. *Perception & Psychophysics, 3*, 367–375.

Masin, S. C. (1980). Scaling of very, very short visual extents. *Perceptual and Motor Skills, 51*, 379–282.

Masin, S. C., & Vidotto, G. (1983). A magnitude estimation study of the inverted–T illusion. *Perception & Psychophysics, 33*, 582–584.

Matthews, M. H. (1992). *Making sense of place. Children's understanding of large–scale environments*. Hempstead: Noble Books.

McBeath, M. K., Shaffer, D. M., & Kaiser, M. K. (1995). How baseball outfielders determine where to run to catch fly balls. *Science, 268*, 569–573.

McBeath, M. K., Shaffer, D. M., & Kaiser, M. K. (1996). "On catching fly balls": Reply. *Science, 273*, 258–260.

McCready, D. W., Jr. (1985). On size, distance, and visual angle perception. *Perception & Psychophysics, 37*, 323–334.

McCready, D. W., Jr. (1986). Moon illusions redescribed. *Perception & Psychophysics, 39*, 64–72.

McGuinness, D., & Sparks, J. (1983). Cognitive style and cognitive maps: Sex differences in representations of a familiar terrain. *Journal of Mental Imagery, 7*, 91–100.

McKee, S. P., Levi, D. M., & Bowne, S. F. (1990). The imprecision of stereopsis. *Vision Research, 21*, 1763–1779.

McKee, S. P., & Smallman, H. S. (1998). Size and speed constancy. In V. Walsh & J. Kulikowski (Eds.), *Perceptual constancy: Why things look as they do* (ch. 14, pp. 373–408.) Cambridge: Cambridge University Press.

McKee, S. P., Welch, L., Taylor, D. G., & Bowne, S. F. (1990). Finding the common bond: Stereoacuity and the other hyperacuities. *Vision Research, 30*, 879–891.

McKenzie, B. E., Tootell, H. E., & Day, R. H. (1980). Development of visual size constancy during the first year of human infancy. *Developmental Psychology, 16*, 163–174.

McNamara, T. P., Hardy, J. K., & Hirtle, S. C. (1989). Subjective hierarchies in spatial memory. *Journal of Experimental Psychology: Learning, Memory, & Cognition, 15*, 211–227.

Mershon, D. H., Desaulniers, D. H., Amerson, R. L., & Kiefer, S. A. (1980). Visual capture in auditory distance perception: Proximity image effect reconsidered. *Journal of Auditory Research, 20*, 129–136.

Mershon, D. H., Kennedy, M., & Falacara, G. (1977). On the use of calibration equations in perception research. *Perception, 6*, 299–311.

Milgram, S. (1970). The experience of living in cities. *Science, 167*, 1461–1468.

Mitson, G. L., Ono, H., & Barbieto, R. (1976). Three methods of measuring the location of the egocentre: Their reliability, comparative locations and intercorrelations. *Canadian Journal of Psychology, 30*, 1–9.

Moar, I., & Bower, G. H. (1983). Inconsistency in spatial knowlegde. *Memory & Cognition, 11*, 107–113.

Moeser, S. D. (1988). Cognitive mapping in a complex building. *Environment and Behavior, 20*, 21–49.

Montello, D. R. (1991). Spatial orientation and the angularity of urban routes: A field study. *Environment and Behavior, 23*, 47–69.

Montello, D. R., & Pick, H. L. (1993). Integrating knowledge of vertically aligned large–scale spaces. *Environment and Behavior, 25*, 457–484.

Moore, C. C. (1907, April) Estimate of distance. *Law Notes*, 5–7.

Moore, G. T. (1979). Knowing about environmental knowing: The current state of theory and research on environmental cognition. *Environment and Behavior, 11*, 33–70.

Morinaga, S. (1935). Visual direction and the moon illusion. *Japanese Journal of Psychology, 10*, 1–25.

Moyer, R. S., Bradley, D. R., Sorensen, M. H., Whiting, J. C., & Mansfield, D. P. (1978). Psychophysical functions for perceived and remembered size. *Science, 200*, 330–332.

Murray, D. J. (1993). A perspective for viewing the history of psychophysics. *Behavioral and Brain Sciences, 16*, 115–186.

Myers, A. K. (1980). Quantiative indices of perceptual constancy. *Psychological Bulletin, 88*, 451–457.

Nakamizo, S., Shimono, K., Kondo, M., & Ono, H. (1994). Visual directions of two stimuli in Panum's Limiting Case. *Perception, 23*, 1037–1048.

Nakayama, K. (1994). James J. Gibson–An appreciation. *Psychological Review, 101*, 329–335.

Neidhardt, E., & Schmitz, S. (2001). Entwicklung von Strategien und Kompetenzen in der räumlichen Orientierung und in der Raumkognition: Einluüsse von geschlecht, alter, erfahrung und motivation. *Psychologie in Erziehung und Unterricht, 48*, 262–279.

Norman, J. F., Lappin, J. S., & Norman, H. F. (2000). The perception of length on curved and flat surfaces. *Perception & Psychophysics, 62*, 1133–1145.

Norman, J. F., Todd, J. T., Perotti, V. J., & Tittle, J. S. (1996). The visual perception of 3D length. *Journal of Experimental Psychology: Human Perception and Performance, 22*, 173–186.

Ohno, S. (1951). An experimental study of inhomogeneity of perceptual space. *Saga Daigaku Kyoiku Gakubu Ronbunshu, 1*, 75–95.

Ohno, S. (1972). Anistropy of perceptual space. In Y. Akishige (Ed.), *Constancies of perceptual world: Epistemological psychology* (Vol. 4, pp. 387–575). Tokyo: Ibunsha.

Ohta, R. J., & Kirasic, K. C. (1983). The investigation of environmental learning in the elderly. In G. D. Rowles & R. J. Ohta (Eds.), *Aging and milieu: Environmental perspectives on growing old* (pp. 83–95). New York: Academic Press.

Okabe, A., Aoki, K, & Hamamoto, W. (1986). Distance and direction judgment in a large–scale natural environment: Effects of a slope and winding trail. *Environment & Behavior, 18*, 755–772.

Ono, H. (1979). Axiomatic summary and deductions from Hering's principles of visual direction. *Perception & Psychophysics, 25*, 473–477.

Ono, H., & Barbeito, R. (1982). The cyclopean eye vs. the sighting–dominant eye as the center of visual direction. *Perception & Psychophysics, 32*, 201–210.

Ono, H., & Mapp, A. P. (1995). A restatement and modification of Wells–Hering's law of visual direction. *Perception, 24*, 237–252.

Ono, H., Wagner, M., & Ono, K. (1995). *Accuracy and precision* (2nd edition). NY: Oxford University Press.

Ooi, T. L., Wu, B., & He, Z. J. (2001). Distance determined by the angular declination below the horizon. *Nature, 414*, 197–200.

Orleans, P. (1973). Differential cognition of urban residents: Effects of social scale on mapping. In R. M. Downs & D. Stea (Eds.), *Image and the Environment*. New York: Adeline Publishing Company.

Orleans, P., & Schmidt, S. (1972). Mapping the city: Environmental cognitions of urban residents. In W. J. Mitchell (Ed.), *Environmental design: Research and practice*. Los Angeles: University of California Press.

Osaka, R. (1947). Anisotropy of visual space: The moon illusion. *Shinri, 1*, 65–98.

Oudejans, R. R. D., Michaels, C. F., Bakker, F. C., & Dolne, M. A. (1996). The relevance of action in perceiving affordances: Perception of the catchableness of fly balls. *Journal of Experimental Psychology: Human Perception and Performance, 22*, 879–891.

Over, R. (1960). The effect of instructions on size–judgments under reduced conditions. *American Journal of Pscyhology, 73*, 599–602.

Owens, D. A. (1986). Oculomotor information and perception of three–dimensional space. In H. Heuer & A. F. Sanders (Eds.), *Perspectives on perception and action*. Hillsdale, NJ: Lawrence Erlbaum Associates.

Owens, D. A., & Leibowitz, H. W. (1976). Oculomotor adjustments in darkness and the specific distance tendency. *Perception & Psychophysics, 20*, 2–9.

Owens, D. A., & Wagner, M. (1992). *Progress in Modern Psychology: The legacy of American Functionalism*. Westport, CT: Praeger.

Pagano, C. C., & Bingham, G. P. (1998). Comparing measures of monocular distance perception: Verbal and reaching errors are not correlated. *Journal of Experimental Psychology: Human Perception and Performance, 24*, 1037–1051.

Parameswaran, G. (2003). Experimenter instructions as a mediator in the effects of culture on mapping one's neighborhood. *Journal of Environmental Psychology, 23*, 409–417.

Park, J. N., & Michaelson, G. J. (1974). Distance judgments under different size–information conditions. *Perception & Psychophysics, 13*, 284–292.

Passini, R., Desilse, J., Langlois, C., & Proulx, G. (1988). Wayfinding information for congenitally blind individuals. *Journal of Visual Impairment & Blindness, 82*, 425–429.

Passini, R., Proulx, G., & Rainville, C. (1990). The spatio–cognitive abilities of the visually impaired population. *Environment and Behavior, 22*, 91–118.

Pearson, J. L., & Ferguson, L. R. (1989). Gender difference in patterns of spatial ability, environmental cognition, and math and English achievement in late adolescence. *Adolescence, 24*, 421–431.

Péruch, P., Giraudo, M. D., & Gärling, T. (1989). Distance cognition by taxi drivers and the general public. *Journal of Environmental Psychology, 9*, 233–239.

Philbeck, J. W. (2000). Visually directed walking to briefly glimpsed targets is not biased toward fixation location. *Perception, 29*, 259–272.

Philbeck, J. W., & Loomis, J. M. (1997). Comparison of two indicators of perceived egocentric distance under full–cue and reduced–cue conditions. *Journal of Experimental Psychology: Human Perception and Performance, 23*, 72–85.

Pitz, G. F. (1965). Magnitude scales of line length. *Psychonomic Science, 2*, 213–214.

Plester, B., Richards, J., Blades, M., & Spencer, C. (2002). Young children's ability to use aerial photographs as maps. *Journal of Environmental Psychology, 22*, 29–47.

Poincaré, H. (1905). *Science and hypothesis*. New York: Walter Scott Publishing Company.

Plester, B., Richards, J., Blades, M., & Spencer, C. (2002). Young children's ability to use aerial photographs as maps. *Journal of Environmental Psychology, 22*, 29–47.

Plug, C. (1989). The registered distance of the celestial sphere: Some historical cross–cultural data. *Perceptual & Motor Skills, 68*, 211–217.

Poucet, B. (1985). Choice of routes through a complex spatial environment by cats. *Animal Behavior, 33*, 1026–1028.

Predebon, J. (1979). Role of familiar size in spatial judgments under natural viewing conditions. *Perceptual and Motor Skills, 48*, 171–176.

Predebon, J. (1987). Familiar size and judgments of distance: Effects of response mode. *Bulletin of the Psychonomic Society, 25*, 244–246.

Predebon, J. (1990). Relative distance judgments of familiar and unfamiliar objects viewed under representatively natural conditions. *Perception & Psychophysics, 47*, 342–348.

Predebon, J. (1992a). The influence of object familiarity on magnitude estimates of apparent size. *Perception, 21*, 77–90.

Predebon, J. (1992b). The role of instructions and familiar size in absolute judgments of size and distance. *Perception & Psychophysics, 51*, 344–354.

Proshansky, H. M. (1976). Environmental Psychology and the real world. *American Psychologist, 31*, 303–310.

Purdy, J., & Gibson, E. J. (1955). Distance judgment by the method of fractionation. *Journal of Experimental Psychology, 50*, 374–380.

Radvansky, G. A., & Carlson–Radvansky, L. A. (1995). Uncertainty in estimation distances from memory. *Memory & Cognition, 23*, 596–606.

Raghubir, P., & Krishna, A. (1996). As the crow flies: Bias in consumers' map–based distance judgments.

Rapoport, J. L. (1967). Attitude and size judgment in school age children. *Child Development, 38*, 1187–1192.

Regan, D., Hamstra, S. J., Kaushal, S., Vincent, A., Gray, R., & Beverley, K. I. (1994). Visual processing of an object's motion in three dimensions for a stationary or a moving object. *Perception, 24*, 87–103.

Reid, T. (1764/1813). *Inquiry into the human mind*. In D. Stewart (Ed.), Vol. 1. Charlestown: Samuel Etheridge.

Reinhardt, R., & Anthony, H. (1996). Remote operation: A selective review of research into visual depth perception. *Journal of General Psychology, 123*, 237–248.

Rieser, J. J., Ashmead, D. H., Talor, C. R., & Youngquist, G. A. (1990). Visual perception and the guidance of locomotion without vision to previously seen targets. *Perception, 19,* 675–689.

Rieser, J. J., Lockman, J. J., & Pick, H. L., Jr. (1980). The role of visual experience in knowledge of spatial layout. *Perception & Psychophysics, 28,* 185–190.

Rissotto, A., & Tonucci, F. (2002). Freedom of movement and environmental knowledge in elementary school children. *Journal of Environmental Psychology, 22,* 65–77.

Rock, I. (1983). *The logic of perception.* Cambridge, MA: MIT Press.

Rock, I., & Kaufman, L. (1962). The moon illusion. *Science, 136,* 1023–1031.

Roelofs, C. O. (1959). Considerations on the visual egocentre. *Acta Psychologica, 16,* 226–234.

Rogers, S. F., & Gogel, W. C. (1975). The relation between a judged and physical distance in multicue conditions as a function of instructions and tasks. *Perceptual and Motor Skills, 41,* 171–178.

Roscoe, S. N. (1979). When day is done and shadows fall, we miss the airport most of all. *Human Factors, 21,* 721–731.

Roscoe, S. N. (1982, October). Landing airplanes, detecting traffic, and the dark focus. *Aviation, Space, and Environmental Medicine,* 970–976.

Roscoe, S. N. (1985). Bigness is in the eye of the beholder. *Human Factors, 27,* 615–636.

Ross, H. E., & Plug, C. (1998). The history of size constancy and size illusions. In V. Walsh & J. Kulikowski (Eds.), *Perceptual constancy: Why things look as they do* (ch. 18, pp. 499–528). Cambridge: Cambridge University Press.

Rossano, M. J., & Reardon, W. P. (1999). Goal specificity and the acquisition of survey knowledge. *Environment and Behavior, 31,* 395–412.

Rovine, M. J., & Weisman, G. D. (1989). Sketch–map variables as predictors of way–finding performance. *Journal of Environmental Psychology, 9,* 217–232.

Rowen, R. B., & Hardwick, D. A. (1983). Effects of landmark salience and direction of travel on young children's memory for spatial location. *Journal of Psychology, 113,* 271–276.

Runeson, S. (1988). The distorted room illusion, equivalent configurations, and the specificity of static optic arrays. *Journal of Experimental Psychology: General, 14,* 295–304.

Russell, B. (1971). *An analysis of mind.* London: George Allen & Unwin.

Ryle, G. (1949). *The concept of mind.* London: Hutchinson.

Sadalla, E. K., Burroughs, W. J., & Staplin, L. J. (1980). Reference points in spatial cognition. *Journal of Experimental Psychlogy: Human Learning and Memory, 6,* 516–528.

Sadalla, E. K., & Magel, S. G. (1980). The perception of traversed distance. *Environment and Behavior, 12,* 65–79.

Sadalla, E. K., & Montello, D. R. (1989). Remembering changes in direction. *Environment and Behavior, 21,* 346–363.

Sadalla, E. K., & Staplin, L. J. (1980). The perception of traversed distance: Intersections. *Environment and Behavior, 12*, 167–182.

Sandstrom, N. J., Kaufman, J., & Huettel, S. A. (1998). Males and females use different distal cues in a virtual environment navigation task. *Cognitive Brain Research, 6*, 351–360.

Scheerer, E. (1986). *The constitution of space perception: A phenomenological perspective.* (Center for Interdisciplinary Research, University of Bielefeld, Rep. No. 102).

Schmitz, S. (1997). Gender–related strategies in environmental development: Effects of anxiety on wayfinding in and representation of a three–dimensional maze. *Journal of Environmental Psychology, 17*, 215–228.

Schneider, B., & Bissett, R. (1988). "Ratio" and "difference" judgments for length, area, and volume: Are there two classes of sensory continua? *Journal of Experimental Psychology: Human Perception and Performance, 14*, 503–512.

Schouela, D. A., Steinberg, L. M., Leveton, L. B., & Wapner, S. (1980). Development of the cognitive organization of an environment. *Canadian Journal of Behavioral Science, 12*, 1–16.

Schoumans, N., Koenderink, J. J., & Kappers, A. M. L. (2000). Change in perceived spatial directions due to context. *Perception & Psychophysics, 62*, 532–539.

Schoumans, N., Koenderink, J. J., & Kappers, A. M. L. (2002). Scale invariance in near space: Pointing under influence of context. *Acta Psychologica, 110*, 63–81.

Schwartz, M. (1999). Haptic perception of the distance walked when blindfolded. *Journal of Experimental Psychology: Human Perception and Performance, 25*, 852–865.

Sedgwick, H. A. (1986). Space perception. In K. R. Boff, L. Kaufman & J. P. Thomas (Eds.), *Handbook of perception and human performance* (Vol. 1, ch. 27). New York: John Wiley and Sons.

Seizova–Cajic, T. (1998). Size perception by vision and kinesthesia. *Perception & Psychophysics, 60*, 705–718.

Shaffer, D. M., Krauchunas, S. M., Eddy, M., & McBeath, M. K. (2004). How dogs navigate to catch Frisbees. *Psychological Science, 15*, 437–441.

Shallo, J., & Rock, I. (1988). Size constancy in children: A new interpretation. *Perception, 17*, 803–813.

Sheehan, M. R. (1938). A study of individual consistency in phenomenal constancy. *Archives of Psychology, 222*, 5–95.

Shepard, R. N. (1988). The role of transformations in spatial cognition. In J. Stiles–Davis, M. Kritchevsky & U. Bellugi (Eds.), *Spatial cognition: Brain bases and development* (pp. 81–110). Hillsdale, NJ: Lawrence Erlbaum Associates.

Shepard, R. N., & Metzler, J. (1971). Mental rotation of three–dimensional objects. *Science, 171*, 701–703.

Sherman, R. C., Croxton, J., & Giovanatto, J. (1979). Investigating cognitive representations of spatial relationships. *Environment & Behavior, 11*, 209–226.

Shimono, K., Higashiyama, A., & Tam, W. J. (2001). Location of the ego-center in kinesthetic space. *Journal of Experimental Psychology: Human Perception and Performance, 27*, 848–861.

Shimono, K., Ono, H., Saida, S., & Mapp, A. P. (1998). Methodological caveates for monitoring binocular eye position with Nonius stimuli. *Vision Research, 38*, 591–600.

Shreider, Y. A. (1974). *What is distance?* Chicago: University of Chicago Press.

Siegel, A. W., & Schadler, M. (1977). The development of young children's spatial representations of their classroom. *Child Development, 48*, 388–394.

Sikl, R., & Simecek, M. (2004). Adjusted size of in–depth and frontal stimuli. Unpublished raw data.

Simpson, P. J., & Nation, K. J. (1997). Head orientation and binaural depth perception. In D. Harris (Ed.), *Engineering psychology and cognitive ergonomics* (Vol. 2, pp. 285–291). Aldershot, England: Ashgate Publishing Company.

Singer, J. L. (1952). Personal and environmental determinants of perception in a size constancy experiment. *Journal of Experimental Psychology, 43*, 420–427.

Sipes, D. E. (1997). Hyperstereopsis as an attenuator for perceptual depth compression (Doctoral dissertation, The Johns Hopkins University, 1997). *Dissertation Abstracts International, 58* (4–B), 2161.

Sjöberg, L. (1960). A study of two R–S function for volume. In G. Ekman & K. Junge (1961), Psychophysical relations in visual perception of length, area, and volume. *Scandinavian Journal of Psychology, 2*, 1–10.

Skinner, B. F. (1985). Cognitive science and behaviorism. *British Journal of Psychology, 76*, 291–301.

Slater, A., Mattock, A., & Brown, E. (1990). Size constancy at birth: New-born infants' responses to retinal and real size. *Journal of Experimental Child Psychology, 49*, 314–322.

Smith, W. M. (1952). Gilinsky's theory of visual size and distance. *Psychological Review, 59*, 239–243.

Smith, W. M. (1953). A methodological study of size–distance perception. *The Journal of Psychology, 35*, 143–153.

Solomon, H. Y., & Turvey, M. T. (1988). Haptically perceiving the distances reachable with hand–held objects. *Journal of Experimental Psychology: Human Perception and Performance, 14*, 404–427.

Stanley, G. (1968). Stimulus–range and magnitude estimates of distance based on object–size. *Australian Journal of Psychology, 20*, 67–69.

Steenhuis, R. E., & Goodale, M. A. (1988). The effects of time and distance on accuracy of target–directed locomotion: Does an accurate short–term memory for spatial location exist? *Journal of Motor Behavior, 20*, 399–415.

Stevens, A., & Coupe, B. (1978). Distortions in judged spatial relations. *Cognitive Psychology, 10*, 422–437.

Stevens, J. C., & Hall, J. W. (1966). Brightness and loudness as functions of stimulus duration. *Perception & Psychophysics, 1*, 319–327.

Stevens, J. C., & Marks, L. E. (1980). Cross–modality matching functions generated by magnitude estimation. *Perception & Psychophysics, 27*, 379–389.

Stevens, J. C., & Rubin, L. L. (1970). Psychophysical scales of apparent heaviness and the size–weight illusion. *Perception & Psychophysics, 8*, 225–230.

Stevens, K. A. (1995). Integration by association: Combining three–dimensional cues to extrinsic surface shape. *Perception, 24*, 199–214.

Stevens, S. S. (1957). One the psychophysical law. *Psychological Review, 64*, 153–181.

Stevens, S. S. (1970). Neural events and the psychophysical law. *Science, 170*, 1043–1050.

Stevens, S. S. (1971). Sensory power functions and neural events. In W. R. Loewenstein (Ed.), *Handbook of sensory physiology* (Vol. 1). Berlin: Springer–Verlag.

Stevens, S. S. (1975). *Psychophysics: Introduction to its perceptual, neural, and social prospects.* New York: Wiley–Interscience.

Stevens, S. S., & Galanter, E. H. (1957). Ratio scales and category scales for a dozen perceptual continum. *Journal of Experimental Psychology, 34*, 377–411.

Stevens, S. S., & Guirao, M. (1963). Subjective scaling of length and area and the matching of length to loudness and brightness. *Journal of Experimental Psychology, 66*, 177–186.

Stevens, S. S., & Stone, G. (1959). Finger span: Ratio scale, category scale, and JND scale. *Journal of Experimental Psychology, 57*, 91–95.

Strawson, P. (1976). *The bounds of sense.* London: Methuen.

Suppes, P. (1995). Some foundational problems in the theory of visual space. In R. D. Luce, M. D'Zmura, D. Hoffman, G. J. Iverson, & A. K. Romney (Eds.), *Geometric representations of perceptual phenomena* (ch. 2, pp. 37–45.) Mahwah, NJ: Lawrence Erlbaum Associates.

Sweller, J. (1994). Cognitive load theory, learning difficulty, and instructional design. *Learning and Instruction, 4*, 295–312.

Sweller, J., & Chandler, P. (1994). Why some material is difficult to learn. *Cognition and Instruction, 12*, 185–233.

Sweller, J., & Levine, M. (1982). Effects of goal specificity on means–ends analysis and learning. *Journal of Experimental Psychology: Learning, Memory, and Cognition, 8*, 463–474.

Tani, N. (1980). A transformation of image map from route–map type to survey–map type. *Japanese Journal of Educational Psychology, 28*, 192–201.

Teghtsoonian, M. (1965). The judgment of size. *American Journal of Psychology, 78*, 392–402.

Teghtsoonian, M. (1974). The doubtful phenomenon of over–constancy. In H. R. Moskowitz, B. Scharf & J. C. Stevens (Eds.), *Sensation and measurement* (pp. 411–420). Dordrecht, The Netherlands: Reidel.

Teghtsoonian, M. (1980). Children's scales of length and loudness: A developmental application of cross–modal matching. *Journal of Experimental Child Psychology, 30*, 290–307.

Teghtsoonian, M., & Beckwith, J. B. (1976). Children's size judgments when size and distance vary: Is there a developmental trend to overconstancy? *Journal of Experimental Child Psychology, 22*, 23–39.

Teghtsoonian, M., & Teghtsoonian, T. (1965). Seen and felt length. *Psychonomic Science, 3*, 465–466.

Teghtsoonian, M., & Teghtsoonian, R. (1969). Scaling apparent distance in natural indoor settings. *Psychonomic Science, 16*, 281–283.

Teghtsoonian, M., & Teghtsoonian, R. (1971). How repeatable are Stevens's power law exponents for individual subjects? *Perception & Psychophysics, 10*, 147–149.

Teghtsoonian, R. (1971). On the exponent of Stevens' law and the constant in Ekman's law. *Psychological Review, 78*, 71–80.

Teghtsoonian, R. (1973). Range effects in psychophysical scaling and a revision of Stevens' law. *American Journal of Psychology, 86*, 3–27.

Teghtsoonian, R., & Teghtsoonian, M. (1970a). Scaling apparent distance in a natural outdoor setting. *Psychonomic Science, 21*, 215–217.

Teghtsoonian, R., & Teghtsoonian, M. (1970b). Scaling apparent distance in a natural indoor setting. *Psychonomic Science, 21*, 215–216.

Teghtsoonian, R., & Teghtsoonian, M. (1970c). The effects of size and distance on magnitude estimation of apparent size. *American Journal of Psychology, 83*, 601–612.

Teghtsoonian, R., & Teghtsoonian, M. (1978). Range and regression effects in magnitude scaling. *Perception & Psychophysics, 24*, 305–314.

Teske, J. A., & Balser, D. P. (1986). Levels of organization in urban navigation. *Journal of Environmental Psychology, 6*, 305–327.

Thomas, J. L. (1987). Locational versus featural information in adult visual memory. *Journal of Human Behavior & Learning, 4*, 16–22.

Thorndyke, P. W. (1981). Distance estimation from cognitive maps. *Cognitive Psychology, 13*, 526–549.

Thouless, R. H. (1931a). Phenomenal regression to the "real" object: I. *British Journal of Psychology, 21*, 339–359.

Thouless, R. H. (1931b). Phenomenal regression to the "real" object: II. *British Journal of Psychology, 22*, 1–30.

Thouless, R. H. (1932). Individual differences in phenomenal regression. *British Journal of Psychology, 22*, 216–241.

Titchener, E. B. (1900/1909/1910). *A text–book of psychology*. NewYork: Macmillan.

Tittle, J. S., Todd, J. T., Perotti, V. J., & Norman, J. F. (1995). Systematic distortion of perceived three–dimensional structure from motion and binocular stereopsis. *Journal of Experimental Psychology: Human Perception and Performance, 21*, 663–678.

Todd, J. T. (1981). Visual information about moving objects. *Journal of Experimental Psychology: Human Perception and Performance, 7*, 795–810.

Todd, J. T., & Bressan, P. (1990). The perception of 3-dimensional affine structure from minimal apparent motion sequences. *Perception & Psychophysics, 48*, 419-430.

Todd, J. T., & Norman, J. F. (1991). The visual perception of smoothly curved surfaces from minimal apparent motion sequences. *Perception & Psychophysics, 50*, 509-523.

Todd, J. T., Tittle, J. S., & Norman, J. F. (1995). Distortions of three–dimensional space in the perceptual analysis of motion and stereo. *Perception, 24,* 75–86.

Towbridge, C. C. (1913). On fundamental methods of orientation and imaginary map. *Science, 38,* 888–897.

Toye, R. C. (1986). The effect of viewing position on the perceived layout of space. *Perception & Psychophysics, 40,* 85–92.

Trillo, A. J. G. (1985). El espacio olfativo. *Investigaciones Psicológicas, 3,* 35–45.

Turano, K., & Schuchard, R. A. (1991). Space perception in observers with visual field loss. *Vision Science, 6,* 289–299.

Turvey, M. T., & Carello, C. (1986). The ecological approach to perceiving–acting: A pictorial essay. *Acta Psychologica, 63,* 1–25.

Tversky, B. (1981). Distortions in memory for maps. *Cognitive Psychology, 13,* 407–433.

Tyer, Z. E., Allen, J. A., & Pasnak, R. (1983). Instruction effects on size and distance judgments. *Perception & Psychophysics, 34,* 135–139.

Van Senden, M. (1937/1960). *Space and sight.* London: Methuen.

Vincent, R. J., Brown, B. R., & Markley, R. P. (1968). Distance discrimination in a simulated space environment. *Perception & Psychophysics, 5,* 235–238.

Vishton, P. M., & Cutting, J. E. (1995). Wayfinding, displacements, and mental maps: Velocity fields are not typically used to determine one's aimpoint. *Journal of Experimental Psychology: Human Perception and Performance, 21,* 978–995.

Vlek, C., & Beintema, K. (1967). Scale–dependence of psychophysical behavior. *Hypothese, Tjdschrift voor de psychologie (Leiden), 11,* 111–125.

Vogel, J. M., & Teghtsoonian, M. (1972). The effects of perspective alterations on apparent size and distance scales. *Perception & Psychophysics, 11,* 294–298.

Von Collani, G. (1985). The horizontal–vertical illusion in photographs of concrete scenes with and without depth information. *Perceptual & Motor Skills, 61,* 523–531.

Voyer, D., Voyer, S., & Bryden, M. P. (1995). Magnitude of sex differences in spatial abilities: A meta–analysis and consideration of critical variables. *Psychological Bulletin, 117,* 250–270.

Wade, N. J. (1996). Descriptions of visual phenomena from Aristotle to Wheatstone. *Perception, 25,* 1137–1175.

Wagner, M. (1982). *The metric of visual space.* Unpublished doctoral dissertation, Dartmouth College.

Wagner, M. (1985). The metric of visual space. *Perception & Psychophysics, 38,* 483–495.

Wagner, M. (1989). Fantasies in psychophysical scaling: Do category estimates reflect the true psychophysical scale? *The Behavioral and Brain Sciences, 12,* 294–295.

Wagner, M. (1992). Keeping the bath–water along with the baby: Context effects represent a challenge, not a mortal wound, to the body of psychophysics. *The Behavioral and Brain Sciences, 15*, 585–586.

Wagner, M. (1998). From spatial perception to cognitive maps: Memory psychophysics and Weber's Law. In S. Grondin & Y. Lacouture (Eds.), *International Society for Psychophysics Annual* (Vol. 14, pp. 50–56). Quebec City, Canada: International Society for Psychophysics.

Wagner, M., & Baird, J. C. (1987). Mistransforming angular size. In M. Teghtsoonian & R. Teghtsoonian (Eds.), *International Society for Psychophysics Annual* (Vol. 3, pp. 73–75). Durham, NH: International Society for Psychophysics.

Wagner, M., Baird, J. C., & Barbaresi, W. (1981). The locus of environmental attention. *Journal of Environmental Psychology, 1*, 195–206. Wagner, M., Baird, J. C., & Fuld, K. (1989). Transformation model of the moon illusion. In M. Hershenson (Ed.), *The moon illusion* (pp. 147–163). Hillsdale, NJ: Lawrence Erlbaum Associates.

Wagner, M., & Feldman, E. (1989). The metric properties of three dimensional visual space. In G. Canevet, B. Scharf, A. M. Bonnel & C. A. Possamai (Eds.), *International Society for Psychophysics Annual* (Vol. 5, pp. 96–101). Cassis, France: International Society for Psychophysics.

Wagner, M., & Feldman, E. (1990). A psychophysical analysis of the development of cognitive maps. In F. Muller (Ed.), *International Society for Psychophysics Annual* (Vol. 6, pp. 234–240). Wurzburg, Germany: International Society for Psychophysics.

Wagner, M., Kartzinel, H., & Baird, J. C. (1988). The perception of length for objects oriented in–depth as a function of distance, judgment method, and instructions. In H. Ross (Ed.), *International Society for Psychophysics Annual* (Vol. 4, pp. 109–110). Stirling, Scotland: International Society for Psychophysics.

Wagner, M., Ono, H., & Ono, K. (1995). *The classic psychophysical methods* (2nd ed.). NY: Oxford University Press.

Wagner, M., & Owens, D. A. (1992). Modern psychology and early Functionalism. In D. A. Owens & M. Wagner (Eds.), *Progress in modern psychology: The legacy of American Functionalism* (ch. 1, pp. 2–16). Westport, CT: Praeger Press.

Wallach, H., & McKenna, V. V. (1960). On size–perception in the absence of distance cues. *American Journal of Psychology, 73*, 458–460.

Waller, G. (1986). The development of route knowledge: Multiple dimensions? *Journal of Environmental Psychology, 6*, 109–119.

Warren, R. M. (1958). A basis for judgments of sensory intensity. *American Journal of Psychology, 71*, 675–687.

Warren, R. M. (1969). Visual intensity judgments: An empirical rule and a theory. *Psychological Review, 76*, 16–30.

Warren, R. M. (1981). Measurement of sensory intensity. *The Behavioral and Brain Sciences, 4*, 175–223.

Watson, J. B. (1914). *Behavior: An introduction to comparative psychology.* NY: Henry Holt.

Watson, J. B., (1919). *Psychology from the standpoint of a behaviorist.* Philadelphia: Lippincott.

Watson, J. B. (1924). *Psychology from the point of view of a behaviorist.* Philadelphia: Lippincott.

Watson, J. B. (1925). *Behaviorism.* NY: Norton.

Webley, P., & Whalley, A. (1987). Sex differences in children's environmental cognition. *Journal of Social Psychology, 127,* 223–225.

Westra, D. P., Simon, C. W., Collyer, S. C., & Chambers, W. S. (1982). *NAVTRAEQUIPCEN,* No. C–0060–7.

Whitaker, D., McGraw, P. V., & Pearson, S. (1999). Non–veridical size perception of expanding and contracting objects. *Vision Research, 39,* 2999–3009.

Wiest, W. M, & Bell, B. (1985). Steven's exponent for psychophysical scaling of perceived, remembered, and inferred distance. *Psychological Bulletin, 98,* 457–470.

Wilcox, S. B. (1992). Functionalism then and now. In D A. Owens & M. Wagner (Eds.), *Progress in modern psychology: The legacy of American Functionalism* (ch. 3, pp. 31–51). Westport, CT: Praeger Press.

Wilkie, D. M. (1995). Time–place learning. *Current Directions in Psychological Science, 4,* 85–89.

Wilson, P. N. (1999). Active exploration of a virtual environment does not promote orientation or memory for objects. *Environment and Behavior, 31,* 752–763.

Wohlwill, J. F. (1963). The development of "overconstancy" in space perception. In L. P. Lipsitt & C. C. Spiker (Eds.), *Advances in child development and behavior* (Vol. 1, pp. 265–312). New York: Academic Press.

Wohlwill, J. F. (1970). Perceptual development. In H. W. Reese & L. P. Lipsitt (Eds.), *Experimental child development.* New York: Academic Press.

Wundt, W. (1874/1904). *Principles of Physiological Psychology.* E. B. Titchener (trans.). London: Swan Sonnenschein & Co.

Yamazaki, T. (1987). Non–Riemannian approach to geometry of visual space: An application of affinely connected geometry to visual alleys and horopter. *Journal of Mathematical Psychology, 31,* 270–298.

Yang, T. L., Dixon, M. W., & Proffitt, D. R. (1999). *Perception, 28,* 445–467.

Yates, J. (1985). The content of awareness is a model of the world. *Psychological Review, 92,* 249–284.

Zahorik, P. A. (1999). Experiments in auditory distance perception. *Dissertation Abstracts International: Section B: The Science and Engineering, 59(9–B): 5145.*

Zajaczkowska, A. (1956a). Experimental determination of Luneberg's constants and K. *Quarterly Journal of Experimental Psychology, 8,* 66–78.

Zajaczkowska, A. (1956b). Experimental test of Luneberg's theory. Horopter and alley experiments. *Journal of the Optical Society of America, 46,* 514–527.

Zeigler, H. P., & Leibowitz, H. W. (1957). Apparent visual size as a function of distance for children and adults. *American Journal of Psychology, 70,* 106–109.

Zhang, J., Huang, Y., Liu, Z., & Hou, Q. (1995). Safe driving and drivers' visual depth perception. *Chinese Mental Health Journal, 9,* 132–133.

Author Index

A

Abbott, E. A., 65
Aczél, J., 31, 38, 53, 156
Aginsky, V., 200
Algom, D., 88, 209, 216
Allen, G. L., 195, 200, 202, 213
Al–Zahrani, S. S. A., 98, 217
Anderson, J. R., 220
Andrews, D. P., 129
Angell, R. B., 24, 43, 154
Anooshian, L. J., 197, 201
Appleyard, D., 196, 202
Aragones, J. I., 192
Armstrong, L., 181, 228
Ashmead, D. H., 228

B

Bailenson, J. N., 62
Baird, J. C., 27–28, 34, 37, 39, 40, 43,
46, 60, 63–72, 74–75, 77, 82–83,
86, 88, 98, 102, 118, 121–125,
132–137, 146, 176, 198–199,
214–215, 218
Baranski, J. V., 98, 217
Barbeito, R., 58–60
Battro, A. M., 38–39, 43, 109
Beatty, W. W., 203
Belingard, L., 207
Bell, S., 201
Ben–Zeev, A., 22, 154, 220–221
Berkeley, G., 20
Bertamini, M., 128
Beyrl, F., 108
Biel, A., 200–201

Bigelow, A. E., 205
Björkman, M., 88, 90
Blank, A. A., 31, 34, 38, 53, 156
Blumenfeld, W., 30, 60
Böök, A., 195
Borg, G., 76, 86
Boring, E. G., 5
Bower, T. G. R., 127
Bradley, D. R., 80, 82
Brambring, M., 205
Bratfisch, O., 82
Brennan, T., 207, 217
Brenner, E., 118
Briggs, R., 208, 214
Brislin, R. W., 126, 128
Brungart, D. S., 228–229
Bruno, N., 47
Brunswik, E., 105–106, 108, 132
Bryant, K. J., 205
Brysch, K. A., 207
Burbeck, C. A., 129
Burroughs, W. J., 34, 63, 208
Butler, D. L., 76, 83
Byrne, R. W., 205–206

C

Cadwallader, M., 27, 34, 63, 208–209
Canter, D., 207, 214
Carey, D. P., 180
Carlson, V. R., 113–115, 126
Carr, H. A., 2, 5, 6
Carr, S., 201–202
Carreiras, M., 209
Chalmers, E. L., 112
Chew, E. I., 88

265

Subject Index

A

Acquisition of cognitive maps, 194–200, 210–213
Affine contraction model, 149–151, 156–157, 165–167
Affine transformation, 19, 149–150
Age, 79, 86, 92, 108, 125–128, 130–131, 139–140, 200–201
Alcohol and size constancy, 109
Alley experiments, 30, 38–43
Analytic geometry, 14, 50–73, 224–225
Anchor points, 193–194, 227
Angularity effect, 207–208, 217–218
Apparent instructions defined, 104
Applications of spatial research, 7–8, 230
Asymmetry of distance estimates, 34, 63, 208–209
Auditory space, 60, 228–229
Axioms for geometries of constant curvature, 31–36

B

Baird's butterfly model, 121–122
Banach space, 17, 71–72, 225
Baseball and visual space, 8, 179–180
Behaviorism, 2, 6–7, 218–221, 230
Berkeley's views on space, 20
Bipolar coordinates, 53–55
Brunswik ratio, 105–106

C

Carlson's perspective–size hypothesis, 113–115
Chapter summaries, 9–11
Child development, 125–128, 130–131, 139–140
Cognitive maps, 4, 189–222
  Acquisition, 194–200 210–213, 227
  Age, 200–201, 227
  Anchor point theory, 193–194, 227
  Angularity effect, 207–208, 217–218
  Asymmetry of distance estimates, 208–209
  Blindness, 204–205, 227
  Categorical thinking, 206–207
  Cognitive science paradigm, 218–221
  Culture, 201–202
  Distortions in cognitive maps, 205–209, 227
  East–West inaccuracy, 209
  Elevation, 209
  Exponents, 209–215, 227
  Freud's unconscious and cognitive representations, 219–220
  Geometry of cognitive maps, 221–222, 227
  Good form, 206
  Individual differences, 200–205, 227
  Integration of paths, 197–199, 207
  Lynch's taxonomy, 191–192, 227
  Mathematical ability, 205